# GRASSROOTS WARRIORS

# PERSPECTIVES ON GENDER

Series Editor: Myra Marx Ferree, University of Connecticut

# GRASSROOTS WARRIORS

# Activist Mothering, Community Work, and the War on Poverty

**NANCY A. NAPLES**

ROUTLEDGE
NEW YORK and LONDON

Published in 1998 by
Routledge
29 West 35th Street
New York, NY 10001

Published in Great Britain by
Routledge
11 New Fetter Lane
London EC4P 4EE

Printed in the United States of America on acid-free paper.
Interior Design by Debora Hilu

Nancy A. Naples, "Contradictions in the Gender Subtext of the War on Poverty:
The Community Work and Resistance of Women From Low Income
Communitites" originally appeared in *Social Problems* 38 (3) 1991: 316–332,
copyright Sage Publications, Inc. Reprinted by permission of Sage Publications,
Inc. "'Just What Needed to Be Done': The Political Practice of Women From
Low Income Women Neighborhoods" originally appeared in *Gender & Society* 5
(4) 1991: 478–494, copyright Sage Publications, Inc. Reprinted by permission of
Sage Publications, Inc. "Activist Mothering: Cross-generational Continuity in
the Community Work of Women From Low Income Neighborhoods" originally appeared in *Gender & Society* 6 (3) 1992: 441–463, copyright Sage Publications,
Inc. Reprinted by permission of Sage Publications, Inc.

Library of Congress Cataloging-in-Publication Data

Naples, Nancy A.
        Grassroots warriors: activist mothering, community work, and the
war poverty / Nancy A. Naples.
                p.        cm — (Perspective on gender)
Includes index.
ISBN 0-415-91024-2. — ISBN 0-415-91025-0 (pbk.)
1. Women in community development—United States. 2. Women in community
organization—United States. 3. Poor—United States. 4. Women political
activists—United States. I. Title. II. Series: Perspectives on gender (New York, N.Y.)
HQ1240.5.U6N36 1998
305.42'0973—dc21                                      97-35178
                                                                        CIP

This book is dedicated to the memories of

Nina E. Fortin

June 10, 1949–October 2, 1987

Donald V. Naples, Jr.

May 27, 1953–November 21, 1985

Peter Canavan

November 30, 1949–April 21, 1996

*No individual struggle for life or*
*dignity is too small or insignificant.*

# CONTENTS

# ACKNOWLEDGMENTS

I owe much to the many courageous and energetic women I met through my work as a social worker and activist in New York City during the 1970s, who inspired me to write this book. I am also grateful to the YWCA of New York City for providing a women-centered environment that helped nourish my commitment to social justice.

Many others contributed to my development as a social scientist. Professors Martin Dosick and Michael Phillips introduced me to sociology and social research, respectively. I thank them for taking a special interest in my education. Professor Marilyn Gittell offered me valuable research experience that helped shape my research on women's community activism. Professors George Fischer, Charles Kadushin, Frank Riessman, Harold Weissman, Bill Kornblum, Gaye Tuchman, and Cynthia Epstein provided valuable advice at various points throughout the study.

Nancy Sennott, Muriel Silva, and Nancy Castleman played a vital role in helping me identify community workers to interview for this study. I would especially like to thank Nancy Sennott, who died in 1988, for sharing with me her work on Philadelphia's Anti-Poverty Action Commission and Community Action Councils. I miss her wise counsel and shared commitment to telling the stories of community action.

Thanks also to David Bradley, legislative director of the National Community Action Foundation, for sharing his experiences and political wisdom, and for his ongoing dedication to community action programs.

Shellen Lubin, Christine Naples Little, and Teresa Shtob assisted with the 1980s research. Lisa Mikhail transcribed tapes from the 1995 interviews. Cheryl Larsson scanned field notes and interviews. Brenda Rogers, Cherry Anaba, Anita Famili, Steve Hoffman, and Kris Kasianovitz provided essential research assistance.

I received funding for transcription costs from a Faculty Research Grant from the School of Social Sciences at the University of California, Irvine. I was able to devote somewhat uninterrupted time to the completion of the book manuscript with the help of two Faculty Development Grants also provided by UCI.

The clarity of the book owes much to the insightful comments of many people who carefully reviewed sections of the manuscript at various stages of completion. The list is a long one. Thanks to Judith Lorber, Sandra Morgen, Cynthia J. Truelove, Maxine Baca Zinn, Esther Ngan-Ling Chow, Doris Wilkinson, Dawn Esposito, Deborah K. King, Kathleen Kinney, Dorothy E. Smith, Walda Katz Fishman, Fred Evans, Tony Smith, Martha Ecker, Lisa Brush, Kimberly Nettles, Mary Sawyer, John Smith, Judy Stephen-Norris, Sonia Michel, Nancy Rose, and Carolyn Sachs. Special thanks goes to Wendy Sarvasy for her critical insights and ongoing interest in the project. Francesca Cancian was a most thorough reviewer and supportive critic who offered valuable comments on multiple drafts. Gwendolyn Mink's and Frances Fox Piven's suggestions were especially helpful. Series editor Myra Marx Ferree who reviewed several drafts of the manuscript offered crucial advice at key points during the writing process. Paula Ross's editorial recommendations helped improve the clarity of the finished product. I also wish to thank the community workers and their daughters included in this study who also read and responded to drafts of the manuscript. Their thoughtful comments and challenging questions have made this a much better work.

I express my heartfelt gratitude to all the women interviewed for this study. They graciously opened their homes, offices, and hearts to me despite their busy schedules. I hope that I have captured some of the vibrancy and sincerity that they brought to their daily struggles to enrich the lives of their communities.

Thanks to my parents, Donald V. Naples and Margaret J. Naples, for all their encouragement and support.

There are no words to describe the debt I owe to Nina E. Fortin. She was my emotional support and intellectual companion from the start to finish of the dissertation that serves as the basis for this book. Her inspired comments and never-ending faith in me and the project carried me through some challenging times. I only wish she could have lived to celebrate the completion of this book.

**Part I:**

**INTRODUCTION**

# Chapter 1

# WOMEN WARRIORS IN THE WAR ON POVERTY

This book presents the only longitudinal study of women community workers hired in Community Action Programs (CAPs) during the War on Poverty.[1] It explores this valuable form of work through voices of women on the frontline of the fight for social justice and economic survival in low-income neighborhoods in New York City and Philadelphia. From their personal accounts we learn of their lifelong dedication to this challenging work—for some beginning as early as the 1940s.

The War on Poverty offered the first government-sponsored attempt to involve the poor directly and formally in decision making, advocacy, and service provision in their own communities.[2] The Economic Opportunity Act (EOA), the legislative cornerstone of the War on Poverty, was signed into law by President Lyndon B. Johnson on August 20, 1964,[3] and quickly became one of the most hotly contested components of Johnson's Great Society programs.[4] It called for Community Action Programs to be "developed and conducted with the maximum feasible participation of residents of the areas and members of the groups" served.[5] Policy makers and African American male and Latino community leaders, who parlayed their antipoverty experiences into political careers or built large welfare bureaucracies, are treated as the only notable actors in most written accounts.[6] By contrast, *Grassroots Warriors* highlights the important stories of women who were hired by antipoverty programs during the War on Poverty.

The implementation of the Economic Opportunity Act, with its emphasis on maximum feasible participation of the poor, offers an historically specific occasion to examine the multifaceted ways the state shapes women's lives—as workers employed by the state, as unpaid community caregivers who link other community residents to the state (e.g., by accessing state resources or gaining state protection), and as beneficiaries of state welfare programs. Many of the women whose experiences form the basis for this book have been single mothers, received welfare, and lived their entire lives in poor, urban neighborhoods that most contemporary policy makers claim should circumscribe their work lives, world views, and political engagement. In contrast to the stereotype of the dependent welfare recipient that forms the justification for contemporary welfare reform,[7] these women contributed vital paid and unpaid services to their communities and provided complex political analyses of local and national struggles for social and economic justice.

In the book entitled *New Careers for the Poor*, Arthur Pearl and Frank Riessman (1965) discuss the rationale for hiring residents of low-income communities as community workers.[8] They argue that noncredentialed resident workers possess a greater investment in the well-being of their communities than workers who do not live in the communities. Further, they assert that resident workers relate more effectively to their neighbors than strangers who do not share the same class and race background. But merely providing dead-end jobs for the poor is inadequate. The jobs must provide entree to institutionalized careers that are also socially useful or at least better than other available options. The concept of "New Careers" found support from the federal government with the passage of the 1966 Scheuer Amendments to the EOA, which established $3.3 million for the New Careers program.

Estimates on the number of jobs provided through New Careers programs range widely. By 1970, Audrey Cohen states that approximately 20,000 people "had enrolled in federally sponsored New Careers projects (p. 10). R. A. Nixon (1970, 7) puts the figure at more than 25,000. Cohen (1981, 10) adds that between 250,000 and 400,000 paraprofessionals were employed in various human service agencies as a consequence of New Careers-related initiatives. Matusow (1984, 251) estimates that 125,000 poor residents were hired by the CAPs as community organizers, day-care workers, counselors, and teachers' aides. However, given the enthusiasm with which local community agencies, schools, and health care facilities, among other human service organizations, moved to hire community, education, and health aides, it remains difficult to assess the number of low-income residents who entered these careers. And to date, little is known about how those hired for those positions fared once they entered these fields.[9] In this book, through the words of women community workers themselves, I examine the strategies they developed to confront problems in their communities, the differences between the resident and nonresident community workers, and how the changing political and economic context influenced their political practice.

Policy makers who helped design the War on Poverty believed that the poor lacked a tradition of community organization.[10] However, many workers hired by the antipoverty programs were often chosen because of their previous community work. Subsequently, through their visibility as paid community workers, these women established themselves as central figures in the ongoing survival of their embattled communities. Moving into the twenty-first century, many continue to help empower others in their defined communities.[11]

This book chronicles how women "build political houses" to fight inequality and discrimination—as one young activist explained with regard to her mother's community work. In many ways, *Grassroots Warriors* explores how a nation builds its "political house" through social policy, democratic implementation strategies, and grassroots community-based activities. These women's stories reveal how social policy can serve as a vehicle for expanding citizenship in concrete ways that go beyond individual practices like voting or paying taxes. The women community workers interviewed for this book view citizenship as something achieved in community and for the benefit of the collectivity rather than as an individual possession. Their position reflects the Civil Rights Movement's admonition that "none of us is free until all of us are free."[12] In this sense, analysis of women's community work offers new evidence for the debate on the state's role in expanding avenues for social citizenship. By centering women's work in the community, I blur the distinction between paid and unpaid work.[13] By highlighting the states' sponsorship of this work I challenge the differentiation between social and political citizenship[14] that form two focal points through which scholars analyze how the welfare state reproduces or counters gender, race, and class inequality.[15]

The central questions addressed in this book are: What motivates women to undertake community work in low-income communities; how does race, class, and gender intersect in their political biographies; what role does the state play in shaping women's community work in low-income neighborhoods; how do processes of bureaucratization and professionalization affect women's community work; how do changes in the political economy and political culture affect their community work; and, finally, how do the community workers ensure the continuity of their work.

The women from low-income communities employed through the antipoverty programs established by the Economic Opportunity Act continued the practice of community work that women traditionally performed. Women's community-based activities have historically involved unpaid work in churches, schools, childcare programs, hospitals, and recreation centers. However, most of the early literature on social reform, charity work, the settlement house movement, and contemporary civic work in voluntary associations focuses on the work of white, middle- and upper-income women.[16] Therefore, the shift in the class and racial composition of those recognized as community workers has important consequences for analyses of poverty, professionalization in social welfare, the role of the state in low-income women's lives, and the politics of community work—as I will demonstrate.

## Dynamics of Class, Race, and Gender in the War on Poverty

In this analysis of women warriors in the War on Poverty, I explore the dynamic relationship of class, race, and gender as it shaped the everyday lives and political motivation of women who found employment in antipoverty programs in New York City and Philadelphia. Exploration of women's community work in poor neighborhoods offers a glimpse into the rich and predominantly informal social networks, historically the essential communal and political resource for those living in poverty.[17] This research also highlights the value of the community workers' political analyses for grassroots campaigns for social justice.[18] The CAPs served as an important organizational location for the development and deepening of community workers' political analyses and activism. The CAPs also provided a crucial site where women affirmed their commitment to address problems in their defined communities as well as a place where they could collectively discuss the nature of the problems and envision effective solutions.

When policy analysts evaluate the effectiveness of the War on Poverty, many emphasize that the "neediest" low-income people were untouched by the programs and that, consequently, the antipoverty programs were a failure even in their own limited terms.[19] For example, critics of the antipoverty programs have argued that those chosen to fill the new jobs as case-work, legal, and healthcare aides as well as parent aides and community organizers were more middle-class oriented than their peers and therefore did not reflect the community at large.[20] Allen Matusow (1984, 251) argues that those poor residents hired by the CAPs were, "not the hard core but the upwardly mobile poor, who too often lacked empathy with those they were leaving behind." The resident community workers interviewed for this study possessed, on average, a somewhat higher level of education than others living in their communities. However, their previous paid employment and income did not reflect a much higher standard of living at the time they accepted paid community work. Matusow also asserts that "middle-class professionals demonstrated little interest in learning whatever it was the subprofessionals were supposed to teach." The small scale of this study cannot directly challenge Matusow's assertions. Yet the findings do demonstrate that this cohort of community workers, both "subprofessionals" and "middle-class professionals," expressed great empathy for their friends and neighbors living in poverty and learned much from one another. How representative these women are is open to further investigation. However, the fact that those who remained in community work positions over the span of thirty years or more calls into question much of what many policy analysts take for granted about community action, maximum feasible participation, and the War on Poverty more generally.

Analysts disagree on the significance of the Civil Rights Movement as a major force contributing to the War on Poverty.[21] However, historical research of this policy era shows that race politics profoundly shaped the political environment of the CAPs once they were established in different communities. For example, Jill Quadagno (1994, 11) demonstrates "how the Civil Rights Movement absorbed community action programs, using them to redistribute political power from local machines to black organizations and black leaders,"[22] although she does not highlight to what extent women took on leadership roles. In a separate analysis of gender dynamics evident in implementation of the Economic Opportunity Act, Quadagno and her coauthor, Catherine Fobes, turn their attention to Job Corps, Title I of the Act, where they discover that Job Corps training centers replicated a gender division of labor by training women for low-paying jobs and family caregiving (Quadagno and Fobes 1995). In contrast, men were trained for better-paying jobs in the skilled trades. Rather than treat the dynamics of race and gender in separate accounts, *Grassroots Warriors* explores how race and gender formed an interlocking subtext[23] of community politics and local community-employment practices following passage of the Economic Opportunity Act.

The race and gender subtext of the state includes expectations about the work that women perform and embedded assumptions about racial difference. These assumptions influence the construction of social policies.[24] Furthermore, social policies have racial and gendered outcomes that position men and women of diverse racial backgrounds differently with regard to the resources they receive or the access they have to state welfare programs.[25] The race and gender subtext also includes the "racialized gender" (Boris 1995) division of labor within the state. For example, women form the majority of social workers, teachers, health-care providers, and middle managers of social-service bureaucracies. Women of color are disproportionately located in the lower rungs of the institutional hierarchies of social work, education, health care, and social service. The War on Poverty included racialized gendered assumptions that informed the design of the antipoverty programs, influenced the implementation of the programs, and consequently shaped the ways men and women of different racial-ethnic backgrounds participated in the CAPs. However, given the mismatch between these assumptions and women's social position within racially diverse communities, women were not always incorporated in ways that coincided with the policy assumptions (also see Naples 1997).

Early reports ignored women's contributions as paid workers, despite the fact that the majority of positions such as community aide, community worker, and parent aide were filled by women.[26] In keeping with the traditional disregard of the economic value of women's work, the Office of Economic Opportunity (OEO), established by the Economic Opportunity Act to oversee the new programs, continued to define women's role in the War on Poverty as that of volunteer. In 1969, OEO published a report entitled *Women in the War on Poverty*, which emphasized that more than twenty million women volunteers had been active in the programs since 1964, stressing their important support roles not their leadership roles. No mention was made of the extensive paid work that women performed. By constructing the pathway to prevention of poverty as expanding employment opportunities for poor men, women's employment needs as well as their actual contributions as staff members and administrators of antipoverty programs were ignored or marginalized. In contrast to the limited picture painted by the OEO, Curt Lamb (1975, 158) found that women comprised a "fair share of leadership positions" in the CAPs, although he did not differentiate between paid and unpaid leaders. In this book, I seek to adjust the historical record by highlighting the experiences of women who found paid employment through the antipoverty programs funded by the War on Poverty.

In order to situate women's community work in an historical context and to examine the state's role in political socialization, I identified community workers who were employed in the CAPs between the years 1964 and 1974. Through analysis of the women's oral narratives, I compare the experiences of African American, Latina (predominately Puerto Rican), and white European American community workers of different class backgrounds as they construct their motivations for community work and political participation over decades of activism.[27] While I emphasize the community work of those women who were originally residents of the communities they served during the War on Poverty, I also include comparative analyses of the community work performed by women who, at that time, did not reside in these low-income Philadelphia and New York City neighborhoods. I originally drew a distinction between the resident and nonresident community workers to differentiate between workers who shared the race and class background of the members of the community they served and those who did not. In this way, I could also identify workers who were hired for their indigenous knowledge of the specific communities and those who were hired for their professional credentials. However, in a few cases, workers who lived in these communities did not share the same race and class backgrounds (e.g., Japanese American Harlem resident Paula Sands). In other cases, workers who were not residents at the time did share the race and class backgrounds of community members (e.g., nonresident Lydia Montalvo who grew up in New York City in a working-class Puerto Rican family). Over the course of the study those who originally resided in the poor communities moved away or gained professional credentials, and nonresident community workers moved into the poor neighborhoods or became more closely identified with the residents after years of community-based work. Therefore, over time, certain aspects of the analysis applied to community workers regardless of resident status.[28] However, because this distinction was so salient during the War on Poverty, I retain it throughout the text, even though over time the clarity of the differentiation blurs.

I interviewed community workers in offices, homes, coffee shops, and parks in many poor neighborhoods throughout these two cities using an open-ended, unstructured interview schedule. Three areas of investigation guided the interviews conducted in the mid-1980s: the development of a biography of the activist woman's personal and work history; an exploration of her political participation and political analyses; and her perceptions of community problems, changes over time, and visions of "community." The in-depth interviews generated a focused life history of key events in each woman's life through a reconstruction of early childhood experiences, community work, political activities, employment histories, family, and other significant relationships. This oral historical approach offered a "context in which to examine the development of political consciousness" (Mohanty 1991a, 33) as well as an opportunity to explore conflicts and tensions in the community workers' self-definition. Follow-up interviews conducted in the mid-1990s focused on gathering an oral narrative of their employment, community work, political activities, and family responsibilities since the mid-1980s; changes in political analyses and practices; children's political analyses and practice, when relevant; and personal and political visions for the future. While these basic frameworks guided the interviews, discussions often ranged far from the topics I chose to highlight here. Not surprisingly, the focus and pace established by each community worker shaped the range of issues covered during the interviews. Other factors such as the time available and the number of interruptions encountered during our meetings also influenced the extent to which I could explore different themes in depth. However, in each case, I covered the basic topics outlined for the study, thus ensuring the basis for comparison across the different narratives. In all but a few cases, I audiotaped and transcribed each interview. In the few cases when the tape was inaudible due to background noise, I relied on the extensive notes I took during the interviews. Transcripts and field notes were analyzed for recurring themes and patterns.

The interviews ranged from one and one-half to four hours and included one or more separate sessions. I met the community workers at all hours of the day and night, fitting into their hectic schedules as best I could. I conducted some follow-up interviews over the phone. Some interviews went late into the night and were picked up again early the next morning. Based on their availability, I interviewed some women during several sessions, and others on only one occasion. I conducted in-depth interviews with a total of sixty-four community workers during the mid-1980s (see Appendices A & B). The forty-two women who lived in the low-income communities that were the target of the War on Poverty when they were hired by community action agencies are defined in this study as "resident" community workers. The twenty-two who were not residing in these communities are defined as "nonresident" community workers. Of the forty-two resident women community workers identified for this study, twenty-six are African American, eleven are Latina (ten of whom are Puerto Rican), four are white European

American, and one is Japanese American. Eighteen of the nonresident community workers are white, three are African American, and one is Puerto Rican. I reinterviewed fifteen of the original sixty-four community workers in 1995. Of these fifteen, I conducted in-depth interviews with three of their daughters to explore some unintended and rarely acknowledged intergenerational effects of mothers' community work—a theme identified in the initial interviews.

The women portrayed in this book tell fascinating stories about community action and the War on Poverty. However, their stories do not represent the experiences and perspectives of all women who participated in community action programs. Their social locations in the large urban neighborhoods of Philadelphia and New York City preclude comparison with women living in smaller cities or rural towns. Some of the women, most notably those in New York City, tell tales of radical activism rarely seen among women in other CAPs throughout the United States. However, analysis of the oral narratives of these particular women illustrates the value of indigenous knowledges for building community, developing political consciousness, and fighting for social justice.

I designed the methodology for *Grassroots Warriors* to capture the complexity of women's motivation for, and ongoing engagement in, community work by allowing them to describe their experiences and perspectives in their own words. The analysis, therefore, starts from the personal narratives of the activists themselves. This approach is informed by feminist scholarship, which, among other things, is interested in "documenting women's experience and observing the patterns found in looking at gender as a category of social experience" (M. Andersen 1983, 15) in the context of each woman's specific social location.[29] I use the term "social location" to indicate the women's multiply constituted "standpoint,"[30] including racial and ethnic identities, class position, family role, sexuality, and gender, as well as geographic, political, and cultural factors that shape their relationship to others inside and outside their defined communities. The notion of social location focuses attention on the shifting nature of the community workers' positionality[31] as well as to the social factors that contribute to their constructed personal and political histories. It highlights the way in which I used the community workers' standpoint as a site of inquiry (D. Smith 1987) for investigating the complex role of the state in contouring low-income women's lives.

## Storytelling and Constructing Histories

The biographical narrative approach offers a powerful method through which to explore the shifts in political consciousness and diverse political practices over time without artificially foregrounding any one dimension or influence.[32] Social movement theories of political participation typically privilege institutional analyses and isolated historical episodes over long-term social psychological processes and community context, although there has been renewed attention to how variation in framing of issues and differences in political culture influence political practice.[33] Overall, however, such approaches miss the rich interaction of individual histories and social action in differing community contexts and, therefore, tell us little about what motivates and sustains political activism. Political activism is influenced by the dynamics of gender, race, ethnicity, class, and political culture that can only be understood through an embedded analysis that foregrounds local practices and individual perspectives.

The oral historical method also permits analysis of political mobilization across different social movements and community mobilizations. By way of illustration, many of the women I interviewed participated in numerous protest movements, including community control[34] of schools, the Civil Rights and Women's Movements, as well as other progressive mobilizations. Local struggles for improved housing or against police harassment, among other community-based efforts that varied across each neighborhood and city, further shaped their political perspectives. The extent to which the community organizations that employed the community workers supported radical political action, promoted democratic process, and valued indigenous perspectives also influenced their social activism.

One of my main motivations for writing this book was to explicate the political lessons offered by women who participated in antipoverty and antiracist community struggles for many decades. However, such an apparently straightforward goal is not without complications. As the Personal Narratives Group (1989, 4) emphasizes:

> The act of constructing a life narrative forces the author to move from accounts of discrete experiences to an account of why and how the life took the shape it did. The why and how—the interpretive acts that shape a life, and a life narrative—need to take as high a place on the feminist agenda as the recording of women's experiences.

I encountered two divergent problems as I proceeded in my efforts to interpret the oral narratives. First, most of the community workers never provided a seamless narrative about "what happened" or what they thought about certain events. In fact, in attempting to present some women's stories I was often amazed at how many different versions I could tell depending on which aspects of their narratives I chose to emphasize or how I combined different facets of their self-presentations.[35] In addition, some women interviewed in the mid-1980s and again in 1995 often told somewhat divergent versions of a similar story or stressed different factors when discussing a particular event or motivation. In fact, the use of oral historical evidence to construct a history of "what happened" at certain points in time has been challenged effectively by historians, most notably Joan Scott (1992). Scott does not suggest we discard "experience" in historical research but that we contextualize and historicize its usage.[36] My methodological solution to this challenge includes locating the women's spoken history in other sources about the periods, events, or actors to which they refer—a typical strategy utilized by oral historians. To do so without disrupting the flow of the stories I relate, I often make liberal use of endnotes. More importantly, although I use their testimony to capture significant moments in their political lives, I resist treating the women's narratives as fully accurate representations of specific events. Rather, I explore their description and analysis of community work as personally meaningful constructions that further shaped their commitment to this form of work. While I also strove to retain the complexity of their lives and political perspectives as they presented them to me, I found that the written form required creating a more linear and less complicated construction of spoken experience than was evident in the interviews that gave rise to the individual life histories.

In contrast to the first dilemma, while some women offered multiple, and sometimes conflicting, constructions of their community work careers and political analyses, other community workers were particularly adept at presenting their political biographies in an internally cohesive fashion that masked inconsistencies and contradictions in their political practice. Over the course of their many years of community activism, these women were interviewed for newspaper articles, spoke on the radio, or participated in a variety of public forums in their capacity as community workers. Consequently, they became particularly skillful in framing their personal histories as well as the political battles in which they engaged in ways that coincide with a consistent political perspective. Given the sincerity and thoughtfulness with which they offered their stories to me, I often was unaware, until the interviews were transcribed and analyzed, of the ways in which some of the women framed their narratives to coincide with a politically coherent persona. This is not to say that these community workers were self-consciously constructing their narratives to appear as such. Rather, I believe, they related their political histories to me in much the same way they integrated these stories of personal and political struggles into their own memories.[37]

However, from my privileged position as storyteller and analyst of the community workers' spoken words, I recognize that the way I gathered the oral histories as well as my organization of the stories also influences how readers will interpret each woman's narrative. In an attempt to counter some of the power of my "interpretive authority,"[38] I shared drafts of the manuscript with the women whose stories I present in detail. This strategy, however, exposed a further dilemma. In asking for feedback on my representation of their lives, I wanted to both ensure that I accurately depicted what they shared with me as well as adequately disguised their identities.

All of the women I interviewed agreed to share their experiences and perspectives with me provided they remain anonymous. Consequently, all individuals have been given pseudonyms (See Appendix B). In the mid-1980s, I viewed this as the most effective strategy. Many of the women were still employed by organizations about which they expressed critical views. Some discussed personal experiences they might not have shared had their names been used in published accounts. However, by the mid-1990s many of the women had retired or moved to other agencies. Children had grown up and could give informed consent for their names to be used. Yet since I started the research with the assurance given that I would use pseudonyms, I continued the practice. In all but three cases, I address each woman by her first name. For three of the women, however, such informality would be considered disrespectful. For them, I use the title Mrs., the mode of address they used in their public life.

This analysis of women's community work highlights the diverse pathways through which women of different race, class, and educational backgrounds come to view community work as a personal calling, political practice, as well as a "New Career." The six women (four resident and two nonresident community workers) highlighted in this opening chapter illustrate both the diverse ways the women came to community work as well as other major themes of the book. Their stories start us on the journey toward understanding the distinctive contributions made by urban community workers to the American social and political landscape. Subsequent chapters take us further into their everyday lives and world views, and highlight how the state played a central role in shaping their careers as community workers. Rita Martinez, Ann Robinson, Teresa Fraser, Wilma North, Lydia Montalvo, and Michelle Dodge are later joined by others whose perspectives provide further insight into the creative strategies designed by the community workers to counter the multifaceted forces that contribute to poverty in America and to ensure the continuity of this work beyond their lifetimes.

### How Six Women Became Community Workers and Why They Stayed

The women whose personal narratives inform this book came to community work through a diverse set of circumstances that highlight the intricate interplay of early childhood socialization, church-based activities, personal experiences of racism and classism, political commitment and political context as well as, to a lesser extent, educational opportunities and career aspirations. Race, ethnicity, class, parenting status, and local and state political initiatives weave a rich tapestry of influences contributing to the uniqueness of each woman's narrative and to the patterned relationships among them. For example, activist mothering—political activism as a central component of mothering and community caretaking of those who are not part of one's defined household or family—is a dominant theme that appears in all the community workers' narratives. Analysis of women community workers' political practice illustrates how women draw on traditional female identities to justify taking revolutionary actions to improve their communities and the lives of their families. Yet many resident workers differentiated their diverse community work activities from "politics" and therefore reinscribed a dichotomy that limited their ability to claim a more powerful political role.

While the state provided opportunities for low-income women to receive pay for these activities, processes of bureaucratization and professionalization established strong pressures toward the depoliticization of community work. The women gained important skills and training from other community members as a result of unpaid and paid community work sponsored by the community-based programs funded through the War on Poverty. Others who had prior experience as unpaid community workers achieved increased status in the community as a result of the paid positions and legitimacy granted by their work. Some women were able to acquire educational credentials and advance their careers as a result of the employment opportunities. For many of the women, especially those with previous unpaid community work experiences, the community action programs appear as a mere backdrop to their lifelong community-based careers. In fact, at points in their narratives, these programs recede from the story altogether. However, as a result of the state's sponsorship of community work, the community workers gained increased visibility and legitimacy as well as resources to expand their political activism and help empower other community members.

The resident workers consistently emphasized how their views on the needs of poor residents and processes of empowerment contrasted greatly with those of social service professionals and most public officials. They described their motivation for community work in highly personal ways often emphasizing early exposure to racism or class oppression. In contrast, the nonresident community workers (the majority of whom are white) were more likely to mention social movement experiences or professional education as triggering their commitment to community work. However, as mentioned above, as some of the resident women increased their education and the nonresident women grew closer to the communities in which they worked, early differences between many resident and nonresident workers were gradually reduced.

In the following abbreviated biographies, I present some family background, growing-up experiences, and motivations for community work, as well as specific political actions and political analyses that were salient in each woman's narrative. In some cases, I stress how community work shaped their approach to mothering as well as how their conceptions of mothering influenced their political strategies. Throughout each narrative, I also highlight the role played by the War on Poverty in supporting or reshaping their community work. The stories told below anticipate most of the major themes addressed in the following chapters.

Rita Martinez's parents, who met in New York City, were born in Puerto Rico. Because her father had to work as a young child after both his parents died, he could not attend school. Rita's mother only completed the third grade but Rita proudly explained how her mother could "outwit any mathematician." She recalled with enthusiasm, "The woman was a wit. She developed a bookkeeping system for her store—she later taught me—which I felt was very amazing." Rita described her mother as an "outspoken person" who, because she could not speak English, had a difficult time finding employment outside of low-paid factory work. However, her mother was active in her community, participating in electoral politics and modeling for Rita the importance of helping others in their low-income Harlem neighborhood. Rita explained that people frequently came to ask her mother for advice. Her mother, invariably, would assist them with any problems they were having with the police or other public officials. Like Rita, many community workers learned the importance of this work from their mothers and passed on this lesson to their children. Women without children related to their community work as community caretaking and emphasized the significance of passing on the legacy of community work to younger members of their communities.

Rita worked as an assistant teacher in a community childcare program earning $8,000 a year when I first met her in 1984. She married at age eighteen and had three children. Rita's apprehension over her youngest child's emotional development led to her involvement in a community-based childcare program funded through the War on Poverty. She took advantage of the educational advancement opportunities offered through the Harlem-based antipoverty program to pursue a personal career goal as a teacher. Rita completed the requirements for a General Equivalency Diploma (GED), got a B.A. from Goddard College, where she gained credit for her "life experience," and subsequently applied for a master's degree in education.

Through her involvement in the antipoverty programs, Rita said that she developed a broader analysis of parents' rights which, in turn, informed her approach to unpaid and paid community work practice. Rita's personal understanding of the relationship between the poor and the political establishment enhanced her ability to engage her neighbors in struggles that directly affected their lives. She explained why she thought poor people could not relate to political debates when their basic needs were not met:

> Many people don't watch…a discussion between [presidential candidates]. They're thinking about when is their next plate of food going to be on the table [and] when are they going to be able to pay the rent. And those are the issues you've got to attack. And you can't just go around talking about taxes. For example…[when politicians are debat-

ing whether taxes should go up or not, the poor] parents are saying, "Taxes, well, what is taxes? I'm thinking about my next plate of food."

Rita evidenced a special sensitivity to the needs of the poor that, she said, "wasn't taught" which, in turn, influenced her community-organizing strategies. She related:

> It was something that I just used to pick up at meetings where I found that parents would not talk, and I would ask them: "Why don't you ask questions? I know you have questions. And your faces' expressions were telling me that you are questioning something. You feel uptight about something, something that was said. I saw something in your face." And they would tell me, "Yeah, it's true." And I say, "Well, why don't you ask?"…My main concern was to have everybody participate and everyone heard.

Rita's concern for a broad-based form of participatory democracy was characteristic of the approaches to community work described by all the community workers, although the extent to which they succeeded in their "empowerment" efforts differed greatly over time and in different organizational contexts.

As many of the community workers emphasized, their approach to working with their neighbors in poor communities contrasted greatly with the lack of sensitivity evinced by elected officials and public-welfare professions who, the workers complained, failed to involve community residents in decision-making processes. Rita recalled one time when "a whole bunch of assemblymen" came to Harlem. She asked a question and said she knew from the response that the assemblymen had no understanding of the needs of low-income people. When she tried to describe the problems in her community, one assemblyman asked her what she meant. She recounted her response as follows:

> And I say, "Just what I'm saying. It's like you're eating sirloin steak and I'm eating mashed potatoes at home without the sirloin steak. That's the difference. And you're going to tell me I need a playground, and I'm telling you I need better schools. The playground will come later." And he looked at me, and he tried to change the conversation. I said: "You can't tell me what I need if you don't live in this community. You can't say to me, 'You need a new playground, or you need a new fountain in that playground.' Come and ask me what I need. And I'll tell you what I need is a job." And many times what they'll say is, "Oh, they don't want to work." And I say every race, every nationality, has a bunch of people that don't want to work…So much is piled on top that you don't care.

Rita's response to the assemblyman and her reconstruction of the interaction highlighted her continued frustration with elected officials who, she complained, did not understand the needs of the poor. Painfully aware of the construction of the poor as people who lack the desire to work, she also understood why some give up on the possibility of finding and keeping employment. Since the poor face so many obstacles to participation in the workforce, they are discouraged from seeking paid employment, she argued. The fact that the event she described took place at least ten years before our conversation reveals the extent to which it symbolized her ongoing struggle for legitimacy with professionals and city officials. Her comment that "so much is piled on" also expresses some of her own weariness with the fight against poverty in her community.

Rita's narrative illustrates three central themes found in my exploration into the motivation for and long-term commitment to community work evidenced by women in low-income urban neighborhoods: the family's key role in the process of political socialization; the role of the state in providing opportunities for low-income women to develop skills and further their formal education in service to their communities; and the perceived contrast between political analyses and practices of women living in these communities and others, especially those nonresidents holding political office. Ann Robinson's construction of her community work career further highlights the diversity of influences that shaped the women's motivation for and continued commitment to community work including the important role of the church and personal experiences of racism and poverty.

Ann Robinson was born in Harlem Hospital to parents who had moved to New York from the West Indies "looking for better living conditions." Ann's father was a factory worker, her mother, who "only went to the third grade," did not hold a steady paid job while Ann was growing up. She was, however, very active in the church. Ann described her family as one that saw little distinction between church activities and community work. Ann's earliest memories are of a household that was always open to others in need. She recalled:

> And one thing I saw within my home—and I guess it was still the Depression around that time—my parents would also have food to share with somebody, be it a child or an adult. And I remember many a night we would be woken up… And I would sleep in the living room because somebody [needed to sleep in] my bed.

She believed that her parents' example fostered her concern for others and laid the foundation for her commitment to community work.

Ann's parents encouraged her participation in a church youth group. Through this group, Ann began working with immigrants who wanted to study for their naturalization as U.S. citizens. In addition to her early childhood and church experiences, Ann explained that living in poverty increased her ability to assist others: "I think again that helped me as I grew older, in what I believed people should have, because I experienced it. I knew what it was."

Ann had five children in a span of seven years. She jokingly added that "something had to be wrong with my psyche. It shows you how brainwashed we were in those days, because motherhood proved your womanhood." Although Ann did not describe herself as a feminist, she offered a grounded explication of the dynamics of gender throughout her political analysis. Widowed in 1943, Ann remarried but her second husband left after he had difficulty finding work. Ann discussed the difficulties she faced as a low-income African American woman in Harlem before she started her paid community work. She detailed how her experience with the welfare system increased her sensitivity to others forced to rely on public assistance: "I used to wonder, even when I was older, about people on welfare and, maybe they didn't try hard enough, they didn't fight the system hard enough." However, she "got a rude awakening one day" when her husband lost his job and failed to find subsequent employment. "The next thing" Ann knew "he was gone." She recalled:

> Life all of a sudden became different. I had to go to school to get free lunch for my children, which changed their status completely because it meant that they had to go to the back of the line with the other children who were on Welfare. It meant that if there wasn't sufficient food, for instance, if frankfurters were being served that day, all the kids were ahead of them, so maybe they would get half a frankfurter, if any at all. It meant a whole change!

Ann emphasized that her subsequent personal troubles with housing and health-care services added to her determination to help improve the quality of life in her neighborhood. She detailed how the class divisions in American society operated to oppress her community, pointing out how landlords, business owners, and public officials contributed to economic stress by, respectively, neglecting their property, charging high prices, and ignoring community residents' complaints. Ann's autobiographical account illustrates how these ongoing struggles against these class factions influenced her analysis of class dynamics.

As the single head of her household, Ann stressed a range of factors that motivated her community activism. In fact, her life illuminates a number of points, depending on which aspects of her narrative I highlight. To begin with, Ann recounted difficulties she encountered as a mother living in a tenement in a low-income neighborhood. Lack of heat, water leaks, and mice and rats roaming her apartment all contributed to her determination to fight against the conditions under which poor people were forced to live. When her son died of pneumonia, she said, "It just triggered me off!" She reported:

And I started fighting them, the Health Department, and others, to get heat in the house, and other things like that. I knew that life didn't have to be like that. There's no reason that my children or anybody else's had to live like that. And when my kids started school I tried to organize the people.

Her struggles with the school system furthered her commitment to community work already established when her children were infants.

Ann recalled another specific turning point in her life where, she explained, she decided to dedicate her life to community service. In 1959, she was very sick and was not expected to live. She asked God to spare her life, help her to get an apartment with heat and a job, then, she reported: "I would spend the rest of my life for people, bringing people resources together, trying to get people outside of our neighborhood to understand what makes us tick." While this historical moment stood out in her mind prior to 1960, Ann already had a strong connection to her church, and through it to community work prior to 1960.

Ann described her community work as a mission. She stressed that she "was able to develop a lot of skills" as a consequence of her church activities. She explained: "And in our church, you had responsibilities, teaching Sunday school, running the programs…talking before five hundred people, so that was good development." Ann held onto her belief in prayer and advised others that God "will help you in his own way." She also emphasized that faith and trust in God "has kept low-income people, or poor people, or black people going."

As I found for almost half of the resident community workers, Ann's parents encouraged their children's participation in church and other community work. The significant interaction between early childhood socialization, church experiences, and community work is especially evident in Ann's story. According to her,

Much of what people today call social work, in the religion that I grew up in was called missionary work, where you extended yourself to people of the community, and the community was anyone in need. It had nothing to do with color, age, religion, whatever. And you shared whatever you had.

As Ann points out, her initial involvement in church work eventually helped her develop the skills she applied as a community worker. However, she underscored that it was her parents' participation in church activities that first prompted her own church involvement as well as her other community work.

Ann's narrative exemplifies the multiple forces contributing to a life-long commitment to community work, a commitment first modeled by her parents and church elders. Ann's ideas concerning her identity as mother and community caretaker further shaped her motivation for community work. She described her involvement in protests against the city-run hospital in her Manhattan neighborhood for welfare rights and improved housing, as well as for expanded childcare services and community control of the public schools.[39] Her ongoing efforts to fight for her children's well-being and her community's self-determination defy the dominant constructions of low-income women as lacking political interest or motivation to work.

Ann's description of police resistance against parents' organizing for community control of their schools illustrates the personal risks that many of the women faced as they engaged in radical political actions in their communities. Ann vividly remembered, "I was quite active [in demonstrations]....And one day we had a meeting [in the school]...And they [the police] shot right into the school house. We had several of our people get their heads beat up." Despite such dangerous incidents, Ann continued to fight for community control of schools and other community institutions.

Despite the problems faced on a daily basis by the community workers as funds were cut back during the 1980s and staff was laid off, most expressed a firm desire to continue the work. The resident women explained their commitment as a logical outgrowth of their own encounters with inequality and injustice. They felt they had a unique perspective that differed from the distanced approach adopted by social-welfare professionals, although as they were incorporated into the professionalized hierarchy of social welfare they often began to describe their work as more social service than advocacy or activism. They also stressed the value of community-based organizations and the Community Action Programs (CAPs), in particular, for providing an institutional base from which resident community workers could develop their skills and create alternative approaches that more directly met the needs of community members. In the next narrative, Wilma North affirms the significance of experiences working in a Philadelphia CAP for her political education as well as for her development as a community leader.

———◆———

Wilma North's family had lived in Philadelphia for several generations. One of five children, Wilma said she "had the best old parents." Her father, who held a variety of factory positions, died in 1966. Her mother, employed as a domestic worker for most of her life, was extremely active in her church. With few avenues available for African American women to develop and demonstrate their leadership skills outside the home, the church offered the principal place for African American women to cultivate and formally exercise power within their communities.[40] Wilma demonstrated this point when she described the importance of the church for her mother's sense of personal power.

As a matter of fact right now she's one of the Mothers of the Church — she's a Church Mother — and she tells me when she feels important she signs her letters "Mother Matthew." And I said, "Why did you write me a letter and sign it 'Mother Matthew'?" And she said, "Oh, I was feeling important that day."

Wilma, like Rita Martinez, was proud of her mother, noting that although her mother only completed the sixth grade "she's got more sense than I've got. She can sit down and do the most complicated crossword puzzles that the *New York Times* can put out." The resident community workers who spoke glowingly about their mothers were, in effect, contesting the negative stereotypes of low-income women of color that dominates the media and public-policy discourse. They expressed much sorrow about how these negative constructions hurt their mothers and rendered invisible their talents and hard work.

Wilma traced her own community activism to the early 1960s when "there was much need and everybody was trying to do something." Several members of her community joined together to start a community organization because, she explained, "...there was a tremendous need for things in our community...which we knew were available in other communities, and so we set about the wheels in motion to try and obtain them for ourselves." Wilma said that the organization was particularly focused on improving the quality of education in the local schools. With three young children at the time, she was especially motivated to participate in this form of activism. Since the PTA in her children's school was not particularly effective in challenging the school administration to correct the problems in the school, Wilma was especially grateful to find an organization willing to take more direct action. She remembers how frustrated she was with the PTA and contrasts this with the excitement she felt when the organization she joined achieved a number of significant changes in the community.

> Well, see the PTA was not my kind of thing. Back in those days the only thing PTAs did was have teas and sell candy....[Well] that's the way I saw it anyway. There was too much to be done to be sitting around gossiping and having tea parties, and I never had time for that kind of stuff. I didn't then and I don't now. And there were things to be done like...[closing] a pinball parlor across the street from the school. Somebody needs to take some action. Or if you need crossing guards, or if there are dilapidated houses, or if you're not getting the kind of response from the police department that you feel the community needs to get....And we did [get it]! We helped hire a very good police community-relations officer at that time. But the biggest thing that I was really happy about was the relationship we established with the Board of Education.

Wilma explained that her organization gained improvements in the schools that the more passive PTA failed to achieve due to her group's effective mobilization of a wide range of community residents. The community-based organization developed a broader constituent base and took a more proactive stance than the PTA. It also proved to other more established community organizations that local residents could join together and improve the quality of life in the neighborhood.

Wilma served as president of this neighborhood organization for several years before President Johnson declared the War on Poverty. She believed her group was successful in their political organizing because, she emphasized:

> Each time there was a meeting, we were there. We were testifying about one thing or another. We did all kinds of things—anything for the betterment of that community. We went before the zoning boards. We went before the school boards.

As a consequence of the work she performed with this community group, Wilma was offered employment in the newly established CAP in her neighborhood: "Yes, that's how I got the job. They told me I was doing it free anyway, I might as well take the job."

Wilma started working for an area office of the Philadelphia Anti-Poverty Action Committee (PAAC) in August 1965 as a clerk typist. During her tenure as a paid worker for PAAC, Wilma improved her position from clerk typist to area coordinator. With only a high school diploma, she managed the area office, wrote proposals, administered funds, and supervised a staff of eight people. Unlike many other resident workers, Wilma did not believe that her lack of a professional credential interfered with her career advancement. She continued to perform unpaid community work along with her paid community work through the 1970s and 1980s while remaining active in her church.

As a consequence of a growing political conservatism and increased government cutbacks, funds for community action declined substantially by the mid-1980s. The political climate was marked by a highly charged conservative and anti-poor rhetoric.[41] The larger more structural changes Wilma described as indicating the success of her community work during the 1960s and early 1970s receded in the description of her community work during the 1980s. In 1984, Wilma showed me a letter of gratitude sent by a man who had been given food by her office as an illustration of what gave her the most satisfaction in her work. In assessing her continued commitment to community work in the 1980s, she shifted focus from improvements in education and housing that marked her story of the 1960s and early 1970s to more individualized interpersonal encounters. Wilma's emphasis on individual service over political action in the mid-1980s indicated how she readjusted her personal and political goals to correspond more with the changed political and economic environment. Community workers who could not make this adjustment found it difficult to remain in increasingly politically circumscribed positions.

Wilma's shifting focus within her community work also fit with her own construction of politics. For example, despite her visible leadership role in her local community, Wilma was amazed that people frequently sought her recommendation on a variety of issues, including politics. She did not connect her central role in the community with politics, which she claimed she didn't "know that much about."

> It's the funniest thing! I don't know why people come to me and ask me things, except for the fact that *I do a lot of civic work*. But I have been asked for recommendations. If there is a need for committee people in my particular division, I have been asked more than one time for a recommendation. *But as far as politics is concerned—I don't know that much about it.* [Emphasis added.]

In addition to differentiating between politics and community work, she made a distinction between political organizations and civic organizations. She emphasized that she was active "only at the school," which was "not politics, only civic."

Wilma did not believe that struggles over the educational and recreational needs of her geographic community were political acts. In describing the contrast between politics and civic work, she discussed how her community "didn't have a recreation center, no place for those children to play" and how the parents joined together to advocate for the use of the local school:

> And so we went to work on that and, of course, we got the recreation center too late for any of my children to enjoy it, but we do have one now. And during that time there was a program sponsored by the Department of Recreation and it was held at the school building, and in the summer they had a portable swimming pool in the school yard. And they put up basketball nets in the yards so the fellahs could shoot baskets. Those were the first recreational facilities that we had in that community. So what I'm saying is no, not anything political. *It was civic—just what needed to be done!* [Emphasis added.]

Like Wilma, many other resident community workers did not interpret their activities as political, because, they argued, politics is not concerned about the needs of low-income people. Community work was defined around the needs of their varying communities. Politics, in their view, was designed to serve those in power, not low-income communities. The firm ideological separation they made between community work and politics frequently interfered with the resident community workers' ability to challenge the established political system despite a large constituency they had established over many years of leadership in their community. However, by working outside the traditional political system, the community workers developed a new language of politics and political practice that more accurately captured their lived experiences and understanding of community needs.[42]

Wilma's story highlights several dimensions of activist mothering as well as the contradictions in the resident community workers' approach to politics. The community workers' ideas concerning their identities as mothers or community caretakers shaped their motivation for community work to a certain extent. How they came to view themselves as activist mothers or community caretakers frequently predated their community work. Once they became active in community work their experiences and acts of resistance defied the dominant definition of motherhood as emphasizing work performed within the private sphere of the family or in face-to-face interaction with those in need. Teresa Fraser's narrative accents the personal price that many community workers and their families paid for their activism.

Jewish community worker Teresa Fraser first became politically active as a teenager when she worked for the Henry Wallace for President campaign in 1948. Teresa's parents were extremely politically active. Her father was a union official and her mother volunteered for different community groups. Both were members of the Communist Party.

Teresa was already active in the community control of school effort in New York when she started struggling with the school system to improve the quality of her son's education. He was dyslexic, although it was not diagnosed at the time. Teresa's efforts on his behalf opened her eyes wider to the racism in the New York City public schools. She recounted:

> I was very embroiled in, more interested in, education as such because my younger son it turned out later had dyslexia, which is now rather recognized and all that but which was not at that time. And so I was able to make a connection between the fact that I had a white, cute son. I mean, if I would go in and ask what's wrong they'd say: "Don't worry. He's so cute." And somewhere I realized that while he was getting…[some] attention or there was an expectation that he was going to learn, that was not true with the black or Hispanic kids. So I got into that whole issue and into the fact that I actually had to make arrangements for him outside the school system. So I'm only saying that in addition to whatever I realized objectively that a lot of this [racist] stuff was going on, it became much more personalized to me because of what happened to him in the education system. And I realized then what a total failure the educational system was. And I'm not saying you have to have a personal experience, but sometimes it helps.

Because of her growing awareness of the racism within the school system, Teresa was especially frustrated over the racism she encountered among the white parents she attempted to organize. She recalled with anger how these parents viciously resisted busing as well as other attempts to integrate their neighborhood schools.

As a result of her activism, Teresa described how her son became the target for vindictive administrators in his public high school. Her lingering frustration over the treatment he received was apparent as she detailed how he was denied his high school diploma because he participated with her in the strike against the public schools in the 1960s.[43]

> My son was out during the strike, and it so happens that the principal was [active in] the Supervisors' union. He called me in, and—anyway, it was a whole scene. And what they did to [my son] eventually was they would not give him a diploma because he missed gym, and it was a big athletic school. And he's a terrific athlete. Believe me, it was just a fake! And they failed him in gym. Which was just astounding. But they couldn't do it anywhere else....[W]e had this whole thing that wound its way through the Board of Education, and eventually he ended up having to take one course in night school, and got a Roosevelt Night School diploma, instead of a regular, academic diploma, which was typical of the kind of nasty things [they did to activist parents and their children].

Teresa portrayed this vindictive action taken against her son as typical of strategies used to discourage parents from challenging public-school officials in that period. Throughout her narrative, Teresa continued to enumerate additional examples of how the New York City Board of Education made it difficult for parents to participate in the 1960s and early 1970s. The different examples Teresa offered revealed how much public-school officials feared parent involvement and oversight.

Parent organizing within and against the public schools in New York City also revealed the ways in which the issues of educational access, housing, welfare, and child care, among other needs, were all interconnected. Once Teresa and her coworkers recognized how other issues were related to the children's difficulties in school, their organizing efforts broadened beyond the educational arena. As Teresa explained, "you found that you couldn't work on schools and leave out housing. You couldn't work on housing and leave out welfare. You couldn't do anything without everything else."

One major problem they identified was the large number of children coming to school hungry. Teresa explained that no breakfast programs existed at that time and the school lunch programs served inadequate and nonnutritious food. Teresa and her co-organizers understood that the children could not learn if they were hungry. In the following excerpt, Teresa describes the evolution of her organizing campaign to improve the accessibility and quality of in-school breakfast and lunch programs.

> One of the things that happened was that there was a terrible lunch program at one of the schools, P.S. 25, and we went to protest about it. And the short version of this is that we called a meeting about school

lunch. We got a tremendous response from the parents. And since I'm a relatively okay organizer, I figured out that if that was what was going to grab people, and that if you called them to a meeting about reading they were so scared that you got ten people, and you called a meeting about food and you got 100 people, so you call a meeting around food. And it really started out just doing it that way, figuring that you could start one place and move ahead, and I became totally derailed into food, which I'm still doing. Because I began to see how critical that school meal was to those kids, and to that family, and it was terrifying!

As more parents became involved in organizing to feed children in school, they began showing up at the schools where they observed other problems. Their growing awareness and collective presence led to organizing campaigns to improve other aspects of the educational system. Teresa reported:

And it was so strange because we were also very visible. Parents wanted to come into the school to make sure that their kid was eating. And so there were many fights, and we did a lot of interesting things. We were pretty notorious for doing stuff that was quite wild.

Among the "wild" actions they devised to expand and improve feeding programs in the schools, Teresa highlighted the following:

We once took a couple of vans and picked up the garbage outside about three schools, and we took it and dumped it at 26 General Plaza having called all the radio stations, TV stations, and newspapers. We got tremendous coverage. And we closed down the Federal Building. They were so scared they didn't know what the hell was coming. And we tried to point out that the food was so bad that the kids weren't eating it, and it was a waste of money and the government was throwing its money down the drain.

This dramatic illustration of the inadequacy of the school-lunch program was followed with a luncheon invitation to all the elected officials in the Bronx. Theresa reported:

We promptly took them on a school bus to a school…where, thank God, though it was not planned again, one of the assemblymen got deathly ill. But it was a terrible situation. You went down into this dingy basement. The kids were sitting like this [with arms folded on the tables not eating the food]. They had terrible food. The workers were working under the most terrible conditions. They didn't have a dishwasher, and in order to really clean the dishes, you can't just give the dishes out the next day without really steaming them in some way, so they would literally wrap their hand with a rag, and they'd stack these dishes in the sink and then rush over and open the hot water full force and run like hell to get out of the way. I mean, it was bizarre! And we said: "We're not suggesting that the world should come to an end, just use paper plates." How far do you have to go? It was revolutionary! They called in the Health Department. These congressmen went crazy. It was wild! And we then gave them a rain check and did our own lunch six weeks later in a school. We got one of the junior high schools. We got a woman who had been cooking in [a public school] in Puerto Rico and a man that had cooked in the army. He was black. She was Hispanic. We prepared and we kept track of the amount of money we spent, and we spent the same amount of money that the Board of Education spent on food and served this wonderful meal. It was fabulous!

Drawing on their collective knowledge, the parents convinced the elected officials that they could efficiently provide more nutritious food to the school children of New York City at the same cost as the Board of Education's wasteful food program. Not only did Teresa and her co-organizers reveal the limits of the school food program overall through these public displays, they also specifically demonstrated to school officials that you could feed large numbers of children fresh and ethnically diverse meals.

We did all the things they said they couldn't do such as got rid of frozen meals, put totally fresh meals in all of the schools that had kitchens, brought them to the other schools that didn't have kitchens. As a matter of fact we helped set up a cooperative trucking service in the neighborhood that moved the food from here to there. We did ethnic meals. We put up a tremendous fight. We increased the breakfast program from next to nothing to six thousand kids eating breakfast a day, and twelve thousand kids eating lunch. That's a very high percentage. We had school food committees, which included the kids and school staff and all of that. And we stopped ordering lousy food. And we did all kinds of things that really, interestingly enough, later became part of the overall system.

Building on the success of these local organizing efforts, Teresa and her co-organizers took their cause far beyond the neighborhoods in which their activism began. Teresa traveled to Albany and Washington to share what she learned in New York City and to pressure legislators to improve the quality and availability of school feeding programs. One incident stood out in her memory:

They had the first White House Conference on Children and…the guy who was the head of the Board of Education's School Food Programs went to testify, and we went and chased him, and everywhere he went in Washington, we handed out leaflets telling the true story about what kind of a bum he was, and the fact that everything he said was a lie, and the school food program was a disaster.

Strategies like this were designed to shame publicly and discredit public officials as well as to gain broader support for reform of the food program.[44] According to Teresa, these strategies effectively garnered media attention and public support.

When the EOA designated funds for CAPs, Teresa and the group she worked with expanded their organizing efforts and received pay for community work. Despite the success of the food program she directed, Teresa lost her position when the supporters of the program failed to win reelection to the local school board in 1974. She recalled, "I was very discouraged when I left there, but it is interesting that now things that we did are almost institutionalized into the regular system." In the beginning of the War on Poverty, high-profile community activists like Teresa were often hired to staff the newly funded Community Action Programs. However, Teresa's story exemplifies how some of the most outspoken and politically radical community workers lost their jobs when they posed a threat to established social service agencies, health care centers, or public school officials.

As the neighborhood and citywide political environment changed, so did Teresa's opportunities to work on various other organizing campaigns. Yet she remained committed to food issues. As the numbers of homeless and hungry New Yorkers increased during the 1980s due to cutbacks associated with President Ronald Reagan's fiscal policies and shifts in the wider political economy.[45] The organization Teresa directs moved into direct-service provision. By 1995, the organization had become provider of food to thousands of hungry and homeless New Yorkers—a service they were not performing in the mid-1980s. When I asked if she thought that this shift in organizational strategy interfered with her effectiveness as a food-policy advocate, she explained that the direct service provided a more accurate assessment of the extent of need than the City's official counts. Armed with the data gathered through direct service, Teresa said she could challenge the official statistics and gain some modest increases in funds to feed poor New York City residents.

Teresa combined her previous political organizing and political analyses with the everyday struggles against the school system, eventually refocusing the target for her activism onto feeding hungry New York City residents. Her narrative highlights the personal cost of activist mothering and the deep commitment required of community workers as they faced increasing community problems and decreasing resources with which to wage the battle. Teresa acknowledged that her experience with her son and the public schools highlighted for her the dynamics of racism within the schools. Her persistent and creative antiracist organizing strategies were recognized by other community workers who identified her as a key role model for them.

After thirty years of activism, Teresa echoed the frustration expressed by most of the community workers; she felt that overall there seems to be little evidence that much progress has been made.

If I'm going to be honest, it's hard to look at anything that I've been involved with and really believe that there's been this progress. It's very hard. When you're fighting an overall system that's so immobile, it's so difficult to move it an inch. And the will isn't there. So you're fighting and fighting and fighting, and people are starving, and people are living in terrible conditions!

What kept Teresa and the other community workers I interviewed engaged in the struggle for social and economic justice forms a fundamental question of this investigation. In answering this question, I also considered why community workers who were not residents of low-income communities chose to work in these relatively low-paying jobs with long hours and little status. Lydia Montalvo provided one answer to this question. Her story also illustrates the way in which the process of professionalization often interfered with effective community activism.

Lydia Montalvo, a divorced mother of two, was thirty-eight years old in 1985 and, therefore, was one of the youngest community workers interviewed. Unlike the resident community workers, Lydia completed college before beginning paid community work. Lydia worked initially as a volunteer for a CAP and did not receive pay for her community work until 1974. Her earliest political work involved fighting for women's access to sports in the Queens high school she attended. She reported that her college involvement in fighting against the Vietnam War, for civil rights, and against sexism ignited her lifelong commitment to social justice—what she described as her preoccupation with relevance. Many of the nonresident community workers credited their participation in the social movements of the 1960s for providing them with a political framework and commitment to community work.[46] However, like the resident community workers, Lydia stressed that the foundation for her struggles against inequality and discrimination was laid by her parents much earlier.

Lydia confronted the pain of racism when she and her family first moved from Puerto Rico to New York City. She couldn't speak English when she entered the first grade. One day when she had to go to the bathroom, the teacher told her that "if I couldn't ask her in English, I couldn't be excused." Lydia wet her pants and "was totally mortified." When she told her parents, they went in the next day "to straighten out the teacher." She explained:

> My parents were not active organizationally. They were very active in school in the sense that they knew exactly what was going on with their children. If there was a problem they were there to discuss it....They wanted to be involved as far as their children were concerned but they didn't see themselves involved with changing the whole system.

Lydia said she received "a more valuable education" from her parents than she "was getting within the confines of the establishment walls."

Lydia also emphasized how the discrimination her father faced as a consequence of his racial-ethnic background left a lasting impression on her. Lydia's father was an experienced accountant in Puerto Rico. When he moved to New York City, he could not get a job in his field because, Lydia explained, "even though he spoke English, he had a heavy accent." Consequently, he worked as a factory worker during the day and a watchman at night. Lydia recalled:

> It had an impact on me because I could not understand why he could not work in his field. That left an impression on me and also a reality that stayed with me, and I think it was the genesis that in one way or the other I had to be involved in helping my community in whatever way.

While Lydia's parents did not participate in establishment political activities such as political clubs or electoral politics, she reported that they discussed politics in the home and modeled strategies of resistance to the racism and classism in the surrounding environment.

In fact, Lydia believes that her father's decision to move the family first from Spanish Harlem[47] to a more residential neighborhood in Queens (where he worked as a building superintendent) and then return them to the Lower East Side of Manhattan[48] was designed to first give his children a strong educational foundation and then to remind them "what it means to be a Puerto Rican in New York City." She recalls how when they returned to Manhattan she and her siblings, at first, "were very resentful because it meant losing friends and systems that were so much a part of" their lives. However, over time Lydia began to see the wisdom of her father's decision making. As she reported, "Later on as I got older I realized how smart he was. And now I am very grateful because it added another dimension in my life which may not have come about if that had not happened." Because Lydia had the experience of living in a predominantly white suburban and middle-class community as well as in predominantly nonwhite and working-class communities, she felt that she could organize more effectively across class and race. She emphasized that this aptitude became an especially valuable component of her effectiveness as a community worker.

Lydia's experiences of discrimination in high school also contributed to her commitment to community work. As her story illustrates, it is difficult to separate the forces of sexism from those of racism as factors shaping the personal lives and careers of low-income women of color. She was told by guidance counselors in the early 1960s that, as a Puerto Rican woman, it was highly unlikely she would attend college and that if she did she was obligated to pursue a service-oriented career.

> When I was going to school there was this whole business of stereo-
> typing and tracking people, and I remember my counselors would say
> to me if I was gonna go to college...because I was a woman, that I
> would be .001 percent of my population and that what I really should
> do was be a teacher or a social worker because that was where I was
> really needed. Now there's nothing wrong with being a teacher, and
> there is nothing wrong with being a social worker because many of our
> community leaders, especially our women, started in that field. It's just
> interesting that no one ever saw me doing anything other than that. To
> the extent that you were going to be given entre this is where you were
> going to be given entre.

She resented the presumption that as a Puerto Rican women her career
choices were so limited at the outset. Further, she was annoyed at the expectation that she should return after college to work for her community
because she "kept thinking that there was another world out there and that
was where the power was, where the decisions were being made." She wanted to go "into that 'white male world' and find out what it was all about."
In fact, she believed that the experience working in this white male world
would eventually enhance her ability to serve her community.

Lydia defied her teacher's prediction and found employment in the white
male world inside the Beltway in Washington, D.C., first as a clerical worker
then as a mid-level administrator in a federal agency. However, her interest in
serving her community, variously defined in her narrative as the Puerto Rican
or Latino community, propelled her to return to New York for a community-
based position. Lydia claimed that she is "much smarter" in her community
work role as a consequence of "all the tricks she learned" working for a mainstream organization. She doesn't believe she can return to that type of work
despite the fact that she had earned more than twice her community work
salary. At the time of the 1984 interview, she was directing a community-arts
agency and earning just under $30,000 a year.

Lydia viewed her community work as a logical extension of her identity
as a Puerto Rican woman. She was especially enthusiastic about the role that
women played in all efforts to benefit the Puerto Rican community. Because
of the sexism she found in these struggles, she participated in the Women's
Movement in the early 1970s and became an early member of the National
Conference of Puerto Rican Women. She explained:

> Basically the [Puerto Rican Civil Rights] Movement was being spear-
> headed by women, and it was the women who would start it and fight
> the different battles that had to be fought, that when the smoke died
> down one of our guys would very nicely and comfortably move into
> that [leadership] position and sometimes walk away with all the glory.
> And I saw this over and over again and it got me very interested and
> involved in the Women's Movement.

Lydia, along with the other Puerto Rican community workers interested in contributing to a feminist movement, did not find a site for their political concerns within the existing framework of the white Women's Movement during the 1970s. Consequently, they developed separate Latina feminist organizations—organizations that are rarely included in histories of the U.S. Women's Movement (see Gluck et al. 1997).

Lydia left the Latino arts organization about a year after our interview in 1985. She said that after six years she had accomplished all that she had set out to and that it was time for new leadership to emerge. She felt it important "to nurture them and then to bring in new, younger leadership to come in and take over"—a concern expressed by all of the community workers. As a credentialed worker with years of experience in an arts organization, Lydia was optimistic that she could earn enough income working as a consultant, but she was unprepared for the resistance she met from the staff of more traditional arts organizations and museums, who saw her as having an "agenda." Because of her efforts to increase access to art and widen the participation of low-income and racial and ethnic minorities, Lydia found that many in the traditional art world thought this meant that she was "somehow trying to diminish the [art] work." However, she argued, she was misunderstood and "never advocated changing, you know, or diminishing the work, that" she believed "in the integrity of the work." She continued:

> I think that the quality and the integrity of the work must remain. What I was basically saying is that maybe there's a way for us to make, even enrich the work and that makes the work even more profound. And that we needed to start sharing what we're doing and to ask people what they thought about it. And to give us ideas about how we might look at it in different kinds of ways....And so, what happened was that, be it with the public funding agencies or with the foundations, I sort of became this person that could not really be contracted with any of these arts organizations because their feeling was that I was going to try to go in there and just change everything they were doing.

The difficulty she encountered forced her to find consulting opportunities outside New York City. Ironically, her work with organizations in other regions of the United States, especially the rural South, enhanced her legitimacy in New York City as someone who could bridge racial and class differences. She also believed that it broadened her own view of the needs of marginalized groups.

When a position opened up for an executive director of a Bronx arts organization in the early 1990s, one of the board members who knew of Lydia's successful consulting work with various groups across the country sought her out. Lydia said she would not have applied for the job without encouragement from the board member because of her earlier difficulty gaining entre into other similar arts organizations. After almost six years away from community-based work, Lydia found herself returning to the South Bronx to fulfill her long-term goal of helping to increase access to the arts by locating arts organizations in a diverse community context. She said:

> I discussed it with several people, including some of my colleagues in the consulting world, their feeling was: "You know Lydia, this is the perfect setup for you. Because you've been talking about how do you have culture-built community and how do you have the fine arts become an anchor for community revitalization."

Lydia viewed her professional position as a way to open avenues for Latinos in this community to participate in their cultural institutions. In that position, she defined her community broadly including gays and lesbians who were usually left out, even by the most progressive community groups in the South Bronx.[49]

Like the resident community workers, Lydia brought to her work a set of personal experiences she believed sensitized her to the ways racism and classism circumscribed the lives of low-income people of color. Unlike the resident workers, Lydia did not situate her work within a particular neighborhood context, although she valued helping to locate arts institutions in working-class and poor communities, notably those with a high concentration of Latino residents. Lydia, along with all the community workers who shared their stories with me, was concerned for the continuity of community work and political participation in low-income neighborhoods and communities of color. Analysis of the community workers' narratives confirmed that the continuity of such work and political commitment long predates the state's interest in supporting this work during the War on Poverty. Michelle Dodge was especially concerned with how to ensure the intergenerational continuity within the African American community of the struggle for social and economic justice and highlighted this dilemma through her analysis of her son's political activism.

---

Michelle Dodge, another nonresident worker, held an administrative post in the Philadelphia Antipoverty Action Committee (PAAC) when I first met her in 1984. Her narrative included a sensitivity to the intergenerational continuity and discontinuity in political activism within the black community. She discussed these issues with reference to her father's influence on her activism as well as her influence on her son's political engagement. Throughout her discussion she stressed how changes in the political economy and political culture shaped the political praxis of black middle-class professionals.

Michelle's parents, who both had advanced professional degrees, raised her in the tradition of service to the black community. Her father was a leader in the black community in Philadelphia and served on the boards of several service and advocacy organizations. Michelle differentiated her activism from her father's by explaining that she "wasn't much of a joiner." However, this statement contradicted the description she gave of her community work career. She perceived her role as less visible and self-consciously less "political" than her father's for a number of reasons. She was ambivalent about taking an active and public role in politics on behalf of the black community "as a result of [her] own upbringing." She explained her reluctance to take on a more visible political role in the community as a result of the fear about reprisals as well as a desire for more privacy than a public presence allows: "Some of it was frankly precaution, because during the time my father was active, there were a lot of threats and then partly my own disinclination to be a part of the fishbowl." Because of her father's high-profile role as an effective leader in Philadelphia's African American community, Michelle also found that "there was a tremendous tendency for people to think that because of who I was I could do certain things," such as gain access to key public officials in the city or resources that were, in fact, outside her reach. When she accepted a position with a city agency, she further reasoned "that it was probably not in my best interests, not personally, but professionally and in terms of the community, to become that involved." She believed a more active political role would compromise her effectiveness as a citywide agency administrator.

Unlike the resident community workers, Michelle had the financial resources to send her son to a private school and, therefore, did not find it necessary to mount personal and political battles to protect her child's educational interests. Although she had some "mixed emotions" about sending her son to a small private school, she liked the fact that she "didn't feel that [she] needed to get involved and worry about the curriculum." She recalled:

> If I had problems I generally went and talked to the teachers and could resolve that. I had enough training personally to do that. But also I am not a joiner by nature. The school he went to is over on Society Hill, and I didn't have a great deal in common with most of the parents. I mean I was single by that time, and I worked every day, and I really didn't have that kind of time.

While struggles to promote their children's education, health, and safety occupied the daily political energies of most of the resident community workers, Michelle's financial status insulated her and her son from these problems.

However, the cushion that Michelle's financial status provided also raised other dilemmas for her. She felt caught between a desire to protect her son, Ron, from racism while still giving him the emotional resources and political perspective to deal with a racist society. In addition, while she wished to encourage her son to contribute to the African American community, as did her father and grandfather, she also wanted to respect his personal and political choices. Finding the balance between these two goals was not always easy but over time, Michelle explained, she grew to trust Ron's political instincts and choices.

Ron Dodge attended a racially and ethnically diverse high school and, according to Michelle, did not face racism directly until he went to college. Michelle questioned how well she had prepared him to deal with the racism he met.

> I criticized some of my contemporaries' parents for shielding their children from the harsh realities of race. And I really never made any effort to do that with [my son] and yet I found out that without my even trying, and partly because things had changed, people were not out on the streets demonstrating anymore, he really didn't see it close up. And so he happened to be at [college]…[and] they had some [racist] issues that arose and actually kind of got explosive while he was on the main campus. I mean he even called me and said, "Listen if you can't get me, I might be in jail."

Michelle commented with some surprise on the strategies chosen by her son and other students who participated in the protest at the college.

> [At the college he attended], most of the white students don't come from places where they've really seen black people…and the incidents were fairly nasty as I understand it.…What was amusing, and I think this is in line with what you were asking about—the contrast in approach—when my son told me, "Well, we've organized [a group] to escort young black women across campus."

Michelle was impressed that her son's generation of college students would prioritize women's concerns in their organizing strategies. She also commented on the way they used television rather than print media to get their messages across to the public.

> But the other thing is they were working on a PR [public relations] strategy that involved going on the *Oprah Winfrey Show*.…I think part of it is just the way the world has changed…because that's what impressed them.…I mean those are the things that got them going about issues and I mean why should they compete for newspaper space when, in fact, they can go on a national television show and get nationwide attention.

Michelle believed that since her son's generation did not grow up within a social movement, the television and other media took on a greater role in

raising their political consciousness. The generational difference in political socialization contributed to the development of different strategies to
confront problems of racism as well as an interest in fighting violence
against women.

In addition to contrasts between how her generation and her son's
generation approached political organizing in response to racism,
Michelle also noted differences in political analysis. For example, her
son commented on the failure of integration and remarked that the
*Brown vs. Board of Education* decision was "the greatest mistake we made"
and that "integration has killed the black community." At first Michelle
was disturbed by his comment then she thought about it further and
decided:

> He's absolutely right! In many respects he is absolutely right. And
> frankly, I was never much of an integrationist anyway. But...there was
> a part of me that said: "God, all this blood and all this time it was, you
> know, [a mistake]?" But it is true that as soon as middle-class blacks
> were able to leave that community, that those that they left behind
> lost a resource that, up to that point, had been available to them—in
> terms of power, political power, and economic power, and so forth.
> And yet, that really is no different from any other immigrant....I mean
> everyone has gone through that and soon as they were able to get out,
> those left behind just sort of stayed there....But he was right in that
> sense. I can't dispute that.

Michelle said she is learning to be sensitive to how her personal political
history limits her framework for conceptualizing political strategies. She
has been forced to rethink some of her taken-for-granted positions as she
reflects upon her son's differing point of view.

Michelle was also surprised when her son decided to join the Million
Man March in Washington, D.C., organized by Minister Louis
Farrakhan on October 18, 1995. Her son explained that "when he went
to the March that it was really a very uplifting experience." Michelle
then asked him, "Have you thought about what you might do in terms
of demonstrating your pledge?"[50] She realized that she could not force
him to take on specific issues. She had always held to the philosophy
that

> ...in terms of our children, I think the worst thing that you can do is
> to try to force a kid to deal with the issues the way you do....Not only
> is the world different, and not only are they different people, but
> what I think that what you can do is just the opposite of what you
> want to do. You can push them in exactly the opposite direction. I
> don't think you can force a kid to become an activist or whatever it
> is you are, you have to let them find their way to make that contri-
> bution [to the community].

Like Michelle, most of the community workers who expressed concern for the continuity of the struggle for social justice were ambivalent about how to accomplish this goal without imposing their political goals on their children and other younger members of their community. Some, like Michelle took a more restrained approach; others were much more proactive in their stance. Regardless of their positions, however, most agreed that the altered political and economic context renders many of the political tactics used during the 1960s and 1970s obsolete or, at best, ineffectual.

In 1995 Michelle was directing a nonprofit community agency designed to expand the availability of low-income housing in Philadelphia. As a participant in numerous coalitions of groups representing the black community, she observed that "more of the old guard [of the Civil Rights Movement] is gone. They've either died or they've retired. They aren't active." She spoke about the changes she witnessed in political strategies and leadership styles of the young black middle class in Philadelphia who are now gaining political visibility within the black community.

> They're not quite Buppies [black urban professionals], but they're close. Although they're politically active, their focus tends to be on long-term gains rather than the short-term stuff....They're no longer the sort of neighborhood board leader, alderman-type folk. They're more the electronic [voting], political types. And so the agendas that they are pushing are economic development and that sort of thing....Yes, the social- service issues are there, but they've refocused so that they're looking more at issues like who's going to be president of the school board, and controlling this.

The strategies Michelle mentioned seemed to reflect a move toward more traditional electoral politics and economic strategies and away from direct action and local-service provision. She illustrated the changes with reference to her son who owns his own business in Philadelphia.

> My own son is now twenty-seven....I didn't make any effort [to lead him into community activism]. I mean he sort of had three generations of [activism], because his father was a community activist, too [as well as his grandfather]. But, I mean, he really made his own choices. Yet in some respects, yeah, I think to the extent that he does he gives back [to the black community], that, yes, it would be more the business type. I mean he actually is running his own small business now. I mean part of that is because what else do you do with a bachelor's degree in economics.

According to Michelle, as a consequence of the success of direct-action campaigns that opened access to formal political institutions and helped expand the black middle class, young black professionals were able to shape their political engagement in ways that were more in line with the

dominant political establishment. Yet the specter of race remained to circumscribe the influence of black middle-class professionals.

Michelle offered one of the most sobering comments on the consequences
of racism for young African American men and continues to wonder about her
son's safety even though he has achieved an upper-middle-class lifestyle. She
explained:

> And the truth is that the difference between a young college-educat-
> ed black male…and a young African American hoodlum, is, in many
> instances, a car stop by the police.…I mean, I'm frankly still worried
> for my son who, because he has his own business, doesn't wear a suit
> and tie. But drives a red B-mer [BMW] and has an earring in his
> ear.…I'm still frightened. Plus I don't think he's the safest driver in
> the world. So, you know, I keep seeing him stopped by the police and
> before he can open his lips and maybe try to share whatever intelli-
> gence he has, you know, finding himself on the ground.

Michelle's class position cushioned her and her son from some of the direct
forms of racism described by community workers of color who grew up in
poor and working-class communities. Yet Michelle knew she needed to
prepare her son for the harshness and dangers of racism in the wider
American society. Because of her professional status, her activist mothering differed from that of the resident community workers. However, as an
African American women she was self-conscious of the need to politicize
her mothering practices. While, worried that she had not prepared her son
sufficiently for the racism he encountered when he went to college, she
also recognized that he had to find his own way and his own political position. She was hopeful that the younger generation of African Americans
would remain committed to the struggle for social justice, albeit in a form
that will differ from the older generation.

The African American and Puerto Rican women who entered paid community work after achieving professional credentials all said they oriented
their professional lives toward working for the "betterment" of their racial-
ethnic groups.[51] Their academic and professional achievements reshaped
their relationships to the working-class and poor members of their racial-
ethnic group. This repositioning added an additional burden for them as
they worked self-consciously to retain connections with their defined communities.[52] Michelle has maintained a commitment of service to low-income
communities of color throughout her professional career, primarily focused
around management of government and not-for-profit agencies. She was
most interested in building strong grassroots community organizations
through which low-income and other marginalized groups could gain a
political voice on issues that touch their lives. However, she was not active in
her community of residence nor did she find it necessary to become involved
in other community groups. For the most part, Michelle was emphatic about

the need to draw a boundary between her professional life and personal life—a perspective that differed from most of the resident community workers I interviewed. Her concern for her son's political engagement, however, reflects a theme that ran through all the community workers' narratives; namely: Who will carry on the struggle against injustice and inequality in their communities?

## Organization of the Book

The assertion that growing up poor and facing discrimination enhanced sensitivity toward others in similar situations was an oft-repeated theme of the narratives of the resident community workers, and was one of the main justifications for the implementation of New Careers in the mid-1960s. Given the primary reliance on oral historical data for this investigation I can only assess the extent to which these attitudes found expression in specific interpersonal encounters and concrete political strategies through the community workers' self-reported behaviors. However, the persistence of this theme along with the multiple illustrations offered by the resident community workers indicates how their constructed standpoints on poverty frequently diverged from dominant perspectives in many respects, even after years of employment in state-funded community programs. In this regard, the community workers differ from "street-level bureaucrats" who are portrayed in some accounts as social control agents of the welfare state.[53] In contrast, all of the resident community workers said they retained their allegiance to the poor for whom they worked, even after years of state employment. While my analysis is limited to the narrative construction of their community work, I also find that the specific encounters and daily activities they described corroborate their self-definitions as allies of the poor against insensitive bureaucrats of the state. This forms a contradictory tension for them as both workers employed by the state and advocates in many community struggles against the state. In chapter two, I describe the background to the New Careers philosophy used to justify hiring indigenous workers in the CAPs and how it became part of the national policy discourse in the mid-1960s. This chapter examines the relationship between earlier innovations in social programming and New Careers and concludes with the community workers' assessment of the implementation of New Careers during the War on Poverty.

Due to their multiple locations as human-service workers paid by the state, unpaid caretakers and activists in their communities, and beneficiaries of social programs, the resident community workers were in a unique position to redirect social-welfare policies for the benefit of themselves and their neighbors. From the workers' perspective, they were especially adept in the role of advocate for community residents, as Wilma North's narrative indicates. Their personal familiarity with the range of social programs, eligibility requirements, and key personnel within the state bureaucracies enhanced their ability to access benefits and assist their neighbors who had difficulty obtaining state assistance for which they were eligible. In addition, they described processes by which they resisted, from within, the decline in funding, the growing bureaucratization and professionalization of the antipoverty programs, as well as the depoliticization of the Community Action Programs.[54] In chapter three, I explore how processes of professionalization and bureaucratization circumscribed the political activism and community engagement of the community workers in New York City and Philadelphia and how the workers creatively resisted these pressures.

The women interviewed for this study came to community work through a diverse set of circumstances as Ann Robinson's narrative illustrates. Chapters four and five present the diverse motivations and personal and political influences the community workers described that led them to take up the challenging demands of this form of labor. Chapter four outlines some of the formal political and professional influences that inspired the community workers, particularly the nonresident workers, to pursue this form of work. Chapter five focuses primarily on the activist mothering of the resident community workers.

Chapter six highlights how the community workers drew on their gendered identities to organize as women and what relationships they formed with the Women's Movement—a theme briefly highlighted in Lydia Montalvo's story. The community workers were also active participants and "center women" (Sacks 1988b) in local struggles to achieve economic, political, and educational equity and to protect the physical safety and health of their communities. They utilized their knowledge and paid positions as resources for these ongoing community struggles as Teresa Fraser details in her discussion of the educational and food advocacy efforts in New York City. Chapter seven describes the strategies the community workers employed to ensure the continuity in community work beyond their lifetimes—a topic Michelle Dodge's narrative foreshadowed. In the final chapter, I discuss the implications of the overall analysis for a renewed war against poverty.

# Part II:
## THE U.S. WAR ON POVERTY

# Chapter 2

# CONTRADICTIONS OF NEW CAREERS

In the provision establishing neighborhood-based community action programs (CAPs), designed, directed, and staffed by low-income residents, the Economic Opportunity Act inadvertently broke down the false separation between paid employment and unpaid nurturing activities traditionally performed by women in poor communities. Many of the workers hired for the community-based programs were already active as unpaid community workers in their neighborhoods. In fact, many were hired because of such experience. Since the previously unrecognized and unpaid community caretaking was historically the province of women,[1] women filled the majority of the newly created positions as casework, health, education, and childcare aides as well as the more general position of community worker (Lamb 1975). Prior to the War on Poverty, women's community-based work was rarely viewed as a "career"—political or otherwise. In much the same way that women's childcare work was devalued since women were defined as "natural mothers," women's community work was, and in many cases continues to be, treated as an unremarkable natural task for women to perform. When researchers and other observers naturalize women's "social housekeeping" role in their neighborhoods and communities, they underestimate the important skills, experience, and networks women develop as a consequence of their community-based work. Yet as I will demonstrate, there is nothing natural about the composite of responsibilities assumed, political analyses developed, and difficult challenges faced by women who serve as community workers in low-income urban neighborhoods.

While most evaluators agree that the War on Poverty was no more than a skirmish,[2] it did contest the professional social service establishment's claim that only with specialized knowledge and training could one effectively serve the poor. Community work is low paid, offers little opportunity for advancement, and is highly unstable. As Rita Martinez pointed out,

> ...It's like, you can't depend...especially on antipoverty programs, you couldn't depend on that it would be [there] for the rest of your working life. It's not like...where you get a post office job and if you're a good worker, you can work for twenty years and get a pension. Poverty jobs were [unpredictable].

In spite of this, many community workers chose to remain in community-based positions even when offered other employment opportunities. The resident workers who obtained professional credentials such as a college or master's degree often turned down jobs that promised higher salaries and professional visibility in citywide agencies. Of the ten resident community workers who received a bachelor's, master's, or higher degree while performing paid community work, only four subsequently accepted positions in citywide agencies outside their communities. In addition, all of the resident community workers remained active as unpaid community workers during their tenure as paid workers, and most, if physically able, continued to serve their communities after retirement. Since the economic viability of many low-income neighborhoods in which they worked had deteriorated over the twenty to thirty years since they first accepted paid community work, many found community work even more demanding in the mid-1980s and 1990s. Given the apparent "irrationality" demonstrated by these women in relation to pay and career advancement, what explains their ongoing commitment to this challenging form of work? This chapter begins to address this question by exploring how the community workers understood and responded to the implementation of New Careers during the War on Poverty.

The first part of this chapter examines the link between New Careers and earlier innovations in social programming, summarizes the main arguments of the New Careers philosophy, and describes the process by which it entered into national policy discourse during the mid-1960s. In the second part of the chapter, I discuss the limits of New Careers, the contradictions of educational advancement for the community workers, and the modest success of New Careers as viewed through the oral testimonies of women hired by the CAPs.

## Maximum Feasible Participation and New Careers: Frameworks for Community Action

The philosophy of New Careers drew from previous experiments in non-governmental antipoverty programs. New Careers, in turn, had significant and lasting impact on the subsequent organization of social welfare. According to Arthur Pearl and Frank Riessman (1965), New Careers would

provide an alternative career path that did not require the extensive training of traditional professional work. As Charles Grosser (1973, 178) pointed out, "fitting the worker to the assignment on the basis of competence
rather than credentials is a radical concept." The philosophy of New
Careers asserted that resident workers could serve as a "bridge" between
middle-class agencies and low-income residents. They could interpret the
community's needs to the professional, nonindigenous staff and act as role
models for their neighbors. As Janet Nola, an African American CAP
administrator in Philadelphia, explained:

> At one point people believed: "Well I'm an expert. I have a doctorate.
> I know better. I know how to do this." But they've realized that you
> have a lot of people that are in the community without that formal
> education that have a doggone good idea what it is that they need and
> a doggone good idea as to how to go about it.

Designers of the Economic Opportunity Act were not the first to highlight
the significance of indigenous knowledge for social-welfare programming in
poor communities. Writing in the 1930s, Chicago sociologist Clifford Shaw
stressed the value of indigenous workers for community service although he
did not factor in a primary role for the state. Shaw believed that "even in areas
with high delinquency and seemingly immendable disorder there exists 'a
core of organized communal life centering mainly in religious, economic, and
political activities'" (Korbrin 1959 quoted in Hallman 1984, 113). Shaw
(1930–1966) asserted that delinquency was an adaptive response by young
people who had no other means for achieving social status. He developed a
program called the Chicago Area Project to address the problem.[3] A focus on
the social context that directly contributes to juvenile delinquency under-
girded Shaw's Chicago Area Project. The second premise of the Chicago
Area Project stated that people engage in activities that provide them with a
meaningful role. Consequently, the Illinois Institute for Juvenile Research,
which sponsored the Chicago Area Project, hired resident workers to organize neighborhood groups and provide youth activities.

The following ad for a paid position with the Chicago Area Project
appeared in 1933 and could be viewed as a precursor for community work
as defined by the EOA of 1964. Emphasis was placed on the applicant's
"thorough knowledge of the people and organizations in their neighborhoods" as well as their "natural capacity for working with adults and youth."

> Help Wanted, the Illinois Institute for Juvenile Research is seeking res-
> idents from certain Chicago neighborhoods to staff a new program
> aimed at reducing juvenile delinquency. Applicants must live in the
> neighborhoods served by the program. They must have thorough
> knowledge of the people and organizations in their neighborhoods
> and a natural capacity for working with adults and youth. Duties
> include organizing civic committees to deal with delinquency and fos-

tering youth welfare activities. The jobs have no minimum education requirements but workers will receive training and supervision from staff workers of the Institute (Hallman 1984, 113).

Once "residents who possessed a natural knowledge of the locality, who could speak the language of the people and who would have easy access to the youth" were identified, they were trained and supervised by staff sociologists (Hallman 1984, 113). However, Howard Hallman (1984, 114) asserts, they were given "considerable latitude within the neighborhoods." For Shaw, the goal was to help the newly formed community groups achieve autonomy. Shaw's contribution to community work rests in his analysis of the indigenous resources, leadership potential, and neighborhood institutions. He also recognized the diverse cultural foundations of urban low-income communities. However, like the designers of the EOA, he focused on the changes needed from within the community rather than on how problems in the wider social and economic environment contributed to urban poverty.

Lloyd Ohlin and Richard Cloward of Columbia University, both heavily influenced by the philosophy of the Chicago School of Criminal Sociology undergirding Shaw's Chicago Area Project, played a central role in developing the model for the CAPs. They drew on the Chicago approach to juvenile delinquency for their book, *Delinquency and Opportunity* (1960). David Hackett, special aide to then attorney general Robert F. Kennedy with responsibility for juvenile delinquency, subsequently recruited Ohlin to administer the funds from the Juvenile Delinquency and Youth Offenses Control Act passed in 1961 during President John F. Kennedy's administration. Cloward and Olin had just finished the plans for Mobilization for Youth, a project designed to put into practice their "differential opportunity theory" of juvenile delinquency, when Ohlin moved to Washington, D.C. to assume his new position.[4] Cloward and Ohlin (1960, 210) argued that "legitimate and functional replacements" must be found that would provide an "access to legitimacy" for "slum youth," therefore the entire community was defined as the target for Mobilization for Youth's (MFY) intervention to prevent juvenile delinquency.[5] Allen Matusow (1984, 110–111) observes:

> Similarities between Mobilization for Youth and later nationwide antipoverty programs were not coincidental. A comprehensive attempt to prevent delinquency by unlocking opportunity, the plan included among other things, public-service jobs for teenagers, neighborhood service centers offering a variety of welfare services in one convenient place, employment of neighborhood people as subprofessionals in service institutions, and organizing residents into groups to solve their own problems.

It was the last feature of this approach, namely "organizing residents into groups to solve their own problems," that caused concern among many social service professionals and public officials. Opposition to MFY's efforts to promote institutional change grew swiftly at both the local and federal levels.

For David Hackett, MFY's model did not go far enough in giving the poor effective control over their neighborhood institutions. According to Matusow (1984), when Hackett was approached to help design a federal program to counter poverty, he recognized that the poor must be given more power than the "expert" model of MFY initially provided. Persuaded by Leonard Cottrell's analysis of how "the disorganization of slum communities" contributed to delinquency and other social problems, Hackett incorporated the goal of developing "community competence" in poor communities through "empowering the poor to take over their own neighborhoods" (Matusow 1984, 117).[6]

Walter Heller, whom President Kennedy had charged with developing an antipoverty plan, adopted Hackett's proposal, which was renamed the Community Action Program.[7] President Johnson expanded Hackett's modest experimental proposal into the War on Poverty. In his State of the Union message, Johnson explained, "I propose a program which relies on the traditional time-tested American methods of organized local community action to help individuals, families, and communities to help themselves."[8] Johnson was not interested in an extended period of study before launching the War.[9] With a limited formulation of the causes of and remedies for poverty and with no time to examine the implications of community action, EOA's framers and implementers were unprepared for the challenge that newly employed community workers posed to the established political regimes in different locales.[10]

When Johnson appointed R. Sargent Shriver, then head of the Peace Corps,[11] to design the legislation for the War on Poverty, Hackett was displaced from his central role. Shriver was not enthusiastic about the feasibility of "community action" and reportedly said, "It'll never fly" (Matusow 1984, 124). Under Shriver's leadership, community action became one of several programs including Jobs Corps, Head Start, and Upward Bound. Followers of Hackett's original plan, including Richard Boone, were given authority to design the community action component of the legislation. Matusow credits Boone, a Chicago school sociologist who worked with Ohlin in the 1950s and who was recruited to help plan Robert Kennedy's National Service Corps,[12] with insisting upon the inclusion of "maximum feasible participation" of the poor in the resulting Economic Opportunity Act.

The concept of New Careers, hiring local residents on the basis of their familiarity with the community rather than their educational credentials, was especially volatile when incorporated within the framework of community action and maximum feasible participation.[13] Analysts disagree over the extent to which designers of the EOA actually intended for the CAPs to organize the poor through maximum feasible participation.[14] In a 1966 study of how twenty cities implemented community action, Stephen Rose

(1972) reports that less that three percent of the CAPs "were in any way designed to organize the poor, to transfer power, or to change the institutional structure." Moreover, in less than two years, political pressures from mayors, other public officials, and traditional social service organizations had already circumscribed the federal government's commitment to maximum feasible participation of the poor in the CAPs.

The political pressure contributed to the termination of support for maximum feasible participation and increased pressure toward professionalization and bureaucratization.[15] The pressure from public officials to control the political behaviors of CAPs and their staff led to a return to the traditional social service approach that community action had been designed to replace. New Careers created a new entry point into the social welfare establishment for workers from poor communities but placed them in low status positions that were often the first to be cut when funds were tight. However, given options to leave their communities for other positions, many community workers I interviewed chose to stay despite the growing demands of their work and the diminished resources.

According to the New Careers philosophy, professionals have less of a commitment to a particular community because they are detached from the particular group they serve and, instead, offer their skills to the highest bidder. High turnover among professionals in the first four years of OEO could support this contention. Because city officials appointed professionals in management positions, tenure in these positions was often determined by factors outside personal control.[16] Brenda Rivers, a white European American community worker who retired from paid community work in 1984, noted that during her seventeen years of employment, PAAC "had something like fifteen chief executive officers." Since the executive officer is filled by political appointments, there was "continual turnover." She noted that "some people lasted only six months...some of them just could not cope with it, some of them didn't choose to cope with it...and we lost a lot of people."[17]

There was less turnover among the resident community workers, particularly in Philadelphia's programs. Brenda pointed out that, with the exception of periods of fiscal cutbacks where large numbers of resident staff were involuntarily eliminated, "turnover was predictable where people died" or retired. Clara Thompson, an African American community worker in Philadelphia who was a full-time homemaker before she took her first full-time job with PAAC, concurred with Brenda's assessment that turnover was low among resident community workers. She reported, "The turnover [in my area office] isn't much at all. We've had workers who have been here for eighteen years, fifteen years...so there's [little] turnover here, I don't know about any of the other offices, but you see a lot of old faces I've been seeing all the time." The case for continuity among the resident community workers can be further supported by examination of the annual Progress Report put out by PAAC. For example, fourteen of the twenty-two resident workers I interviewed in Philadelphia in 1984 were listed as community workers or council representatives in the Philadelphia Antipoverty Action Committee's 1966–1967 Progress Report (PAAC 1967).

The retention of resident workers can be explained by three factors beyond personal commitment to this form of work. First, without the educational credentials, the resident community workers found few other forms of work available to them. Second, since their expertise lay in knowledge of particular communities, their experiences might not be defined as transferable to other locations. Resident workers were hired primarily because of their identification with a specific community. Several community workers pointed out that their identification with their particular communities often interfered with career growth. Furthermore, many did not seek alternative positions because, they explained, the satisfaction they drew from their community work was tied to working within their defined communities. Third, cutbacks in funding also prevented upward mobility within the organization. Thirteen resident community workers advanced professionally without finishing high school or college but the lack of credentials continued to circumscribe their legitimacy within the wider social service arena.

Ann Robinson's experience illustrates the contradiction inherent in the implementation of New Careers since credentialed status remained a basic criteria for gaining credibility in the social welfare field. Ann recalled the discrimination she felt as a result of her noncredentialed status and was angry that poor people with little education were made to feel ashamed. Although Ann never continued her education beyond high school, she advanced in her community work career to become director of a community-based organization in Harlem. She described one experience she had at a meeting with credentialed, middle-class workers:

> I was at a meeting and we were talking about poor people, and one of them [the credentialed workers] referred to them: "You know how those people are, you can't get them…to do…"et cetera. So I said, "Really? What did we do to get you out? The same thing we did to get you out, gets them out. They're ashamed. Society makes you ashamed. Why is it hard to say, "Well, I know what hard times are. I understand." It doesn't take anything away from you.

Ann discussed how she was constantly reminded of her lower-class status by professionals who could not accept her as an equal. For example, Ann encountered resistance from colleagues who could not believe that someone who did not have an advanced degree could successfully function with other profes-sionals.

> It was weird, because sometimes with the very people who I'm having to train, to break in, things are fine; 'til all of a sudden they find out that you don't have it [the professional credential]….I was speaking at a conference, and there was a professor who I will not name…he

asked me, "Where did you get your degree from?" So I said, "The streets of East Harlem." So he kept on talking, "Where did you say you got your master's from?" So I say, "I don't have one." And he says, "So what are you doing up here?" I told him, "Times have changed!"

Ann Robinson faced the contradictions of New Careers throughout her community work career. Even as she became recognized for her expertise as a community worker, she was challenged for not having the appropriate credentials. Further, by crossing class lines she also became witness to the classism of credentialed colleagues. Ann recalled another unpleasant encounter at a conference on housing:

> Things were going fine, and finally, [one of the panelists] said something about poor people. And I just couldn't take it anymore. And I said, "Pray tell me, what is a poor person supposed to look like and sound like?" Anyhow, near the end he told people, "You see her there, she's just pretending! There's no way that she can function and articulate as well as she can unless she has a master's. She's just saying that to give to the people in her community." But there was someone from New York, and he told them that I didn't have [the college degree].

Ann needed someone else to verify her noncredentialed status. First insulted by the insinuation that she could not express herself well without an advanced degree, Ann suffered further humiliation by the need to call on someone else to corroborate her claims. While she experienced difficulty as a result of her lack of a professional credential, Ann believed that her role as enabler for others' academic advancement was more important than her own. Ann found ways to negotiate the limits of New Careers—in some instances, calling on her religious faith or, as in this case, her self-definition as an enabler of others' advancement. However, she remained angry that her extensive experience as a community worker continued to be undervalued because she did not have the professional credential.

## Limits of New Careers

In addition to Ann Robinson, twelve other women interviewed said they advanced in their careers without the benefit of professional credentials. However, the career path they described was a short one and once a community worker reached the position of supervisor or coordinator of a community-based program she had reached the end of the career ladder unless she chose to move to a citywide administrative position. Three of the thirteen women who advanced in their careers reluctantly elected to leave their community-based positions and take positions in a citywide agency.

For those who remained in their communities, the increase in poverty in their communities and the decrease in funding for social welfare programs augmented the problems these women had to confront and placed a ceiling on the maximum salary they could earn for ever-growing responsibilities. Puerto Rican community worker Carmen Hernandez explained the latter problem with reference to the growth of bureaucracy within her New York City CAP. She noted that the resident community workers "weren't educated people when" the War on Poverty started.

> They were people who saw that there was a need in the community, and they went about their business doing it, because when they first started doing it, they weren't making any money—$3,500 a year. And some of them have been there for fifteen years and still don't make $15,000 and that's the sin!

However, for the resident community workers, their jobs were more than a place to earn a salary. They constructed their work in terms that defied the dominant approach to employment. In their oral testimony about their relationship to community work, they criticized the low pay, lack of job security, and limited career path, but they also felt that paid community work was more than a place to earn a living. Paid community work provided an opportunity to perform work that could help rectify the problems within their communities. Many performed this work without pay before the CAPs were funded. Now they could concentrate their energies on the work that mattered most to them, rather than be torn between other low paying jobs that often took them out of the community. However, since the resident workers rarely distinguished between their unpaid and paid community work, they were less likely to make demands for better pay and better working conditions than workers in other types of working-class jobs.

Grace Reynolds, a white community worker in Philadelphia, had only an eighth grade education when she began with PAAC. Due to her years of paid work with PAAC, she said, "I'm not in poverty now. I'm not far from it, but...I have a pension from the city for working for ten years, so that was my social security which just keeps me a little above poverty." Grace cleverly advanced her community work career despite her lack of a high school diploma. She took the test for a teacher's aide position and for program coordinator, doing well on both tests. She recalled with delight how she found employment, first as a teacher's aide then as a community worker by "stretching the truth" that she had finished high school.

> When it came time to show your diploma I said: "I don't have it with me"—stretching the truth. They believed me, and I was [ranked] third, but they didn't need another coordinator, but I could get the teacher's aide job. Well, I was thrilled...I was [a] teacher's aide there for six months, and I loved it, but I had a lot of grandchildren myself, so I had a lot of experience. Then the [area office] started the I&R [Information & Referral] worker position. ...I said, "Well this is what I joined up for to see if I could help people and this would be some-

thing that would help people." So I put in my application for that and naturally I was hired.

The paid position enabled Grace Reynolds to "go off welfare." She said the salary "wasn't much, but it was enough to work on." After six months, she took another paid position as an I&R worker that "was a little bit better paying job...about $3,000 per year." She was promoted to I&R supervisor in 1971 and retired in 1986. Over the years she was also elected to chair the Community Action Council (CAC). After she retired, she continued her activities as an unpaid community worker helping to establish and promote services for the elderly in her community.

Some resident community workers who did not pursue professional training were passed over for promotions in favor of younger, less experienced workers with advanced degrees. African American community worker Frances Rider was one of the five workers who described the frustration she experienced as a result of this process. She had only a high school degree when she started working for PAAC. She retired from another community-based program in Philadelphia after twenty years of paid community work. Her frustration is apparent in the following excerpt:

> They brought in a girl to be my supervisor. I was in charge of the mental health care for ten years dealing with senior citizens...and then you bring someone in from left field who doesn't know anything and make them over you, over this person who has been doing it all along!...And she came with a salary of about $20,000! I'd been there twenty years and wasn't making $20,000.

Like Frances Rider, most resident workers were angry at a lack of financial reward they received after years of service and were also insulted that new, inexperienced staff were placed in supervisory positions over them. In many ways, the powerful professional and bureaucratic apparatus of the social welfare establishment thwarted the successful implementation of New Careers. Advancement in New Careers, ironically, often meant obtaining professional credentials.

## Gaining Credentials and Training

Professional or credentialed status provided the primary path to career advancement and financial reward within paid community work, despite concern that professionalism would compromise the effectiveness of the resident workers. Pearl and Riessman (1965, 196) believed that "the indigenous nonprofessional is very much task centered and 'now' centered and this is his strength and his weakness." They insisted that professional status distances an indigenous worker from his community. The effectiveness of the indigenous worker, in their view, was directly tied to retaining the same class orientation as their "clients." Since professionalization requires adopting middle-class values, the acquisition of professional credentials would negate the distinctive advantage that indigenous workers have over non-indigenous workers.[18]

Despite emphasis on class similarity for effective community work, many of the antipoverty programs offered incentives to workers who wanted to continue their education and, by extension, experience upward mobility. Some workers regretted that they did not take advantage of these opportunities. Most of these women said they lacked the time or the financial resources to attend college. However, others declined the offer to continue their formal education explaining that the knowledge they gained as result of their community work was more valuable than "classroom learning." Most who returned to school did not, in fact, find that the educational content enhanced their community work. Because of their view that the best education came from working in the community, the community workers saw the use of credentials to determine who should fill certain positions in social-welfare programs as a limited and discriminatory process.

Those who managed to attend college while working full time as community workers were often critical of the experience.[19] Puerto Rican community worker Angela Garcia returned to college after years of community work but found that the institutional demands of higher education did not meet her needs. Among other complaints was the lack of choice over which courses to take and at what levels. More important, she did not see any value placed on the knowledge she acquired from her community work experiences. Working with parents in her first paid community work position, she gained vast experience that she brought to bear in subsequent community work. She described her approach to parent organizing as follows:

> I always felt...that we were missing the point...So, for the last years ...I worked with developing parent programs, and I was responsible for the parent programs, so I became parent director, then assistant to the executive director, and just started to write proposals and get funding to do parent training. As a result of that, I became very knowledge-able...and negotiated with members of the board at the chancellor's [office] and the directors of programming at the board, I really got a hands-on experience beyond belief that is not written in any books.

She gained the knowledge about organizing from her work with parents in Brooklyn, the Bronx, Manhattan, and...Queens." She felt that her efforts to empower others transformed her. Angela's emphasis on the significance of experientially-based knowledge matched the philosophy of New Careers. However, as the process of institutionalization proceeded within CAPs, this indigenous form of expertise became increasingly devalued. Many employed through New Careers who did not achieve professional status

quickly found themselves placed at the lower rungs of the social welfare
hierarchy.

## Pursuing Higher Education

Brenda Rivers was one of the five community workers who advanced
from high school to graduate school while working as a paid community
worker. She explained the difficulty in trying to attend college on a part-
time basis while working full time as a paid community worker.

> I wasn't going to school full time. These were all evening part-time class-
> es, usually two evenings a week. Sometimes I carried three courses and
> went Saturday mornings too…One problem when you go part-time is
> that you have to fit in the courses you've got to have in order to graduate
> and the more courses you get, the less choice you have…I went sum-
> mers, six week sessions, which are loaded because they put you through
> a whole thirteen weeks of work in six weeks.

Like many of the community workers who wanted to continue their formal
education, Brenda discovered that most of the traditional college programs
did not serve her needs. After she finished her college degree, she wanted to
go on for her master's but found the schools in her area unsupportive of her
desire to attend on a part-time basis. She complained that these colleges
expected students to drop everything and go full time for two years.

Those who did achieve a college education had mixed reactions to the
question: "Did your studies help you in performing your community
work?" When Puerto Rican resident community worker Carmela Calas
first started as a community worker she had just graduated from a New
York City high school. She decided to return to school after working for
several years because, as she described it, she knew a lot but realized that
credentials are necessary to advance in the field of social work. She completed her college degree and graduated with a master's degree in 1978.
Following graduation, she was hired to direct a community-based program for the elderly in Manhattan's Lower East Side. While she believed
the degree has helped her career mobility, Carmela said college offered
her "nothing new."

The community workers who gained their academic credentials
through alternative programs expressed a much more positive assessment
of their educational experiences. Angela Garcia concurred with Carmela's
negative assessment of traditional college curriculum and structure.
However, several years after she dropped out of a traditional college she
enrolled in an alternative program that validated her community work
experiences as well as provided an opportunity for her to expand her
knowledge base.

Angela was the first one in her family to graduate from high school.
She started her paid community work while she was working on her col-

lege degree. Although she was greatly disillusioned with her college experiences in a traditional academic program, she recognized the importance of the credential for her career and persevered. She worked the graveyard shift at a bank, left the office at 8 A.M. and went to school, returning home at 3 P.M. to sleep before she had to return to work. After nine years she "got into a disagreement about education" and quit college.

> Remember, I was thirty-two years old then, and to go back to school, and knowing what you know but you know that you need the piece of paper, and wanting to take the courses that they say you can't because you're in the freshman year and not in the graduate [program], and I wanted to take some of the graduate courses,' cause they were more exciting than the boring subjects that I was taking... And, by 1967, I had had it with the system, and I decided I didn't want to go to school anymore. That was it.

While she worked for pay at night and went to school during the day, Angela volunteered for a summer Headstart Program. After she quit college in 1967, she took a paid job as a school "paraprofessional" and, in 1970, accepted a job as a counselor for a Latino organization devoted to the educational advancement of Hispanic youth. This job was more demanding than her previous one. She described her dedication to it as "an act of love":

> I worked there from 1970 to 1978, and that's really when I got my feet truly wet. And I tell people all the time it was an act of love. Because...if you were there in those times, you [were paid] from 9 to 5, but there was no such thing as 9 to 5. You did after-work. You ate and breathed that job, because there were so many things that were happening.

She became an expert in negotiating with admissions and financial aid offices for the acceptance of Hispanic students in colleges across the country. She was subsequently promoted to Educational Opportunity Counselor. Through her job, Angela learned about the alternative-degree program offered by Goddard College. She applied and was amazed when they gave her credit for her "life experience." To qualify for graduation she did a study of the Puerto Rican community that connected her background and political concerns. Angela described with enthusiasm the opportunity to read in a variety of subjects and the doors that her college credential opened for her.

> I went on to books that I'd never had the time to read...And it was exciting. I read about forty-four books. I love to read. I have a big library in my house. My escape from the world is literature....And so then I graduate, that was in '73. Of course, that opened a lot of doors

within my community, because then I became the director, which they never would have given me without the degree. I mean, the thing is that that paper was very, very important.

Angela found that, although there are many people working in the community who are "super-qualified, they're not going to make it unless they have a degree." And, unfortunately, only a few people from her community go on to get the credentials. "They're very rare," she noted.

## Importance of Mentors

Given the difficulty of supporting a family on the relatively low salaries provided by the CAPs, coupled with the long hours, community workers who did advance their education and careers frequently identified a mentor who helped promote them. About one-third of the resident community workers interviewed mentioned mentors who as CAP supervisors took a special interest in encouraging the resident community worker to finish college or take another challenging position within the organization. This type of mentor is similar to those discussed in the literature on corporate or professional advancement (see, e.g., Lorber 1984).

Ann Robinson was working as an unpaid community worker and receptionist for a CAP when she took a week off due to illness. When she returned, her position had been filled. With the support of her supervisors, she extended her community work in East Harlem from unpaid labor to paid employment. She found the professional staff extremely responsive to her work in East Harlem. Her immediate supervisor was especially supportive. She remembers a sign in his office that said, "Come and let us reason together."

> So I could go and sit down with him and tell him about…what's happening…and what I felt needed to be done. I just went off, and I got involved, and I'd come back and keep him attuned to what was happening. And many times, through his connections and his board, they would be supportive of many things we got involved in.

Over the years, Ann developed her leadership abilities and eventually was hired to direct a community-based childcare program in East Harlem. In 1984, she was earning an annual salary of $20,000. She continued working part-time as a teacher in this program even after she retired in 1995.

African American community worker Martha Framer's career was advanced by a male supervisor who encouraged her to take a management-level position. She began as a secretary and when she was promoted to a position of administrative secretary she "had assumed a lot of responsibilities." Martha recalled that her supervisor

> …encouraged me to try something else, more along the line of man-

agement. He knew that I had been planning to go back to school and so forth, and he felt it might be a good opportunity for me to try my hand at something else. Because honestly, I have never liked typing, and I never liked filing. I always felt I was doing my boss's job and he was making $10–15,000 more than I was and…I wanted to try something else.

With her supervisor's encouragement Martha applied for a job to direct a pilot program with the agency. She explained, "They wanted to try to do something called a multiservice center and to offer more than just social services in the area offices." She continued, "I never ever thought I would get the job, primarily because at that time my background was more clerical… I just didn't anticipate it. I went in for an interview and was recalled. Next thing I know I had this job." In 1984, Martha was employed in a mid-management position in PAAC. She remained with PAAC until 1990 when she accepted a new position as a health educator with another city agency.

African American community worker Pat Easterly also worked for PAAC in a management position in 1984. She first started working for PAAC in 1966 when she accepted a job as a receptionist. Pat married in her early twenties, had two children, and separated from her husband in the early 1980s. She was also encouraged to continue her education by a male supervisor. Pat recalled that her supervisor would tell her, "Why don't you go back to school and take some courses because I am not going to be here that long, and I would like for you to move into my position…at least be able to recommend you." She explained:

> And there were some areas that I did not have experience in as far as interviewing prospective employees and that type of thing and I think I had a fear of those types of situations, you know. He began to let me sit in with him when he was doing it, and I learned to become more relaxed with that and I did decide that, yes, I should go back to school in order to prepare myself to be able to move on.

Ann, Martha, and Pat benefitted from the encouragement of their male supervisors. However, it was more typical for community women to identify the support given by other community workers, especially women community workers, for their political development, as I will illustrate in chapter six. Not surprisingly, the institutional mentors were more typically singled out for promoting career mobility than for encouraging the community workers' political development.

## Limits and Possibilities for Credentialed Community Workers

Completing college did not always provide a path to career advancement and job security. Puerto Rican resident community worker Carlotta Mendez, who obtained a master's in social work, lost her job in New York City due to cutbacks in government funding during the mid-1980s. Carlotta reported that community work tapped into a significant part of her personal makeup, "what apparently was in my gut. I like community involvement....I really like to work with [community] groups. I'm quite good at it!" Carlotta decided to use her talents for the benefit of her own community rather than on the behalf of white Americans. She recalled, "Somewhere along the line I made a decision...that if it were true that I was good at what I did, then why am I giving it to the white Americans? Why don't I use those skills within my own community? That was a very conscious decision." She remained in the community work position until she was laid off.[20] Prior to the "budget crunch" she "had no intention of leaving" community work.

She reported that she had a great deal of difficulty translating her community work experiences into a paid position in the private sector, even with the master's of social work degree. After almost thirty years of community service, managing large programs, and negotiating with public officials, she could not find a position.

> And I said, I was fifty, and I had decided, "Ah hah, that is it." The beginning of my second half century. I walked away from it. I literally walked away from it and decided...I'm not going to work for CBOs [community—based organizations] anymore. How do I make the bridge between being a social worker and working for the private sector?...I could not do anything with the private sector. So I failed completely. Here it is early '84, and I'm still unemployed. There are no opportunities.

In the meantime, she worked as a part-time consultant to a variety of community-based organizations serving the Latino community. After several years without full time employment, Carlotta was hired by a citywide Latino social services agency. Her difficulty in parlaying her community work experience into a better paying position illustrates another major limitation of community work as a New Career. In addition, for those who parlayed their experiences into other employment, as Carlotta eventually did, the administrative and citywide positions they accepted often took them away from direct contact with their communities. These women missed the daily personal connection with members of their communities. This loss of connection, in turn, dampened their enthusiasm for their jobs even when their work included efforts to improve the quality of life in their communities.

## In-Service Training

Many CAPs provided in-service training to the newly hired community workers. Analysis of the oral narratives reveals that, for the most part, the training provided was perfunctory and seldom contributed to the workers' career advancement. Only seven of the forty-two resident community workers mentioned in-service training as a significant part of their experience with a CAP. All of these women worked for PAAC. African community worker Marcy Barnett discussed her experience with PAAC's in staff training programs. She had a high school diploma when she accepted a job as area coordinator. According to Marcy, PAAC offered the staff training that was not responsive to their real educational needs. According to Marcy, PAAC did not offer the support for the resident community workers to finish their high school education. She recalled:

> After about a year, PAAC said they were going to make them [the resident community workers] come back to school. Well, most of the women did not have a high school education, and I had talked to them and I felt that if they were going to make them go to school, why make them go back to learn what they already…[knew]? Let them go to school and finish high school. But they couldn't see this.

Marcy stressed that PAAC's decision to provide the workers with short term training programs, which duplicated the skills they already possessed, "didn't make sense."

In contrast, African American community worker Alice Porter spoke enthusiastically about the in-service training received by the first staff employed in her PAAC area office. The women staff "came from their kitchens—they had never done office work before." The staff was given training in interviewing and assessing and solving community problems. She believed that the more experienced community workers "did a good job" when they conducted in-service training for the staff and that there was "promotion from within." Alice was hired in 1965 as a community worker, and recalled, "That was one of the lowest-paid workers in the program at that point." In a few months she was promoted to the position of supervisor that she still held in the mid-1980s. She retired from the position in 1989. As a result of her experience, she believed there was "upward mobility" in PAAC, although the illustrations she provided indicated limited career progression.

The differing perspectives offered by the resident community workers on career mobility reflects, to a certain extent, the personal expectations each woman brought to her career. Most never pursued community work as a way to improve their status or income. However, satisfaction with their careers as community workers also reflects three other factors: (1) the extent to which there were opportunities for promotion; (2) how often, and how many, staff were laid off due to funding cuts; and (3) the extent to which bureaucratic procedures circumscribed the community workers' ability to accomplish their jobs as they defined them. Personal, economic, and political factors interacted to create different patterns of influence on each woman's assessment of her community work career and led to some important differences among the resident community workers.

## The Modest Successes and Pronounced Failures of New Careers

Although few meaningful programs remain from the War on Poverty, they had a tremendous impact on the lives of the community workers and many of their neighbors. The state's sponsorship of resident community work affirmed the ongoing community work of women from low-income neighborhoods by: (1) creating additional organizational sites through which community work could be accomplished; (2) increasing the power base of, and providing legitimacy for, informal community leaders; (3) training new community workers for leadership positions; and (4) legitimating demands for decent housing, welfare rights, quality education, and safe and environmentally sound neighborhoods[21]—themes that will be further illustrated in the following chapters.

The state-sponsored employment introduced several conflicts into the lives of the resident community workers. First, professionalism forced some workers to move from their community-based positions in order to advance in their careers or, for those who did not gain advanced credentials, to lose much-deserved promotions. Second, centralization of decision making frequently required the workers to compromise their personal goals in order to work within the formal structure. Third, bureaucratic demands added administrative and political constraints to the service and advocacy provided by the resident workers. Finally, institutional pressures and professional socialization led some community workers, who were promoted to management positions, to view their management jobs in much the same way as the traditional social service workers they criticized.

Commitment to their communities contributed to a blurring of the lines between paid responsibilities and unpaid activities. Most community workers neither viewed their jobs merely as a source of income nor defined them as "9 to 5." Once motivated by their concerns for their community, this relationship with their neighbors supported their involvement over the years. Their self-described approach to community work contrasts with the availability of the traditional social service establishment. Angela Garcia emphasized the difference between the service provided by the groups developed by the Latino community and that given by the traditional agencies: "You have dedicated people…but the agencies that are supposedly helping you out are 9 to 5. And when everybody else goes home, we're still there. We're in the neighborhood, and we're still working!"

Because of the interconnection between paid and unpaid community work, the involuntary loss of a paid position as a result of budget cuts did, in some cases, diminish a community worker's commitment to community activism. Ethel Pearls, an African American community worker in Philadelphia, was forced into retirement in her mid-fifties when the program she directed was defunded. She missed the intense involvement she had in her community and contrasted her involvement in the mid-1980s with the community work she performed before and during her employment.

Ethel said she "was always a community worker." When she heard about PAAC, she did not hesitate to run for the Community Action Committee (CAC) in South Philadelphia. Since she was a single mother of four, she decided to resign from the council to take a paid position as area coordinator.[22] Ethel left the Antipoverty Program when she was offered a job as director of community affairs at a local health center. The position paid $4,000 more per year for essentially the same duties but with less administrative demands, including supervision of six people rather than eighteen. She described with bitterness her failure to find another paid community-work position after she was laid off in 1981. She could not believe that, after giving her "whole heart," the health center's administration gave her "no warning," she and thirty-one other people were given only seven days notice. She "felt very hurt." Her children "couldn't understand" why she was let go and then could not find another position. They said, "Mom, with all the people you helped?" Ethel believed that one of the main things that prevented her subsequent employment was the lack of professional certification. For two years, she "put in a resume everywhere, but there were no vacancies at that time" in human services. She expressed anger and disillusionment that all her life she had been helping people and when she needed help no one was there. She tried to get a job in the health center's kitchen but was told that it wouldn't be appropriate since she once had an office and staff in the center. As a consequence, Ethel withdrew from much of her previous unpaid community work. In 1984, her only involvement was in the church. She said, "I've done what I told everybody else not to do. I've given up."

The decrease in funding for social services also contributed to a deterioration in the quality of life in the poor neighborhoods of New York City and Philadelphia thus increasing the pressures on the community workers who remained in their community-based positions. Without a wider social movement in which to situate their struggles, the community workers were often discouraged about the possibility of achieving the major social and economic changes needed to improve their lives and that of their neighbors. In addition, many were especially emphatic about how the elaboration of bureaucratic demands inhibited their political efficacy as community workers.

The tensions between New Careers and organizational control was embedded in the EOA even before the external pressure hastened the process toward bureaucratization. The initial antipoverty legislation espoused a belief that the older social service organizations were out of step with the needs of the poor due to professional distance from their clients. However, since part of the defined goal for the federally funded CAAs was to create efficient organizations that would coordinate the myriad of not-for-profit agencies and local government institutions to better serve the low-income communities, those agencies that demonstrated a professional orientation were those most likely to receive funding.[23] This tendency compromised the commitment to maximum feasible participation of the poor and led to the development of a new set of bureaucratic social welfare institutions as well as reinforced the power of traditional ones.[24]

African American resident worker Mrs. Ruth Dever described the early excitement over the antipoverty programs and the subsequent bureaucratization of PAAC. Active in her neighborhood association, the United Way, and community youth programs before the antipoverty programs came to Philadelphia, Mrs. Dever noted that "in the beginning of the program, of course, there was a great deal of enthusiasm that has since fizzled out." She also described how, within the first few years, PAAC increasingly circumscribed her community work and inhibited the area offices from meeting the varied needs of the community. She noted that "being a part of a bureaucracy, you get schooled into the fact that you do certain things under direction" and this direction rarely met the needs of the community residents. For Mrs. Dever, the process of institutionalization meant a movement away from the original intent of the CAPs; namely, to be more responsive to the needs of community residents than the established social service agencies.

Despite the lack of a high school diploma, Mrs. Dever was promoted in 1972 to I&R worker and supervised three part-time and two full time staff. Five years later she was promoted to district manager. By this time, she had completed her high school degree and taken some courses at the local community college. However, at the age of sixty and after eighteen years of work and increased administrative responsibility she earned only $15,000 a year. When I asked her in 1984 if she had plans to retire she said that she thought often about retiring because of difficulties associated with the work. She explained:

> A lot of people who were really enthused become really cold and what not. Sometimes you're fighting staff as well as problems—not in the sense of being angry with them, but having to pull them along....And people come in and sometimes they vent their frustrations on you, and you have to make them understand where they're coming from.

Ironically, as Mrs. Dever moved into a management position, she adopted a relationship to her staff that mirrored that described by some of the nonresident workers who were supervising resident staff. Mrs. Dever complained that she fought with resident staff who resisted her attempts "to pull them along" and improve their efficiency. She expressed an even greater degree of frustration with the limited contact she had with community residents that resulted from her promotion to area coordinator.

Many resident workers like Mrs. Dever who accepted management positions also complained about the increased demands of the bureaucracy. As directors of community offices the women were required to perform administrative and supervisory work that took them away from direct contact with community residents. She reflected on the difficulties she faced as an administrator:

> One thing I miss with the administration is the touch I had with the people. Now, I'm dealing more with supervisors and things like that. I miss that touch....Of course, sometimes you're on the phone and sometimes in the office and then you get involved and get back in and find you're a little rusty.

Mrs. Dever said that if she were to retire "perhaps I would be connected in some way by coming back and volunteering." She hoped that, in this way, she would again have more direct contact with the people in her community than she had in her administrative role.

Mrs. Dever did retire in 1986, primarily to care for an elderly aunt. The cost of paying for a home health care worker was greater than her take home pay. Although she was reluctant to leave her job, the financial considerations outweighed her commitment to paid community work. In 1995, Mrs. Dever said that she remained active as an unpaid community worker through her church, although she continued to volunteer for the local CAP as she had predicted more than a decade earlier. She now survives on Social Security and a small pension from her years at PAAC. She complained that if PAAC had paid more, the pension would have been higher so she would not have to worry as much about money in her retirement years.

### Bureaucratization and Resistance

It is difficult to measure the proportion of community workers who left community work for other work or became unemployed as a consequence of fiscal cutbacks. Many women did retain the same positions they held in the mid-1960s, although most reported little increase in pay. Others, like Carmen Hernandez, who were given the opportunity to leave their communities for either citywide social service or other types of employment chose to remain even when it meant turning down a salary increase. Carmen explained:

> And people laugh at me now, because I say, "You know, I have not yet made the money that I made when I was eighteen years old."...I went to work on the Stock Exchange in '65. I was in the Research Department....I was there six years. And that was my first job....And I said, "Oh no, this is crazy!"...I turned down [a non-community work] job in '77....But I really didn't want the job. I didn't want the move.

Not only did she turn down a higher-paying position outside the community, she also resigned from her paid community work position "for the betterment of the program…to get on the board to make that change." Here we see evidence of how resident community workers' perceived their role as social change agents as more important than their career considerations. Of course, such a choice did not come without risk, as alternative employment was rarely available in the communities in which they resided.

Analysis of community work as a New Career reveals a number of contradictions: (1) the career path was a limited one; (2) even with professional credentials community workers had difficulty finding comparable work once the programs were eliminated; and (3) jobs were quickly incorporated into the professional hierarchy thus diluting the major advantage of New Careers' workers—namely, to challenge the ineffectual approaches of the social welfare establishment.[25] However, New Careers did provide significant job experience and political education for women residing in the poor, urban neighborhoods of New York City and Philadelphia that continues to benefit these communities as subsequent chapters demonstrate.

## Conclusion

The philosophy of New Careers can be traced back to the 1930s and found in the work of Clifford Shaw's Chicago Area Project. It was carried forward by University of Chicago sociologists, notably Lloyd Ohlin, who, along with Richard Cloward, also stressed the value of community-based organizations and indigenous workers for fighting juvenile delinquency. During the War on Poverty, New Careers provided low-income women with access to education and social service careers and enhanced their ability to improve the lives of their families and neighbors. Yet by assigning these workers to low paid and increasingly deadend jobs, it also circumscribed their career mobility and income.

Drawing on their own standpoint for "assessing knowledge claims," the resident workers' emphasized "concrete experience as a criterion of meaning" (Collins 1990, 208) and were, for the most part, skeptical about the value of classroom learning for community work, although a small number of the resident workers did increase their educational credentials. Those who advanced in their careers often mentioned the significant role played by mentors who encouraged them and provided the concrete support needed to juggle the multiple demands on their time. However, New Careers provided only a narrow opportunity for career advancement for community workers. As funding decreased, many women were left in dead-end positions or were frustrated by their inability to translate their community work experience into other types of paid employment. However, their employment contributed to a major shift in emphasis from previous community work that stressed instilling the poor with middle-class values, denied the significance of indigenous culture, and blamed the individual for his or her inability to leave the ranks of the poor and achieve economic security.

The newly legitimized community workers from low-income urban neighborhoods, particularly those using their positions to advocate for broad-based institutional change quickly threatened public officials. The state limited the resident workers' control and political power through increased bureaucratization, professionalization, and decreased funding for community action programs. These processes circumscribed the resident community workers paid work and, for some, constrained their political activism. As a result of accepting administrative positions or finding few other job options after layoffs, resident workers like Ethel Pearls experienced an increase in alienation from their communities that dampened their enthusiasm for community work.

All the resident community workers explained that community work in low-income neighborhoods requires dedication to a long, slow process that nonresident workers often lack. And, like Angela Garcia, many resident community workers insisted that their experiences as residents of the poor neighborhoods gave them an advantage over the credentialed nonresident workers—a distinction that was consistent with the New Careers philosophy. They often drew on this distinction to justify resistance to certain bureaucratic demands and to attempts by credentialed professionals to discredit them in public forums. While workers in the two cities described both practices, the resident workers in Philadelphia were more likely to stress the problems with centralized administration and increasingly bureaucratic practices, while New York City resident workers were most concerned with the tension between credentialed and noncredentialed workers. The differing political cultures and antipoverty program administrative approaches were key in explaining the different emphases in their stories, as the next chapter highlights. The differences in bureaucratic structure and politics of the antipoverty programs in New York City and Philadelphia offered community workers divergent grounds upon which to construct community work careers as well as to develop political analyses and engage in social activism.

# Chapter 3

# COMMUNITY ACTION IN DIFFERING POLITICAL CONTEXTS

The amendments to the Economic Opportunity Act of 1964, beginning as early as 1965, chronicle the increased controls placed on the antipoverty programs by the federal government as staff and low-income residents organized for more power and resources for their communities.[1] Funding for community organizing activities was eventually eliminated, while staff were increasingly prevented from engaging in a wide variety of political actions. However, differences in political culture and institutional politics led to variations in the extent to which professionalism, bureaucratic practices, and limits on political advocacy circumscribed the community work of women employed in the community action programs.

While the War on Poverty and the community action programs it spawned are not social movement organizations,[2] the community workers often discussed their work in social movement terms. They described their commitment to community work as part of a larger struggle for social justice and economic security for people of color and low-income residents of all racial-ethnic backgrounds. Most situated their communities within the boundaries of New York City or Philadelphia, though they viewed themselves as participants in a larger political effort that was manifest to them in the extensive local community struggles being waged in others cities across the U.S. However, their social locations within these differing urban political contexts and their employment by the state influenced how they could express their political beliefs.

Social movement theorist Sidney Tarrow (1992, 181) argues that "political culture" remains a critical factor in explaining the connection between "the social structural bases of politics...[and] its institutional outcomes." Referencing the work of Gabriel Almond and Sidney Verba (1964, 29ff),

Tarrow (1992, 182) discusses the significance of the symbolic dimension or "civic culture," which Almond and Verba define as "a mix of participant and supportive, traditional and modern, values and orientations supporting liberal democratic practices." [3] The revaluing of the symbolic and cultural processes that create the dynamic spaces in which social movement goals are defined and in which individuals and groups find that their values resonate corrects for the one dimensional reliance upon observable material resources focused on by resource mobilization theorists.[4] However, political culture must also be understood in the context of the material resources, historic patterns, and institutional practices that provide the grounds for the development of "collective action frames"[5] or other political ideology.[6] For example, as Frances Fox Piven and Richard Cloward (1980, 139) point out, "Structural arrangements are one large determinant of the patterns of political activity that emerge in any political system. Structural arrangements encourage, or block, the articulation of political groupings and help to direct those groupings to focus on some issues and not on others."

In a study of women community workers and political activists, Marilyn Gittell and I (1981) found that the political organization and political culture of the city influenced the nature of the relationships between women active in community-based organizations and those from women-specific organizations like the National Organization for Women (NOW) or labor unions or the city government agencies. Chicago, for example, has a strong tradition of coalition politics and, therefore, provided a context for feminist or women-specific organizers to work with community-based activists. In New York, however, the sheer size of the city frequently prevented working relationships from developing between community workers and those representing citywide agencies or coalitions. As a consequence of these findings and those of previous research,[7] I designed the study for *Grassroots Warriors* to include women community workers in Philadelphia as well as New York City in order to examine the effect of different political and organizational structures on women's community work.

The pattern of implementation, as shaped by the political culture and institutional politics in each city, contoured the abilities of each CAP to incorporate effectively the radical democratic possibilities of the community action title of the Economic Opportunity Act; namely, to support the use of grassroots political action when deemed necessary for social change efforts, to promote democratic process, and to value indigenous perspectives in decision-making and hiring practices. In analyzing variations across different CAPs, I noted two major forces that constrained the political activism of the community workers and highlighted the significance of political culture in shaping community work. These forces, that of bureaucratization and professionalization, are expected outcomes of the institutionalization process to a certain extent. However, what is of interest here is not that bureaucratization and professionalization occurred through the CAP implementation process, but how these phenomena developed differently in each city and created varying constraints on the community workers political activism and job satisfaction.

Analysis of the implementation of CAPs in different cities reveals the diversity of organizational structure and the different approaches used to involve the poor in program design and delivery.[8] Philadelphia and Los Angeles tried holding elections for representatives of the poor. New York, on the other hand, utilized a community-based convention approach. Delegates were chosen at the neighborhood level to represent the churches, schools, and other community organizations. The representatives at the convention then elected a citywide antipoverty board (Wofford 1974, 83). Since the limitations placed on the CAPs from the federal level increasingly narrowed local control in decision making over program design, neither centralized nor decentralized approaches achieved maximum feasible participation of the low-income residents even at the local level.

Philadelphia's citywide response to the EOA, the Philadelphia Antipoverty Action Committee (PAAC), was established as a centralized program with twelve area offices in poor communities around the city.[9] The twenty-two member central advisory board was comprised of a representative from the Mayor's office, representatives from nine established social service agencies, and twelve elected representatives from the poverty communities. Programs were developed at the central office with input from the twelve local areas. Since the Philadelphia antipoverty agency operated as a quasi-city agency, all employees were prohibited from overt political action as a condition of their employment (see Appendix E).

In contrast to Philadelphia, New York City developed a more decentralized community action agency structure. Despite the establishment of a central citywide board and the limitations placed by the OEO, the community-based programs in New York City assumed more autonomy in program design than the area offices in Philadelphia. This contrast in approach can largely be explained by the unique history of the New York programs which, in turn, is linked to the city's complex political organization and political culture. For example, as mentioned in chapter two, Mobilization for Youth (MFY) was designed before passage of the EOA and implemented in the early 1960s as a joint project of the social-service agencies serving the Lower East Side and New York School of Social Work at Columbia University. In fact, MFY served as a model for the Community Action title of the EOA.[10] MFY, originally established to prevent juvenile delinquency, found an institutional home in the Henry Street Settlement House on the Lower East Side. Richard Cloward (1964, 1) explained the goal of MFY's community organization strategy as providing staff and resources "to help local groups participate...in the social issues—encouraging residents to choose issues, frame them in their own terms, and act within their legal rights to deal with the problems they encounter daily" (quoted in Fried 1969, 138).

Harlem Youth Opportunities (HARYOU), also established in advance of the EOA,[11] was one of the few New York City CAAs that initially adopted the radical stance of MFY. In 1964, under the leadership of African American psychologist Kenneth Clark, HARYOU published a report, *Youth in the Ghetto*, on the consequences of powerlessness and included a proposal to counteract the problem. HARYOU developed an analysis that emphasized the role of race and class in perpetuating poverty among African Americans. They argued that American institutions were unable to respond to the problems due to bureaucratic rigidity and middle-class insensitivity. The solution was for low-income and African American communities to confront racist and class-biased institutions. David Greenstone and Paul Peterson (1973, 42) note that both MFY and HARYOU (later HARYOU-ACT)[12] "took the lead in demanding that the CAP provide for the broadest possible participation of the poor, and, in particular, that it fund the variety of community organizations that had been forming in neighborhoods around the city."[13]

An unanticipated finding of this study relates to differences between the political analyses and activism of community workers in New York City and Philadelphia. Such differences must be interpreted in dialogue with the divergent political and organizational structures in which community work was embedded. Overall, the women in Philadelphia generally offered less radical political analyses and approaches to community action than the community workers in New York City. This finding should not be read as implying that women in Philadelphia were generally more conservative than those in New York City. Those with more radical political perspectives would not find the CAPs in Philadelphia as fertile a ground for their community activism as they would find in some New York City CAPs. It is likely that through a process of self-selection community workers in Philadelphia, who held a more radical analysis, would search for other sites for their political engagement.

## Philadelphia's Community Action Agency: A Centralized Approach

The city government conceived and implemented PAAC in collaboration with established social service agencies in Philadelphia.[14] When Mayor James Tate first submitted Philadelphia's plan to OEO, he was denied funding until he involved the poor in program design and administration. The first Antipoverty elections in Philadelphia were held in May 1965. Only two and a half percent of those eligible voted in these, the country's first elections for poor representatives to serve on an antipoverty board.[15] Eligible candidates could not have an annual income that exceeded a range of $3,000 to $6,000 depending on the number of dependents (Bailey 1973,

175). Those interested in running for the Community Action Councils (CAC) were required to submit a petition with fifty signatures of residents in their local neighborhoods. Twelve representatives were elected for each of the twelve poverty areas defined in Philadelphia. From these local councils, one representative was chosen to sit on the citywide committee of thirty-one giving the poor forty percent representation. While the city administration as well as the established political parties were said to exert little control over the election process, only three percent of those eligible to vote in the election actually participated in the first elections (Greenstone and Peterson 1972). The 1966 Antipoverty election attracted 5.4 percent of the eligible vote but only 3.5 percent turned out the following year.[16] The 1969 election drew a little less than 3.5 percent—16,057 voters as compared to 17,315 in 1967 (Greenstone and Peterson 1972).

Matusow (1984, 256) reports that despite the mandated involvement of the poor on Philadelphia's policy board, Samuel L. Evans ran the show. Mayor Tate appointed Evans vice-chair of PAAC and, from that position, Evans "set out to insulate the program from the influence of the poor and run it in Tate's political interest." He helped diminish the poor's influence on the board by announcing that the elected poor representatives "were not bound in voting by their neighborhood councils and by personally courting them with lunches, dinners, and private caucuses." Evans also worked to isolate the different area offices from each other. Matusow reads Philadelphia's CAP history as an exclusive top down one with the poor representatives acting as pawns in Evans's political games. He argues that Evans bought the poor off with jobs; that "of the 144 poor people who sat on area councils in 1966, 118 had obtained employment either with the poverty program or the city government" (p. 257).

Yet from the standpoint of the women community workers, the relationship between their employment and election to the policy board was much more complex and could not be explained as patronage. In fact many of the women had already obtained employment through a local area office before they ran for election. When paid workers serving on the boards were cited as having a conflict of interest, many resigned their elected positions. Matusow is correct in depicting Philadelphia's centralized administrative structure as creating an inhospitable environment for maximum feasible participation. However, the local representatives and community workers did resist attempts to coopt their participation. For example, a watchdog group was established called the Maximum Participation Movement whose members included some officers and members of Community Action Councils.[17] Furthermore, the community workers remained committed to the empowerment of community residents through participatory strategies. Wilma North reported that her community always had representation to the citywide council because of the active participation and successful organizing strategies utilized by the neighborhood association she had worked with for years. She explained:

Most of the people who ran for council came from neighborhood block council and...they formed kind of a slate with other members throughout the community, and I think at that first election, four members of [our] block council were elected to the area community action council—PAAC council. And we've always had representation from that area on the council....I think right up until the last election.

## Council Representatives as Paid Workers

Those who were elected to the council were often the most obvious choices for the paid positions in the twelve area offices (and vice versa) and consequently could be accused of monopolizing the already limited opportunities for participation (see E. White 1973). Paid positions for which residents were hired included community organization aides who, in 1964, earned $3,900 per year and council assistants who were paid $5,000 to manage the area office. Community organization (CO) aides were eventually given primary areas of responsibility including youth; employment and job development; culture, recreation, and leisure time; housing; resource development for the aged; as well as community organization. Initially, council assistants could not hire or fire the CO aides who were selected by CAC representatives. Not surprisingly, this caused tremendous problems for the council assistants who could not supervise their staff effectively (see Sennott 1974). Within a year, each area office also employed information and referral (I&R) workers and I&R aides. In some offices, this new social work component led to the employment of credentialed workers who received a higher wage than the resident workers thus adding to the tensions within each area office. The social work staff were subsequently placed under a social services supervisor who was employed by the central PAAC office and this further divided the area office staff (Sennott 1974).

A great deal of controversy arose over the suspected conflict of interest of paid staff who were also elected to the CAC.[18] Under the leadership of acting executive director Barbara Weems a partial solution was found to the prohibition against CAC representatives accepting paid positions. PAAC was reorganized giving supervisory responsibilities to four coordinators who were hired to oversee the operations of three area councils each. Since the CAC members were no longer directly responsible for area operations, it was now possible for CAC representatives to accept paid positions in the area offices. However, many PAAC community workers did resign as CAC representatives. The formal resolution of the "conflict of interest" controversy reflected the increasing bureaucratization of PAAC and the expanded centralization of control over the CAC (Sennott 1974).

When PAAC opened an area office in her community, African American community worker Mrs. Ruth Dever received encouragement from her neighbors to run for one of the twelve area council seats. She served as council secretary for two years but quit the council in 1966 to take a paid position as an I&R aide for the area office for which she was paid an annual salary of $3,900. She commented with a smile, "they weren't calling us paid volunteers but it was just about the same thing." The I&R position was Mrs. Dever's first paid job. Due to a medical disability, she had not been able to accept full-time employment that required traveling from her community. However, since the job was integrally related to her previous unpaid activities she was highly qualified for the position. While some community workers retained both positions, Mrs. Dever resolved the tension by resigning her position on the council. She explained that, "I wasn't going to be accused of having two hats and so the next election I just refused to run, although some [paid workers] did remain on the council."

Unlike Mrs. Dever who decided to resign from the council, Grace Reynolds, who first ran for the CAC and won in 1965 kept her seat on the council when she took a paid job as an I&R aide the following year. She remained on the council because, she said, she "didn't get in there just to get a job. I got in there because I was concerned about people." She believed she could be more effective in her community if she retained her policy-making role. She continued to serve on her area council even after she retired from PAAC in 1976.

For those women who were both employed by PAAC and elected to the council, the decision to resign one of the roles was a difficult one. Most said they were committed to serving their communities to the fullest extent possible—as staff and as members of the CAP councils. Furthermore, these women were frequently the ones who were identified by their neighbors for council positions. But without paid employment, most low-income representatives could not continue their council service. Therefore, some of the most dedicated resident community workers could not participate fully in the decision-making CACs. Brenda Rivers, who did not serve on the council, also noted that since no money was available for the expenses incurred by the poor who were elected to the CAC their participation was severely curtailed. This was especially problematic for women with children since no funds were allocated for childcare expenses. Brenda recalled:

> They did allocate money for expenses at one point—it was harder than hell to get it, but they did and it primarily covered things like…public transportation, taxis at night to get home, lunches, suppers if it was necessary. I don't think they ever put anything for babysitting….It was strictly for transportation and food.

Brenda Rivers emphasized the waning commitment to maximum feasible participation in hiring that accompanied the bureaucratization and professionalization of PAAC. For the first ten years, "you had to live in the community where you worked." In the move to "professionalize" the work, the PAAC administration asserted that "if you're a community worker you ought to be able to work anywhere." Brenda believed that this change was in response to the fear that "people were responding too much to their Community Action Council rather than from the direction of the central office." The strategy "mixed...[the community workers] up with a wild hand," she reported. As African American resident community worker Othelia Carson stated:

> They were trying to control the area offices from the central office....They made each area office do the same activities, rather than responding to...what each neighborhood needed....And it was no good because what we needed out here they didn't need in North Philly....[But] they said that workers should be able to work in any neighborhood.

Othelia asserted that when workers moved into other areas, "it's just like going to a foreign country." Othelia's response illustrates one of the primary ways the community workers defied dominant understandings of labor. For the resident workers, their jobs were not merely a collection of definable skills; it was their relationship with their particular community that formed the basis for their community work. They could not apply their community work to any neighborhood or any situation because the work was not limited to the activities they performed. The work embodied years of community building and relationships with particular people and institutions.

Martha Framer, who started with PAAC in 1969 in a clerical position and was promoted in 1976 to an administrative position, also discussed what she believed was the "irrationality" of "professionalizing" the PAAC workforce. Martha commented that the decline in PAAC's commitment to hire indigenous staff contributed to the tension between the central office and the community-based staff. Furthermore, the expectation that community workers should function in any community across Philadelphia, she said, "scattered [the community workers] all over and it's more costly for the employees—car fares, et cetera—and that has been a hardship on them and affected their willingness to change."

According to Martha, the workers resisted the shift to professionalization and bureaucratization. She reported that from her earliest days at PAAC "there were always some complaints about how difficult it was to get the area staff to follow directions and to implement" the programs designed by the central staff. Worker resistance and opposition to the authority of the central office continued despite Martha's persistent efforts to increase staff "morale" and "productivity." She reported:

> I'd say, almost fifteen years later...problems do exist. I believe that I have tried every innovative way that I'm aware of and still researching to find some other ways to increase their morale. Hopefully that would

increase their interest and to provide them with more up-to-date and active information. Hopefully that would enhance their knowledge of the program and would eventually help their actual performances in the job. I'm perplexed at this point because...what we've been doing is trying to begin to get everyone at least to a basic minimum level of performance, and I would say after a year and a half of trying to do that, I'm concerned because to me we're not making any headway.

In her efforts to improve worker morale Martha inadvertently designed strategies that increased the workers dissatisfaction with the central office. Most of the women interviewed in Philadelphia believed that PAAC had the potential to serve the community and to involve community residents, but that the desire by the central administration to control area activities undermined those goals.

## Bureaucratization of PAAC

Overall, the PAAC workers emphasized that the process of bureaucratization decreased their ability to meet the differing needs of the twelve poverty areas. In 1984, at the age of sixty-two, Othelia Carson was employed as an outreach worker for PAAC and earned $10,000 a year. Her husband was disabled. Othelia accepted her first paid position as a PAAC community worker in 1964. She asserted that the area offices had more autonomy to design their own program in the early start-up months of PAAC. As PAAC became more bureaucratized and the central office exerted more control over the area offices, the council was prevented from designing programs that differed from other areas. Othelia echoed the view of many PAAC workers that in the early months, the area councils "had a say."

> Now, at that time the council would get together, and they would go out into the areas. They hadn't set up offices then—they were getting ready to set them up. And they would say what was needed. Now maybe [Area] J didn't need what [Area] K needed. Maybe J needed more help with education, maybe K needed more help with the housing.

But within a short time the central administration of PAAC decided that "each area would have to have a supervisor and so many outreach workers and different things like that" and, consequently, standardized the program across the city.

Brenda Rivers reviewed the bureaucratic changes in PAAC from her initial employment in 1968 until she was laid off in 1982. During her tenure at PAAC she advanced her education and was promoted to a citywide mid-management position. She left PAAC when the program she directed was defunded. She recounted:

> Initially...some of us took off like a shot and were doing a dozen different things and some offices were sitting twiddling their thumbs with

> nothing to do....So that they turned it around and restrained some of
> us who were going fast and pulled up the ones who were inactive, or
> virtually inactive, and got them all involved in the same programs.

Rather than allow each community to determine their own programs, the
centralized office took increased control over program design and implementation. Brenda explained that, within a short time, "PAAC became the
voice of the city," primarily the mayor's office. Any program which "had
much substance to it somehow or another got waylaid along the way and
things came from the top down for the most part and did not go the other
way very often."

According to Brenda, one of the most significant turning points that
furthered the staff's loss of control was connected to the debate over the
jurisdiction of PAAC. A special committee was established in 1967 to
determine the form of organization best suited to PAAC. Despite Sam
Evans's central role in "discredit[ing] community action," Mayor Tate
placed Evans in charge of the panel to reorganize PAAC (Matusow 1984,
257). The major debate concerned whether PAAC should be organized as
a private nonprofit corporation or a part of the city government. After
considerable discussion, the decision was reached to establish PAAC as an
independent commission within the city government.[19]

The jurisdiction debate included whether or not staff would have civil
service status. Brenda noted that those employees who were knowledge-
able about the importance of civil service unions for protecting their
interests as workers struggled unsuccessfully against the administration
who opposed unionization. Brenda believed that the resolution that
established PAAC as an independent city commission limited the power
of the staff to serve their communities as well as to protect their rights as
workers.

> Some of the people in the administration did not want that [union-
> ization] to happen and managed to convince them [PAAC workers]
> that they probably would not be able to pass the civil service tests,
> and, therefore, they shouldn't be pushing for that, were finally
> turned over and did not push to be included under civil service, not
> realizing, of course, that the tests would have been new ones that
> could have been adjusted to their abilities. And because of the idea
> that they would all fail and all lose their jobs, the majority voted not
> to....So that settled that one. That was when we lost.

Brenda also believed that the lack of civil service status inhibited the ability of PAAC community workers to upgrade their positions by applying
for jobs in other city agencies. She explained that PAAC workers "were
considered temporary employees and therefore where jobs were offered
throughout the city which were upgrading jobs we were not eligible to

take the exams for them." The fact that the central office used the workers' noncredentialed status to convince them to vote against civil service status further indicates the contradictions embedded in the implementation of New Careers.

Administrators used personnel policy practices that prevented staff from engaging in political activities to limit further the autonomy and decision-making power of the community workers. As African American resident worker Josephine Card stated:

> When people started learning how to lobby, and started going to politician's offices and banging on those doors, and started writing letters…'cause now they had gone too far.…[The administrators] immediately started trying to undermine those programs. And then they started putting all these things in personnel policy practices, so if they received public funding, you can't be on political lists, etc.…Our staff is laced with that stuff now. It wasn't in the beginning, but now it is. They've laced you so you cannot do anything. You know what a force that would be, if you had all the poor people protesting about something?

Josephine tied the increasing constraints on workers' political activism to the threat they posed to the social welfare and political establishment. Not surprisingly, as Alice Porter, an area coordinator in PAAC, remembered, community workers resisted this process of depolitization.

A block captain and active in a variety of community groups in her neighborhood before joining PAAC, Alice accepted a paid position following separation from her husband in 1966. She described how PAAC tried to curtail political work of the paid staff who frequently circumvented the rules because, she emphasized, "nothing could stop us." As a quasi-city agency, all PAAC workers were prohibited from overt political action as a condition of their employment. According to Alice, the community workers had great mistrust for the two-party system that they believed represented the interests of rich white men. Therefore, they did not find it difficult to remain "nonpartisan." They focused on the problems that were of the most concern to their communities and continued to advocate for solutions. For example, Alice said she reinterpreted the formal agency rules prohibiting "partisan" politics and actively participated in political struggles to protect the interests of her community. She viewed these efforts as an extension of her job as community worker and advocate; consequently, she said she did not feel constrained by the regulations. However, most other workers emphasized the contradictions between advocacy for their communities and their responsibilities as workers employed by the state.

By 1967, federal appropriations for the antipoverty programs were reduced drastically. Most communities were forced to make serious cuts in program provision and staff. In Philadelphia, according to the community workers interviewed, most layoffs were made on the basis of seniority and worker evaluations. The remaining programs were further circumscribed by federal guidelines, which severely curtailed the activities defined as community action. Further retrenchment occurred in 1978. Reductions in staff and program services also occurred when funding for the CAAs were collapsed under the Community Services Block Grant in 1981.[20]

## Institutionalization and Retrenchment

PAAC's board retained its policy-making role until 1984 when the mayor shifted its role to advisory status. As Janet Nola, a PAAC administrator interviewed in 1995, recalled,

> In the beginning up until '84 our board was a policy making board. But there was so much dissension among the board that actually hindered the operations. So that year the mayor decided in '84 to make it an advisory board.

Janet defined the decision to end the board's policy-making role as a rational step by the Mayor to increase efficiency. When I asked her what, in particular, she thought contributed to the Mayor's decision, she explained:

> Different parts of the city wanted different things, wanted jobs for their friends....It wasn't about programs really, you know. I mean it was just about basically jobs and power....We couldn't move. I mean we had to have approval from them and it would be fights about other issues, not dealing with the programs per se. So when they became an advisory board it was just a matter of keeping them informed as to what we were doing.

To my question "was there much dissension when the board's role shifted to advisory status?" Janet said, "No, it was very quiet" in the mid-1980s.

> They're still elected by the community, but like I say, they are not really that involved in the decision-making process. It's more so we inform them, and we ask them to bring us input, give input in different things that they feel…is needed in their particular communities.

When I expressed surprise at the lack of resistance by local communities and board members, Janet explained that as a "very political city" Philadelphia faced a great deal of disagreement among the different groups represented on the policy board. Her response included a theme that appeared in many of the resident workers' narratives; namely, a definition of political that equated it with "self-interest" rather than concern for broader "community" needs. By "very political," Janet meant that in Philadelphia people got involved in political activities for their own gain. Rather than represent the low-income communities, she felt that most board members had "their own motives" and that "infighting" among them curtailed their efforts to improve the lives of the poor.

While Philadelphia has its own unique political history, as Janet Nola points out, the commitment evidenced by the women who served on the antipoverty board at the local community level in Philadelphia mirrors that expressed by the resident community workers in New York City. In both cities, workers tied their commitment to a concern for others in their communities rather than self-interest. Resident community workers in both locales were more enthusiastic about their work on the antipoverty policy boards than Janet Nola. For many of the resident community workers, this was their first experience in a formal leadership role. However, since CAP legislation mandated participation by different segments of the wider community, including established social service agencies and government officials, the competing interests frequently generated disagreements that often prevented policy boards from taking effective action on a variety of problems faced by residents in low-income communities.

The centralized approach to CAP administration in Philadelphia laid the groundwork for the shift away from comprehensive antipoverty strategies developed in the 1970s to targeted economic development efforts in the 1990s—a citywide response to the Empowerment Zones and Enterprise Communities (EZEC) Program included in the Omnibus Budget Reconciliation Act of 1993.[21] The Enterprise Zone Program targets specific geographic communities with tax reductions and relief from certain government regulations to encourage business and industrial development. When I spoke with administrators in 1995, they enthusiastically discussed the creation of three Empowerment Zones designed to feature different approaches to economic development.[22] Former PAAC community workers, however, were less optimistic about the new approach. They explained that the management structure created for the Empowerment Zones shifted the basis of power from the community residents to developers, city bureaucrats, and leaders of established social services agencies.[23]

Overall, the community workers employed by PAAC described greater problems with centralization and bureaucratization than was evident in the narratives of the community workers in New York City. However, women in both cities emphasized how the process of professionalization circumscribed their political efficacy as well as their careers as community workers—a theme I illustrate with reference to MFY.

## New York City CAPs: Decentralization in Implementation

The history of the CAPs in New York City is more complicated than that of Philadelphia due to the difference in organizational structure and political history. As mentioned earlier, some CAPs in New York City, like MFY, were organized prior to passage of the EOA. Others evolved out of existing community organizations. Still others were developed by local community groups and block associations in areas like Bedford Stuyvesant and the South Bronx. Due to historical factors, Harlem and the Lower East Side were the first to respond to the funding opportunities provided through the EOA. The South Bronx was also highly visible in developing CAPs at the start of the War on Poverty.

The large proportion of the first EOA funds designated for New York City were directed toward MFY and HARYOU since they had the benefits of early organization and political support. In addition, Albert Einstein College received $289,652 to establish four emergency mental health centers in the East Bronx and train neighborhood people to provide initial care (Jonnes 1986). Within a short time, however, various community groups and local leaders discovered ways to attract some of the antipoverty funds (e.g., Youth in Action in Harlem; Massive Economic Neighborhood Development [MEND]; the East Harlem Tenants Council; and Hunt's Point Multi-Service Corporation and Simpson Street Development Association in the Bronx). By 1978, at least four hundred antipoverty programs operated in New York City. Despite the existence of a large number of independent CAAs, the city of New York gradually circumscribed their autonomy.

### Community Convention Approach to Management of CAPs

Mayor Robert Wagner established New York's Council Against Poverty and the Poverty Operations Board in June 1964. Both groups were comprised exclusively of city officials and chaired by the president of the city council, Paul Screvane. In March 1965, a proposal designed by city staff was submitted to OEO. This proposal, which called for a city-run antipoverty program controlled by public and existing citywide, private agencies, was sharply criticized. After a revised plan was vetoed by Governor Nelson Rockefeller, Wagner issued another executive order that reorganized the Council to include one hundred seats on a policy board executive committee to administer the antipoverty programs and a professional planning committee to review funding requests from local groups. The administrative arm was called the Economic Opportunity Corporation. Forty-two percent of the seats on the Council were designated for representatives of the poor and for private organizations like HARYOU and MFY. In addition, the city's antipoverty proposal designated sixteen poverty areas in which "community conventions" were developed to serve as local advisory boards (Greenstone and Peterson 1972).

When John Lindsay took over as mayor in 1966, he supervised the consolidation of the Council Against Poverty into a single board of sixty-two members (Jonnes 1986). He commissioned a study by Mitchell Sviridoff to determine the most efficient way to reorganize the city's antipoverty programs. Sviridoff proposed that the city's social services be organized under a large umbrella agency known as the Human Resources Administration

(HRA). Wagner's proposal called for the establishment of six community progress centers which weren't completely set up until the end of his tenure as mayor. Sviridoff recommended that these centers become community corporations that could sponsor local leadership. The study group also added six new poverty areas to the original sixteen. Three more areas were later added for a total of twenty-five areas (Hallman 1969). The antipoverty programs were placed under the jurisdiction of the HRA, along with the manpower programs,[24] the Welfare Department, and the Youth Board.

Subsequent elections for the community corporations were held in 1970 and 1972. The city set out to restructure the citywide agency into a new Community Development Agency (CDA). Twenty-six areas or Neighborhood Development Areas (NDAs) were designated as having a high concentration of poverty. Eight additional areas were identified as Secondary NDAs. In each NDA, an Area Policy Board (APB) was established with thirty-three members elected from the community—seventeen representing the poor, up to eleven from the public sector, and five from the private sector. All recommendations for funding were selected by the APB and then submitted to the mayor for approval.

The process of professionalization intensified with the increased centralized control over CAP funding. For example, Ann Robinson who was elected to the Council Against Poverty recalled that in New York City the professionals did not allow the poor to speak for themselves. In fact, she recalled, "Many of the professional people would tell the poor who were elected to the antipoverty board: 'Well, you know you really can't express yourself. Let us speak up for you. We can get them to understand it better.' And gradually people began to back out." The process of professionalization and its relationship to attempts to depoliticize the community workers was furthered by amendments to the EOA that required increased bureaucratic standards and professional staffing in order to qualify for funding (see Appendix D).

New York City community workers identified for this study worked in numerous CAPs located throughout four of the five boroughs: Manhattan, the Bronx, Queens, and Brooklyn. To situate the experiences of each community worker in each neighborhood would require an extensive discussion that is beyond the scope of this study.[25] While I cannot provide background on all the CAPs in which these women were employed, I will briefly highlight the organizational dynamics of Mobilization for Youth, the program that provided the template for the Community Action component of the EOA. As a model program, MFY's professionally designed and lead approach to community action inhibited implementation of the legislative mandate for maximum feasible participation to a certain extent. Professionals were often attracted to MFY because it offered them an institutional base for community organizing that was unavailable through other more traditional social service agencies. Ironically, despite its failure to achieve maximum feasible participation, MFY was considered one of the most radical CAPs in the country.

## Mobilization for Youth: Professional Innovation

The idea for Mobilization for Youth (MFY) was presented by Richard Cloward and Lloyd Ohlin, Columbia University social work professors, to the Board of Directors of Henry Street Settlement House in 1957. MFY received funds from President Kennedy's Commission on Juvenile Delinquency and Youth Crime (PCJD) set up in 1961[26] and the Ford Foundation's Grey Areas Project in 1962.[27] As discussed, MFY subsequently became the model for the CAPs to be funded under the EOA. Since MFY was designed as a model program, most of the early staff were young professionals interested in the unique experience and autonomy that a new innovative community-based program offered. Less emphasis was initially placed on employment of resident personnel than in many other CAPs. Hattie Jones (1969,62), however, noted that MFY utilized indigenous staff to "explain the slum to them [the professionals] and, just as important, explain their presence to the slum."

Although only five percent of operating funds were devoted to community organization,[28] this program quickly became the target of "intense public attack" (Fried 1969, 137). MFY supported numerous protests and community actions especially those associated with the Civil Rights Movement. MFY staff participated in the 1963 March on Washington, supported local black and Puerto Rican leaders in efforts to develop a Police Department civilian review board, and sponsored voter registration campaigns for poor residents. They organized community residents on behalf of welfare rights and a contentious rent strike. One of the most contested actions taken by MFY involved their support of a group of Puerto Rican mothers, Mobilization of Mothers (MOM), who were pressuring the Board of Education to remove a hostile principal from one of the local elementary schools. Rendering invisible the leadership of MOM members, local principals attacked MFY arguing, "Workers paid with public funds...have no right during their official working hours to misuse public funds by secretly proselytizing to their own private beliefs and affiliations to the innocents who do not realize that they are being used to further someone's desire for a social revolution..." (quoted in Fried 1969, 140).

The FBI began surveillance of MFY in 1963 and, in August 1964, they accused the agency of irregularities in financial management, employing Communist sympathizers, and encouraging the summer riots in Harlem.[29] The agency came under investigation from both the federal and city governments. MFY's Board also retained their own special counsel to conduct an independent investigation of the charges. Alfred Fried (1969, 151) notes that the Greenwich Village branch of the NAACP was the only agency to come out in support of MFY during the first days of the attack against them. Eventually other organizations, including the National Association of Social Workers and the American Jewish Congress, joined in support. Most notably absent were some of the large labor unions in New York and the most prominent social agencies. The pressure placed on MFY diminished its community organizing activities even though none of the charges was substantiated.[30] For example, Alfred Fried (1969, 159) reports that MFY's support of the rent strike as well as "the Parent Education Program (which included Mobilization of Mothers under its umbrella), had been rendered difficult or impossible."

Sabrina Brock, an African American community worker, was employed during MFY's first years of operation. During the early years of MFY, Sabrina reported, the staff was frequently caught between their goals of community organizing and traditional social service. While the agency was under scrutiny from numerous professional groups and political officials, tensions between these often competing goals intensified.

Following graduation from social work school in 1964, Sabrina Brock found employment in MFY, and she remained there until 1967 when she accepted a position teaching community organization to social work students. Sabrina described the exciting atmosphere that surrounded the initial development of MFY:

> More than anything else, there was the attitude of the administrators …in the whole development of an [exciting] atmosphere… Everybody came to Mobilization, anybody who wanted to try to do anything. We all converged. And…the combination of the kind of staff, the kinds of programs that were generated, with the permission of the agency, everything could go. [But] it had to be thought through. It had to be justified. There was no carte blanche ticket. But anything that had quality, any issue—education, housing, employment, welfare rights. I was one of the first welfare rights [organizers]….We set up the first welfare rights groups in the city in '66. And we were the first in the country.[31]

Sabrina worked in a special unit which "tried to demonstrate that one-to-one work could be more effective if you involve all kinds of community resources in the work….So it was short term, emergency, advocacy, crisis intervention, all that stuff that later got written up in the textbooks, we were doing."

According to Sabrina, MFY's neighborhood centers differed from traditional social services in treating the poor with respect. However, she felt that, as with any program located in poor neighborhoods, over time they too became "crappy."

> The neighborhood service centers were more benevolent social work services. People came there and they were treated like human beings. But basically they were the poorest of the poor….I think some social welfare commentator said when you develop services for the poor, inevitably they become poor services. So even though there was an intellectual and social commitment, the neighborhood service centers were crappy—you know, poorly furnished, long waits, even though everyone who was dedicated broke their hearts.

She found that "in the first two or three years, people who might survive anyway come to the door" and by "the fourth or fifth year of MFY, you were really getting people who were so disenfranchised, so demobilized, that mobilizing them was a twenty-four hour thing. They would just live on the edge socially, financially" and "just when you were hitting the so-called hard core," the funds began to dry up and the political pressure intensified.

Sabrina recalled how the staff responded to the problems they encountered on the Lower East Side by increasing their advocacy efforts. Reflecting on the belief held by MFY staff at the time that they could empower members of the community, Sabrina said:

> And there was this whole kind of advocacy, you had to do something for these poor people, and, indeed, it is a mixed bag. People were so resourceless. It was hard to tap into the real power that they potentially have, a naive quality that any social agency, anybody working in community development under government and social aegis could empower people—that was interesting. We all felt like we were pedalling to save the world.

Sabrina quickly became cynical about the attitude of the professional staff that they could "empower" the poor who were living with so few basic resources. She no longer felt that the professional staff acting as outside organizers could effectively mobilize community members. As Sabrina questioned this professional "will to empower,"[32] MFY was under pressure to curtail much of its radical community action. Sabrina recalled how these pressures translated into an intense professionalization that further compromised MFY staff's ability to improve the lives of the residents on the Lower East Side.

Sabrina questioned MFY's commitment to hiring resident community workers. Sabrina did not think the administrators of MFY were as committed to employing local community residents because, as a model demonstration program, they were under pressure to "produce."

> I think that the units that I was in, it wasn't that there was no intention [to hire local residents], but it was less. The first unit that I was in was a totally all professional case work unit. They chose these cracker jack workers who had a lot of skills because this was either going to work or it wasn't. They couldn't have any novices or beginners, which of necessity many community people who might have been great natural helpers had to be. Because they had never been exposed to the variety, the vicissitudes of the bureaucracy that things had to be slugged out with.

According to Sabrina, MFY did try to involve neighborhood residents in community work activities especially in housing and in education, and they did serve on advisory boards. However, as the process by which funding decisions were made became routinized over time, the role of those representing the poor on advisory boards was increasingly circumscribed.

Despite her criticisms of MFY, Sabrina felt that the experiences she gained were well worth the battles she fought. She enthusiastically relayed the conflicting pressures she faced as a community worker with MFY:

> Mobilization for Youth had been attacked by then [1966]. Everybody was a lot more careful, but this was a logical expression of the programs they'd been developing—neighborhood service centers, community involvement, an advisory board, day care. Any issue that touched people's lives, they had tackled in some way—not perfectly, and as a matter of fact very imperfectly, because there was this whole liberal baggage....What was self-determination and what did real advocacy look like? It was all mixed up, and multi-problem families, culture of poverty, and all that load of crap. But, nonetheless, that was a life experience. And it was the first time any of us had a whole agency, had a whole cultural environment, that gave enough. We were attacked for everything we did. The welfare department attacked us. The city attacked us....But I don't know that that romanticism that we have about the sixties—it was tough! It was not clear, "okay, go out, go forth, and do your thing." Everything had to be haggled out, hashed out, had to be reasonable, had to be professional.

Sabrina described how political pressure along with cutbacks in funding quickly constrained the effectiveness of the MFY staff who were interested in mobilizing the poor. Yet, despite the pressures, Sabrina found MFY provided one of the most supportive working environments of her professional career.

## Conclusion

The Philadelphia CAPs were designed in direct response to the federal legislation and were limited by the political environment and the haste with which they were developed. Processes of bureaucratization and professionalization further circumscribed the political activities and program innovation of the Philadelphia programs. In the years immediately following the passage of the EOA, community workers in both cities experienced a greater degree of autonomy in their work. The early excitement reported by the community workers hired in the first years of funding quickly gave way to disillusionment as the programs became increasingly circumscribed by centralized authority and reliance on professionals. Low-income residents' claims to authority within CAPs shifted from organization to organization, from city to city, and changed over time. Differences between the experiences of community workers in Philadelphia and New York City lessened as the processes of institutional control, professionalization, and funding cuts circumscribed the range of political actions that were viewed as feasible, especially given the increasingly conservative political environment.

The declared War on Poverty was short-lived, but the war continues for the women whose stories are told here. What explains their motivation for such challenging work and how they remained engaged as life-long community activists constitutes the foundation for the next two chapters. In these chapters, I highlight the personal influences, daily conflicts, and the complex political analyses evident in the community workers' narratives. I further contextualize their perspectives by attention to how the dynamics of gender, race, and class contoured their everyday lives and political strategies. Chapter four explores the influence of religious teaching, social welfare traditions, and radical social movements in shaping the community workers' personal and political commitment to work on behalf of low-income communities and highlights the experiences of the nonresident community workers. Chapter five discusses the practice of activist mothering and other informal processes that influenced the motivation for community work that was especially evident in the narratives of the African American and Latina resident workers.

## Chapter 4

# PATHWAYS TO COMMUNITY WORK

Jewish community worker Jill Anders participated in anti-Vietnam War demonstrations during college but said that the Peace Corps really raised her political consciousness. She joined in 1968 after graduating from college and was sent to Latin America with her husband who saw it as a way to obtain a draft deferment. She was highly critical of the training she received in the Peace Corps since she thought that it was designed to

> eliminate anybody who they thought would make trouble. They saved all the future businessmen of America [from being drafted], basically. The idealistic sort of socialist types who were part of the early Peace Corps were completely out [by 1968]. And now it was much more bureaucratic—future business people, a lot of people who wanted to go into foreign service, who were hoping to expand daddy's business to [Latin America]. Those were the people—a lot of MBAs. And the whole scene was very different. And I came into direct contact with U.S. imperialism. I mean, I had heard about it before, but now I saw it every single day, and it was amazing.

Jill and her husband lasted only eight months out of the two-year term. However, she described how she was profoundly affected by the poverty she witnessed in Latin America and how this experience furthered her political commitment.

> The people lived in unspeakable poverty....People would live in cardboard homes, with like one dress, no shoes, in incredible places. There were sanitation ditches with shit floating down the street, kids

playing in it, and you know, all these kids with distended bellies. Unbelievable health problems. And it was just so shocking!

Even more remarkable, Jill recalled, was the fact that the Peace Corps volunteers were housed in nice country-club settings with live-in maids. She and her husband moved into a poor working-class barrio, rather than stay in the wealthier part of town. She exclaimed, "No one in the barrios had a refrigerator, but us." Jill and her husband had numerous confrontations with the Peace Corps trainers and were on the verge of being thrown out when the residents in their barrio joined together and signed a petition to support their staying in the community. After a few more frustrating months, they resigned from the Peace Corps and returned to the United States, "much more politicized, much more ready to struggle."

Jill contrasted her radical politics with her parents' approach, which she defined as politically naive. Both her parents had advanced degrees and held professional positions while Jill was growing up. She expressed great respect for her father who she saw as "a social reformer in his own way." She said that her father became disillusioned when he came to see how politicians were not interested in doing the right thing. She explained, "I really respected him for being a crusader. He was like a public health crusader but he did it individually. He didn't know about organization. He didn't know about developing a movement." She differentiated her father's lack of awareness about "developing a movement" with the political work she began when she moved with her husband to a small college town for graduate school after leaving the Peace Corps. Here she became caught up in the radical activism of the 1960s but initially with little conceptual understanding of the New Left politics in which she participated. She described the enthusiasm she felt upon returning to the United States with her husband and taking off as an activist.

> The day after we arrived…there was this…concert that was a benefit for the [local]…tenants' union. And we joined [the organizing effort] that night, and we went to the meeting within a day or two to, you know, roll up our sleeves, and we were ready to go. And I can look back now, being an experienced political person, and realize that they must have thought, "who are these people coming in, willing to spend [their time on this]." We didn't have any friends [there]…so we had a lot of free time. And we had a great need for social networking. We were very excited politically. We were both chomping at the bit to get going.

The group she joined was committed to grassroots organizing efforts, and she began by going "door-to-door" to organize tenants. She recalled:

> And I used to come home from [work].…I'd take my dress off, put my jeans on, and go door-to-door organizing. To me, it was such an exciting thing to do. First of all…we were organizing against the worst landlords, but you got to talk to people in their homes, about their

homes, about their politics, the aspects of their daily lives. It was very informative and very exciting to me, and I just really enjoyed it tremendously.

This experience led her to redefine herself as an activist. She found the community organizing invigorating and felt that she could make a difference in people's everyday lives as well as contribute to their political education. Within a short time, she joined a socialist group through which she continued to work as a grassroots organizer. She enthusiastically recalled:

> It was the first time I started thinking of myself as an activist. And I loved it. It was so exciting to do something that you wanted to do, that you thought was right, that you could have a say in, that, you know, was assuming some control over your life, in a world where you really have so little control over your life....I loved the whole process, I loved the whole experience....And that year I joined a [socialist] group....I looked at it and said, "Right! Right! I agree with that! I agree with that! That must be me."

In hindsight she realized that her enthusiasm for the work masked how little she actually knew about "politics." However, following her intuition, she joined a group that did not manifest the top-down authoritarian approaches that she saw evident in other leftist political groups of the time. She reflected on her decision-making process:

> I really knew very little. When I think back, it wasn't stupid that I joined it, but I didn't know what the hell I was doing. I had no idea what I was joining. But I made a pretty good selection, I think, given the choices. Well, it was that group and the Communist Party that were active. And I definitely never had Stalin's politics....I was always one of those small "d" democrats. That was just like where my gut was. And part of it was antiestablishment....I didn't like a person on the basis of their being a heavy leader, you know, assuming too much control and authority. It was just something in my personality [that] I didn't like [that kind of leader]. So [because of] my politics, of course, I was going to oppose the ideologies that [were] associated [with authoritarianism].

She described the group she joined as "a tiny little group of very young people, all in their late teens, early to mid-twenties" who "didn't know what...they were doing." She recalled much abstract discussion of the ideology of Marx and Lenin rather than more grounded political analyses. However, she emphasized, "it was very exciting" and she "learned a lot!"

Due to the small size of the town, she found herself front and center in numerous community and labor struggles including drives to increase voter turnout and support local strikes. She recounted some of the organizing efforts:

And we would have meetings every three weeks of three hundred people. It was really a mass movement. On election day, we had three
thousand people working with us, in a city of one hundred thousand
people. It was incredible! We had all these cars with these big posters
on top, these big signs that said "Shuttle to the Polls," and we got
everybody to the polls. All these different people doing organizing.
Again, I was doing this compulsive door-to-door organizing. I didn't
feel like I had done my share even though for about a year I was the
political coordinator. And I was just thriving on it. It was so exciting!

Jill also ran for political office—a plan devised to promote the platform
of her party rather than to win the election.

One of the elections I ran for office in an unwinnable position, but my
function was as labor liaison. I spoke in front of all those labor unions.
That was such an experience! And I was this little pisser. I was twenty-
three years old. And I was speaking in a hall of like nine hundred men,
steelworkers or auto workers. I would say what we [the political group]
thought. We had worked out this fifty-page legal-size single-spaced typed
platform on everything you could imagine. It was a lot of good ideas.
And that's what I spoke on, and it was very, very exciting. Again, I would
still never get that opportunity except [in this small town].

Jill was grateful for the experiences she had as a result of joining this leftist political group and described how she thrived on the activism. Not surprisingly, her graduate studies were a mere backdrop to her political work.

I was in the right time and I was in the right place and I was very fortunate and I busted my ass. I'm a sixteen hour-a-day person and at least
eight of those hours were spent on politics. And I enjoyed every
minute. We would take sandwiches for lunch and dinner. We would
leave home in the morning, and we would pack up our sandwiches for
the whole day. We'd get home at midnight. We'd get up at eight in the
morning. We'd get to our nine o'clock classes. We'd get our classes
over with and then we'd go to the office.

When she moved to New York City in the early 1970s after she graduated,
she continued work with a local chapter of the same political group. Jill's
description of her community work contrasts sharply with the indigenous
perspective of the resident community workers of color who fought racism
and poverty on a daily basis. She came to antipoverty activism through a
political analysis and a more distanced understanding of how race and class
operate as systems of oppression in America. She recalled:

We waded through every black struggle, but it really was an all-white
group. But the best aspect of the process was class politics, very good class
politics....even though I didn't know what...class politics was when I

joined this organization. It struck me in the sense of the underdog, the inequalities in society, that whole approach and that people had to have certain elements of equality...especially economic equality.

After an extended period of time working on external issues, Jill began to see the need to help "democratize the organization." She explained, "I did a lot of feminist stuff within the organization itself, trying to democratize the organization, trying to improve the process within the organization, trying to develop ways to get women more involved within the organization, [in] decision making and [day-to-day] functioning." Finally, after many years of work with the group, she reached the conclusion that "it was too small to be effective or even meaningful." She came away with a deep understanding of the limits to "pushing that [left] perspective." She believed, "It's really pompous to think that I have a perspective and I'm applying it to this arena. It just seems foolish, and that kind of charade I couldn't just go with."

By the mid-1970s, Jill had accepted a community work position at a Bronx community organization and taken her political energies into community-based antiracist and antipoverty struggles as well as feminist activism. In this regard, she stands apart from many of the resident community workers who did not see themselves as feminists or, when they did, did not find a site for their work within Women's Movement organizations (a theme I will return to in chapter six). In this chapter, I outline the diverse pathways into community work the women described in their oral narratives (most notably, missionary work, social reform, and radical political action).

## Formulating the Pathways

Aside from personal experiences with poverty or discrimination that motivated community activism, the community workers' narratives contain reference to five different trajectories. The first trajectory relates to the religious tradition of missionary service. The second links to the social work profession. A related trajectory connects to the tradition of professional service within the African American community. The fourth path to community work draws on the radical organizing of the Communist and Socialist parties and the political groups associated with the New Left, as Jill Anders's story illustrates. The Civil Rights Movement forms the fifth major influence for community workers. And, finally, for a small number of nonresident community workers, the Women's Movement of the late 1960s and early 1970s offered an important spring board for their political commitment. These categories overlapped in different women's oral histories; however, for clarity of presentation I discuss them in separate sections below.

## The Power of the Local Church

Religious traditions of community work predate all other paths to work on behalf of the poor. Local religious institutions provide influential sites through which members learn about the needs of poor community residents and, in turn, model ways to extend religious teachings into their daily lives.[1] The racial, class, and denominational differences between and within these traditions differentially shape women's early experiences of community work. These differences are highlighted through the stories of the women who emphasized their connection with religious teaching when explaining their commitment to community work. Eighteen of the twenty-six resident African American community workers listed church-related activities as their first community work experiences or as generally significant for their training as community workers. In contrast, only three of the Latina community workers (all resident community workers) and three of the European American women (all of whom were nonresident community workers) highlighted their religious beliefs and church experiences—all but one describing community work they performed as members of the Catholic Church. Although none of the women made specific reference to traditions like liberation theology, black ecumenism, or feminist spirituality, themes identified in their narratives overlap with those found in these progressive religious perspectives.[2] The most recurrent themes include: (1) an emphasis on social justice through increasing economic, political, and social equality and (2) empowering the poor to act on their own behalf.

## The Catholic Worker Movement

Working on behalf of the poor and drawing on the New Testament and the teachings of Jesus Christ, Dorothy Day, who cofounded the Catholic Worker movement with Peter Maurin, combined radical social movement goals of the 1920s and 1930s with community work (see Day 1952).[3] Her work predated the liberation theology movement which I will describe below. However, as June O'Connor (1991, 98) notes:

> Day's views and values anticipate those voiced in the liberation theologies of Latin America, Africa, and Asia: a decision to see life from the standpoint of the poor and to stand with the poor in a struggle for justice, an approach to theology rooted in praxis, a view of religion as a spur to revolutionary action, a desire to help bring about the transformation of society grounded in the values of justice, peace, freedom, and love.

Beginning with the distribution on May Day of 1933 of twenty-five hundred copies of their newspaper, the *Catholic Worker*, Day and Maurin helped inspire what Day called "a family spread across all the cities and states of this country" to help the poor (Coles 1987, 13–14). The assistance they provided transcended service provision and included social action at the local, national, and international levels. Writing during the Depression, Day stressed that "the State is bound for the sake of the common good, to take care of the unemployed and the unemployable by relief and lodging houses and work projects" (quoted in N. Roberts 1984, 116). Day spoke out as a pacifist during World War II, marched alongside Cesar Chavez and the farm workers, and linked her campaign for social justice with the Civil Rights Movement of the 1960s. Furthermore, as Nancy Roberts (1984, 159) points out, the *Catholic Worker* was "the first Catholic publication to advocate civil disobedience as a legitimate form of antiwar protest."[4] Of particular relevance to the War on Poverty is the fact that Michael Harrington, whose book *The Other America* (1962) played a central role in focussing national attention on the extensive poverty in the United State hidden behind a curtain of apparent wealth, was an editor of the *Catholic Worker* during the early 1950s.[5] According to Roberts (1984), Harrington's experiences with Day and other Catholic Workers formed the basis for his influential book.

Dorothy Day continued to struggle against poverty until her death in 1980. Despite her outspokenness on issues of national and international concern, Day emphasized "working from the bottom" as the primary political and spiritual approach of the Catholic Worker Movement. In his biography of Day, Robert Coles (1987, 90) describes "the essential thrust of all Catholic Worker efforts" as "an intense, persisting localism, not as a step toward an eventual national effort, but itself the ultimate effort. This localism included both spiritual and political work."

These "localist politics" (Coles 1987) were manifest in the Hospitality Houses Catholic Workers established throughout the United States. Unlike many of the early Settlement House workers, "helpers" in the Hospitality Houses did not preach middle-class values to the poor. Developed during the Great Depression, the Hospitality Houses were designed as an immediate response to the problems of poverty and homelessness witnessed by Day and other Catholic Workers. The commitment to living among the poor was made on the basis of faith, not moral superiority. O'Connor (1991, 96) explains that while Day "never articulated or appropriated a feminist perspective on society and history, her radical critique of social arrangements together with her desire to 'reconstruct the social order' makes an alliance of her aspirations and many feminists' aspirations possible even now."

Due in great measure to her activist work among the poor on the Lower East Side, several of the community workers from New York City mentioned Dorothy Day as an inspiration for their community work. For example, Latina community worker Maria Calero, who had met Day, said she was "very, very impressed" with her. For Maria, Day epitomized the best of women's approaches to organizing which Maria contrasted with the less effective "male style" she found in groups like the Young Lords or the Black Panthers as well as the new left student movement of the late 1960s. She explained:

> Now of all the movements I saw, hers [Day's] was the least theatrical. She was directly involved with delivering a service....She had a belief in people that was beyond belief. She really believed in people. She had no desire to educate them or to reform them or to heighten their conscious-ness. She had a spiritual belief that, while the Young Lords was dominat-ed by strong macho guys...so was the Panthers, so was the movement at Columbia University, the Catholic Worker movement was not.

Like Maria Calero, many other community workers made a distinction between the organizing styles of women and men—stressing that women's approach was more consensus-building and concerned with enhancing the participation of other community members. The distinction the communi-ty workers made between women's and men's leadership styles parallels the differentiation Karen Brodkin Sacks (1988b) makes between "center women" and "spokesmen" in the labor and community struggle she stud-ied. Centerwomen played a key role in linking other members of a com-munity to one another as well as facilitating the leadership role of more vis-ible community members. Sacks (1988b, 79) explains that centerwomen helped mobilize "existing workplace social networks, as opposed to indi-viduals, around class-conscious or at least job-conscious behavior and value" in the union struggle waged at Duke Medical Center during the 1970s. The organizing campaign was successful due to the interaction of centerwomen and spokespersons or spokesmen who served as "public speakers, representatives, and confrontational negotiators" (p. 79). While this distinction helps make salient the often less visible role of women as organizers, women do play visible leadership roles as well. In fact, the com-munity workers I interviewed served their communities as centerwomen as well as spokespersons. However, the community workers who acted as spokespersons insisted that their approach was more communal in orienta-tion than spokesmen who they viewed as self-promoting. Those who relat-ed to community work through their religious beliefs, in particular, consis-tently constructed their leadership style as community oriented.

### Liberation Theology and Everyday Practice

In 1968, when many of the women in this study were gaining their first experiences in CAPs sponsored by the War on Poverty, Latin American bishops were meeting in Medellín Colombia, and beginning to take up the call of liberation theologians, most notably Gustavo Gutiérrez, to address directly the economic and political oppression of the poor in Latin America. A decade later, excluded from the official proceedings, the libera-tion theologists created a document arguing for "a preferential option for the poor" and a reaffirmation of *comunidades de base* (grassroots communities) as the site for the development of "people's theology." Writing in the preface to a collection of essays by Gutiérrez (1983, vii), Robert McAfee Brown explains that these frequently lay-initiated communities "joined their Bible study and liturgical life to everyday concerns for transformation of the unjust economic order, challenges to the political dictators, interventions on behalf of the thousands who have 'disappeared.'"

In the United States, diverse liberation theologies developed in direct relationship to the social movements of the 1960s and elaborated the connection between social justice, equality, and how oppressed groups develop their "own theology of liberation" (Brown 1993, 95). "A preferential option for the poor," a central tenet of liberation theology, is derived directly from Biblical teaching and is used to argue for radical political action to fight poverty. Brown (1993, 31–32) explains:

> We are told that the *Bible* indicates God making a preferential option for the poor. Religious leaders proclaim that the *church* must make a preferential option for the poor. The phrase has its critics (who usually misunderstand its true meaning), but it has persistently made its way into the literature and, much more important, the lives of those who try to embody a theology of liberation....The gospel, of course, proclaims that God loves *all* people, not just some. But when we observe that in God's world the poor get a decidedly unfair share of the world's goods (due chiefly to human greed), the fact that God does love *all* means that there must be food, shelter, jobs, and human living conditions for all and not just for some. To create a situation of "liberty and justice for all," then, it is necessary to start to make some changes, and the phrase we are examining asserts that we must start with the poor—that is, make an "option" on their behalf. This means that when a legislative proposal is under discussion, or a plan for a social program is being floated, the question to ask is, "Will this, or will this not, improve the situation of the poor?" If it will, it should be supported, since it will bring about a consequent broadening of the degree of social justice in society. If it will not, it should be opposed, since it will simply entrench the nonpoor with greater power than ever (emphasis in original).

For Brown (1993, 32), "attempts to close the gap between rich and poor are part of the mandate of the gospel, and those who find such proposals threatening need to reflect on the fact that the notion of a preferential option for the poor is not just the newest theory to come from radical economists, but is the clear thrust of the biblical message." In addition to the emphasis on "the preferential option for the poor," liberation theologians stress the significance of liberation and conscientization, namely, "*working* for justice (liberation) and *educating* for justice (conscientization)"[6] (p. 75, emphasis in original). As Gutiérrez (1973, 7) asserts, "To know God is to do justice."

Sister Margaret Fogarty was one of only two community workers interviewed who followed explicitly in the religious tradition, both of whom were nonresident and white community workers—although many members of religious communities from diverse racial-ethnic backgrounds worked in soup kitchens, schools, counseling centers, youth groups, senior citizens homes, and health clinics throughout low-income urban neighborhoods during the 1980s when I first began this study. Most of these workers also had professional credentials and performed their work through established social service agencies as well as church-based programs. Some, like Sister Margaret, took advantage of government funding to support their community-based programs.

Although Sister Margaret did not define her work with reference to liberation theology, she explained that it was her identification with the Catholic Church's mission that was the prime motivator for her work in the South Bronx: "I was here for the satisfaction that I felt that through my own talents and abilities I could help formulate a people. And you know…the mission of the church is to form a people!" Sister Margaret took this mission to mean organizing people to create a sense of community and "bring about social change. And that's how [workers in the local Catholic Church] got involved in motivating and educating people to take an active role in their neighborhood."

While some resident workers also described their work as a mission, their racial-ethnic and class identification with the community in which they lived and worked led them to express more direct affinity with other community members than nonresident workers like Sister Margaret. As a consequence of personal identification with their defined communities, they viewed their mission as a very personal expression of their concern for their neighbors or racial-ethnic communities. The resident community workers could not abstract their sense of mission from the particular community context. Unlike Sister Margaret, most resident workers did not tie their social missions to specific religious institutions. In contrast, Sister Margaret's primary allegiance was to her religious faith and the Catholic Church. She had grown to love the people of the South Bronx and would find it difficult to leave for other religious work. However, as she explained, "Each year I have to make that decision, whether I will stay or not." She also recognized that her position as a church worker gave her more freedom to work on behalf of the poor than low-income residents.

> In the early sixties, it was very difficult. People who had families—I mean, it's difficult for us, but, I don't have a husband to worry about. I don't have children to worry about, so it's much easier for me as a single person to say I'm going to stay in the neighborhood.

Although Sister Margaret did not have the daily demands of a family to pull her away from community work, she also did not have the same kind of personal connection with the geographic community that kept many of the resident community workers committed to their communities over many years.

Growing up in a predominantly Italian American working-class neighborhood in Brooklyn, Sister Margaret said she had "very little exposure to different cultures." At age seventeen she decided to dedicate her life to religious service, entered a convent, and taught in a Catholic school after graduating from college. She learned to speak Spanish while serving in a parish school on the Upper West Side of Manhattan. She spent time in Puerto Rico to improve her fluency and was subsequently sent by her religious order to teach in an elementary school in the South Bronx. As an educator in the South Bronx during the early 1960s she felt she could not ignore the problems that were affecting the lives of her students so she started working with a local community organization. She has been performing community work in the South Bronx ever since. In 1995, she was directing a community development organization she helped establish in the mid-1960s.

The local Catholic Church funded the organization she directs. Sister Margaret explained that this organization "came about in the sixties as a response to the social service needs of the people." She views the organization as "the social service arm of the church" or "the Christian witness in the neighborhood." She recollected:

> If you think back to the sixties, I don't know if you're familiar with this neighborhood, but we had, well we still have the ghetto situation...but we had big problems with arson, the burned out buildings. All one precinct, in fact, was considered Fort Apache. It was considered Fort Apache because it had the highest crime rate, and I'm very happy to say that it [the crime rate] has gone down since. I don't know exactly where we stand, but it has gone down considerably.

Sister Margaret took great pride in the successes of the community betterment campaigns she helped organize. For Sister Margaret, community development activities that involved community residents were more effective than simply "tak[ing] people by the hand" as social service providers typically did.

Sister Margaret distinguished between her organization as the "social services arm of the Church" and traditional social service approaches which create dependency in their clients. She explained:

> It's very easy, like take an analogy to social services, it's very easy for someone to come along and take people by the hand, but then you're forcing people to be dependent. And you have to do it all the time. Now we do have social services. You see clients. You've been here this morning, you've seen the whole gamut of people with problems, various problems, and everything. But there are certain needs. It is easier for me to pick up a phone and say, "This is Sister Margaret Fogarty, can you help Nancy with"—but we have to train people to help themselves.

In the above passage, Sister Margaret articulates a construction of "empowerment" that mirrors the conceptualization offered by some nonresident workers, especially those who became community workers following their training as social workers. Literature on radical social work and community psychology emphasize empowerment as a strategy to enhance the personal and political power of individual residents in poor communities.[7] However as Barbara Cruikshank (1995) notes, social reform discourse on empowerment often shifts focus from collective processes designed to gain political power for a community to an individual social-psychological process.[8] In the above excerpt, Sister Margaret emphasizes building individual competence. In contrast, a more radical approach to empowerment stresses processes by which community workers strive to enhance the political and collective power of community residents. Sister Margaret did reference this more radical construction of the empowerment process in other points during our discussion.

In fact, both individual and collective formulations of empowerment pervaded the community workers' narratives, although some workers privileged individual processes over collective ones. Furthermore, Sister Margaret's "outsider" status in the South Bronx contributed to constructing these collective processes in more distanced terms than was evident in the resident workers' narratives. Sister Margaret emphasized that her work was designed to empower community members "to take an active role in *their* [emphasis added] neighborhood." However, like the resident community workers I interviewed, Sister Margaret saw her work of "motivating and educating people" as benefiting the entire community not simply building individual self-esteem.

Running through Sister Margaret's narrative was a concern for empowering the residents of the South Bronx through concrete, visible achievements. She felt that even small successes would create the grounds for hope that, in turn, would increase the residents' participation in improving the quality of life in their community. She explained:

> Interestingly enough, we have increased population, but the crime rate has gone down. So it shows the different attitudes of people. Like, I think one of the attitudes now is that there has been, through the work of the dedicated people…that sign of hope that's been reinforced. So when you see something visible, an improvement of a housing stock, when you see schools being built, when you see the extended health services, when you see expanded social services, that gives people hope. And they say: "Gee, there's something good going on here, and I want to be attached to it."

Sister Margaret's narrative was dense with examples of the kind of work she and her organization performed in the South Bronx over almost thirty years of "service." The community work she described revealed a complicated mix of service, advocacy, and direct action. As community actions sponsored by her organization helped improve the housing and safety in the neighborhood, Sister Margaret reported, residents began to participate more freely in the public life of the community thus greatly increasing their quality of life as well as their political consciousness.

The most notable and visible sign of Sister Margaret's organization's success in the South Bronx was the improvement in the availability of safe and affordable housing in what was some of the most desolate areas within the community. Although Sister Margaret was (and in 1995 continued to be) an influential community leader in the South Bronx, her religious affiliation along with her less powerful role as a woman prevented her from gaining the same status as male community leaders in the South Bronx.[9]

Many of the community workers complained that the organizational mandates from government officials or agency administrators inhibited their political activism. Sister Margaret faced another, somewhat more formidable, constraint on her activism. While convinced that her political activism was central to her ability to serve the people of the South Bronx, she was strongly aware that the Vatican might not approve of her actions. She explained:

> And first of all, people trust us, because they know we're not going to abuse the people and we're not going to embezzle the funds, so we have a very good reputation....Then the Pope came out and said anyone [in religious life] would not be allowed [to participate in politics], you know, it would be disobedient, so I had to step back. But that doesn't prevent me from being involved. I may not be involved politically myself, but as far as this office, well people would say, well if you're grooming people, if you're training people, if you're developing people, well I feel personally, I'm not gonna...hold back any, if I still feel that I have something to contribute. This is my neighborhood. It's our neighborhood....I'm still interested in the development here. And I feel that I have something to contribute. If this is the way I can do it, and I have the leadership for it, then as long as I'm fruitful [I'll keep doing it].

Like many other community workers, Sister Margaret justified her continued engagement in activism by linking it to her community caretaking role. Over the years she became deeply invested in the well-being of the South Bronx neighborhood in which she lived and worked. However, she remained an outsider in the community and, unlike the resident community workers, continued to question her relationship to the community. "I mean, I have to take stock," she confessed. "It's very difficult." She explained:

> People think it's easy with all the changes in religious life—[that we] have carte blanche. That's not true. We still have our vows. We have our sense of obedience. We have our responsibilities. And even though a superior doesn't say to me, "Okay, Sister Margaret, I want

you to go to Afghanistan next year," I have to make that decision if I'm
going to stay here or if I'm going to go to Afghanistan next year. So I
feel that I have been fruitful, and each year I have to make that decision, whether I will stay or not.

Despite her thirty years as a community worker in the South Bronx, Sister
Margaret's primary allegiance was to the Catholic Church. Aware that her
superiors in the Church might have other assignments for her or that other
communities might need her service, Sister Margaret never felt "settled
permanently" in the South Bronx.

Three Latinas and eighteen African American women also said they
gained valuable community work experiences from their participation in
church activities. However, while twelve of the eighteen African American
women who were active in the church before 1964 continued to participate
in a variety of church activities in the mid-1980s, none of the Latinas mentioned ongoing church-related participation. For example, before she began
working for a CAP, Angela Garcia was extremely active in the Catholic
Church in the South Bronx. In fact, she credits the Catholic Church for providing her first community work experiences. However, in her opinion, the
Church offered only a limited approach to the problems in low-income
communities. She took the lessons she learned and crafted a more liberatory
theological approach that better fit what she observed in the South Bronx.

After Angela graduated from high school she joined a church organization called the Legion of Mary. Group members traveled throughout the
community praying with people in their homes. Angela worked with the
group for five years. She "knocked on every door, visited everyone in that
area, in that parish," and became involved in helping other parishes establish Spanish Legions of Marys. Through her community visits she recognized the limitations of prayer in meeting the daily survival needs of her
low-income neighbors. She explained: "That, of course, really woke me up
to the fact that praying and going to church on Sunday and getting people
to do that was not enough, and there were other problems that we, as members of our organization, wouldn't get involved in, but you felt that there
was something else [that could be done]."As a result of her work with the
Legion of Mary, Angela broadened her approach to community work
beyond the context of the church. Even after she began her paid position in
a community-based organization, she continued to view her community
work, not as a job, but as a social mission.

## African American Women in the Church
Unlike the Puerto Rican women who were brought up in the Catholic
Church, many of the African American women found in their local churches lifelong institutional homes in which they could express their spiritual
and social concerns. Numerous authors have documented the significance
of the church in the African American community.[10] In addition to the

important services provided to poor communities, the church also provided a context for organizing the African American community, particularly evident during the Civil Rights Movement.[11]

Only three of the white European American women (all of whom were nonresident community workers) and one of the Puerto Rican resident community workers mentioned her mother's active involvement in church activities. However, nineteen of the African American women emphasized their mothers' participation in their church. Josephine Card of East Harlem described how her "whole family...were all in some part of [the Baptist] church." She believed that her church work formed the foundation for her community work, that "the church was a catalyst for a lot of the things I do now." Her parents took her and her five siblings to church each week for special services at six in the morning.

> We used to have breakfast at the church, and then we'd go to the hospital to visit. They used to take all of us. I had one sister and four brothers...and we'd go to the hospital, and they would have prepared baskets of fruits and nuts and things like that, like toothpaste and cologne and powder, and we used to have to go with them to the hospital and go visit people and give them the gifts and talk to them and sort of visit with them.

Josephine said she continued church work, "always, even now." She saw a connection between her involvement with the church and her community work because, she explained,

> It was through the church that I understood the importance of working with people....It's not really different. See, I don't see it as being a separate kind of function. I think it's all part and parcel of the same thing....And I found out if I use a very basic principle to do unto others as I really wish them to do unto me, and treat everybody as if they all belonged to God, then I wouldn't have any problems. And I did that all through my life....And if you have this talent, or this skill, or information, then you share it. And that's basically what it's all about.

Josephine's religious beliefs informed her approach to community work as well as sustained commitment to this challenging work despite the overall deterioration in the quality of life for many within her community.

Like Josephine, Ann Robinson's religious faith helped her remain deeply committed to community work through difficult financial times and frustrating struggles. Ann also drew on her religious beliefs to make sense of the growing economic and social problems in her East Harlem neighborhood over her more than thirty years of community work. She stated:

> Some of it makes sense because of my religion, what I believe in, and reading in the Bible....A lot of what I see happening now because I'm

in a Pentecostal religion and reading in the Bible from Daniel....There
were things interpreted in Daniel and things in Revelations but, according to the things I heard and read and am seeing now, a lot of this has
to happen. They told in Prophecy where children would be against parents and injustice in the courts and...all these different wars in the
name of religion. It's more and more of those things coming to be but I
still have hope because I believe in the Great Being, and I believe there
is a movement even within the church. They're forgetting about the
labels whether your Catholic or Presbyterian, Methodist, Baptist.

On the one hand, Ann accepted the problems in her community as
inevitable and predicted in biblical accounts. On the other hand, the coalition building among different denominations to fight against the problems
associated with poverty encouraged her. She did not agree with those who
use the Bible to justify ignoring the plight of the poor. She explained that,
in her view, "they have...much hatred in their hearts."[12]

I know they will say the Bible says "by the sweat of your brow." I'm
aware of that but there is also, if they would go back to...the New
Testament when Jesus had all those people, a crowd of people, he
would always make sure they were fed. And I know they will pick up
another point that says "the poor will be with you always." True. But
there is enough work [that can] be done [to help the poor].

The church had become increasingly more important to the African
American resident community workers like Ann Robinson who I reinterviewed in 1995. Churches provided the primary sites for soup kitchens,
literacy training, childcare programs, and collection of clothing and monetary
contributions after poor communities lost government funding through cutbacks begun in the 1980s. In addition, some of the community workers who
had retired or were laid off from their paid community work positions and lost
their formal link to community-based organizations had shifted their community work activities to their churches. For the community workers who linked
their commitment to their religious faith, the church was more than a community institution that provides resources for the poor and an organizational
presence in their urban neighborhoods; it was a place where they gained the
emotional support and spiritual guidance to negotiate the difficult challenges
of community work. Those who entered community work through professional career paths like social work or law described their commitment to
community work in different terms, although some overlap with the "missionary" construction of community work appears in the oral narratives of
nonresident African American and Puerto Rican women who viewed their
work as a way to serve or "give back" to their communities.

# Social Work Professionals as Community Workers

The notion of "community work" had little meaning for people before the 1960s (Radford 1978). While there is a tradition of community action that we can trace from the industrial revolution, the community worker as an occupation is a more recent phenomenon. Community workers in the social work tradition can trace their roots to the professionalization of the charity organization and settlement house approaches to poverty. James Taylor and Jerry Randolph (1975, 7) offer the following definition of community work that follows from the social work tradition:

> Community work is an attempt to help with human needs, and to increase people's success in coping with their problems. The person in trouble is imbedded within a network of family processes and community systems. Your help will be most effective when you use those systems to support your efforts.

In my usage of the term, community workers also include those whose primary activity is organizing community members to challenge institutional systems that do not promote the well-being of community members. This process might entail the use of radical political action as well as more established forms of politics like voter registration and electoral campaigns.

Some community workers I interviewed came to this work through their training as social workers, others were motivated by their political ideology to focus on grassroots campaigns for social and economic justice. National coordinating groups like Citizen Action and Association of Community Organizations for Reform Now (ACORN) provide national visibility for the diffuse network of community organizers and community workers engaged in improving local residents' economic security, health and safety, and social citizenship although only one of the community workers I interviewed mentioned these organizations.

The proliferation of literature[13] and training programs such as those offered by Midwest Academy in Chicago and Highlander Center in Tennessee further demonstrate the growth of this form of citizenship work. These approaches are more closely related to the radical organizing tradition of the union movement and New Left than to the social work tradition.[14] However, links can be found in the social work literature on community organizing which emphasizes the importance, as Jim Jacobs (1982, 96–97) states, that "central to community organizing is the belief that the 'community' is the major social category toward which political work is directed." Each community has its own "social and economic network of people." These networks are organized by complex relations of class, race, ethnicity, religion, and gender. Yet, community is not a self-evident phenomenon, it is the consequence of daily interactions and political struggle which "has to be constantly reevaluated in relation to critical political priorities" (Martin and Mohanty 1986, 210).

Of the six nonresident women who linked their community work to the social work tradition (see Appendix A), only one came to community work directly through her education as a social worker. She studied with Richard Cloward at Columbia School of Social Work during the early sixties and gained employment in MFY. In fact, this individual, Jewish community worker Joyce Armato, described herself as a disciple of Cloward's. Through her experiences at MFY, Joyce developed a philosophy about community organizing that included an emphasis on teaching "technical expertise."

Settlement houses like Henry Street, institutional home to MFY, continue to provide services and some advocacy and leadership training for low-income residents in New York, among other large cities in the United States. Sabrina Brock credited her early experiences in a settlement house for giving her the skills and desire to pursue a career in community work. She explained:

> I was a member of the Settlement House [in the Bronx], which was another progressive influence in the neighborhood, which, of course, gave me a whole sense of community work....So through the settlement house I immediately was recruited as...the articulate youngster who was sent to conferences, and that gave me a kind of education as a spokesperson for youth that I wouldn't have gotten [otherwise].

With her parents off to work each day, the settlement house provided a key resource for her early political socialization.

> The Settlement House was the other big influence [besides my parents], 'cause my parents stuck us there because they were working parents....They both worked full time. How else could they survive? My father was in the shipyards. My mother did a variety of service jobs— saleswoman, restaurant counter woman, unskilled, low paying labor for women.

After school, Joyce would help organize clothing and food drives, and, she recalls, "distribute leaflets, and generally participate in community struggles, whatever they are." To support her college education, she found work in the settlement house during the school year working part-time with teenagers and children and in the summers as a camp counselor.

In 1960, Sabrina remembered taking one course called "community organization" in social work school but did not recall hearing people talk about community work at the time. Through another course on group work she was required to perform an internship in a community agency. She enthusiastically expanded her ongoing work with the settlement house and then a children's home to include organizing youth groups.

> So I was in [the] settlement house and then a children's home, where I organized groups with kids, and my groups were always doing these weird things, like talking about civil rights and sex, and the role of girls

to be strong and intelligent and capable. And that got me into a lot of trouble with my [social work] placements. I was considered someone who allied herself with agitating forces in the community, and I was getting called on the carpet constantly for these activities, which were just beyond the pale of the agency's requirements.

Sabrina said she found herself challenging the agency's procedures in her social work placement and was highly critical of many aspects of the agency's policy toward the poor. Following graduate school, she felt fortunate to gain employment in the newly established MFY where her more "radical" approach to social work was reflected in the program design.

### African American Women and Community Service

Historically, African American women like Sabrina Brock have contributed significantly to the well-being of other members of the African American community.[15] Paula Giddings (1984) notes, that more so than white European American women, African American women of "all economic stations" were involved in efforts to help the poor (also see Gordon 1991). Intense racial discrimination faced by African American women of all classes encouraged educated African American women who formed social organizations to retain their concern about, and ties to, poor African American communities. One well-known African American philanthropist, Mary Church Terrell (1863–1954), acknowledged that, "Self-preservation demands the [Black women] go among the lowly illiterate and even the vicious, to whom they are bound by ties of race and sex...to reclaim them."[16]

The African American women who performed community work did not do so through the Charity Organization Societies[17] or white dominated settlement houses where racism prevented them from contributing their knowledge and skills.[18] They served as informal caregivers or "community othermothers"[19] or worked through African American community institutions, especially the African American churches. Despite the important community work they performed, educated African American women were also refused membership in white women's organizations. In the face of such exclusion, they created their own organizations, such as the Neighborhood Union and the National Association of Club Women (NACW), that offered important services to the wider African American community.[20]

For middle-class African American women there is a long history of visible unpaid service to their communities combined with employment in a service career such as social work or teaching that long predates the War on Poverty.[21] Michelle Dodge of Philadelphia, for example, who was introduced in the first chapter, was raised with a commitment to political activism and service on behalf of the African American community that exemplifies this tradition among African American middle-class professional women. And, for all of the African American community workers, participation in the

Civil Rights Movement and other radical movements of the 1960s deepened their resolve to fight injustice experienced by members of African American communities.

## Radical Politics and Community Organizing

The community work tradition in radical political organizing can be traced back at least to labor organizing campaigns of the 1930s and 1940s (see Fisher 1994). Radical political parties such as the Communist and Socialist parties also helped mobilize local communities to pressure for state support. The Communist Party and other radical political groups organized the unemployed as workers and as community residents. During the 1930s, the Communist Party of the USA developed unemployed councils, farm and labor coalitions, as well as tenants unions.[22] The party also worked to cross the racial divide. They asserted that all races were needed for the working-class revolution to succeed. While the local organizing efforts of the radical parties were devised primarily as a way to develop a national movement opposed to capitalism, the neighborhood organizations provided a framework for local activism. However, as the labor unions grew in size after the mid-1930s, the Communist Party focused increased attention on the labor movement to the neglect of neighborhood-based organizing (Fisher 1994). Despite the withdrawal of the Communist Party's support for community-based organizing, the tradition of their community work did provide an important contrast to the social work approach. Local councils respected the ethnic diversity of the residents and the existing cultural institutions, although racism continued to pervade labor organizing generally. The organizers also encouraged the development of indigenous leadership, although organizing campaigns seldom targeted women workers.

Sabrina Brock, like many of the women in this study, grew up in "a political family." In Sabrina's case, her parents were members of the Communist Party, and their activism influenced her political activities even as a teenager.

> My father was a unionist in the shipyards, and he was in the American Labor Party. And invariably, as the American Labor Party hooked up with the Democratic Party, they were involved in that. So a lot of my community sense and political sense was generated long before the so-called sixties. My father was sitting in Washington in the forties. We were marching for various things. I wasn't a red-diaper baby, but I was certainly a red-diaper kindergartner. As a child, I was involved in a lot of the programs that were coming out of the socialist, communist, progressive [groups], all the terminology that was used to describe the activities left of the Democratic Party.

Due to his radical political activities, Sabrina's father was "harassed by the FBI." She recalled, "We used to think the FBI would come and take my father away. And they indeed followed him to get him to name names."

Sabrina's childhood experiences provided her with an opportunity to develop her leadership skills as well as political analysis. She explained:

> And out of that history, growing up with [a politically active family], it was a lot more interesting, combined with then the Settlement House and the kind of socializing activities they put us through to make us nice, good citizens, particularly as black ethnic youth. It was real indoctrination to social consciousness and participation. So by the time I was in my teens, I was actively involved in struggling [against problems in my community], through…demonstrations, political and educational work in the community, and in this case with youth.

The political education Sabrina received from her parents included some features of activist mothering to be discussed in the next chapter. However, her parents also taught her a much more explicit critique of capitalist society than other community workers described. She drew on this political analysis as an important resource as she developed her political perspective. Sabrina explained that involvement in the social movements of the sixties "gave expression to stuff that" she and others "were struggling through and then got scared around the McCarthy period."

Sabrina's exposure to the Communist and Socialist Parties and left labor groups developed logically from her parents' activism. However, her engagement with the Communist Party formed but one channel through which she expressed her political concerns. Because she had early exposure to radical political organizing, her activism was not limited to a single outlet, like the Communist Party or other left political group, as it was for some younger activists interviewed.

Sabrina was a generation older than Jill Anders and Liz Grasser, who became involved in the Communist and Socialist parties while in college. Jill and Liz both described a personal commitment to these parties that consumed all their political energies for a significant period of their lives. Since the political parties they joined required such total commitment, both Jill and Liz eventually found that they no longer could give the extensive time and energy the party loyalists required. Both also described frustration with the authoritarian leadership style of these groups. Liz Grasser, a nonresident Jewish community worker in New York City, was thirty-seven when I first met her in 1984. She explained why she left the socialist group she was involved with in the 1970s: "It was difficult balancing the degree of involvement that you had to have to kind of feel like you were pulling your weight in the party.…And then there were some incidents where I was not thrilled with the level of democracy." The contradiction between the rhetoric of the New Left and women's positions within these groups was a theme stressed by the younger activists and was illustrated in Jill Anders's narrative at the opening of this chapter.[23]

## Community Workers and the Social Movements of the 1960s

Although women played a vital role in both the Civil Rights and the Student Movements,[24] the rhetoric of the movements that stressed equal rights and shared leadership contrasted with women's unequal status in decision making within these movements. At the same time, the community organizing projects of Students for a Democratic Society (SDS) and the Student Nonviolent Coordinating Committee (SNCC) provided places for women to develop their organizing skills and to achieve their own successes.[25]

The Civil Rights Movement as well as other national political struggles drew on the organizing skills of women in cities and small towns across the U.S. These social movements owe their success to the community work of women like many of those described in this book who went into the streets of their communities and organized others for the March on Washington or Resurrection City[26] or welfare rights' campaigns.[27] For example, SNCC organizers utilized the existing institutions in different locales to reach out to community members. The churches, as the most important formal structures in African American communities, permitted organizers to contact large numbers of community residents. Since women played a central role in these churches, African American women also provided a firm foundation for the work of SNCC and other civil rights organizations. As SNCC founder Ella Baker noted, "the movement of the 1950s and 1960s was carried largely by women since it came out of the church groups" (quoted in Giddings 1984, 284).

However, of the twelve resident community workers (ten African American women and two Puerto Rican women) who played a leadership role in the protests during the Civil Rights Movement, most said they found little support from the national leadership for their local struggles. African American community worker Francine Evans, who was a resident of the Lower East Side of Manhattan, admired the Reverend Martin Luther King, Jr., but reported that she "could not relate to the people from New York who went with King." She explained that she "couldn't get any of them to march" when her community was fighting for a new medical facility or when housing was needed. Francine believed that the local struggles were just as important to the lives of her community as the national campaign for civil rights. She felt that many of the national African American leaders did not understand the significance of the community-based struggles for safe housing, adequate medical care, and quality education, among others, that were waged in low-income black neighborhoods across the country during the 1960s and 1970s.

Betty Glass, a white European American community worker, was motivated to engage in community work following her involvement in the Civil Rights Movement. Her father was a corporate lawyer, and her mother was active in the League of Women Voters. Betty moved to New York City after graduating from an ivy league college to participate as a community activist in Harlem. As a white, middle-class women, Betty initially did not know what role to play in the predominantly black political group she joined upon her arrival. When the War on Poverty was announced a year later, Betty accepted a position as director of a Head Start program in East Harlem. She explained that the position was not an end in itself but a means by which she could continue her political involvement in Harlem. While directing the program, Betty pursued her unpaid organizing work against "slum lords" who were neglecting to maintain their buildings in the community. For white women like Betty Glass and Sandra Cole (another non-resident white community worker from New York City), politicization during college or in personal relationships with black men thrust them into the Civil Rights Movement and provided them with a different social location within the movement than was evident in the narratives of the African American and Puerto Rican community workers.[28]

Sandra Cole gained her first paid community work through her employment in a New York City settlement house after she completed her master's in social work. She was not politically active in college but after moving to New York and then dating an African American man for a short time, she became extremely interested in the Civil Rights Movement. She attended the March on Washington in 1963, her first formal political action, with her boyfriend. She enthusiastically recalled:

> But it was an incredible experience, to see people all along the way waiting outside all night long, just saying: "We're with you. We can't be there but we're with you." I think anybody who did that march can never get over that experience. It had to be life changing. When Martin Luther King spoke, and you felt the power of that speaker, I mean I can't listen to his records yet without getting tears in my eyes, so however you want to term politics, whatever he was saying, or whatever he was doing, I would do it.

Sandra's general interest in civil rights grew into a deep political commitment. However, gender dynamics within the Congress on Racial Equality (CORE), the civil rights organization she joined, tempered Sandra's enthusiasm. She complained, "I mainly did shit work in CORE....I did the typing, and I can't type. I cleaned and I'm not a great cleaner. You know, I was willing to do all kinds of things. Because that's how I started in, at that level." Sandra remained an active member of CORE in New York City until a shift in leadership made it difficult for her as a white women to continue in the organization. Her experience in CORE prepared her for community activism. Eventually, she found a position where she could combine her interest in grassroots organizing with her interest in women's issues.

For Sandra Cole, the Civil Rights Movement served as a primary foundation for her subsequent career as a community organizer. She moved from concern for the civil rights of African Americans to a broader analysis of the intersection of gender, race, and class. Sandra completed her graduate degree in social work in 1968, and found employment with MFY where she helped organize working-class women in a campaign to improve services in their neighborhoods. She next obtained a job in another community organization in Brooklyn where she combined her passion for community-based activism with her commitment to women's leadership development.

Despite her professional status as a social worker, Sandra did not view her work as a "job." She explained that it felt more like "home" than work, and described how she used familial strategies to organize women in Brooklyn. She explained:

> They were like my mother and my relatives who had really shaped me. [It] was my mother and her sister sitting around the coffee table. That's how I organize, sitting around tables like this, having coffee. And I like that. Somehow I felt that I had found a place, a family.

She emphasized how comfortable she felt in a multiracial women-dominated environment and contrasted it with her experience working with CORE. Here she refers both to gender and race politics as a way of interpreting the different experiences.

> Somehow this felt better than being stuck...in CORE where there was no sense of family. I would certainly say that. I mean, there was a family in the sense that we were fighting something together, and I learned about race politics, and I saw all that. And I was pretty tough...and [at one point] there were [only] three whites, and people would challenge our presence, and I didn't leave. I mean, if the whole group had said I should leave, I would have left, but one person threatened me physically. I mean, I had things happen where somehow a little courage came out....I always had some of that sense of standing up against great odds and that started young. I could do that. I'm not afraid to stand up.

Sandra worked closely with CORE for six or seven years but it was her work with working-class women that most felt like home to her despite her own middle-class upbringing. As a white women, she was clearly more at home in the more diverse multiracial working-class Brooklyn community than in East Harlem. However, she also stressed the importance of the women-centered environment promoted by the community organization in Brooklyn for enhancing her feelings of home. Sandra's exposure to the Women's Movement and the development of a "feminist consciousness" helped her unite the different aspects of her personal and political lives as I will explore in Chapter 6.

# Conclusion

Among the five pathways to community work (religious tradition of missionary service; professional social work; tradition of professional service within the African American community; the radical organizing of left political groups, the Civil Rights Movement; and the Women's Movement) local churches were most frequently mentioned as providing experiences central to many community workers' commitment to community work—especially the African American women who grew up in low-income urban neighborhoods.

Some of the nonresident community workers came to community work through their commitment to social reform or via social work and other professional identities. African American women, in particular, described how their desire to work on behalf of African Americans and other people of color motivated their professional careers. Most described working as advocates and political activists as well as providing needed social services. Other nonresident community workers came to this work through an explicit desire to put their radical politics into action. The community workers who had been active in the New Left found the rhetoric of New Left parties frustrating and their political strategies vacant of practical outcomes. These nonresident workers defined community work as a way of life—one that differed in significant ways from the resident community workers' more personally defined (albeit politically constituted) lifelong commitments to community work.

The goal of empowering the community residents bridged the discourses of the radical political workers such as Betty Glass and Sandra Cole and the more social service oriented nonresident workers. In contrast, the women who were indigenous to the low-income communities expressed a far more personalized construction of community work, even when their narratives included participation in radical political parties or social movement organizations. For the social service oriented nonresident workers, the infusion of professional discourse into descriptions of their community work further distanced them from direct identification with residents of the communities in which they worked; although this feature of professionalization similarly affected the community work practice of resident workers, particularly those who acquired professional credentials.

A number of the women, especially the African American women, who stressed the importance of the church or settlement house experiences for their community work, credited their parents with encouraging their participation. In the next chapter, I explore how parents, particularly mothers, provided early exposure to community work and offered analyses of structural inequality that informed the community workers' political perspectives. I describe these and other forms of activist mothering and demonstrate how activist mothering contributes to the economic, social, and emotional survival of many poor residents as well as places contradictory demands on women in their triple roles as paid workers, unpaid community caretakers, family caretakers.

# Chapter 5

# ACTIVIST MOTHERING, COMMUNITY CARETAKING, AND CIVIC WORK

Puerto Rican community worker Nina Reyes's political engagement on the Lower East Side of Manhattan spanned a period of thirty years. During this time, Nina said she was involved in any and all community actions that affected her local community. From struggles for improved sanitation to child care to voter registration to elder care, Nina's trajectory as a community worker illustrates the theme (emphasized by Wilma North in chapter one) of doing "just what needed to be done" to fight the problems associated with poverty in the urban United States.

Nina moved from Puerto Rico to the Lower East Side with her family when she was ten years old. Raised by her grandmother who worked as a janitor, Nina credits her grandmother "for all my values and ideals because she guided me to be...the best I can." Nina met her husband in high school, married, and went right to work as a secretary in a downtown Manhattan law firm. She became active with her husband through the local settlement house and together they developed a new community-based organization designed to advocate for the issues confronting local residents. She first explained that they felt a need to establish the organization as a response to the infusion of funds, new programs, and "strangers" into the Lower East Side as a result of the War on Poverty. As Nina recalled, "When the antipoverty programs came, they all came in one shot, and nobody knew what was going on. See, a whole bunch of strangers were coming into the community that nobody knew. So that's why we became involved."

Nina also emphasized another event that triggered her community work career. In relating her community work history she was reminded of her response to the sanitation strike that occurred during the same year the antipoverty programs were funded and described it as a key event in her initiation as a community worker.[1] She recalled:

> I will never forget how we got involved. Remember the sanitation strike? We got involved when we saw our community becoming a disaster. We got to the point that we rented a truck and picked up the garbage in the street. I had one child at the time, 1964. We used to take our daughter everywhere we went.

Not surprisingly, as a mother of three children, day care became the next major campaign to draw her political energies. Throughout the early part of the 1960s, Nina undertook community work as an unpaid activity while working full time in an office in downtown Manhattan. When the War on Poverty was declared, she found community-based employment in a day care program funded through the EOA. Nina next became involved in a campaign to register Puerto Rican voters while she also worked to expand day care availability for residents of the Lower East Side. She translated her political engagement in the community into paid community work but remained active in campaigns that went beyond her job definition. She continued to emphasize the importance of voter registration and was active in several local elections.

Nina and her husband played important leadership roles in the community organization they helped to create until the early 1980s, when, she reported, it was besieged by internal conflicts and a type of "dirty tricks" politics. She explained why they resigned from the organization: "The leadership was changing, and there was too much politics, too much dirty tricks. And when it comes to that I don't want to deal with it. I don't like when you have to do harm to somebody to help somebody else."

Nina's use of the term "politics" as a negative construct echoes the way many of the resident community workers defined the term. It also draws upon one popular use of the term that associates politics with unethical behaviors and infighting.[2] Following in this vein, the community workers also differentiated between neighborhood or "civic work" and political activities or politics. For the most part, as highlighted in Wilma North's abbreviated biography in chapter one, most of the resident community workers expressed a distrust of public officials who, the community workers believed, did not care about the problems experienced by those living in low-income neighborhoods.

Nina expressed her frustration with the increased problems in her community since the 1970s and the persistent cutback of funds to support community work programs. When I asked her how she remained committed to community work despite the difficulties, Nina interpreted her lifelong commitment through her deep personal awareness of how racism circumscribed the opportunities of the poor—a response given by most of the African American and Latina resident community workers.

How do I keep it alive? Because I see the hurt. It's like something that bothers me, and I must say it. You know all these stores, Japanese stores, Korean stores, what I see there is mostly people from Mexico [working in them], and those people work! And when I see them, for some reason I see my father, when my father came to this country. That he had to work so hard for so little money....My father was very good with numbers....When he came here he went and worked in farms in Philadelphia. And then he moved to New York, and he worked in supermarkets like that, driving the deliveries and all that. When, just because he didn't have that knowledge of English he had to work for so minimal, low pay. My father was a very smart man....My father loved poetry. My father read poetry, and he loved to read....He couldn't do more in his life because of the oppression that we live in. And every time I see these Mexican people, it breaks my heart. And I see my father.

Because she had witnessed her father fighting such oppressive forces, Nina was especially concerned about the treatment of Latino immigrants and was highly critical of California governor Pete Wilson's attacks against Mexican immigrants who, she exclaimed, "are being taken advantage of." With a heightened awareness of the problems faced by immigrants to this country, Nina said she reached out to "newcomers" in her neighborhood and attempted to introduce them to the programs designed to help them learn English, continue their education, or secure food and shelter.

This form of community caretaking was a consistent theme that appeared throughout the oral narratives of the resident community workers and comprises a central component of activist mothering. The notion of activist mothering also highlights how political activism formed a central component of the community workers' motherwork and community caretaking. As a sociological concept, the term captures the ways in which politics, mothering, and labor comprised mutually constitutive spheres of social life for the community workers. It serves to counter traditional constructions of politics as limited to electoral politics or membership in social movement organizations as well as constructions of motherwork and reproductive labor that neglect women's political activism on behalf of their families and communities.

Traditional academic practices fragment social life and falsely separate paid work from social reproduction, activism from mothering, family from community, and dynamics of race from class and gender. A close reading of the resident community workers' oral histories reveals the inseparability of these multiple dimensions of social life and analysis. For example, in order to correct the limited notion of class and labor associated with orthodox Marxist theorizing, feminists in the dual systems tradition[3] argued for assigning greater significance to activities defined as social reproduction.[4] However, the separation of productive or wage labor from social reproductive labor reproduces the gendered division of labor within sociological analyses and prevents a socially contextualized appreciation of the ways that women, in particular, make sense of their own activities. For example, the notion of activist mothering draws attention to the caretaking activities of women who do not have children of their own and who conceive of their community work as mothering.[5] For the resident community workers, paid work formed one component of their mothering practices just as mothering practices formed one component of their paid labor. The notion of activist mothering also draws attention to the caretaking work of women who do not have children of their own and who conceive of their community work as mothering activity. Throughout the narratives, I frequently found it impossible to determine which activities comprised unpaid community work and which ones exclusively related to their paid community work. This analysis contests the divisions between paid and unpaid work traditionally used to discuss women's work. Such a broadened understanding of labor also provides a contextualized strategy for exploring the intersections of race, class, and gender in constructions of mothering work and paid labor.

## Mutually Constitutive Spheres of Social Life

Feminist scholars of women's community activism argue for the importance of examining family as well as neighborhood institutions and social networks for the development and expression of political consciousness.[6] Analysis of the community workers' political practice illustrates the contradiction between women's performance of apparently traditional female roles and the revolutionary actions they take for the benefit of their families and communities—a phenomenon I explore through the notion of "activist mothering." Temma Kaplan (1982) uses the term "female consciousness" to describe women who make political claims on the basis of their gender roles and participate in radical political action. In a similar vein, Maxine Molyneux (1986) differentiates between "practical gender issues" and "strategic gender issues" to capture the way women activists organize around their practical everyday needs for food, shelter, day care, and housing versus organizing around their gender-specific identities. Obviously, this distinction often breaks down in practice as analysis of women's community work demonstrates. While all the women organized around specific survival needs and community-based concerns, many also mobilized around strategic gender issues.[7] Activist mothering as a construct derived from the everyday practices of the community workers described in their oral narratives centers the myriad ways these women challenged the false separation of productive work in the labor force, reproductive work in the family, and politics. This analysis of activist mothering provides a new conceptualization of the interacting nature of labor, politics, and mothering—three aspects of social life usually analyzed separately—from the point of view of women whose motherwork historically has been ignored or pathologized in sociological analyses.[8] It also highlights how political positions form and are reconstituted through an intricate mix of personal, ideological, and material forces.

The resident community workers lives were shaped by experiences of racism, sexism, and poverty. They learned to mother as activists fighting in their homes and communities against the debilitating and demoralizing effects of oppression. When we limit our analysis of mothering practices to those activities that occur within the confines of a nuclear family, we miss the material conditions that contribute to differing family forms as well as the social construction of gender and political activism. For example, experiences of racism marked African American and Latina community workers' first encounters with injustice in North American society. These experiences informed the antiracist mothering practices they utilized within their own homes and served as a basic target for community work. The conceptualization of activist mothering draws attention to the historically specific context in which many of the women interviewed developed their political analyses and strategies.

## Defining "Activist Mothering"

I did not begin this research with an interest in mothering per se, although I did wish to examine how mothering activities contributed to, or inhibited, political participation. As I reexamined the activists' personal narratives, I recognized how a broadened definition of mothering was woven in and through their paid and unpaid community work which in turn was infused with political activism. The traditional definition of mothering—nurturing work with children who are biologically or legally related and cared for within the confines of a bounded family unit—failed to capture the community workers' activities and self-perceptions of their motherwork. The term "activist mothering," generated through close reading and rereading of the narratives, better expresses the complex ways the resident community workers, especially the African American women and Latinas, made sense of their own activities.

Activist mothering not only involves nurturing work for those outside one's kinship group, but also encompasses a broad definition of actual mothering practices. The community workers defined "good mothering" to comprise all actions, including social activism, that addressed the needs of their children and community—variously defined as their racial-ethnic group, low-income people, or members of a particular neighborhood. In addition to testifying before public officials, all the resident community workers participated in public protests and demonstrations for improved community services, increased resources, and expansion of community control. Ann Robinson, for example, described her involvement in protests to improve health care, public education, child care, and social services for those residing in her Manhattan neighborhood. Resident community workers who did not have children also viewed their relationship to their communities as one of caretaker. Since most of the resident community workers shared the same race and class background and grew up in the same neighborhoods as those on whose behalf they worked, they saw themselves as beneficiaries of their community work efforts as well.

All the resident community workers with children said that, for the most part, a large portion of their community work derived from concern for their children's well-being. The four African American women and three Puerto Rican women who did not have children traced their motivations for community work to a variety of social problems manifest in their communities and viewed their activism as community caretaking more than politics. The term activist mothering highlights the community workers' gendered conceptualization of activism on behalf of their communities, often defined beyond the confines of their families, households, and neighborhoods. Central to their constructions of "community" was a convergence of racial-ethnic identification and class affiliation.

Activist mothering includes self-conscious struggles against racism, sexism, and poverty. Racial discrimination was one of the consistent themes expressed by all the African American and Puerto Rican community workers, and struggles against racism formed a basic undercurrent for most of their community work. Similarity between Latina and African American community workers also emanated from their social location in low-income communities. As residents of poor communities, many of the women described how the deteriorating conditions as well as the inadequate education and health services that threatened their children's growth and development fostered an ongoing commitment to community work. Their own mothers helped interpret experiences with racism and classism and instilled in their daughters a belief in their ability to overcome these obstacles. As we saw in Lydia's narrative presented in the first chapter, fathers also contributed to the cross-generational continuity of activist mothering. Therefore, the conceptualization of activist mothering challenges essentialist interpretations of mothering practices.

Literature discussing women of color's activism further highlights the ways that racism and a commitment to fight for social justice infuses their political analyses and political practices.[9] Women of color as activist mothers, especially those living in poor neighborhoods, must fight against discrimination and the oppressive institutions that shape their daily lives and, consequently, as mothers they model strategies of resistance for their children. For example, African American women's struggle against racism infuses their mothering practices inside and outside their "homeplace."[10] Lessons carved out of the experiences of "everyday racism" contribute to mothering practices that include "handing down the knowledge of racism from generation to generation."[11] Referring to this practice in her discussion of homeplace as "a site of resistance," bell hooks (1990, 46) explains: "Working to create a homeplace that affirmed our beings, our blackness, our love for one another was necessary resistance." Hooks argues that "any attempt to critically assess the role of black women in liberation struggle must examine the way political concern about the impact of racism shaped black women's thinking, their sense of home, and their modes of parenting" (p. 46).

Patricia Hill Collins (1990) describes the broad-based nature of mothering in the African American community and highlights the work of community "othermothers" who help build community institutions and fight for the welfare of their neighbors. She argues that the activities of othermothers who form part of the extended kinship networks in the African American community pave the way for the political activism of community othermothers. According to Collins (1991a, 129), "[a] substantial portion of African American women's status in African American communities stems not only from their roles as mothers in their own families but from their contributions as community othermothers to black community development as well." Collins (1991a) and Stanlie James (1993), among others, argue that African and African American women exemplify this tradition of othermothering and community othermothering that can be found in a variety of places and across time.[12] However, these patterns are not natural expressions of a black woman's social or cultural identity. Rather, as analysis of women's community work demonstrates, they are developed in dynamic relationship with particular historic conditions and transmitted through self-conscious socialization practices and political struggles. For example, as Collins and James both point out, African and African American women pass down cultural traditions as well as survival and resistance strategies from one generation to another (also see K. Scott 1991).

Whiteness cushioned the four European American resident community workers from facing the dynamics of racial oppression until they became active in community-based struggles. For one of the four women, such recognition never materialized. Harriet Towers of Philadelphia did not see racism as a problem in her community work and defined the neighborhood in which she worked as "an integrated one," adding, "I've never been prejudiced myself. I could always work with most everyone." When pressed on this point, she insisted that she always got along with everyone, regardless of race. However, early awareness of class inequality and poverty was central to the narratives of all four white women who were living in low-income neighborhoods when President Johnson launched the War on Poverty. Grace Reynolds of Philadelphia described her childhood as one totally defined by struggles for economic survival. Her mother died when she was young. Her father was a laborer, and the family was very poor. Her involvement in the antipoverty programs was her first political activity. Brenda Rivers said she first recognized the need to become active at the community level when, as a new mother, she moved from a small rural town to Philadelphia. Brenda, a mother of a biracial child, stressed antiracism campaigns as well as struggles against the causes of symptoms of poverty in her geographic community.

Like many of the women of color, white community workers Harriet

Towers and Teresa Fraser both described how the political education they received from their parents influenced their commitment to community work. Harriet reported that although her mother was ill most of her life, she was active in the church. Her father, who was a corrections officer, "tried to do everything he could" to help the prisoners. She saw his work with prisoners as an early role model for her commitment to community work.

These four white women's motivations for community work as briefly presented here illustrate four of the processes by which political awareness is raised and political commitment is shaped: fighting to improve the quality of their own children's lives (Brenda Rivers and Teresa Fraser); struggling for economic survival (Grace Reynolds); early childhood socialization (Teresa Fraser and Harriet Towers); and church or civic organizational experiences (Harriet Towers). Most resident African American women and Latina community workers interviewed (including those like Lydia Montalvo who were not living in low-income communities during the War on Poverty) described all four of these patterns when discussing their motivation to participate in community-based struggles for social and economic justice.

The following discussion illustrates the themes that emerged as aspects of activist mothering in the community work of the women who were living and working in low-income communities in New York City and Philadelphia. I center the experiences of the resident community workers, although, as already pointed out, many of the nonresident community workers, especially the women of color generally and white nonresident workers from working-class backgrounds, also described many of these patterns. I begin by outlining the key dimensions of the community workers' activist mothering and then explore how racism and class oppression contributed to their community work as well as the strategies they developed to fight against discrimination. In the next two sections, I describe the activist mothering performed by the community workers' mothers and discuss the tensions between family-based labor and community work. I conclude by demonstrating how the community workers defied dominant definitions of mothering and politics through their activist community caretaking.

### Activist Responses to Discrimination

The African American women and Latinas I interviewed uniformly identified many experiences with racism and sexism as part of their earliest childhood memories. Rita Martinez of East Harlem said she was "guided" into pink-collar work, despite the fact that she expressed a desire to pursue a career as a teacher.

> My whole life, since I could remember back, I wanted to be a teacher. And I had mentioned this, and this is very vivid to me, I had mentioned this to an eighth grade teacher…and she said, "I don't think you'll make it. You don't have the temperament. You fly too fast." And here's a fourteen year old, and she's saying this. At fourteen, who does not fly off the handle? Think, at fourteen, even at twenty-one you are still sometimes

too fast. So that discouraged me. See, the thing that hurt me most was that I cared for that teacher so much. We were very close. And when she said that, I believed her.

Rita was dissatisfied with the training program for beauticians in which she was subsequently enrolled and quit high school at the age of sixteen. Given this personal history, she was particularly excited by the opportunity to fulfill her lifelong dream of becoming a teacher through a CAP in East Harlem.

For the four women who moved to New York City from Puerto Rico or the Dominican Republic, lack of facility with English increased their encounters with racism. Maria Calero was divorced with three children when I met her in 1983. She was working as a program director for a city-wide nonprofit agency in New York City. As a teenager, Maria moved to New York City from the Dominican Republic with her family. Her first paid job was as a factory worker. She "hardly spoke the language" and was unprepared for the racism she found. She recalled:

> I remember feeling that I was not a part of the society at all....I had come to this country when I was fifteen so my experience was different from those Hispanic women who were raised and went to school here. I came from an homogenous society...to a society that strongly discriminated.

Maria was also astounded by the racism she encountered within the Hispanic community.

> My father is black Hispanic, and my mother is white Hispanic. But my identity was Hispanic, and they were calling me black or nigger. I just got very confused about the racial conflicts within the Hispanic community. But I remember feeling that I was not a part of the society at all, that I was outside of the society.

Maria believed that the contrast between her early childhood experiences in a racially "homogenous" society and her experiences of racism in this country increased her sensitivity to injustice and discrimination. She was the only community worker to argue that an "outsider" perspective had value for political analysis. However, like other resident community workers, she also valued an "insider" indigenous perspective for its sensitivity to how race, class, and gender dynamics patterned the experiences of poor people of color throughout their daily lives. In fact, Maria's narrative highlighted the interaction of outsider and insider vantage points for shaping personal experiences as well as political analyses.

Although she said she was raised in "a very traditional manner, in a male-dominated family," Maria reported that she was keenly aware of the broader political environment. She stated:

> Somehow I always had the room to think about issues of social concern. For example...I married very young, but I was concerned in the early sixties about police brutality. I was very much concerned about civil rights issues, and I was very personally aware of discrimination issues.

Maria detailed the problems with police brutality in her Harlem community and also emphasized how "Hispanics had enormous problems getting registered to vote because you had to pass a test" that presumed a certain facility with written English. Her awareness of racism and class discrimination was heightened when she gave birth to her first child and began to investigate the high school dropout rate and how racist teachers had lower expectations for Latino children.

By the time her two daughters were of school age, she had grown increasingly pessimistic about their receiving a decent education in the New York City public schools. She explained:

> I really had to think about what schools my daughters would go to. I wanted them to be educated, and I wanted them to go to college, and I wanted them to participate, and I think I had many more dreams for them than I had for myself. But in allowing myself to think a lot about how they were going to be educated and what was going to happen to my daughters, I began to ask questions about the Board of Education, about public schools, about how were Hispanic children being educated in the public schools, and discovering the dropout rate, the stories from people who were very smart but sent to vocational schools because I began to read studies about teachers' expectations, about how racism got in the way of teaching children. I began to think a lot about education in terms of what was really learning. I wanted them to be educated, but I also wanted my children to be thinkers. And I got very concerned about that.

Her concern for her children's education led to her first leadership experience in a parents' advocacy organization. There she said she deepened her understanding of the limits of the public-education system in New York City, enriched her community work skills, and met many women who modeled for her a kind of political analysis and political practice that drew her further into community activism.

A third of the thirty resident workers with children described their first community work activity as a response to the quality of their children's education. For example, Wilma North traced her career as a community worker to her dissatisfaction with the educational quality of her children's school. However, her activist mothering led her into other struggles—as she explained, "anything that had to do with the betterment of [my] community and the welfare of those children going to the elementary school"—long after her own children graduated.[13]

## Mothers' Activist Mothering

Many of the resident community workers' mothers provided, as one worker stated, a "strong foundation" for their desire to serve their community. A total of seventeen mothers were described by their daughters as informal caretakers in their communities. Five (or forty-five percent) of the Puerto Rican women and twelve (or forty-six percent) of the African American women said their mothers were involved in a variety of helping activities in their neighborhoods. These activities included taking neighbors to the hospital, helping care for the elderly, advocating for increased childcare programs, fighting school officials to expand educational opportunities for young people, struggling with landlords and police officials to improve the housing and safety conditions in their community, and interpreting for non–English-speaking residents.

At the time of the interview, Carmen Hernandez was director of the same education program in East Harlem that had employed her as a bus driver in 1969. Carmen characterized her mother, who was still active in her neighborhood, as "a frontier community person" who fought for other children's rights as well as her own. Carmen recounted:

> Back in the '50s and early '60s, when it wasn't right for parents to get involved, to be in the classrooms, and to question teachers, she was doing that. She'd ask: "Why?" "How come?" "Give me a reason." "I won't take it just because you said it." "Show it to me." "Let me read it so I can understand what's going on, because verbally that doesn't connect with me."…And I used to look at her, and she got her point across. And she would fight for different children's rights, and she didn't care whose child it was.

Carmen's description of her mother as an activist and a frontier community person mirrors Patricia Hill Collins' (1990) account of how African American women's broad-based mothering practices contributed to their role as community othermothers. Among the many lessons Carmen learned from her mother's activist mothering was the importance of questioning and "dialogue in assessing knowledge claims" as well as the "ethic of caring" (Collins 1990, 212, 215). Mothers also taught their daughters how to create and sustain community ties. These community-building and sustaining skills served as one foundation upon which the daughters developed as community workers in their own right.

Josephine Card was in her early fifties and worked in a program for the elderly in her East Harlem community, earning an annual salary of $18,000 in 1985. Josephine learned from her mother's example how important informal networks are to the survival of low-income people like herself. Josephine's mother was a school teacher in Georgia but could not find a job in her field when she moved to New York City in 1929. Her mother had recently died but Josephine continued to feel her mother's spirit with her. She explained:

There are a lot of things I do, and I get tickled because I think about her and what she would have done, and I know just what she would have done with a lot of stuff. She was a very bright woman. Everybody in the community came to her for anything. If they had problems with bills, if they had problems with burying somebody that lived somewhere else, they'd come to my mother. My mother knew all the funeral directors, and she knew all the ministers in the churches and she knew everybody....She'd always know who to call. And they'd use her almost like for community consulting. I'm serious!   My mother's house was always like a revolving door.

Even after her mother's death, Josephine drew on her mother's teachings to inform her approach to community work, especially the lessons on networking with others to promote community well-being. For example, Josephine decided to accept a paid position for which she at first thought she was unqualified. When during the job interview the members of the board of directors of the new community-based agency told her the names of some of the people with whom she would be in contact through the position, she found that she knew everyone they mentioned. She took the job, and through it she reaffirmed her sense of connection with her community. She remembered: "They wanted a lot. Well, it just so happened that every name they mentioned to me in this community I knew personally. I mean, I really knew them well. So, it was like old home week coming here [to this agency], and I've really enjoyed my work here." The networking skills she learned from her mother helped Josephine in her own community work, enhanced her success as a paid worker, and increased her feelings of personal connection with other members of her community. Josephine's experience further demonstrates the blurring between family-based experiences, paid labor, and social reproductive work.

## Negotiating Community Work and Family-Based Labor

The above discussion illustrates the broadened definition of mothering that infused the community work of the women in this study. For many, this continued the activist mothering practices they witnessed as children in their parents' home. The fusing of community work and family-based labor frequently meant opening their homes to those in need. Ethel Pearls of Philadelphia described how she invited young people, especially those with children, who had no other place to live or who were having difficulties in their own homes to stay with her and her family. By 1984 when I interviewed her, Ethel's children were grown and out of the house. She continued to offer her home to others even after she was laid off from her paid community work position. She explained: "They always tell me I had a household of people and if anybody just doesn't have anywhere to stay, they come here." Ethel introduced me to a young woman staying in her house and related:

> She's trying to find someplace to stay. I got bedrooms, so until she gets herself straightened out, she and her baby [are] here. I could never have a fancy house, I guess, but my house is usable. Some people have homes that aren't liveable....I don't have anything fancy. I couldn't because everybody just comes along sometimes and just want to talk, and I don't want to say to them: "Don't sit there."...I'm 60 years old now, and God has been good to me. I don't think I've lost anything by trying to help.

Ethel's children's home life resembled that of Ann Robinson's childhood as described in chapter one. In both homes, family and friends as well as strangers were welcome if they needed a place to stay or food to eat. Historians of the African American family point out the importance of resource sharing for the survival of low-income people, and personal testimony from my research reveals the continuity of this practice among low-income women in contemporary urban neighborhoods.[14] This practice is not limited to the African American community. The Latinas I interviewed were also taught the importance of sharing resources with others in their community, a practice they took into their own activist mothering.

The intricate relationship between community work and family-based labor also generated tension between a worker's caretaking responsibilities for her own children and her caretaking work in the community. Some of the women expressed regret that the extensive hours they spent on community work took them away from their own children. Pat Martell of the Lower East Side, for example, grieved the time she lost with her children, especially her youngest child. Her husband had a steady blue-collar job when she started as an unpaid community worker outside the home. Pat was subsequently offered a paid community work position in a local CAP. After she accepted the position, she became "so involved in what was going on in the community" that she was unable to spend much time with her two children. She gave birth to another child while working for the CAP. With the support of her daughter's aunt who babysat for her during the day, Pat continued community work. She recalled:

> The youngest one, I was working up until the doctor put me in the hospital a week before she was born, and I went back to work when she was three weeks old. I kind of regret that....She's been raised well, though. And her aunt—I don't know what I'd do without her—took care of her. She's okay, but I've missed a lot. I've missed so much. I look at her sometimes, and I think, my God, she's ten years old and I don't really know her....We haven't done a lot of things and that's on my conscience right now.

Pat's story again illustrates the blurring between family-based labor and community work as well as the contradictions that result from the overlapping demands. The paid community work position quickly became vital to the economic survival of Pat's family. Her husband lost his job as a skilled laborer and accepted employment as a driver, a position that paid little. The salary from community work helped to keep her family just above the poverty line. Through her community work, Pat provided needed income for her family while she remained actively involved in improving their quality of life in other ways; however, it also meant that she had less time to spend with her children. Her dilemma haunts all mothers who must find a way to secure their family's economic and emotional well-being. Fortunately, the resident community workers were situated within an extensive network of other-mothers who assisted them with child care and supported their community work. All of the community workers with children mentioned the importance of other women who helped them negotiate the competing demands of unpaid and paid community work and parental responsibilities.

Tensions between family-based labor and community work increased further when paid work took the worker from her home community. A total of three African American women and three Latinas accepted higher paying positions outside their communities. Five of these six women had children. They encountered two of the most common difficulties faced by employed women with children—the lack of quality child care and the inflexibility of employers who refused to recognize the childcare needs of their employees. As a single parent, Maria Calero could not live with the uncertainties and low pay of neighborhood-based community work. She accepted a "professional" position in a city agency. She recalled:

> I had no day care for my son.…Finally, I found day care on the Upper West Side [of Manhattan].…I would take two buses to be at the day care at a quarter to nine in the morning. My boss then had a real position about feminists and would say…that I had to be a professional, that my circumstances were of no importance to him. I had to be at my job at nine o'clock in the morning so whether [my son] was clinging or not, I had to leave [him].

Maria expressed much sadness over the pain that this abrupt process of separation caused her son each morning. She believed that this experience had a lifelong negative impact on her son which she could never repair.

Despite the difficulty balancing parenting responsibilities and paid employment in a citywide agency, Maria explained how this work experience enhanced her sense of personal and political power. Yet she also said that it took her away from the original enthusiasm that motivated her community work. In her desire to increase her family's economic resources and advance her professional career, she "became uninspired in the job" and increasingly alienated from her personal goals. Her experience of alienation affected how she related to her children. She felt that the position she accepted in order to increase her ability to support her family directly interfered with her emotional and physical availability to her three children.

In contrast, East Harlem community worker Josephine Card shifted her site of work from noncommunity-based factory work to community work. This shift enabled her to remain more involved in the care of her seven children. She left this position as a school aide when her youngest child was born but continued unpaid community work. Through this work, she learned about the antipoverty programs and applied for a paid position. She accepted a job as an assistant supervisor in the CAP in her neighborhood and was promoted to supervisor three months later. The community work position that Josephine accepted was "only a few blocks away" from her home. Her previous jobs as a factory worker, cashier, and school aide did not offer her the same challenge that the community work position provided. She gained a wide range of additional experiences. She designed programs, provided direct services to her community, spoke in public, and, "at one point," supervised a staff of twelve. For Josephine, the community-based work enhanced her availability to her children as well as her increased self-esteem.

Community work activities of women living and working in low-income communities loosened the supposed boundary between home and community in other ways. In addition to the long hours required by community work, the lack of financial security was another source of stress for the worker and her family. Salaries were often withheld when the organizations ran into funding difficulties. For the most part, salaries were low and increases, rare, or at best, inconsequential. Since the community workers seldom distinguished between their unpaid and paid community work, those who were able to accept the uncertainties of community-based employment often continued working without pay during times of financial crises. Carmen Hernandez, a mother of six, laughed when she told me that she made more money working in a downtown Manhattan office when she was eighteen than as a community worker with twenty years' experience. When she was offered a job in 1977, which would provide a large increase in salary, she turned it down because she didn't want to leave the community. Not only did she decline a higher paying position outside the community, she also resigned from her paid position to become a voting member of the agency's board of directors. During most of the 1970s, she juggled her unpaid community work with college, family responsibilities, and the delicatessen she opened to replace her paid community work position. She was busy an average of twelve hours a day. Sometimes she thought:

> Gee, I must be really crazy, because I have some real fantastic skills, and I don't want to go nowhere else. 'Cause I've had several good job offers....I'll never be rich. I'm comfortable. I'm happy. So I really don't think I want any more than that. As long as I'm happy!

Carmen said her decision to stay active in her community and to situate her paid employment there gave her the chance to be closer to her five children. She valued the opportunity to watch them grow, to get to know their friends, and to be available to them. Overall, the community workers' activist mothering had contradictory effects on their children's lives. On the one hand, their activism often took them away from their families and many women described the frustration they felt when they did not have enough time to spend with their children. On the other hand, their activism also improved their children's health care and education as well as provided a foundation for upward mobility, paving the way for their college education, among other opportunities. However, some children experienced reprisals and other forms of discrimination because of their mothers' activism as Teresa Fraser's narrative in chapter one attests. Yet, by educating their children on the political organization of their social world and modeling activist mothering, some community workers also contributed to their children's commitment to work on behalf of their defined communities—a theme I explore in chapter seven.

## "Civic Work, Not Politics"

The community workers' construction of their community work as community caretaking shaped the strategies they used to confront specific problems and informed their views of politics more generally. Like Wilma North, many of the resident women interviewed did not view their community work as explicitly political. More than half of the resident community workers constructed a firm boundary between their community work and politics. Some used the term "civic work" to define the diverse actions they engaged in as community workers. Others defined giving testimony at public hearings; their involvement in demonstrations; their struggles against irresponsible and, frequently, racist public officials; and their outspoken participation in local coalitions and advocacy programs as "citizen activism" or "community activism." As Carlotta Mendez said of her community work:

> No, not political in the classical sense, probably more community activism. We used to run a housing clinic. That's amazing! I can go back thirty years and what was needed then was exactly what's needed now—housing clinics! We used to volunteer our time in the evening and counsel people as to where to go to get their heat turned on—that type of clinic. We were not yet at a level in the community where there were a whole lot of Puerto Ricans running for public office.

Carlotta noted that it was unusual for Puerto Ricans to run for public office in the 1950s and 1960s. However, she saw her work and those of other community workers in her neighborhood as "not political in the classical sense" because, in her view, there was a difference between the concerns of community activism and politics—narrowly defined as electoral politics. This theme was echoed by many of the community workers interviewed, as the following discussion illustrates.

Most of the resident workers did not define themselves as political people, feminists, radicals, or socialists as some of the nonresident workers did. They simply believed they were acting to protect their communities. Simultaneously, they held a radical critique of establishment politics that contested the dominant definitions of "the political" and accurately saw the limitations of dialogue with and incorporation into the dominant political system. Because the resident community workers believed that politics was a formal system by which wealthy men (and, sometimes, women) vied for power for its own sake, they distinguished themselves from politicians who they viewed as out for their own gain.

Most of the women interviewed believed that people running for public office rarely cared about the poor. Even when they expressed an interest in dealing with the problems of poverty, when they got into office most public officials never followed through with campaign promises to low-income people. Gloria Alvarez, a resident community worker on the Lower East Side, said she stayed "away from politicians" whose disregard of important community problems made her angry. Gloria believed that, in contrast to community workers, politicians were not really interested in improving the lives of low-income people. Their only concern was to hold onto their positions of power. Because of mistrust of the political establishment, few resident community workers expressed an interest in working with a particular political club or candidate for office.

African American community worker Mrs. Louise Long maintained the distinction between civic work and politics, but also recognized that political power could be harnessed for the good of low-income people. According to Mrs. Long, it was the race, class, and gender of politicians that interfered with their service to her community. She did not believe that these middle-class politicians, who were usually white men, understood the needs of African Americans and other people of color nor were they willing to pay attention to the poor who did not have the power to advance the politicians' careers. Mrs. Long wanted to see a political club established that would be "for the people." She explained:

> You know what I'd like? I would like to get a storefront and we pay the rent on our own. I really would like to do this. I would like a storefront someplace on Henry Street or something, that the people involved would raise funds and pay for it on our own, and start a club, and register the young people, and have a political club. I would like to start with that aim. I would like to set a figure and set it up on a chart and reach for this goal....Not for power, but for people to see [how they could make change].

Mrs. Long emphasized that she did not view such a political club as a place where individuals would gain power over others but a place where residents could discover how to influence city agencies and politicians to improve the quality of life for poor residents of the Lower East Side. However, she was discouraged from pursuing this project by the lack of resources as well as the resistance she expected from the established political parties.

Only ten of the resident community workers had any first-hand experience with establishment politics. They worked in campaigns for candidates they believed would best serve their defined communities. Only one of these ten women ran for political office. All of these women viewed their participation in established party politics as a continuation of their community work. The following quote from African American community worker Eve Parker, who was elected as a New York delegate for Jesse Jackson in his first bid for the Democratic presidential nomination in 1984, illustrates this point.

> I'll tell you something. I'm not a groupie! That's number one. I don't like belonging to groups. That's not really my thing. When issues come up, like people like Jesse Jackson who has a message, and I knew the struggle he would have, that's when I rise to that occasion.

Eve distinguished between politicians with "a message" and others who are only interested in power. Unfortunately, she complained, she did not find many people running for public office who had anything to offer the poor.

Several women did have personal aspirations for public office but met with resistance from the traditional political parties. The Puerto Rican women consistently described situations where capable Latinas were passed over by the Hispanic leadership, who preferred to support a man for elected office, even if he was less capable. Two women described different campaigns in which the Puerto Rican leadership supported an African American man rather than a Puerto Rican woman. The community workers vividly described how these cross-race and within-gender alliances effectively circumvented women's formal political leadership in two significant local elections. They both discussed how these local political battles simultaneously brought different constituencies of the community together while natural allies became divided against one another. Since women were the least powerful members of the fragile coalitions within these two communities at the time, they were unable to counter the male-dominated political alliance formed to thwart the women's elections.

The resident community workers sustained a high profile as "civic workers" in their communities; however, acceptance of the narrow definition of politics did compromise their political efficacy in relation to the formal political establishment. The gendered and racialized dynamics of local politics further constrained their entry into electoral politics. Fortunately, in creating their own community-based form of politics, they continued to resist dominant constructions of their "social place" as poor women and publicly claimed their right to a safe, secure, healthy, and economically sound existence for themselves and their communities.

## Small Gains of Community Work

One consistent feature shaping lifelong commitment to community work was the value placed on daily interaction with neighbors and co-workers. These meaningful interactions were often cast as a form of "emotion work" particularly valued by women (or for which women were better suited).[15] For the most part, the community workers said they approached their work on a daily problem-solving basis. They explained how they gained great satisfaction from their ability to help even one of their neighbors. Yet the deep-seated problems associated with urban poverty did wear down their enthusiasm for community work to a certain extent. The nonresident community workers, were especially discouraged by the federal, state, and city governments' failure to fight urban decay, economic inequality, and racism. To counter the frustration they often felt, the community workers explained that they tried to keep sight of their daily accomplishments such as helping others in their community overcome the myriad of problems associated with poverty.

For example, Alice Porter proudly spoke of three people she relocated to decent housing the week before the interview. Clara Thompson and Othelia Carson of Philadelphia also discussed how they found satisfaction in their community work by helping their neighbors escape some of the problems of poverty. Clara recalled:

> Well, there was a woman who told me I was very instrumental in getting her child to continue in education. This particular child—I don't know if she looked up to me, had confidence in me—sometime you know an outside person can be more than a family member. And this particular one, when I would speak to her, say different things, she would listen.

Othelia Carson described how people who had nowhere to turn would be told of her program and come for life-sustaining support. She recalled one single mother who had no money and no place to live, Othelia referred her to a place where she could get food and shelter. "This is something that makes me feel good," she exclaimed.

> The husband had beaten her and left her and the children....She came in the office and she needed help and...I referred her to some places [for help] and every once in a while I see her, and she looks like an altogether different person. At that time she looked like someone you could just push up in the corner and just beat and would just stand there and take it.

As a partial result of the help she gave this woman, Othelia was pleased to report that "now...you can see the confidence [this woman] has built in herself."

Ann Robinson said she was especially committed to improving and expanding the educational opportunities for young people in her Harlem community. She stressed that through the antipoverty programs, many low-income residents were encouraged to complete their high school degrees, attend college, and "to branch out to other things."

> We have young people who came through the school systems....People who have had some college and dropped out were able to go back....We had someone who became a pharmacist, and [some who became] nurses, and through all of this, even though our communities have deteriorated, and the burnt buildings that you have here, there are some people who never go back to the level of despair that had been there prior to [the antipoverty programs].

Ann and others interviewed also emphasized the value of the CAPs for helping to enhance the connections among community residents. When political battles occurred within the community, these programs served as organizational bases for mobilizing community members and helping to empower different constituencies who were previously denied legitimate avenues for political participation. The community workers defined mobilization and political awakening of low-income residents as among the most significant contributions they could make to the continuity of struggle for social and economic justice.

As I found with the nonresident workers, the interrelated goals of individual and collective empowerment were salient in the resident community workers' spoken accounts in both the mid-1980s and mid-1990s. Steve Burghardt explored the tension between these two dimensions of empowerment in his 1982 book, *The Other Side of Organizing*. Writing primarily for nonresident community organizers, Burghardt argues that the key to longevity in this challenging work is finding the balance between personal and social-structural dimensions of change. He asserts that "so many organizers leave community practice after a few years" and "'burn out'—not because the work is finished, but because they are too exhausted, personally, to continue" (p. 49). On the one hand, the community workers who remained active from the 1960s or earlier discovered how to balance the personal and political aspects of their lives, to a certain extent, and therefore avoided "burning out." Obviously, the workers who "burnt out" are not represented in this analysis. On the other hand, the community workers' focus on the satisfaction gained when providing individual service in the 1980s and 1990s is a major shift away from the more collective aspects of empowerment that captured their political energies in the early years of the War on Poverty, and, in this regard, provides evidence of depoliticization.[16]

However, it is important to further contextualize this shift. Since the wider political environment no longer supported the more radical political actions that typified their community activism in the 1960s and early 1970s, many community workers explained that the reduced use of collective action was less a personal political decision than a reflection of wider trends.

Organizational pressures toward "standardization, routinization, and other distancing and alienating case-processing practices," also may have contributed to a valorization of the small gains of daily practice.[17] Like "street-level bureaucrats," the community workers employed in poorly funded community-based programs for many years might "believe themselves to be doing the best they can under adverse circumstances" while "adjusting their work habits and attitudes to reflect lower expectations for themselves, their clients, and the potential of public policy" (Lipsky 1980, xii–xiii). Michael Lipsky defines street-level bureaucrats as "public service workers who interact directly with citizens in the course of their jobs, and who have substantial discretion in the execution of their work" (p. 3). Most of the resident community workers did not play the disciplinary role of teachers, police, public defenders, social workers, and others employed directly by large state bureaucracies. However, the resident community workers did control some important, albeit minimal, resources and, in certain instances, had discretion over prioritizing community residents' needs in the distribution of these funds and services. Furthermore, in constructing their connections with other community residents as one of mutual respect and support, it is also possible that the community workers neglected to consider how much power they had in these interactions as Barbara Cruikshank (1995) cautions. Failure to acknowledge their power within their communities could also compromise the community workers' efforts to promote the leadership abilities of other community members and to ensure the continuity of community work—a topic to which I will return in chapter seven.

## Conclusion

The contradictions that arose from the community resident workers' negotiation of family-based labor, unpaid community work, and paid work expose how the so-called separate spheres of social life are braided in and through the social relations of community. Most of the resident community workers viewed both their unpaid and paid work as caretaking or nurturing work despite the radical political activities involved. Their involvement in social protests, public speaking, and advocacy as well as grantwriting, budgeting, and other administrative tasks were viewed as a part of a larger struggle—namely, doing "just what needed to be done" to secure economic and social justice for their communities. The dialectical relationship between the dominant discourse on the political and the community workers' practice of community caretaking contributed to a unique form of community-based political activity that differs profoundly from the civic work of middle-and upper-income men and women who volunteer for not-for-profit associations.[18]

The resident community workers also challenged traditional notions of gender and mothering in their work and served as models for their children as well as others in their community. All of the women interviewed said they held onto a strong sense of their personal power and, for many, the example given by other activist mothers helped strengthen their belief, already established by their own mothers, in their power to affect change in their communities. As funds were withdrawn from their organizations and problems within their communities increased, many of the resident workers drew comfort from the help they could offer other residents. Shifting focus from processes of collective action to individual service was an effective way for the resident community workers to remain committed to the work under increasingly harsh economic and political conditions, although it also contributed to a process of depoliticization. For many, this shift in emphasis was an adaptive response to the increasingly conservative political environment as well as a result of the control placed on them by government funding agencies.

The resident workers grew up with a consciousness of discrimination and injustice that further fueled their commitment and informed their political analyses. Dynamics of racism and classism were particularly salient in the narratives of the African American and Latina community workers. However, analyses of sexism and their relationship to feminism were complicated by the ways in which patterns of race and class shaped the community workers' political praxis, and their perceptions of, and direct experience with, the Women's Movement. In the next chapter, I examine experiences of sexism, gendered patterns of organizing, the varied relationships the community workers' had with the Women's Movement, and the creative ways they wove their personal concerns into community work.

**Part IV:**
**THE GENDERED POLITICS OF COMMUNITY WORK**

# Chapter 6

# DYNAMICS OF RACE, CLASS, AND FEMINIST PRAXIS

In 1974, Josephine Card was hired by a women's health organization in New York City to help open up women's clinics in her community. The group identified Josephine through her work administering a health care program in East Harlem. Despite her active engagement in this feminist health organization, Josephine did not define herself as a feminist nor did she view her activism solely in terms of women's issues. She explained why, in the early 1970s, she came to view the women's health movement in New York City as a white, primarily Jewish, women's movement:

> The [women's health organization] was going around opening up women's clinics, and that's when the whole abortion thing got to be very popular, and they opened up women's clinics and [were] teaching women about their own bodies, that whole movement, which was not a black movement, primarily, I believe, a lot of Jewish women [were in it]. 'Cause all the women I met, practically all of them were Jewish....When [the director] came to the office one day to speak to me, she said that she heard there was this woman up in East Harlem with a [health-care program], and they wanted to know more about it....So she came up to talk with me, and I took her all through the clinic, explained to her what we did and why, and how we had our resources, and a couple of weeks later she asked me to join her [organization]. And I did. And then when they got involved with their project of opening clinics, they asked me would I do it because...[she said:] "We've got a lot of talent, but we don't have anybody who is [experienced as] a clinic administrator."...So I did go out and work with them.

Josephine subsequently gained a great deal of experience and knowledge by representing the organization in national and international forums. She enthusiastically recalled, "It was very interesting, because...I was able to travel to Europe and [to] that first conference they had down in Mexico [in 1975]. I was there, the International Women's Year Conference....I was there!" Despite her long-term association with the feminist health organization, Josephine maintained the view that the women's health movement was a white women's movement and despite her affinity for the issues addressed by the movement she remained an "outsider within" (Collins 1991a).

Like Josephine, not all the community workers would describe themselves as feminists; however, their efforts coincide with those found in explicitly feminist struggles.[1] To begin with, many of the community workers' challenged manifestations of inequality and discrimination in their communities. And, like feminist activists, most community workers described ways they opposed the patriarchal organization of the state and other institutions by bringing so-called "private" needs into the public arena, contesting narrow and sexist definitions of women's abilities, and working against anti-participatory practices that privilege the perspective of dominant groups (Fraser 1989, 158).

While many of the community workers, especially the resident community workers, did not define themselves as feminists or view community work through a feminist lens, most distinguished between the approaches of women and men, emphasizing that women's ways of organizing were more effective in mobilizing as well as empowering members of their predominantly African American and Latino low-income communities.[2] They also noted how women, more than men, were concerned with nurturing the leadership skills and political empowerment of other community members. Furthermore, while not all of the women interviewed for this study had mothers who served as models for their community work, most did identify other women in their communities who served as mentors for them.

## Women's Ways of Leadership

Drawing inspiration from people who she called "the Dorothy Day type of people," Maria Calero described the style she felt most represented her approach:

> I would always ask myself: "Can I translate this to Mrs. Rodriguez in the corner, and tell her, and we can have a conversation about it?"...For me, what was important was the connection between getting something done, and maybe that's like having kids and raising a family.

As for many of the other community workers interviewed, Maria found paid employment directly out of her unpaid community work. She emphasized that the job offer resulted from her "knowing how to organize and being a volunteer [in a community agency in the Bronx], and being in the presence of strong women."

Mentoring relationships among community workers did at times cross racial-ethnic lines. In fact, two white women, Teresa Fraser of New York City and Brenda Rivers of Philadelphia, were identified by other resident community workers as mentors and role models for them. Maria Calero was particularly appreciative of the political education she received from a number of women she met through her activism in the community control of schools struggle. Maria mentioned that Teresa Fraser played a key mentoring role for her community work career and politicization. Maria was also impressed by the leadership style modeled by Ellen Lurie, the woman who headed the parents advocacy organization she joined in the early 1960s.

Ellen Lurie, author of *How to Change the Schools: A Parents' Action Handbook on How to Fight the System* (1970), worked as a community worker in East Harlem and became active in the parents' organization of her children's elementary school. Her activism led to her appointment to the Local School Board 6 in Upper Manhattan. She worked to help keep the schools open during the school strikes of 1967 and 1968, and served as training director for United Bronx Parents, an educational advocacy organization she helped found. Lurie died in 1985. In 1993, in honor of her work on behalf of school children in New York City, parents of children in District 6 named a new elementary school after her.[3]

Maria Calero remembered how astonished she was by Lurie's outspokenness and confidence:

> I began to attend meetings as just a volunteer for an organization called United Bronx Parents....And it was headed by this extraordinary white woman called Ellen Lurie. And...the people there were all Puerto Rican women, and I remember thinking, what is this white woman doing here? She's crazy. And she was saying how we have to participate, and how she belonged to this group of people who were going to take over the Board of Education, and [she said:] "This was your taxes, and this was your money, and you hired those people." And I just kept thinking of this crazy white lady. And the next day, or two days later, I read in the *New York Times* that they had taken over the Board of Education and had declared it the People's Board of Education. I think that that was the most extraordinary kind of [thing]!...And I heard her talk, and I thought: "Wow!" She became years later my mentor and my friend.

As a result of her efforts on behalf of school integration and her outspoken criticism of the New York City Board of Education, Lurie was chosen to serve on the People's Board of Education.

This struggle against the Board of Education led to the expansion of United Bronx Parents, which originated when parents in a Bronx elementary school joined to protest their children's expulsion from kindergarten. Teresa Fraser, who was an active member of United Bronx Parents, explained that the children were "suspended from kindergarten for some very silly, minor infraction." United Bronx Parents then became the vehicle for expanded parent organizing following the People's Board of Education. When the War on Poverty was declared, this organization applied for funds and increased their efforts to organize the parents of children in the public school system.

Working closely with Lurie, Fraser, and other organizers, Maria Calero became a leader in the struggles to protect parents' rights within the public school system and to improve the quality of education for children in New York City, throwing herself wholeheartedly into the struggles for community control of schools. She explained her organizing philosophy:

> I really believed that if a parent made a concrete contribution through involvement, through daily involvement in a school, in terms of the choice of teachers, in terms of the choice of principal, in terms of the curriculum of that school…that the teacher was accountable to the parent, that the parent had an intimate relationship with the teacher and they all together contributed to educate the child, that would strengthen the person about the contributions that they could make to the block or in the neighborhood. But you have to have that kind of relationship. It was the most difficult experience in my life. I did a lot of crying in that period. And it was a period of enormous turmoil in this country.

Maria explained that this process of politicization transformed her in many ways. She recalled that she began to see many things in her environment in a different light. She described this period of her life as both exhilarating and emotionally upsetting. She was not alone. As she emphasized, during this time, the entire country was undergoing challenge from the diverse social movements of the 1960s.

## Fighting for Community Control of Schools

During the late 1960s, parents in New York City developed into an organized force demanding community control of schools. Since mothers were oftentimes the ones to negotiate with the schools on their children's behalf, they were in the forefront of these battles. Frustration with the New York City Board of Education fueled their protests against a centralized and insensitive bureaucracy. This dynamic is especially evident in the following excerpt in which Teresa Fraser described how the People's Board of Education developed spontaneously from the dismissive behavior of formal Board members.

> There was a finance hearing at the Board of Education and it was one of these typical things where nothing—I know because I was really involved in it—nothing special was planned.…Hearings were a very

big thing. Everybody went to hearings. PTA people. I was one of the officers of the Parents' Association for years. We went down and carried on about where the money was going. Some lady from Brownsville asked if she could speak earlier than her time because she had to go pick up her kids, and they said, "No." And the person who was at the microphone, whoever's turn it was, said, "She can have my time."…And whoever it was running the meeting said, "No way!" And people got pissed and said, "Let her talk!" And I'm telling you, I swear to God this was not a planned thing. And they got up and recessed. And people were just furious. And they came back and they called off the hearing on the Board of Education budget because some lady from Brownsville wanted to speak so she could go pick up her children. And…a couple of other people were in the audience, said if they're not going to listen, we will listen. And that became the People's Board of Education.

The parents and their allies stayed in the building for three days and three nights. Teresa recalled with amazement that the Board of Education officials "tried to freeze" the parents out of the building by turning on the air blowers.

Teresa enthusiastically described the innovative work they did to help involve parents in their children's education while also providing programs for the parents. Working in multiracial coalitions, the organizers invented numerous strategies to involve Spanish-speaking parents. She recalled that "some of the things that happened…were really unusual" at the time especially as they tried to organize across the lines of race and ethnicity. She was particularly proud of the curriculum development and bilingual workshops they planned to reach out to Latino parents and their children. She explained:

> In the first place, I would imagine we were one of the first, if not the first, truly bilingual [programs]….[I]t sounds ridiculous to think about it [now], but we mimeographed a very nice thing with pictures of Puerto Rican leaders and writers and important people. That had never been done! And we distributed it. I mean, it was an amazing kind of thing that things that are taken for granted now in a kind of way, and it a little preceded the "Black is Beautiful" period, but essentially it was the beginning of that whole time. And we ran sessions with parents that had hundreds [in attendance]….The material was completely bilingual….We rented the same kind of equipment they use at the United Nations, and we had translators and people sitting with earphones. It was unbelievable! People don't do it now. It was incredible! But what happened is when you do direct translation, it doubles the time that you take up. And people can't do that. People have an evening and that's it. They have a couple of hours. What we did was we would have a plenary session, with various important speakers or interesting speakers or whatever, and I'm telling you, it…was jammed, standing room only, big school auditoriums. And then we'd break

down into workshops....You could sign up for an all Spanish work-shop, or an all English-speaking workshop. So the workshops them-selves, although it [separating people into smaller groups] wasn't the best thing...but on the other hand, we got so many other things done that it really didn't matter. So in terms of transmitting information, at least people were comfortable being able to speak.

As a consequence of their creative and persistent efforts, Teresa and the co-organizers helped to develop a cross-race coalition that worked to address the different issues facing the various constituencies.

One of the most important and successful campaigns led by the parents' advocacy group involved getting access to the reading scores for the public schools.

[Ours] was the first group that got the reading scores, which turned out to have made a tremendous contribution to what happened, again mostly because...[well] when you have a kid who can't read, your ten-dency is to assume, what did I do wrong? And the school system and the whole system lends itself to that, particularly with black and Hispanic parents, who also feel very often, certainly in that time, feel very isolated and alienated from the school system.

Teresa stressed how parents were made to feel responsible for their chil-dren's learning problems by administrators and teachers who treated each individual as if his or her failures were personal ones, not connected to "mis-education" in school. Once parents came to realize the collective nature of the reading problem, their ability to push for changes in the school system improved (also see Stern 1998).

### Engaging with the Social Movements of the 1960s
During this period of intense activism at the neighborhood level, many of the community workers were also involved in the social movements of the 1960s. For example, Maria Calero participated in protests against the Vietnam War among other collective actions. While she also felt drawn to the organizing efforts of the Women's Movement and the Young Lords, in both cases she found the analyses lacking. Skeptical about the radical claims of all the social movements of the 1960s, she viewed the neighborhood as the most important site for affecting change, preferring to work to help meet the immediate needs of her community. She explained her view as follows:

So I did march with the Lords when they protested the welfare cuts or when they took over the church. I also knew that there were cultural statements being made, and I thought that they were important to be made, but I certainly didn't believe that we were soldiers in the army. And I remember reading then Marcuse[4] saying that everybody was ready to pick up arms, and I didn't believe that....I always saw that if I had to believe in something, that I had to have an impact on...[for example] the children in that neighborhood [who] had to be vaccinated.

Since Maria measured the value of political ideology by its direct benefit to those living in her community and other poor areas, she found much of the rhetoric that dominated the radical left during the 1960s and early 1970s wanting.

Maria's involvement in these social movements was further tempered by her experiences growing up in the Dominican Republic. She said this made her more cynical in her analysis of what would contribute to change in the United States. She explained:

> I wanted, yes, to have all these thoughts about changing the world, but I did not believe the revolution was around the corner. I had been raised in the Dominican Republic, where the Sixth Fleet, you could see it arrive in the Caribbean on the horizon, the government of these macho types would immediately crumble because they knew that this was the most powerful government in the world....So I had more of a real fear of this country. I knew that these people were not fooling around, and they're not gonna let their children tumble a power structure as strong and as invested, entrenched, in this nation, [and] an economic system that was so powerful.

Maria felt that her childhood experiences outside the United States provided a different lens through which she understood what was politically possible. She described herself as both an insider within the Latino community in the United States, and an outsider due to her place of birth. She also constructed her outsider experiences as both personally painful and politically beneficial. Her shifting relationship to outsider/insider status illustrates how "'outsiderness' and 'insiderness' are not fixed or static positions" (Naples 1996, 83). This further demonstrates the difficulty with the resident/nonresident distinction drawn at the start of this study as well as the taken-for-granted assumption of the New Careers philosophy that indigenous status will be fixed over time (Cloward and Ohlin 1960). Community processes and patterns of personal transformation repositioned community workers' relationships with other community members. In Maria's case, her feminist activism further marginalized her from the male-dominated Latino community in which she located her political work in the 1960s and 1970s. Her identity as a Latina positioned her as an "outsider within" (Collins 1991a) the Women's Movement as well.

While she criticized the New Left for its abstract and implausible political ideology, Maria expressed an affinity for the goals of the Women's Movement. However, she did not see a central place for herself within this movement. She explained: "I would participate sort of at the edge of the women's peace [movement]....I read Betty Friedan's book and was very fascinated with what she said. I didn't think she was speaking to me directly, but I at least knew that this lady made sense." Since she did not find a site for her political interests within the mainstream organizations of the Women's Movement, Maria became active in a group established by Latina feminists in New York City called Action Latina. Of particular interest here is the fact that Maria placed the group Action Latina "at the edge" of the Women's Movement. Such a move represents her personal experiences with the white-dominated Women's Movement. It also mirrors historical accounts of the movement that neglect to include the multifaceted women-centered organizing of women of color (see Gluck et al., 1998).

### Negotiating Race and Class Dynamics in the Women's Movement

Many nonresident community workers, especially the women of color interviewed, said they did not find "a role to play...as an activist" in the Women's Movement. As African American worker Edith Harper explained:

> I have always identified with it philosophically and emotionally and in every other sense, but have not been one of the people out there organizing the [Women's] Movement. My sense is, and I'm on the outside so I can't really say, that the movement was initiated by women who were not grassroots. It was not a working-women's movement, and therefore the issues that people focused on were somewhat removed from the everyday concerns of the average woman who goes to work, comes home to a family, whatever. So it did not involve and include everybody. I think that now the people in the movement have certainly decided that they do, in fact, want to include various other groups, and to become more of a coalition, and therefore there's keener sensitivity to various issues that may or may not seem to be relevant to them, but their relevance to other people makes them valid to deal with.

Edith was working with a childcare information, referral, and advocacy organization in the mid-1980s. She reported that in the 1970s when she first became active in the day care field she did not find any of the major women's organizations supporting community groups working to increase the availability and quality of day care. However, by 1983, she found that many women's organizations were "actively pursuing us to be connected, and to make sure that they are supporting us and wanting to know how to and in what ways." She was pleased that the "Women's Movement types" had finally come on board with direct support of day care initiatives, but remained critical of these women's groups because it took so long for them to become involved with this issue.

Despite the perceived distance from the issues and approaches that were central to the Women's Movement organizations of the early 1970s, many of the nonresident community workers identified strongly with a primary message of feminism; namely, that women deserve equal treatment in society. Feminism resonated with their lived experiences as political activists and women workers. White European American Beverly Towner, who was brought up in a middle-class family, found her way to feminism through her experience as a shop steward for a day care center. She recalled:

> And I think the thing that really propelled me into activism is that as...one of the [union] representatives in contract negotiation ...[with] day care owners, I'd come to these meetings and the owners would be there. They're all nonprofit [day care centers], and the money comes from the city, and the city negotiator would be there, and they'd all say things like, "Taking care of children is so much of a pleasure for women, that really they should be paying us for the privilege." Also things like, "Well, you're really lazy. Taking care of children is not hard work." And we kept stressing the educational component, and the strain of taking care of kids who were hardly verbal. And I watched teachers, and I think the most amazing teaching job is with these kids, because you give give give, and you don't get back very much. If you're not in the mood, you can go downhill rapidly. If you're a high school teacher, or a college teacher, you give out and then you get this feedback. There's none of that. It's very chaotic. So I saw how people's [stereotypical] attitudes were [negatively] affecting the salary and the prestige of day care workers. And just about all the workers in the day care center were women. About all of them were black, too. So I got so interested in that [and]...I really became committed.

Beverly described her deepened commitment to community work as a consequence of recognizing the ways in which gender, race, and class circumscribed black women's lives. She did not see Civil Rights Movement organizations addressing issues like day care during this time and, furthermore, as a white women, did not feel there was a place for her in these organizations. She did find political allies within the Women's Movement and, around the time of the contract negotiations, joined the New York Radical Feminists. Unfortunately, she quickly realized that "as much as I really liked being a member, as much as it had raised my consciousness, they were always going to be a discussion group. They were never going to be a force." She eventually joined the National Organization for Women (NOW), which by this time was focusing on issues of child care among other "women's issues." As a white woman, she did not experience the dissatisfaction expressed by Josephine Card or Angela Garcia who could not identify with the approaches taken by white-dominated Women's Movement organizations of the 1970s.

Women of all racial-ethnic working-class backgrounds were generally less likely to feel an affinity with the Women's Movement than their middle-class counterparts. In 1984, I asked Sandra Cole how the women in her racially diverse working-class neighborhood in Brooklyn viewed feminism. She complained that:

> There's no reality of feminism when it comes down to here. Women are still not talking at any community meeting about women's issues at all. They don't know how to think about community development, economic development, from a woman's perspective. They know how to talk about rape and battering, but they don't even know how to talk about rape and battering from a *feminist neighborhood perspective*. They're talked about as outside the context of where people live, politically, emotionally, and I think that's off....I think that whole Women's Movement is outside of the [neighborhood] context....Women who organized in this country had to separate themselves from family and neighborhood so that we could think as women, and that we couldn't do it unless we separated ourselves, so that what we haven't discovered is that we don't have to do that anymore and that we're still doing it. We're creating institutions outside. We're not making our neighborhoods and our families accountable to the changes that are going on. So that women are still saying that they are out there doing feminist things, [but] going home with the same kind of family [emphasis added].

Sandra Cole highlighted the significance of women's attachment to their community for grassroots politics and said she worked in dialogue with women in her community-based organization to develop, what she termed, a "feminist neighborhood perspective." However, she expressed frustration that they often did not claim the political identity of "feminist."

Despite the resident community workers' widespread critique of the Women's Movement and of feminism more generally, there were some significant differences between the Latinas and the other community workers. For example, while most African American community workers agreed that women needed to be in decision-making positions in local, state, and federal government (or in the words of New York City community worker Mrs. Long, "You need women down there [in City Hall and Washington, D.C.] with them men"), only a few of the African American women interviewed for this study mentioned a need to organize separately as women. Even when African American community workers like Josephine Card participated in Women's Movement organizations or focused on women-specific issues in their community work, they did not identify themselves as feminists nor define their work as exclusively women-specific. In contrast, almost half of the Latinas emphasized the need for political organizing separately as women. It is important to note here that the Latinas were, on average, younger than the African American and white resident workers interviewed (see Appendix A).[5] Furthermore, African American women interviewed were less likely than the Latinas to claim that sexism inhibited their ability to perform community work. Since the African American women I interviewed did not perceive their leadership roles circumscribed within the community-based institutions of the African American community, they were less motivated to form separate organizations.

## Puerto Rican Feminists and the Women's Movement

Carlotta Mendez discussed how she grew to "define three parts" of her identity—her race, ethnicity, and gender—when, as a Puerto Rican, she faced sexism and racism from black males during her early community work. She was asked by the African American and Latino male leadership to give up her position in a CAP in a predominantly black community to a black man. She was "shocked" that, politically, she was not considered an appropriate person to fill the job. Throughout her many years as a community worker, she continued to struggle against sexism in the Puerto Rican community. In 1985, she emphasized:

> I think it's critical that the Puerto Rican community conserve its institutions created to serve its population and deal with some of the problems that confront us. But I am more and more convinced that in terms of discrimination, a lot of what has happened to me inside and outside the community has to do with the fact that I'm a woman.

Since neither the male-dominated Latino organizations nor the white women-dominated Women's Movement organizations reflected her political priorities or valued her leadership, she felt it was important to create separate Latina political institutions.

Angela Garcia captured the sentiments of many of the Puerto Rican women when she stated that "being Puerto Rican, your womanness is just there, where the consciousness of the Women's Movement is busy defining that." As evidence for her assertion, she criticized many of the issues promoted by the Women's Movement. For example, she believed that an issue like educational equity would involve poor and minority women more than issues like the Equal Rights Amendment. She complained that when she approached "Women's Movement types," they couldn't get it "through their heads" that gay rights or abortion are not the main concerns for the Puerto Rican community. She explained, "The issue of gay rights is not an issue in our community. It happens, it's there, and it gets taken care of. But it doesn't become a public issue—which is the problem that many of us have [as practicing Catholics]." She emphasized that issues like gay rights or abortion served to alienate practicing Catholics. Angela described her personal view on the issue of abortion:

> I'm a practicing Catholic, but I don't take abortion as an issue and publish it, and make a big thing about it. I know where I stand on reproductive rights. I think a woman has a right to decide. That's been

my argument with God. And that's been my argument with the people who say they represent God.

Angela believed that "abortion gets done" in the Puerto Rican community but she did not think there was a need to "make such a point of it." In defining issues like gay rights and abortion as outside her "political focus," Angela participated in rendering gay, lesbian, and pro-choice Puerto Rican activists outside her community. In doing so, she was also narrowly defining who she felt were legitimate members of her "community" and inhibiting coalition building with others who might prove logical allies in certain political struggles.

While highly critical of the priorities set by Women's Movement organizations, the Puerto Rican resident community workers were even more troubled by the racism they experienced within the movement. In addition to lack of understanding about the concerns of low-income people, Angela Garcia felt that the established organizations of the Women's Movement did not welcome women of color. She related:

> Another thing I see as to why many Hispanic women haven't come into NOW or into the National Women's Political Caucus, we know that there are women who are there and were involved from the beginning, [but] never assume the leadership role, except [a] few....[And Hispanic women] would never then go out and recruit from their own community, because their own community wouldn't go in there.

An individual woman of color did not need to have a personal experience with racism within a Women's Movement organization to discourage her participation. These organizations gained the reputation among women of color for racist practices.[6]

Maria Calero described her personal experience with the insensitivity to the different issues confronting Latina and African American women by those women representing the Women's Movement. She remembered "a time when the Women's Movement was pretty strong when there was a debate among the women in the Lower East Side, whether we would identify ourselves with the Women's Movement, because we identified ourselves with our own group, and it was just terribly conflicting about who were we, except we knew all the agencies were dominated by men, even the Hispanic management we were aware of was pretty lousy." One incident stood out in her memory:

> I remember...one day somebody asking me to an interview at WBAI [a New York City public radio station], and being terrified that this lady was going to ask me the inevitable question, "Are you a feminist?" Which eventually she did, and I had to—a moment of consciousness for me—I had to say, "Yes." But I was scared to death. And that was the first time I publicly said it, "Yes." I was scared that now I was going

to go back to the Lower East Side and I was going to be banned from the Hispanic community. But of course I'm a feminist. The black women in that program were pretty upset that she broached the question, and they didn't want the question to be asked.

As a consequence of insensitivity to the complexity of racism in American society and gender dynamics within civil rights movements, the predominantly white Women's Movement failed to attract the support and organizing skills of many of the resident community workers I interviewed for this study.

Angela was particularly articulate about the political tensions she experienced as a Puerto Rican woman that led her to help create Latina-controlled organizations. Her discussion reveals the limits of the Civil Rights and Women's Movement organizations. She reflected on her split identity in her political work:

> I lead two lives as they say. One is as a woman and working in women's groups and identifying as a woman and then the other as a Puerto Rican dealing with Latino women and dealing with those issues, etc. I find myself sometimes on a fence because I don't like what I see sometimes and also because I know that no matter which way you jump you're going to get burnt no matter what. The women's groups and women's issues are not winners for us [Puerto Rican women]. The reason being that it's white dominant and what you're basically doing is following the white woman as the leader, as the one who is determining what is going to happen and what's not going to happen. And over here when you do the Latino thing the [Latino] leadership is there; however who runs it and makes the moves are the men.

Angela often felt "on the fence" witnessing the limits of the white-dominated Women's Movement organizations and the male-dominated Latino organizations. She also recognized that even when women get into positions of power they are often handpicked by men who control them to a certain extent.

> What ends up happening is that some of the women who you work with are taking their orders from men although they're here in these groupings. And it's the men, very interesting, it is the men who are selecting the [women] leaders....You look at women who are in key positions no matter where you look at them in government, they're not there because they're women [or] they have done something for the Women's Movement. They don't come out of the shop because Bella [Abzug] called up or Gloria [Steinem] called up or Betty [Friedan] called up....So you always have to do it through the guys....And the point is that once these women [are] into these positions then you have to deal with them whether you like them or not, whether you

think they are going to do the correct thing or not and sometimes they surprise you, and they come through and sometimes they say, "I can't do it," and I say, "I understand." You got to follow whose putting bread on the table.

As a consequence of their dissatisfaction with the white Women's Movement and male-led Latino organizations, Lydia Montalvo, Maria Calero, Angela Garcia, and Carlotta Mendez played important roles in the creation of the National Conference of Puerto Rican Women, the National Council of Puerto Rican Women, National Puerto Rican Women's Caucus, the National Latina Caucus, and the Hispanic Women's Center. But, as Angela Garcia emphasized in 1985, as women "there are [also] a lot of ad hoc things [women] do" to enhance women's position in the Hispanic community. In addition, despite her criticism of the Women's Movement, Angela strongly claimed a feminist identity.

I'm one of those positive feminists. I really believe that there should be no apology for being a feminist, and I believe feminism means the equality of people, men and women. And that the struggle is to balance off—[make women and men equal]. I think more voices need to be heard in a positive feminist way than the "I'm not a feminist but." This politics of language is very key here.

By playing the "politics of language," namely, by publicly declaring feminism as a positive identity and countering the negative stereotypes attached to the term by the media and political conservatives, Angela hoped to encourage more Puerto Rican women to claim a feminist identity and participate in challenging the sexism within their community.

Carlotta Mendez commented on the growing acceptance of feminism among younger Puerto Rican women contrasting her experiences in the 1960s and 1970s with the 1990s. Defying expected gender norms of the 1960s and 1970s, Carlotta said she did not know that she was "supposed to be inferior." She explained:

And I would sit there with guys, and I don't know I'm supposed to keep my mouth shut, you know, so I'm going along. And that became a problem and at that age…I was the only woman in the particular age range, and I was challenging and attempting to be equal, too. And it was not a conscious feminist move, I just didn't know better. And that became a major hassle.

In the 1995 interview, Carlotta reflected again on her involvement with the Women's Movement reporting that to be a feminist in the Puerto Rican community during the 1990s is not as unusual as it was in the 1960s and 1970s.

I may have been seen as an oddball in the '60s or '70s when I began to relate to the Women's Movement as a Puerto Rican woman but in the 1990s it's not strange. We have a new generation of women who also [are] feminists...and the guys themselves have been educated. So it's not that I have an easy life if I'm doing the feminist bit for the Puerto Rican community but certainly it's not where it was twenty or thirty years ago.

## Sexism and Its Influence on Community Work

While the Latina resident community workers felt that the male-dominated institutions of the Latino community kept women from assuming more leadership positions, they also reported a range of experiences with sexism in their personal relationships that further inhibited their ability to engage in community work to the extent they desired. East Harlem community worker Rita Martinez's husband was also active in community activities, serving on several boards of directors of local not-for-profit agencies. He initially resisted his wife's interest in community work and rarely assisted her in the home. The conflict over her community work put a strain on her marriage. She explained the difficulty in terms of contrasting cultural expectations between herself and her husband:

> I became so involved that I would go from work, and then go home, feed the kids, and then come back and go for a meeting. And it was hard because I had to take my kids with me everywhere. [My husband] was active in this community, and he did a lot of organizing tenement housing buildings and he had to go to their meetings, so we were never home together. And then when he was, I wasn't. And I would ask for him to babysit. And he would say, "But I never see you!"...What happened was that it was all right for him to do it because he's a Puerto Rican man. In terms of Puerto Ricans, they're very macho. The woman is in the house. The man is not in the house. So that was a conflict. And we needed a lot of discussion....But I think after awhile it did us good. He knew I was doing it for the children.

Rita was frustrated that her husband resisted her community participation, even though he was active himself. Yet after criticizing his so-called macho behavior, she said he finally came to understand that she was "doing it for the children." Rita could not claim her right to participate in community work for her own sake, nor could she successfully renegotiate gender expectations within her household. She and her husband came to a mutual understanding that Rita's community work was a necessary aspect of her mothering role. However, this construction of her political participation and community caretaking served to reaffirm the gender imbalance she initially complained about.

In contrast, Gloria Alvarez of the Lower East Side described her Puerto Rican husband as extremely supportive of her community work. She related:

I've been married to my husband for twenty-three years....My daughters love him. And I know how good he is. But anything that I am very active in, he's with me. He's supportive of everything that I do. He says I'm a fighter...and he gives me suggestions. He helps. He doesn't mind the hours. He believes in what I'm doing.

The contrast between Rita's and Gloria's husbands' support for their wives' community work illustrates the danger in generalizing about patriarchal practices within the Puerto Rican community. While gendered cultural patterns exist within racial-ethnic groups, analyses of the concrete practices of specific members reveal a wide variety of experiences that do not correspond with stereotypical views. The examination of gender inequities within a specific racial-ethnic group must be sensitive to the diversity of actual practices that shape women's lives as well as to changes over time.

## Toward a "Feminist Neighborhood Perspective"

Most of the resident community workers believed that their socially marginal position in society as low-income women contributed to their special understanding of the importance of community for low-income people.[7] Their participation in community-based organizations further sustained their commitment to struggle on behalf of their communities. The women I interviewed developed their commitment to, and political analyses of, community work in dynamic relationship with others in CAPs and other "assertive community organizations" (McCourt 1997) as well as informally as they engaged in daily struggles for the betterment of their local neighborhoods.

CAPs increased the organizational sites through which community activist women forged a sense of connection with others facing similar problems in their neighborhoods and, consequently, the programs served as a key location in which definitions of community were constructed and sustained. One method by which we recognize how our personal experiences are part of broader collective processes is through interaction with others encountering similar issues or problems. Interactive or group reflection on the connection between personal problems and political processes formed the basis for the consciousness-raising strategies adopted by the Women's Movement of the late 1960s and early 1970s. The consciousness-raising group process enabled women to share their experiences, define and analyze the social and political mechanisms serving to oppress women, and develop strategies for social change. While few of the women I interviewed would define their collective discussions with other women who shared similar experiences as consciousness-raising, they often discussed the value of spontaneous as well as ongoing conversations for recognizing the broader dimensions of politics, inequality, and discrimination.[8]

Sandra Cole was especially articulate about the significance of feminist consciousness for her community work. The now-familiar feminist adage of "the personal is political" is well illustrated in her story. Shortly after graduating from college, Sandra had an unwanted pregnancy that she decided to terminate. At the time, abortions were illegal but, desperate to end the pregnancy, she turned to an illegal abortionist. She did not tell her friends about it, keeping it a closely guarded secret until she encountered feminism. She explained:

> I didn't care if I died....The person who I was involved with wasn't there to be helpful. Other people were helpful, but I didn't tell my women friends that I lived with.... but we didn't talk to each other. I mean, think about it. I always want to remember that women did not talk to each other then, because I want to know that this is how we've transformed. I mean, you and I could talk a hundred times easier...about everything in our lives in a minute, and we didn't do that then. People didn't do it. One of my friends said, "How come you didn't tell me? Why didn't you tell me you were having an abortion?" I said, "What would you have heard?" She said, "You're right. I couldn't have heard it." And, so I got an abortion on a kitchen table in the South Bronx, in a tenement building, and got on the train before I started bleeding and went home and got married to the boy next door.

Sandra's marriage did not last long but she kept the secret of the abortion for years until she attended a demonstration against the Catholic Church's position on abortion.

> Well, I had no feminist consciousness at all. And it happened at one moment....And it was when I was working here [in the Brooklyn neighborhood organization], still had my Civil Rights connections, and somehow, and I don't remember who told me, there was going to be this demonstration at St. Patrick's Cathedral against its stand on abortion....[And] it would be my opportunity, you know, to get out my views about the whole abortion situation I had gone through. But, of course, I would do it as [if to say] my clients had gone through all this. I mean, we didn't say we had abortions in those days either. And I went up there with twenty people demonstrating at St. Patrick's Church.

After the demonstration, several organizers invited Sandra to join them for a discussion that turned into one of the most important events of her life. Here she started to make connections between her personal experiences and the collective concerns of other women that completely transformed her political perspective. She recalled:

> And we sat down, and we started talking about feminism. And I was like [clicks her fingers a number of times]....like everything [clicks] just like that. And, of course, a lot of women went through that. Like a lightbulb....It was like, oh! oh! oh! And then I got involved in this...very, very exciting, consciousness-raising group!

Sandra expressed the excitement she felt as she made connections between her personal experiences as a woman and the political analysis that developed in the consciousness-raising group. However, she recalled, the feminists she met could not understand the relevance of her community work.

> They didn't understand how what I was doing in the neighborhood had any relationship to feminism....I was fighting for a day care center, and the whole community was battling against me. I was pretty clear [how it was connected to feminism]. And it was men who were fighting [me], [and] it was the political system, and my life was being threatened....I mean it was like a big thing that went on for about three years, and...that was the first time I had to take leadership. I was going to leave, but for those few women in the neighborhood who said, "No, you can't leave."

Sandra was successful in her fight to establish a day care center in her Brooklyn neighborhood but regretted that her feminist community did not view this effort as a target for their activism.

Sandra remained in her community work position and took what she defined as the best of feminism into that setting. For Sandra, "the consciousness-raising thing is really key" because she believes:

> Women who have gone through that process [of consciousness-raising] hold true to their feminism. Women who haven't lost what it means to be a feminist very fast...and that those [who have gone through consciousness-raising] are people...[who] really can hold true. I can count on those women to this day. Whether we agree with each other is something else because there were certainly [tensions within feminist groups].

The community workers like Sandra Cole who participated directly in Women's Movement organizations and consciousness-raising groups were often frustrated by their inability to convince "Women's Movement types" of the value of community organizing in working-class neighborhoods. However, they recognized a specific form of feminist praxis in their local communities that could be linked with more explicit feminist agendas if broadened to include what Terry Haywoode (1991) defines as "working-class feminism."[9]

Haywoode (1991, 152–153) points out that "in many urban neighborhoods a new and important form of political organization emerged in the 1970s and early 1980s...grounded in the informal networks of association which had already been established by the working-class women who were residents of these neighborhoods and became connected with ideas about organizing developed in the Women's Movement and in other progressive social movements of the 1960s and early 1970s." This working-class feminist form of organizing featured the mobilization of women's "pre-existing networks of communication and organization."

Haywoode emphasizes that the key to urban working-class women's effectiveness was the way they understood the social organization of community, for "women know a great deal about community life because it is the stuff of their every day experience" (p. 183). Other features of working-class feminism include drawing on traditional gender roles as well as religious and cultural traditions (also see Pardo 1998). While the working-class women Haywoode worked with criticized the Women's Movement's negative assessment of the family and its broadened understanding of sexualities, they "heartily embraced the concept of an increased public and employment role for women" (p. 184). Haywoode discovered an articulation of women's issues as "community issues" in working-class women's organizations. Since the dominant discourse of the Women's Movement of the 1970s did not articulate links between gender, racial, ethnic, class, and "community issues," many of the community workers (especially those who were residents of the low-income neighborhoods of New York City and Philadelphia) did not see themselves within it even when their political work dovetailed with constructions of feminist praxis.

## Weaving Private Concerns into Public Work

Throughout their careers, the resident community workers sought to integrate their personal concerns for their various communities into their work. Consequently, the workers introduced into public discourse issues traditionally viewed as private and personal. They redefined individual problems with the welfare and health care systems as collective, community problems. They viewed police harassment of one member of their community as an offense against the whole community. As the community workers experienced dissatisfaction with the state's role in their neighborhoods, they joined together to challenge the state's definition of their problems and the limited ways in which the state addressed these problems. The positions they held within the state provided a contradictory site for contesting oppressive features of the state as well as rechanneling resources to more effective uses.

Historically, women's work at the local community level includes negotiations with community-based services and public institutions. The community workers frequently recounted their frustration as their concerns were met by unresponsive public bureaucracies. This in turn led the women to organize protests in their communities. As discussed, the schools became one of the most significant sites of contestation. In fact, fourteen (or 33 percent) of the resident community workers interviewed described the problems their children were having in the public schools as a primary catalyst for their community activism. Japanese American community worker Paula Sands who resided in Harlem explained, "There were times we had to do things that were outlandish in the eyes of the public" because "there were a lot of issues that came up which constantly pointed up the inability of the staff to recognize the legitimate claims of parents." Paula also believed that the dominant educational system was not set up to educate low-income children.

> Educational institutions were not really prepared to teach youngsters in low economic neighborhoods. There was not a will to learn about minority youngsters, nor a will to protect minority youngsters and their potential and to assume they had the potential if it was encouraged and brought out to its highest. There's no reason to think that every single youngster in Scarsdale, [N.Y.] has some natural potential and automatically is going to college any more than anywhere else—but if you got strikes against you, its 'cause you're not going to be able to [achieve as much].

The racist and classist behavior of the middle-class professionals and an irresponsible public education system led resident community workers to protest the injustices their children encountered in school. While the conditions of their lives as low-income and minority women brought them to action, their community activism offered them an experience of self-empowerment that further enhanced their ability to push for broader changes in their local communities.

### Shifting Standpoints on Poverty

Community workers were not always in agreement about the solutions to the problems of poverty and what community workers should do in order to help improve the lives of the poor. A few women felt that if an individual completed high school and worked hard on the job, he or she could leave the ranks of the poor. Others insisted that the society must provide the poor with better education and expanded employment opportunities to help them out of poverty. In contrast, other workers felt that the rich, who rule our society, are not interested in eliminating poverty; therefore, the poor must gain control of the major political, economic, and social service institutions in America. These contrasting views illustrate that sharing similar experiences as well as race, class, and gender backgrounds does not necessarily lead to similar political analyses.

Ann Robinson and Marcy Barnett are African American women who were born in low-income urban communities in the mid-1920s. They each came to paid community work in the 1960s following informal family and church-based activities, personal experiences living in poverty as well as a commitment to help improve the quality of life in their neighborhoods. Both had only a high school degree when they obtained paid community work. After approximately twenty years of experience, they each emphasized contrasting views of how to combat poverty. Ann stressed the need for organizing her community to counter the problems of poverty. She emphasized the importance of the antipoverty programs for helping to expand her analysis of the structural problems inhibiting parents and other residents from gaining control over their communities. In contrast to Ann's more structural emphasis, Marcy, who had recently retired from a paid community work position, believed individuals needed to take the initiative and improve their economic condition to counter poverty. Marcy explained, "See, people have to motivate themselves. Is this what I want or do I want to do better? It has to begin with you because that's the only way things are going to get better."

Echoing the now dominant approach to welfare reform, Marcy believed that it was important for low-income people who could work to be forced to work. "Make them take jobs, then they would have a sense of independence," she said. She was extremely critical of the welfare system, which, she believed, prevented poor people from taking care of their own needs. She asserted: "But as long as they can go to the centers and get their check and their food stamps and do what they want to do...they're saying, 'Why should I motivate myself?' Make them motivate them-selves. That's why I say it had to begin with you." Marcy Barnett's analysis of the causes of poverty informed her community work as well as how she socialized her seven children.

> Just like I told my daughters, "Children, if you don't want anything for you, then I don't want anything for you. But you may not stay in my house and get a welfare check. Now if you want something for you, I'm going to help get something for you." And I sincerely meant that....You find four generations getting a welfare check. Now, don't misunderstand me, I have nothing against welfare if you need it—if you can't work, if you have a handicap...you're out of work, and have a family to take care of—use it. But you're healthy and you're going to sit back and wait on a check. No, that's wrong!

Despite her belief that people are individually responsible for their own economic destinies and that workfare is an effective strategy for ending women's dependence on welfare, Marcy also recognized that the solution must include access to decision making on the part of low-income people. While she strongly adhered to the ideology of the work ethic, her commitment to expanding democratic participation and political access for the poor evoked themes of the War on Poverty that has long been eclipsed by the coercive and nonparticipatory features of contemporary welfare reform. Her perspective again illustrates how emphasis on individual competence building coexisted with collective empowerment processes in community workers' narratives, although Ann's construction gave greater priority to collective strategies than Marcy's.

Ann's East Harlem neighborhood offered a more radical context for her work than Marcy's Philadelphia neighborhood. However, Marcy did not say she wanted to see more militant action on the part of her neighbors and coworkers. While Marcy differed from Ann in emphasizing the individualist "work ethic" as an important solution to poverty, she also stressed the importance of expanding poor people's access to the political decision making. The contrast between Marcy's and Ann's analysis of how to counter poverty in their communities reveals how political perspectives can vary among those who share similar social positions, thus contesting essentialized standpoint perspectives that equate particular ways of knowing with specific social identities.[10] The question raised here for an assessment of New Careers is to what extent sharing the same social background as those in the poor communities does in fact provide a privileged vantage point for community workers. The overriding answer derived from this analysis is that indigenous knowledge does offer a valuable partial perspective on poverty that differs from dominant constructions; however, aspects of the dominant perspectives on poverty also appear alongside alternative analyses in some women's narratives. The overriding contribution of the community workers, however, is their long-term commitment to combat poverty and inequality from the grassroots when others in more powerful positions have long ago abandoned the fight.

## Conclusion

When we examine the community workers' perspectives on gender identity, we find, in many cases, a unique feminist theory and practice, particularly in the leadership and mentoring they provided other women in their communities. However, there were some key differences between the African American and Latina workers in their construction of feminist praxis. While Latinas and African American women reported numerous experiences with sexism, Latinas were more likely to emphasize the ways sexism inhibited their ability to engage in community work to the extent they desired. While none of the African American community workers I interviewed desired a formal relationship with the Women's Movement, many of the Latinas expressed a political affiliation with feminism and, in some cases, the Women's Movement. Yet they found it essential to create organizations that stood apart from both the male-dominated Latino institutions as well as the white female-dominated Women's Movement organizations. They hoped that these autonomous groups would reflect their unique experiences as Latinas. However, efforts to develop broad-based coalitions with other women's organizations or to link with gay and lesbian groups were limited by fears that issues like abortion or gay rights would alienate other members of their predominantly Catholic Latino communities.

In contrast to the priorities set by the Women's Movement, the resident community workers of all racial-ethnic backgrounds concentrated their political energies on issues closer to their everyday lives. Many became active in struggles to ensure an adequate education for their children and most who were living in New York City became extremely involved in the movement for community control of schools. Critical dialogue among the women who participated in the CAPs served to deepen the community workers' analysis of the gendered inequities in the institutions that shaped their lives, although few articulated a "feminist neighborhood perspective" in terms comparable with Sandra Cole's analysis. However, through processes that parallel consciousness-raising, the community workers recognized how police, school officials, welfare case workers, and health care providers mistreated women, the poor, and racial-ethnic minorities in everyday encounters. This growing awareness helped strengthen their resolve to fight for their community's rights.

Unlike the construction of middle-class liberal feminist praxis, the community workers did not generally emphasize individual achievement as the primary goal of their community work. Although they often described individual empowerment as a major component of their work, the community workers defined these efforts as necessary for the process of collective empowerment. While they emphasized that individuals should be treated with respect and have the opportunity to gain access to jobs and education, they did not view individual upward mobility as an end in itself. Rather, they understood individual empowerment as a way to enhance the social and economic capital available to their communities. In this regard, the community workers' narratives exemplifies the difficulty in detaching individual processes of empowerment from collective empowerment strategies; although some workers did, at times, privilege individual competence building over collective strategies, especially as the political climate changed.

While the community workers offered different analyses of what contributes to poverty in America and what solutions were most effective in fighting inequality, all of the women interviewed for this study were committed to developing new leadership as well as preserving the organizing skills and knowledge gained over years of community service. They attempted to bequeath this legacy to their communities through their words, actions, and lifelong commitment. The older women expressed a desire to scale down their community work activities but believed they could not do so unless others came forward to replace them in the community. In the next chapter, I explore the processes by which they contributed to the continuity of community work and highlight the limits of the contemporary context for promoting the political engagement of low-income youth.

# Chapter 7

# INTERGENERATIONAL CONTINUITY OF COMMUNITY WORK

Sabrina Brock's parents played a key role in raising her consciousness about injustice, economic inequality, and racism. She honored the activist mothering she received and credited this early foundation for her endurance as a community worker. In 1995, she discussed how her identity as a community worker was forged out of these early experiences:

> I can't say that I always wake up with unbridled enthusiasm for the day. You get tired. But I think I've been privileged to have my baptism in my values and in my politics early on in my life supported by my family and supported by some watershed experiences. And…I got enough support in the small communities and in the small ways that I was organizing to know that that was something that I couldn't turn my back on. That was who I was. My identity was forged out of those experiences and those values. And that's what kept me young, strong, you know. I guess I'm weary now, but I ain't giving up. I'm going to keep on keepin' on.

Sabrina "keep[s] on keepin' on" despite the difficulties posed by the contemporary political and economic environment because of the firm commitment and political values instilled by her parents as well as an accumulation of personal political experiences that continue to sustain her. However, transmission of political commitment and values from one generation to another is not a simple and unmediated process as Sabrina found when she tried to incorporate her own daughter into her activist work.

Sabrina discovered that no legitimate role existed for her daughter in the community actions that drew her mother's time and energies. Although she brought her to demonstrations and other community actions, Sabrina complained that organizers never developed ways to engage younger people in these campaigns and that her daughter, Emma, resented being "forced" to attend her mother's political events. She explained:

> She grew up in that trough, being born in the 1970s. She doesn't come of age until really that land of the 1980s and she didn't become…[an] activist but she spent most of her life on picket lines, demonstrations, or whatever. She used to quip: "The only time I've ever seen Washington was to stand in front of the Pentagon or the White House with a barricade, a police barricade, demonstrating. I never saw the Smithsonian museums or why people really go to Washington."

According to Sabrina, the lack of wider context and specific strategies to engage her daughter's political interests and her daughter's resentment that her mother spent so much of her time on political activism, contributed to Emma's "resistance to struggle." She stated:

> It's been a resistance to not having more of my time because I was always at a meeting.…I always tried to build her into it but we haven't learned as activists that if we're going to take our children with us we have to provide a way for them at their level to participate and feel engaged. We haven't done that well.

Reflecting back over her attempts to incorporate her daughter into her political activities, Sabrina now recognizes the limits of such strategies. Missing from her efforts and those of other activist parents were approaches that would permit their children to engage in their own way and through their own interests and abilities.

Furthermore, many of the community workers complained that their children's needs were sometimes put on hold as the political demands on their time increased. Sabrina defined broadly the needs for nurturing. Not only did one's children require care, but all those participating in activist struggles need to be nurtured. Sabrina complained: "We don't nurture each other as activists. You know, we just drain each other, requiring more work, more work, more work, more work." She felt that activists were so caught up in the day-to-day struggles that they rarely took time to play or socialize without an activist agenda.[1]

In our discussion of her twenty-two year old daughter Emma's activist orientation, Sabrina at first emphasized Emma's "resistance to struggle." After some reflection she remarked that her daughter has yet to come into her own political personality. However, later in the interview Sabrina noted that Emma was particularly concerned with environmental issues such as protection of dolphins and other sea life—an activist arena in which Sabrina was never particularly interested. Sabrina commented on her daughter's environmental interests and analyzed the process by which she believes young people develop their own political visions:

> And I think that like the tomato soup commercial of years ago when the two guys are there stirring the thing and one says, "Well, did you put peppers in the sauce?" "It's in there." "And did you put onions?" And he says, "Yeah, it's in there." And he says, "Well, did you put the garlic in?" "Yeah, it's in there." "You mean it's all in there?" "It's in." I think my kid is in process and all the values and the experiences are in there, and what I want for her is to be able to sort out within a value context where she's going to make her stand. And so if she can commit to dolphins and clean water, ultimately they're mammals and they might translate back to humans.

Sabrina did not view Emma's interest in environmental concerns as a legitimate focus for political activism. For Sabrina, it appeared that environmental activism was acceptable only if it directly benefitted human beings. Sabrina has no interest in building coalitions with groups advocating for environmental issues in their own right. While she was concerned that her daughter would not continue the legacy of activism she bequeathed, Sabrina also narrowly defined what would be acceptable political engagement.

One of the major reasons that people might resist becoming active in social movements on their own behalf, according to Sabrina, is the risk of jail or even death. She discussed these fears in the context of her own political history as well as what her daughter might have internalized. She contrasted the risks of activism with the comforts promised by compromising and living within the consumer culture.

> Because I think some of the legacies of the movements were also, you died. You were assassinated. They will kill you....You know when people realized you go to jail or you died [they became fearful]. And I think this country never faced the hour in that way like they have in other countries. And so when they finally rise up, they're willing to sit in those risks, you know. And I don't think it has to come to that. I just think that's the message....You can be happy and have more clothes and more hair and more lipstick and have more boyfriends and money and cars, and housing and marriage and whatever....[However] if you choose this way you will go to jail, and you will die, you know. And...I think those meta-messages are always there, as well as the constant devaluation of cooperation, collectivity, [and] community building.

As Sabrina's perspective suggests, rather than understand children's resistance to the struggle for social justice as a consequence of their more politically conservative worldview or as individual self-interest, we must examine the extent to which awareness of the physical attacks, arrests, and assassinations of progressive community leaders—especially those connected with the Civil Rights Movement—effectively discourages activism among black youth. Those who were brought up in activist households were particularly situated to witness the extent of police harassment and other forms of intimidation against outspoken community leaders like their mothers or fathers. When placed up against the comforts that accrue with a more sedate middle-class lifestyle, the risks of political resistance appear even greater.

Children of activist mothers who witnessed the dangers of participation as well as the extensive time commitment required by community work might be discouraged from engaging in community-based struggles for social and economic justice as Sabrina argues. However, even those who wished to continue the legacy faced a different political environment that shaped their political perspectives and political strategies in ways that diverge from their parents' approach to politics. Class location further influences the political possibilities for younger activists. As a consequence of their activist mothering on behalf of their children, the community workers mobilized resources and social networks that contributed to their children's upward mobility. Children of activist mothers who achieved middle-class status and who continued the legacy of community work and political activism did so with a different relationship to their communities and through different political strategies as Michelle Dodge's narrative (presented in chapter one) highlights. Loss of community-based programs combined with an increase in poverty within the low-income communities that were the target for the War on Poverty also inhibit the development of younger leaders from these communities who could continue the legacy of community work.

## Activist Mothering: The Next Generation

Ensuring the intergenerational continuity of community work posed a central problem for the women in Philadelphia and New York City as their energies and goals changed with age. Throughout their careers, the community workers encouraged younger members of their communities to continue the struggle against injustice and for racial and economic equality. The community workers modeled a lifelong commitment to this activist work and contributed to their children's personal political formation. They also served as political mentors to other young people in their communities and educated them about how racism, classism, and sexism contoured their social location. The community workers developed strategies to train other members as activists in their communities and to pass on the legacies of their struggles (also see Gilkes 1988). As Carlotta Mendez bluntly put it in 1995:

> I'm a woman in my 60s, and I came out of college in my 30s and have been active all these years so I'm talking to [other] women [and we wondered]…where the hell is the next generation. And there was a gap there….Yes somebody has got to pick up. In twenty years I'll be dead!

Despite their desire to pass on the torch, those who held dear the philosophy of personal freedom and autonomy to choose one's life path were reluctant to impose their life choices on others. For those who wished to instill a sense of obligation in their children and other younger community members to "give back" to their communities, the shortage of viable progressive leadership and alternative political institutions further interfered with their efforts. Lack of a wider political context in which progressive views and democratic political activities are legitimated and supported increased the obstacles the women faced as they sought to pass on the legacy of community work to the next generation. Yet, despite these obstacles, many of the women proudly discussed ways their children and other younger community members continued as activists in their own right.

### Activist Daughters and Their Political Socialization

Several days before one of our interviews in 1984, Gloria Alvarez's youngest child fell ill, forcing her to miss a demonstration for low-income housing on the Lower East Side that she helped to organize. She recounted:

> I couldn't attend that one because my five year old had a very high fever, and I had to take her to the hospital. And I was mad because I wanted to attend that demonstration, and I ended up at the hospital, and they didn't find anything wrong with her. [I asked myself]: "Why am I sitting here when I should be at that demonstration?"

While Gloria could not attend, she was pleased to know that her oldest daughter, age twenty-one at the time, went to the demonstration. She was proud of her daughter who also loved to participate in their community's struggles. She said of her daughter, "She takes after me. She's very active. She's a fighter, too!"

The community workers modeled activist mothering, often with unintended influence on their children's political socialization. Elsie Rodriguez, a Puerto Rican community worker in Philadelphia, believed that her son and daughter learned from her example and continued the community-work legacy. She emphasized that they "saw me working and how I got involved....I was an inspiration!" She believed she was especially influential in her daughter's life: "And that's why my daughter, I feel, she's very active. She's even more active than me, because she's already started and she's very young, and I've encouraged this in her."

Maria Calero of New York City also described her oldest daughter, Elena, as "a real activist" who attended "lots of community meetings" with her mother when she was growing up. Maria enthusiastically shared, "I really love her. I really respect her. And we disagree, we have political disagreements. She's much more idealistic than I am." Maria also proudly characterized her younger daughter Becky as a "humanitarian," someone "concerned about the cruelty of human beings against human beings."

While her oldest daughter was particularly interested in struggles against class inequality during the mid-1980s, Maria said that Becky was most intent on fighting against racism. Their different political perspectives often generated tensions for the two sisters. However, Maria respected each daughter's views. Maria said her only concern was that they both grow into their own political visions. In 1984 when I asked if she thought that her own activism influenced her daughters' political commitments, Maria responded:

> Oh, my God, yes! Sometimes I even worry about that. Sometimes I think Elena is caught in the sixties ,'cause she went to all the meetings with me. And I have this fantasy that she wants to re-create the sixties. And I feel very sad about that, 'cause I want her to just create for today's reality. I don't want her to re-create the sixties, the problems of the sixties, the so-called movement.

In 1995, Maria further remarked on her daughters' political development and worried about how they viewed Maria's contemporary political engagement. Maria was working as a multicultural educator for a private organization located far from the poor neighborhoods of New York City. She was concerned that her daughters might now see her as a "sellout." Yet in separate interviews with her daughters, it is clear that they continue to hold their mother in high regard. Both sisters said they were strongly appreciative of the political education they received from both their mother and father.

Like many of the community workers interviewed, Elena Calero emphasized that she became "more political" than most of her peers because of the exposure she received growing up. As she explained, "the framework was there" so that when "I experienced...what felt to me like direct racism, direct classism, I think I kind of understood what [my parents] had been saying—you know, like things made sense somehow. Although [high school] was probably a real bad time to have to learn those lessons." After years of struggling against the inadequacies of the New York City public-school system, Elena's mother decided to send her to a private high school. Here Elena faced both racism and classism. Following a painful period of adjustment, Elena decided to organize other students against the discrimination they encountered. She credited her mother's validation and role modeling for helping her resist internalizing the negative messages and subsequently to fight against them. Elena described that period of her life as follows:

> And then I went to this high school and then I had a really...bad experience and just felt very much like "other" the whole time I was there. And I think that...and the fact that I was validated at home. You know, it wasn't like she would say, "Oh, no, no, no, you're just overreacting!" You know, if I came home and said I heard this terrible joke, or this was

said in class, she would acknowledge that, yeah, I was in this basically all white environment of rich, rich kids, and I wasn't going to fit in. So I think if I had not been, you know, being raised in kind of a politicized environment that confirmed my own thinking...And so I was free to kind of go off to school and become little miss organizer after school. So I do think that's important. If you don't have the support and that your parents say, "oh, just fit in and get over it," you probably reacted differently. And...I think the lesson of being "other" is so profound that, you know, if it happens to you at five or if it happens to you at fourteen, or if it happens to you at forty, it just changes your whole perspective on life and the world....I have friends who went into all white boarding schools, but they didn't have any support at home and they, like, lose it, you know, have nervous breakdowns, become drug addicts. So I really think the fact that I had a politicized home base enabled me to kind of get through it by the politics. Because I became [a major organizer]....I tried to organize the few [students of color] in high school, the students who were there, and that was very hard for many of us.

Elena's awareness of how racism and classism construct people as "others" who feel apart from the dominant society was established by her parents early in her life. When she began to face the consequences of these processes, she drew on these lessons and took a leadership role in fighting against the racism within her high school. She drew courage from her mother's support and, through these struggles, began to develop her own political personality.

When Elena graduated and went on to college, she was so relieved to be out of that oppressive environment, she recalled, that her activism "just took off!" She was particularly active in the Latin Students Association. She felt she was a "step ahead" of her classmates because of the "indoctrination" and familiarity with critical perspectives she received from her parents. She recalled:

So sometimes I would get really frustrated because they wanted to process stuff and I wanted to organize stuff. 'Cause to me, I knew what the problem was. It was very clear to me. Whereas they were like, "Well, is it this or is it that?" And I would say, "No. We need more students. We need support....We need to have an admissions policy that looks at XYZ issues. We have to have scholarships available, etc..."

Elena understood that her political socialization prepared her for the leadership role she assumed in college. She explained how this early training and her own leadership qualities brought her to the attention of the school administrators as well as her peers:

And...that's how I rose to be a leader, I think. Because I just happened to have been able to figure a few things out faster and not [that I was] smarter, just because I had been raised around people who constantly built political houses...and then the other thing was, I think...I obviously...had leadership qualities. [And] the deans would encourage it in me. We had two deans who were just wonderful, wonderful people and they really would push me....[Well] you see a group and you see someone with a big mouth and...you use those to help you shape the group...I got a lot of attention from some of the deans and that would kind of feed into [my being] like a leader.

Elena was surprised when her mother would "react negatively" to her activism and ask about her studies. She was, she admitted, putting more time into organizing than into her schoolwork. However, these struggles prompted her subsequent decision to pursue a career as a lawyer. Although Elena said she regrets how dogmatic she was at the time, she now views it as "a phase in my life," one that further prepared her for her career in public interest law.

In 1995, Elena was employed by a legal advocacy agency where she worked to improve education, housing, and legal services for the poor. She credits her mother for instilling in her the belief that women can hold important positions in the world while also fighting for social justice. She was concerned that too few girls learned this lesson growing up:

And I think there's a whole class of young girls who have absolutely no idea that there are judges and lawyers who are women and so it concerns me....And I think you need to know that. I think you need to see those people. I mean, I think I am clearly who I am because of my mother. And I saw that when she didn't agree with something, she fought against it. She was involved. She went to meetings, and I didn't like it because she came home late, and we complained because we had to make dinner. But now in retrospect I am very clear that I am who I am because of my mother. And you know, I think she's unique, to be honest with you. I know my friends don't have mothers like her. Some have professional mothers, some have regular traditional mothers, but none of them are like her.

Elena grew to appreciate the value of her mother's activist mothering as she developed her own activist identity. Over time, it became clear to her that friends who had "regular traditional mothers" missed out on the political socialization that shaped much of her personal values and professional life.

## Dynamics of Race Ethnicity in Political Praxis

Elena and Becky Calero, whose father was of white North European descent, both commented on the dynamics of race-ethnicity within their family. Their narratives highlighted how such dynamics differently shaped their personal political biographies. Throughout their lives, they had to negotiate their mixed racial-ethnic background that has also divided them from each other in painful ways.

Elena is able to pass as white and recognizes how her skin privilege cushions her from the more explicit forms of racism that neither her sister nor mother can avoid. When she is in a public place with her mother, she must bear witness to the negative treatment her mother receives. But Elena is also concerned that race is used as the central factor to explain the problems in this country and that "there's a big class difference in this country and if no one talks about it, you know, then it bothers me." She explained:

> And I believe that race is a big part of what motivates this country and why things are done the way they are [in the United States]. And I totally know that when my mother and I go someplace I get treated one way and she gets treated another way. And I know that, and so I don't discount the power of racism, but I also think that perhaps there are class issues....And I know so much about that kind of [wealthy] life, the other world, because of [attending the private high school]...I've seen it, observed it, [and was] close up to it. And then also to be really poor and I just know [what] that's like.

It is possible to conclude that because of her skin privilege, Elena's class position became more central to her politics. In contrast, her sister, who does not benefit from the whiteness in her biracial background and has a large network of black friends, centered racism in her political analyses.

Becky emphasized that Elena "looks straight up white." She explained, "She doesn't look interracial to me. She looks like a white girl. And me, people never know what the hell I am!" She reported that most of her friends are black and that, especially when she is out with them, she has experienced harassment from police and others. She described a number of frightening and abusive incidents and commented that they happen, not once a week, but "in between frequent and infrequent." More recently, she has experienced incidents she described as "very subtle":

> And if you're not aware then you would think I was crazy for saying there's such racial tension....If you're white and you don't have any black friends that you are with all the time, then, no, you're not going to notice. You're going to think everything's beautiful, the world's beautiful, 'cause you're never going to feel it. But because I'm always around my black friends, it happens. And we're tuned into it. We're aware of it. Certain times it can be very subtle.

When I asked her if she felt her mother prepared her for the racism she faced, Becky remarked that she was "raised so proud" and that she has become more aware of how racism works as a consequence of her friendships with young black men and women.

By linking Becky's and Elena's political perspectives with their racial-ethnic identities and differing experiences of racism, I evoke the historical materialist claim that "epistemology grows in a complex and contradictory way from material life."[2] This analysis also demonstrates the complexity with which racialization processes operate within families as members negotiate the dynamics of racism in the wider society.[3]

## Dynamics of Class, Status, and Political Context

Having a mother or father who is politically active in his or her community is not a guarantee that a child will continue as a community worker or
develop similar political beliefs. Several women interviewed in 1995 pointed out that while their children hold progressive views they are not as active
as their mothers or, if they are politically active, they channel their activism
through more traditional political clubs and institutions. Like Sabrina
Brock, several other community workers thought that their children had
enough of community activism as a consequence of growing up in an
activist household. As Lydia Montalvo said of her children, "I think that
they sort of feel sometimes like that's too depleting." She believed it best
not to "force them to care about these things. I think that that is something
that has to come from them naturally." She is, however, "hoping that"
interest in activism "will come."

Lydia shared a recent experience that both encouraged and amused her.
She and her two children attended an event honoring the Young Lords. She
was an active participant in the Puerto Rican Young Lords during the late
1960s but, she explained, her children had not really understood what that
participation meant or how the group had fought for justice on behalf of
the Puerto Rican community. She reported:

> I took them to this event [a showing of a film on the Young Lords] and
> they were kind of intrigued. And, oh, my gosh, you know, "Mother,
> you associated with these revolutionaries?"...And they thought that
> was very cool. Because, I would guess, maybe they didn't see me quite
> in that realm....And so they got very intrigued and they wanted to talk
> to all these people...and [ask] what did I do.

While she was encouraged that her children's interest in political activism
was piqued, she recognized that "It's not the same time. It's not the same
environment." Moreover, as her children grew into young adulthood, Lydia
said she could not identify any viable political organizations that would
speak to them. Like Lydia, many of the community workers expressed sadness at the lack of a broader progressive political movement in which
younger people could focus their political passions.

In addition, most of the community workers' children have improved
their social status and class position as a result of attaining professional
degrees—oftentimes a direct consequence of their mothers' activist efforts
on their behalf. Their upward mobility removed many of these young people from the low-income communities in which they grew up. It also put
them in contact with other more middle-class friends who do not share
their political views or commitment to political activism. Becky Calero was
frustrated that none of her friends wanted to participate with her in different struggles against injustice, but she was unwilling to wait for them to
join her. She missed a more activist engagement with her environment and

felt compelled to channel her political concerns. She confessed, "I feel like I need to be more [politically active]. I feel like I'm not doing enough. It's starting to really itch me. So I feel like I'm not doing enough. I need to get out there more. I need to start going to more rallys, doing more stuff." For Becky, the activist model set by her mother imprinted itself on her to such an extent that she is uncomfortable in a more passive role. Becky said she wishes "there was something like the [Black] Panthers" where she could direct her political concerns.[4] Her longing for a group like the Black Panthers reflects the centrality of antiracist work in her personalized politics.

> I just don't feel like there's anything out [there like that]. I would definitely turn my little house into a Panther place where everyone could come and luckily back then that's when there was really possibilities of major changes happening....I just don't feel like there's anything [now]. There's no place. I don't even know where to go to find anything to get involved with to make a change.

Becky was especially frustrated with the negative tenor of the dominant discussions on welfare, poverty, crime, and race relations. She explained:

> The discussions at the different levels, you know, local, state, and federal, it's just so negative, and people blaming one another—mean-spirited. That word just keeps coming back to me. There's just something mean and, you know, inhuman about the solutions they're offering.

Becky had yet to find an outlet for her political concerns generally. Since she did not feel attached to any particular geographic community, she was not drawn to any particular community-based struggles.

In contrast, Nina Reyes's daughter Johanna, who no longer lived on the Lower East Side, remained active there in community-based struggles, particularly to improve education and housing. As someone who no longer lived in the community, she acknowledged the challenge of finding a clear role for herself in these struggles. Johanna was trained as a lawyer and worked as a lobbyist for expansion of low- and moderate-income housing in New York City. Her status as a middle-class professional also altered the nature of her relationship to the low-income community in which she grew up. Johanna moved from the Lower East Side where her parents continued to perform community work to a middle-class suburban neighborhood north of New York City. However, she said she felt more affinity with the issues confronting residents of the Lower East Side than she did in the neighborhood where she now resides. Johanna participates in the community-based struggles as a board member of a Lower East Side community organization. She travels after work to attend community meetings and offers her legal expertise to various campaigns for social justice. She related, "Well, to me it's like this…unofficially I live on the Lower East Side. And my involvement and my heart and everything is on the Lower East Side. And so for all intents and purposes this is where I live."

While many of her peers in the professional world were concerned with financial security and maintaining an upper-middle-class lifestyle, Johanna's commitment to social justice pulled her in another direction. She viewed her parents as role models for her and commented on how their special interest in helping people overrode their concern for status and wealth. Johanna explained:

> I think it takes a special kind of people to do public-interest work. I think you generally have to have an interest in helping people. If you're in it for just the job or just the money you can just forget it. Because, it's not—for what you put into it—you cannot be compensated economically. You really can't, you know. I feel that my mom has worked at [a local community organization] for thirty years and when you come to see, and even my dad, when…it will come time for them to retire what they will have for a pension is nothing. How they dedicated their life!…Really!

In contrast, she felt that "what most people do is you try to choose higher and higher and higher so that you can have some kind of economic status." For Johanna, the lessons her parents taught about fighting for social justice overrode her concern for achieving a secure middle-class lifestyle to a certain extent.

However, despite her commitment to fight for social justice, Johanna experienced conflict with her boyfriend whom she described as "a real go-getter and he's very entrepreneurial and he wants to make money." When she returns to the Lower East Side she sometimes feels caught between these two different worlds.

> Sometimes I do [feel cornered] because, you know…I've studied…a lucrative profession and most people go into it because they want to make money. And for me, I think very little about making money, although I won't lie to you, I do want to make money…but that's not the driving force. I mean, I can't think of anyone that'll say they don't want to make money, but I don't think that's the driving force [for me].

Johanna often had difficulty trying to negotiate the tension between her personal politics and the middle-class professional world she inhabits with her boyfriend. When I asked how she balanced the two worlds, Johanna explained that she drew on her deep connection with her parents to resist distancing herself from her community of origin. Community activism was a family affair:

> But I think in that sense my parents' interest has really driven me....We've always been involved in voter registration drives. I mean, I could remember being eleven and twelve years old sitting on Delancy Street with my parents on hot summer days and registering people to vote, you know. I can also tell you my mother's always been involved in elections. And it's kind of hard to just talk about my mom without talking about my dad because a lot of the things have been joint things that we've all done.

As a vital member of her family, Johanna felt drawn to contribute to the community actions deemed important to her parents. She did not describe her involvement as obligatory. Rather it was a natural extension of her concern for her family and the community in which she grew up. In this regard, Johanna's description of her community work coincided with that offered by the older generation of community workers.

The community workers who as activist mothers educated their daughters and sons about the wider political environment said they did not expect their children to follow directly in their footsteps. Most hoped that their children would continue their educations and advance to more middle-class lifestyles and were both surprised and pleased when their children incorporated an activist stance into their professional work. Yet, as Sabrina Brock's comments reveal, underneath expressions of support for their children's choices were often strong expectations that they contribute to their communities in some significant and recognizable ways.

## Passing the Torch

Passing the torch to younger people included communicating the value of antipoverty, antiracist, and antisexist work to others residing in poor communities. Yet the community workers also remained sensitive to the structural barriers to political participation and community work faced by poor urban residents. In addition to the economic and social decline of their communities, a major frustration experienced by some of the community workers was that many people do not remember the history of the struggles fought in their communities. Consequently, the community workers, resident and nonresident alike, viewed passing on the knowledge they gained after years of community activism as a major component of their work. However, what counted as important historical moments and cultural experiences to pass on varied greatly.

### Constructing Community and Constituting the Legacy

Close examination of differences across the oral narratives revealed divergent definitions of community that partially explained the diverse perspectives on, and approaches to, what constitutes the legacy of community work. For example, Carlotta Mendez and Francine Evans emphasized contrasting notions of "community" in descriptions of their community work. Carlotta defined her community in nongeographic terms as Puerto Ricans stateside as well as in the Commonwealth. She wished for continuity of cultural identity among Puerto Rican youth and worked toward the development of educational and political forums to educate them about their cultural history. Carlotta's political approach to training new leadership that emphasized their identities as Puerto Ricans contrasted with Francine's more geographic emphasis. However, since housing segregation reaffirmed racial-ethnic and class homogeneity, Francine inevitably evoked the centrality of race-ethnicity as well as class in her political construction of her geographic community. Not surprisingly, as a consequence of her approach to "community," Carlotta had long focused her community organizing on a citywide basis while Francine remained attached to her geographic community throughout her thirty-five years of community work.

In 1995, Carlotta Mendez directly tied her satisfaction with her community work career to the development of new leadership and spoke enthusiastically about her efforts to support the political socialization of Puerto Rican youth. Carlotta was one of the few community workers who also emphasized the need to educate the youth from her racial-ethnic community about their cultural history. Among other initiatives in this arena, she worked to establish "a course on Puerto Rican history and culture for the core curriculum of New York City public high schools." She discussed the importance of passing on Puerto Rican cultural history and political identity to youth with reference to an annual Puerto Rican youth conference her organization sponsors. The leaders in her organization feared that

> the kids…would get caught up in the larger black thing or youth thing and what you have to do is pull them out and tell them we have a slightly different focus because we are committed also for the last thirty years to a reinforcement of the cultural self. You have to have an identity in this country. You can't be an American. You have to be a Puerto Rican. Everybody has some sort of hyphenated identification in this country even if your white European, Irish American, German American. With us it's even more critical because we're people of color so that is also of concern and they're only going to get it through this type of thing [the Puerto Rican youth conference].

Ironically, Carlotta's emphasis on identity politics did not match the perspectives offered by Becky and Elena Calero and Johanna Reyes who did not define their identities as Latino or Puerto Rican as the primary basis through which they saw their political engagement. While Becky centered antiracist work in her construction of how she would like to focus her political energies, she did not build it exclusively around her Latina identity. It is also fascinating to note that neither Becky, Elena, nor Johanna centered their gender identities in discussions of their political analyses or political activities—although all three did express some affinity for feminist issues.

## Constructing Feminist Identities

While Carlotta and some of the other Puerto Rican community workers stressed the need to organize separately as Latinas, the younger women did not express such an interest. Johanna Reyes said she defined herself as a feminist and thought that it was important to have protections for women in the workplace. She described some experiences with sexual harassment and was relieved to know that she would have some legal recourse if the situations became more difficult to handle. But she offered the following assessment of her relationship to feminism:

> So in that respect I am a feminist because I feel that we should have equal rights. I still like for a man to open the door for me and some feminists are totally against things like that. They're very what I'd call hard core in the sense that they want everything equal. I still like being a lady. I still like being treated like a lady and respected.

Johanna's analysis of the value of equal-rights legislation and laws against sexual harassment for her position as a professional women mirrors that of earlier generations of liberal feminists. However, she was quick to say that, despite her views on feminism, she enjoyed "being treated like a lady." In this regard, her view of feminism and femininity contrasted with Carlotta's approach. Carlotta, who was thirty years older than Johanna, emphasized that she did not want to be treated differently by men.

Becky Calero's argument with feminism was less about constructions of femininity, than about priorities for action. While Becky said she would define herself as a feminist, she felt that the real focus needs to be on male youth. Given the terrible "statistics" and life chances of a young black male in today's society, especially with regard to unemployment, imprisonment, and police harassment.[5] Becky felt that more attention needed to be paid to their problems than to issues affecting women and girls. She explained:

> I would definitely say I'm a feminist. But I guess to me the emergency that is going on is our male youth. So that's my only focus. I really feel that we have no men, no leaders coming up. Our male youth are in trouble big time. And our women are in trouble too. The young girls, the young black women, the young Hispanic girls are not doing so great either. But…boys really need some leadership. They really do. I think they're in big trouble. So to me that's my focus. You know, 'cause black males are the ones who are getting most discriminated against. They're the ones who are getting beaten up.

Since Becky understood that the Women's Movement and feminist organizations, by definition, were not interested in the problems of young men of color, they obviously did not provide institutional sites through which she could address her political concerns.

Elena expressed more conflict than her sister about using the term *feminist* to describe herself. She felt that the divisions between women's groups on her campus and tensions between white women and women of color, and between heterosexual women and lesbians associated with the feminist groups on campus deterred her from considering herself a feminist. Her ambivalence over adopting this political identity is unmistakable in her response to my question, "Do you define yourself as a feminist?":

> Not really. It's funny. That term is so loaded, that I…don't call myself a feminist. But to me it's just like the way things should be. I don't know, the term was so loaded in college. We had so many fights with the women of color and the white women and the gay women….So I have to say I did develop a disliking for the term, but I felt it does apply to me….I really admire the feminist movement and I know that I wouldn't be where I am without it, so I'm totally grateful and indebted, you know….[But] it's weird because I have to say it's not a term I use in my vocabulary very often….It's not what I think of when I think to describe myself. Whereas if you ask me, I probably would never say feminist. I would say a lot of other things.

While she felt indebted to the feminist movement for making possible her access to a career as a lawyer, she preferred to use the term "activist" to describe her political identity. She further explained her complicated view of feminism assessing the feminist platform from her vantage point as a Latina community activist.

> And I believe in social justice. Like, I probably would not say I'm a feminist. I'm not exactly sure why, except that it has negative connotations on that, going back to college. But I read feminist literature. I buy feminist literature. I don't send money to white feminist organizations, but…I believe in abortion rights. Probably the platform. I probably totally support one hundred percent the feminist platform, although now there are all these different splinters. I do wonder if the abortion issue should be at the top of the agenda. I can't say that they've totally convinced me, you know. And I think that sometimes it worries me that that's what turns a lot of people off, even though I totally believe in abortion rights and I'm not at all pro-life.

Elena's discussion of what feminism means to her reflected similar points raised by some of the older Puerto Rican community workers. She wondered, as did they, whether abortion should be the top priority for the Women's Movement although she herself is pro-choice. Furthermore, since she believed that many women have moved into professional positions, she did not feel the urgency that Carlotta Mendez felt in claiming feminism as a political identity.

In many ways, her interest in encouraging young women corresponds with Carlotta's concern for developing the leadership skills of Puerto Rican youth. However, Elena centered class in her analysis rather than racial-ethnic identity. She asserted the need to instill in working-class girls the belief that they could enter jobs that were traditionally male-dominated. She explained:

> I'm not convinced yet that [feminism] has yet had an impact on the girls who go to public school....I actually do make a point of going to the schools and I am probably more proactive than some people because I don't think that they see women [in professional jobs]. I don't think they know that [women can be lawyers, for example] and they don't know it because it's not part of their world and they don't know the difference. Like I know the difference. I know what it's like to have all male teachers and I know what it's like to not know any [women] lawyers and like there were few [women] lawyers and doctors, and so on, but they don't know that difference. So you can tell them, "Oh, there are more women lawyers and more women doctors" but it doesn't really have an effect on their lives, and so I don't think they are able to model themselves, and so I think it's a class issue that needs to be developed. And I think there's a serious class issue in this country. I think that we can talk about the race issue and even that we feel uncomfortable talking about, but we never talk about things as a class issue.

Elena was interested in serving as a role model for young working-class women whom she felt would not have the opportunity she did to see that women could become professionals.

## Training the Next Generation

Carlotta Mendez described in great detail her approach to nurturing young leadership in poor New York City neighborhoods. She stressed training them in decision-making strategies and political debate usually associated with middle-class America. She explained:

> Kids in usual American middle-class [communities] learn how to sit on committees. That's what this world is all about and you shouldn't wait until you are thirty to do it. You should learn how to do it when you're eighteen. Sit on committees. Negotiate across the table. Reach out for resources. So you let them do all of that because it is a learning experience and they usually don't do it until ten years later. I have made a commitment that it will happen. We will find the monies to make [the Puerto Rican youth conference] happen

but we also trust them [to organize the event]....And we help them do that. But it is also exciting because they may say to give us an example "we want green curtains" and I may come back that I think they should be white curtains. I love it when they give me a hard time and argue against me on a point, and I don't care whether I win or lose the point, I just think it is exciting to sit in a room with kids that are learning how to argue a point. And they may not see that is what is happening. But I enjoy the hell out of it to see them arguing a point against me and willing to take me on and not accepting that I know best. And that is all what drives me and excites me, getting our kids to think, understand, compromise and negotiate positions, and not to accept that age means that [they have to always follow what their elders say].

Carlotta enthusiastically reported on her work to assist Puerto Rican youth in organizing an annual conference in New York City. She felt it important to define the conference around the interests of Puerto Rican youth rather than open it up more generally at this point because, she explained, "they get a sense of comfortableness with themselves and how to wheel and deal and we [the Latino community organization]...continue to reinforce that that [youth conference organizing] committee operate pretty independently."

Carlotta's interest in educating Puerto Rican youth about their cultural heritage connects to the fear expressed by many of the community workers that the lessons gained in the course of political struggle would be lost. African American community worker Francine Evans was especially artic- ulate about this process. Speaking from her back room office in a storefront on (what was in 1984) one of the most desolate streets on the Lower East Side, Francine Evans shared her frustration about the loss of historical per- spective on the successes achieved during her thirty-five years of commu- nity work. She was disturbed by the way some of her neighbors merely acquiesced to the government cutbacks and to the increased bureaucratic elaboration in the institutions serving her community that evidenced a lack of respect for the residents—in part a consequence, she felt, of the loss of historical memory. She described how she worked to increase participation among the very poor of her neighborhood and to increase their under- standing of the struggles waged on behalf of poor people on the Lower East Side. Francine detailed some of the important, albeit subtle, gains she wit- nessed in her own community work. She believed that "a lot of people can't see" the changes "because they weren't part of it."

I have a lot of people going out and saying, "Well, there's no blacks [participating]." Well, I know better. I'm out there every day. And when I need their support, they're there. So that when you listen to them [the critics] and they don't know what they're talking about, you really feel ashamed.

Francine tied the lack of awareness of the ways in which blacks in her community participate in local struggles to the general loss of historical memory about these campaigns.

By way of an example Francine referred to a successful community action designed to maintain a local health facility in her community and discussed how most community members now seem unaware of this history. She recalled a recent meeting at the clinic

> where we were screaming about the long wait...and this one woman got up and said, "Well, every hospital has it's own way!" Francine angrily responded, "This isn't every hospital!" It was built by the people on the Lower East Side and one of the things we said, we weren't going to sit down there hour after hour waiting for our medication; nor were we going to sit there hour after hour waiting for doctors who tell us to be here at 8:30 in the morning and they don't come in until eleven. This was not everybody's hospital. This is [our hospital]!

Francine remembered the hospital as "a well-run multi-ethnic facility" and demanded that the history of the local struggle for control over the facility be passed on to current community residents.

Francine Evans is a large, commanding women. She recalled, with satisfaction, an encounter she had with a police officer who tried to block her from the medical center when the residents were struggling for community control of the facility. She recounted:

> So I was walking up the stairs one day and this great big cop was coming down. I said, "You know, there's not room for two of us on this stair. I would suggest that you go home sick today because I intend going up those stairs. And it doesn't make me any damn difference which one of us goes down..." And I continued up the steps and he continued to back up. So we got to the top and I went on in the office.

As a result of this meeting with the hospital administrators, the community residents were given an office in the clinic. She told the officials, "That doesn't mean that I'm going to stay the hell out of here. I intend to be here every day to know what's going on." She was placed on the hospital's advisory council but made it clear that she would not be a token member. Her active involvement made the administrators "very, very angry," she recalled.

Francine's extensive community work experiences led to her belief that "if you continue to battle along the same line, meeting after meeting," those in power "have to give in."

> Because as you get different people heard...so that the rooms that we used became increasingly crowded and more and more people turned up. We went to a picket line and that resulted in our getting our own

office. We had an office right there in the facility. We knew when the
doctors came in and went back out again.

The long, slow struggle paid off for the community residents. They gained
a voice in the operation of the hospital as well as important organizing
experiences that they parlayed into other struggles for community control
of neighborhood services such as education and housing.

Francine recognized the crucial role she played in encouraging others to
struggle for change. She said that she now understood

> that a lot of people who were fighting for change got their strength and
> their faith in what they were doing from me. They hadn't been in a sit-
> uation like Resurrection City, and not been to conferences where they
> met people from all over the country. So that all they saw was what was
> happening on the Lower East Side. And every now and then you hear
> someone say, "We can't get that changed." We can, and we will. The
> change is gradual.

Francine emphasized that her extensive experiences in community organizing and her participation in the Civil Rights Movement gave her a broader
understanding of the slow, gradual progression toward social justice.

### Limits to Leaving an Activist Legacy

All community workers agreed that the development of new leadership was
vital to the ongoing survival of low-income communities. The African and
Puerto Rican women were especially emphatic about the need to ensure the
continuity of their work. For example, Elsie Rodriguez said she would like
to give up the ongoing struggles to improve life in her Philadelphia community; however, she feared that no one would replace her. She complained
that there's a "lull" in the struggle for civil rights and explained that it
"burns" her up to see the attitude of young people today who say, "Well,
that's not our problem. Let George do it." Eve was ambivalent about the
cause of this attitude. Is it selfishness or fear about the state of the world
that causes young people to ignore the needs of their community?

> I have to catch myself, because everyone is not the same as me. And
> maybe when they get older they'll start getting involved. Right now their
> thing is survival— 'me first.'...But I tell them there won't be any "me"
> if people don't get with it and they'd better snap to it real soon. 'Cause
> at the rate they're going, I don't know what's going to be....It is
> scary!...We're just a breath away from people destroying the whole
> world. It's very frightening!...They're aware of it. They're just freaking
> out. They think the drugs are the answer to it. It's too much for them.

Although she understands why young people in the 1980s were not taking
an interest in their communities, she resents them still "because they're not

paying any dues." Her response to those who complain about the society is, "What the hell are you doing about it? That's my answer to them. And I don't think I'm being unsympathetic. It really makes me angry!" After fifteen years of community work, she's tired and she "feels like resting" because, she emphasized, "It's a long haul!"

Francine Evans was particularly articulate about constraints on political participation experienced by the poor who "work the worst jobs for the least amount of pay." She described how she taught young people about the ways the rich people "make a fantastic profit off the backs of" poor people. She also talked about the work that mothers do "cleaning in hotels and people's houses. They work in the dress factories, with the noise plus the fatigue, pushing the material into the machines, that goes on for five days a week." Because of the tiresome work that poor people must perform in order to earn a living "they don't feel like coming out to a board meeting," she said. In the following quote, Francine illustrated how she encouraged the involvement of her poor neighbors while acknowledging the constraints in their lives that interfered with their full political participation.

> I've seen them in meetings just nodding off. "Why don't you go home?" I'd ask. "You're sure I don't have to stay?" they'd say. And I'd tell them, "But your name is on the attendance sheet. They know you were here." And they go on home.

Francine was concerned for the young people growing up in poverty. She explained, "The children are hard hit because it takes two salaries to run a pig sty." She described the contradictory experiences of young people who grow up in poor housing watching the wealthy lifestyles of those on television.

> And the clamor of landlords saying they don't make any money....They live in nice houses and these people live in crap. They're not gonna fix a window that's broken. They're not gonna fix a ceiling when it falls down. So that we have the most horrendous housing....But the children are seeing terra-cotta kitchens on TV, baby blue bathrooms on TV. They don't live like that. And they know the difference.

As a consequence of the discordance between their lives as poor people and that of the rest of American society, Francine finds that "a lot of times [young people from her low-income community] are nodding out, copping out." She defined the physical and emotional consequences of living in poverty as the primary factor inhibiting collective action and the historical memory of social change efforts.

Most community workers expressed concern that the young people in their communities were confronted with so many negative social influences that they may not survive their childhood years. Children living in poor neighborhoods are faced with gang warfare and other forms of violence, drugs, sexual abuse, and other social ills that profoundly limit their capacity to work on behalf of their communities. In 1984, African American community worker Mrs. Delia Parsons described her concern over the increasing drug problem among the youth as well as the growing problem of prostitution in her Lower East Side neighborhood.

> Drugs are a terrible problem down here. That's gotten much worse. I would say the past ten years is a whole different world....Wherever you go, people are yelling out on the street what they're selling, and you don't get used to things like that. It just can't be. And you see so many of our children caught up in this, and it's a quick way to make a dollar, and they're all involved, and then you see young people over there, prostitutes. It's mind boggling! And sometimes you just try to erase it, 'cause what can you do? So, it's terrible!

Mrs. Parsons did not know "what's going to happen to this [younger] generation" and did not see "much hope" for young people living in poverty in her neighborhood.

African American community worker Marcy Barnett found the 1980s a "very hard time for young people." Economic restructuring of the workforce had increased the problems of unemployment and underemployment for those younger members of Marcy's Philadelphia community. Many could find only part-time, low-wage positions that offered few benefits and little opportunity for advancement. However, Marcy believed that part of the problem in developing new leadership in the 1980s in Philadelphia was that older people refused to step down to make the way for the younger generation. She stated that, "if we as older people keep the job, then what are the younger ones going to do?"

> You have to help young people on their way. That's the only way the world's going to keep turning. And they keep on becoming discouraged...and you have to help them how you can....Young people tell me I'm very easy to talk to, and they like to talk to me because I encourage them....Everybody needs words of encouragement. As old as I am, I need it sometimes too.

For those young people interested in helping to improve the quality of life in their neighborhoods, most of the women interviewed in 1995 felt that few neighborhood organizations serve as local sites where younger community residents could develop their leadership skills and learn about the legacies of the struggles fought on their behalf by the foremothers and forefathers. With the increase in homelessness, unemployment, and drug abuse, many of the remaining community-based organizations in low-income communities that were the target of the War on Poverty are fighting more basic battles for economic and social survival than they faced in the late 1960s.

## Conclusion

The community workers' activist mothering and political analyses influenced their children's political commitment to a certain extent (although, of course, the relationship is not determinant; namely, not all of their children became political activists nor shared their mothers' political analyses). On one level, class mobility reshaped their children's attachment to a specific low-income or racial-ethnic community. On another level, the shift in the larger political environment during the 1980s and 1990s limited the sites through which the younger generation could find a locus for their political activism or gain leadership training.

Less visible to the community workers was the process by which their definitions of community (the basis upon which they built their community work careers as well as their political analyses), served to limit how others could be drawn into this form of work. For young people who gained professional status, the geographic sense of community work may not serve as a basis for their political engagement especially in the contemporary conservative context. Furthermore, community as defined by specific racial-ethnic identity no longer held sway for younger people like Elena and Becky Calero who are from multiracial backgrounds or who are embedded in racially diverse friendship networks.

In 1995, neither Elena, Becky, nor Johanna Reyes identified their Latino background as the primary dimension upon which they constructed their personalized politics. Elena did describe a period during her college years when she centered her Latino identity; however, in her early thirties, her activist energies focused on fighting poverty and classism, although many of those on whose behalf she worked were people of color. Becky, in contrast, was primarily interested in fighting against racism in a broader political context than cultural identity politics permits. And, of particular note, is the lack of centrality for gender politics as expressed by the younger women. While each of the daughters interviewed would define themselves as feminists, they do not articulate their political interests with explicitly feminist organizations or causes. Clearly, a sample size of three cannot provide the grounds for a more confident assessment of the complex intersection of gender, race, ethnicity, and class in the political analyses developed by the community workers' children nor in the political motivations of younger women more generally. However, these findings further highlight the limits of analyses of political participation that fail to explore how shifting constructions of community influence political identities and the formation of a personalized politics.

Of great concern to many of the community workers was the loss of historical memory about the struggles fought within their communities during the many years in which they had been active. Community workers, like Francine Evans, discussed ways they tried to keep the memories alive as well as the limits to these efforts. Most described the pressures faced by young people growing up in low-income urban neighborhoods, as well as how hard parents had to work to support their families on minimum wage jobs, as primary factors inhibiting participation in community action. While the resident community workers, understood the constraints, most expressed frustration that so few community members were ready or able to take up the torch. These concerns became particularly salient as the community workers' reached retirement age or grew weary of the never-ending battles against inequality and injustice. As with other dimensions discussed throughout this book, the community workers did not hold one common position on how to encourage new leadership or on what were the important lessons to share. Also evident in the narratives of those community workers who were most interested in promoting younger leadership was the central role the older women continued to play in their neighborhoods and wider community. While they expressed a firm commitment to passing the torch to younger activists, they inadvertently may have monopolized key decision-making roles and defined political agendas in ways that marginalized newer actors.

In the final chapter, I consider the relevance of lessons garnered from the oral narratives of the community workers for contemporary discussions of the welfare state. To wage a renewed war against poverty, I highlight the need for broadening the definition of labor to include work in the community, the value of community ties for fighting against poverty, and the importance of empowering low-income residents to participate in the political institutions that shape their social and economic lives.

**Part V:**
**CONCLUSION: LESSONS FOR A RENEWED WAR ON POVERTY**

# Chapter 8
# SHIFTING STANDPOINTS ON POLITICS AND THE STATE

Key to the feminist project of the last thirty years is a reconceptualization of the term "politics."[1] Feminist research demonstrates the extent to which women's militancy has been masked by the traditional categories used to assess political action.[2] Furthermore, because most discussions of politics assume individual self-interest as a motivation for participation, contemporary political analyses rarely incorporate actions that derive from a concern for the collective good or commonwealth. In addition, when we adopt a definition of politics that is limited to voting behavior, membership in political clubs or parties, and running for public office, we obscure the political practice of community workers, the grassroots warriors. Since much of the community workers' activity occurred outside the formal political establishment, traditional measures underestimate the extent of their political participation. Many of the resident community workers I interviewed rarely engaged in electoral politics, especially through established political parties, although many participated in voter-registration drives. Few expressed an interest in running for public office. Rather, they challenged the authority of city and state agencies, landowners and developers, and police and public school officials. They maintained a close watch over the actions of elected officials to ensure that the interests of their communities were served. Furthermore, they were vocal participants in community-based protests against racism and other forms of discrimination in their neighborhoods.

The political analyses and political practices described by the community workers developed as a dialectic between ongoing personal and collective experiences of injustice. Changes in the wider political economy and shifting historical political forces at the local neighborhood, city, and federal levels further shaped their perspectives. The women brought their personal, political, and work histories into negotiation with these shifts and developed some overlapping as well as disparate political visions and practices. On the one hand, participation in common struggles did increase the sense of connection among participants even when backgrounds differed. Through ongoing and localized struggles many resident and nonresident community workers came to share political strategies and views on empowerment. On the other hand, the resident workers were less likely than the nonresident women to define their commitment to community work as politics, although they were quick to acknowledge how and why they were forced to act in politically recognizable ways.

The contestation over what constitutes politics was evident in many of the resident community workers' narratives. The dominant discourse on political participation highlights activities associated with traditional political parties, electoral campaigns, and self-promoting interest groups. While more radical political actions such as demonstrations and strikes were recognized as politics, many of the women interviewed differentiated these forms of protest from traditional politics on the basis of a distinction between collective versus self-interested actions. This is not to say that the community workers did not understand the political nature of collective action, rather they distinguished between the individual, self-promoting class basis of traditional electoral and interest group politics and collective campaigns for civil rights and economic equality. Within this broad-based distinction, however, less agreement was found in their explanations for the continuing poverty in the United States or in the specific strategies they found necessary to counter economic and social inequality.

From analysis of these women's narratives, I identified a broad-based notion of "doing politics" that included any struggle to gain control over definitions of self and community, to augment personal and communal empowerment, to create alternative institutions and organizational processes, and to increase the power and resources of the community workers' defined community—although not all of these practices were viewed as "politics" in the community worker's terminology. Analysis of women's community work provides insight into the valuable political analyses  derived from a localized or grounded political practice, as well as the constraints of such praxis. Despite the limits placed on their political efficacy by the processes of bureaucratization and professionalization, the resident community workers in this study can be viewed as "organic intellectuals" in local struggles (Gramsci 1971).[3]

The community workers developed their political philosophies in dialogue with the concrete activities that shaped their daily resistance to inequality and injustice. However, as their narratives illustrate, they do not necessarily produce similar analyses nor adopt parallel political strategies (also see Katznelson 1981)—although significant patterns were evident in their relationship to the dominant political arena.[4] The themes of community control, access to the political process, and concern for the quality of life and equitable treatment of residents in their communities was woven consistently throughout the narratives of all the community workers, nonresident and resident alike. The variety of issues they addressed in their communities—variously defined—required their participation in a wide array of specific political strategies including testifying at public hearings, organizing voter registration drives and educational forums, performing legal advocacy, and speaking before community groups and the media as well as leading public protests. Their paid employment as community workers offered one more site through which they fought for the rights and well-being of their communities as they defined them.

Racial, ethnic, and class differences were evident in the career trajectories as well as the political analyses offered by the community workers. This book demonstrates how gendered identities as women, daughters, mothers, or workers intersected with racial, ethnic, class, professional, and political identities to create a complex and oftentimes contradictory set of forces that informed their consciousness of inequality as well as motivation to fight for social and economic justice. Since political socialization takes place across many spheres of social life, the oral historical method helps explicate how and why women of different racial-ethnic and class backgrounds engaged in community work on behalf of themselves and other residents of low-income communities and how their political practices changed over time. Most community workers, especially those from poor and working-class backgrounds, articulated the importance of early childhood experiences for shaping their commitment to fight injustice. They honored the memories of those who served as models for them as they developed their own political analyses and skills. In honoring these memories, they also recognized their responsibility in passing on the legacy of community work to younger members of their communities.

Many resident community workers interviewed for this study described their community work as a logical extension of their desire to improve the lives of their families and neighbors. Most detailed a variety of community problems that sparked their initial community activism; although most resident community workers described problems with the public schools as the most significant specific catalyst for their political mobilization. In addition to struggles to improve the quality of their children's schools, the resident workers became involved as community activists as they confronted a range of issues in their neighborhoods including health care, housing, sanitation, crime, and safety. Not surprisingly, the problems they addressed in their work shifted in response to changes in the local political economy, although some of the community workers remained committed to one or more specific arenas such as childcare, housing, education, health, or food policy.

The community workers stressed the role of personal experiences with racism, sexism, and poverty for enhancing their commitment to community work as well as deepening their political perspectives.[5] Throughout their daily lives they fought against racism and class oppression. However, they also defined their commitment to community work through their gendered social positions as mothers and community caretakers. In this regard, they expressed an overriding concern for enhancing the connections among community residents to sustain the fabric of their communities.

For most African American and Latina community workers, concern for their geographic community overlapped with concern for their racial-ethnic community; therefore, they also described their community work as designed to promote the rights of African Americans or Puerto Ricans or Latinos. Few African American resident community workers I interviewed felt a need to organize separately as women. However, while many of the Puerto Rican community workers identified such a need and did, in fact, help create Latina organizations, they rarely described political campaigns in which they worked with other women's organizations. Out of the sixty-four community workers I interviewed, only Lydia Montalvo mentioned working in coalition with gay and lesbian groups. This organizing effort was connected to a community-sponsored art exhibit that featured gay and lesbian artwork. Lydia received complaints from some community residents when she arranged to present gay and lesbian images in the community show. She reflected on why she encountered such resistance in the South Bronx: "I mean a community like this knows that we have gay people, but actually being confronted with images that remind them that there are gay people and yet they're still part of this community, is something that they're not always interested or willing to [deal with]." Despite pressures from some residents in her community, Lydia felt it important for the community-based art museum to feature the lives of all of the diverse members of the community. However, most other community workers felt that gay and lesbian issues were marginal to the priorities they set for their community work. As Sabrina Brock remarked, "I've supported my friends who are gay, but that's the one movement that I haven't actively participated in in any strong way." By 1995, some shifts had taken place. Most illustrations of coalition-building efforts were given by Latino community workers and related to collaborations between Latino organizations and AIDS health-services programs sponsored by gay organizations.

By doing "just what needed to be done," the resident community workers in this study contested the analytic separation of unpaid work from paid labor, personal interests from public issues, and nurturing from social activism. On the one hand, by putting their radical politics or religious commitment into professional practice, the nonresident community workers challenged the processes of racial segregation and class divisions said to undermine the development of a cross-class and cross-race Women's Movement. On the other hand, constructions of community used by the resident community workers to identify who comprised their social and political constituencies also tended to reinforce some of these divisions. For example, as mentioned above, gay men, lesbians, and others who did not fit into the normative heterosexual paradigm did not appear in most community workers' accounts of their "community."

The community workers' experience of communion developed through ongoing geographic, antiracist, and antipoverty struggles in varying urban neighborhoods under shifting political-economic circumstances. Participation in these struggles over an extended period of time brought the perspectives of the resident and nonresident women closer together. As resident community workers took their personal concerns into their paid work and the nonresident workers brought their religious and political ideologies into their paid positions, both groups challenged the hierarchical and regulatory methods of the social service establishment. Their perspectives began to merge as the resident women advanced in their careers and the nonresident women developed closer ties to the low-income communities. In some cases, resident workers who attained advanced degrees did relate a more professionalized social service discourse in subsequent interviews.

The professional socialization process further revealed the contradictions in the New Careers philosophy. To advance in their careers, many community workers felt that they needed to complete a college or graduate-level degree. Years of employment in community organizations that grew more bureaucratized and professionalized served to temper the community workers' political activism to a certain extent. As the political environment around them grew increasingly conservative and the problems in their communities escalated, many community workers moved into service provision and away from community activism and policy advocacy. However, regardless of credentialed status or political perspective, the resident community workers believed that they were uniquely qualified to interpret the needs of their comunities and that their special relationship with their communities informed how they viewed their paid community work.

## Political Participation and Institutionalization

Carlotta Mendez's evaluation of the Economic Opportunity Act and its emphasis on maximum feasible participation of the poor reflects the sentiments of most of the community workers whose oral narratives formed the basis for this book. She enthusiastically reported:

> It provided the training ground for people to learn how to do things, even though a lot of it was infighting....It paid them wages and it gave them responsibility and people moved out of that parallel structure and into the mainstream. And when people say that the only thing that the program did was to give people jobs—it was the most important thing it could have done!

The expansion of local citizenship and community-based employment that occurred during the War on Poverty, and highlighted in Carlotta's account, stands in stark contrast to the constriction of citizenship and urban disinvestment that characterizes contemporary policy context (see, e.g. Slessarev 1997).

The community workers firmly believed that the key contribution of the community action programs was the involvement of residents, particularly women from the communities in which the programs were established. Women as unpaid community workers have had a tremendous impact upon the state. In fact, women's unpaid work and community activism were essential for the formation of the U.S. welfare state. Social reformers such as Jane Addams, Mary McLeod Bethune, Florence Kelly, and Frances Perkins crusaded tirelessly to expand the state's role in social welfare.[6] In addition, women's activism opened new spaces for middle-class women's paid employment within the state. Along with the development of paid work in the fields of social welfare, health care, and education that accompanied the expansion of the welfare state, some middle-class activists found leadership positions within the state.[7] The War on Poverty provided spaces within the state for women of color from working-class backgrounds to receive pay for the work they performed on behalf of their communities.[8]

The incorporation of low-income women as community workers in government-funded programs highlighted the "lines of stress and disjuncture" (D. Smith 1987, 204) in the institutional arrangements of the state. The workers contested the state's limited definition of paid labor, narrow interpretations of community needs, arbitrary bureaucratic demands, reliance on credentialed knowledge as a basis for decision making, and the separation of politics or political action from state provisions of social welfare. But state-sponsored employment also changed the nature of the work most notably by pressuring community workers to temper radical political activism.

The process of institutionalization also compromises the political efficacy of social movement organizations as Frances Fox Piven and Richard Cloward (1977, 317) emphasized in their discussion of the National Welfare Rights Organization (NWRO). Some analysts also argue that the gender politics within the NWRO contributed to the shift away from grassroots organizing on the part of the national leadership. While welfare mothers initiated and led welfare-rights groups in different cities prior to the founding of the NWRO in 1966,[9] the national organization emerged in 1966 under the leadership of former university professor George Wiley. Guida West (1981, 367) reports that "conflicts over male dominance...gradually surfaced and led to fragmentation" of the NWRO.

Like West, many movement participants and feminist scholars emphasize how movement organizations and other institutions reproduce gender inequality, although they are divided over the extent to which these institutions can be transformed through feminist activism.[10] Hester Eisenstein's (1995, 69) analysis of femocrats[11] in Australia counters Kathy Ferguson's claim that "bureaucracy and feminism are natural enemies." However, Ferguson (1984, 4) asserts that since "the bureaucratic organization of public life directly controls the work of most women who hold jobs outside the home and affects the entire society in a way that is antithetical to the goals of feminist theory and practice, it is a crucial target of feminist concern." She defines "the best avenue of resistance to bureaucratic capitalism" as the "formation of alternative organizations," but recognizes that "this is not an option readily available to everyone" (p. 208). In fact, this solution is most out of reach for organizations located within low-income communities.

Researchers concerned with the political empowerment of low-income neighborhood residents recognize the limitations of community-based organizations. These constraints relate to the problems of bureaucracy, dependency on outside funding, and increasing control over staffing and program design by state funding and licensing agencies. Many writers agree that problems of bureaucratization lead community organizations to focus inward—toward their own survival—rather than continue to effectively serve their communities.[12]

In Philadelphia, the community workers described how they became incorporated into the centralized bureaucracy and how their ability to engage in political activities was quickly circumscribed. New York City community workers complained about the ways professionalization undermined their claim to expertise as experienced community workers. As a partial consequence of these interrelated processes, along with the increased conservatism in the wider political environment, by the mid-1990s many women in both New York City and Philadelphia were more involved in the provision of services than in the community activism and advocacy that characterized their community work in the early 1970s.

## Policy Innovation in the Short-Lived War on Poverty

Many observers point out that attention to black America during the War on Poverty created the grounds for backlash against antipoverty measures during the 1970s. The perception by the white middle class that they were footing the bill for ever-increasing services to the poor led to diminished support for welfare state programs, especially those that targeted specific groups and neighborhoods.[13] Other analysts highlight how the service orientation and decentralized implementation strategies of the War on Poverty sabotaged the establishment of a national assault on unemployment which would offer a more effective way to counter poverty.[14] For example, Daniel Patrick Moynihan (1969, 187–88) wondered: "Would it not, then, have been wiser for the antipoverty program to direct its efforts to the creation, for example, of trade union organizations in minority groups, using the contracting powers of the government and the protective sanctions of The National Labor Relations Board to create units of economic and political power, which, once established, would thereafter have an independent life of their own?" Margaret Weir (1988,183) further argues that the control offered to African Americans during this period over particularistic local programs "reinforced incentives for black leaders to seek race-specific policies" rather than more "universalistic solutions" (p. 183). By targeting African American unemployment specifically rather than the problem of unemployment more generally, antipoverty strategies in the mid-1960s inhibited the establishment of a multiracial coalition to press for broader structural solutions. Weir concludes that "the racial targeting of the War on Poverty helped to create the conditions for a powerful backlash that would severely damage prospects for meaningful cooperation between blacks and labor in support of employment programs" (p. 184) and "created rifts in local Democratic coalitions by providing meager resources that became the focus of contention" (p. 185).

Yet, as this analysis of women's community work demonstrates, the dynamics of gender and race within the War on Poverty also had unintended consequences for politicization and political participation of residents in low-income communities as well as for the establishment of community organizations through which they could express their political interests. Without such experiences and the expansion of community-based institutions it is unclear how these residents might have participated in more broad-based coalitions to fight for structural solutions to poverty and unemployment. While I agree with Weir's general critique, I argue that without a more contextualized understanding of the way in which the claims of "community action" and "maximum feasible participation" were taken up in practice and served as a framework for broader political participation of low-income individuals and their communities, we should not close the book on this period of social policy innovation.

Commitment to maximum feasible participation of low-income residents has disappeared from the welfare reform legislation of the 1980s and 1990s. Emphasis on comprehensive, multiservice community-based approaches to fighting poverty has receded from public discourse along with calls for local community control over the assessment of community needs and design and implementation of antipoverty programs. While contemporary welfare reform stresses individual state control over the reduced funds for social support, it does not legislate that community residents and welfare recipients have an active decision-making role in program design, resource allocation, and implementation.

The Community Services Block Grant program through which the CAPs have been funded since 1981 was touted by some federal legislators as a model for the contemporary block grant approach to welfare reform. Since the Personal Responsibility and Work Opportunity Reconciliation Act of 1996 drastically reduces the funds available for low-income residents, it will undoubtedly increase the rate of poverty more generally and place further demands on the remaining community workers and the CAPs (see, e.g. Center on Social Welfare Policy and Law 1995). As Jane Jenson

(1997) points out, demands for decentralization in the name of democracy and moving social services closer to local communities, opened spaces for "off loading" of the fiscal problems of the other levels of government.[15]

By strengthening and developing community organizations in poor neighborhoods, policy designers of the War on Poverty expected to enhance the mediating institutions in which individual residents could gain the skills, education, and resources to move out of poverty as well as to improve the quality of life for all those living in these neighborhoods. Further, the hope was that participation in these institutions would increase poor residents' sense of connection to the wider social world and improve their access to resources outside their neighborhoods. By gaining experience in decision making and acquiring leadership skills, these residents would develop the necessary framework for participating more fully as citizens. New Careers has long since been replaced with a narrowed conceptualization of Public Service Careers and incorporated into the professional social-service hierarchy. As the women I interviewed retire, it is unlikely that they will be succeeded by younger community workers. However, their political analyses and organizing strategies have much to teach us about effectively waging a renewed war against poverty. Analysis of the community workers' experiences and perspectives demonstrates the significance of three key lessons: (1) a broadened definition of work to include socially meaningful labor in the community; (2) attention to mechanisms for developing and sustaining the social ties that link residents to each other and to social institutions; and (3) procedures that ensure a broad-based form of participatory democracy.

While it seems foolish to envision a renewed war on poverty given the contemporary shift away from comprehensive state-sponsored antipoverty measures, progressive policy analysts must generate alternatives to the coercive behavioral measures that dominate contemporary poverty debates (see Naples 1997b). With the narrowing of citizenship rights through welfare, immigration, and anti-affirmative action policies of the 1990s, antipoverty and civil rights activists must reintroduce broadened notions of community action and maximum feasible participation into the discourse on social welfare.[16] At the very least, this effort will help direct attention to the structural conditions that create poverty, the communities in which low-income women and their families reside, and the valuable work that low-income women perform on behalf of individuals and families living in poverty.

Focus on community-based employment, community action, and maximum feasible participation will not replace the need for a broad-based coalition of groups to press for structural solutions to poverty, discrimination, unemployment, and underemployment. However, analysis of urban women's community work illustrates how community action and maximum feasible participation operated in practice and served as a framework for broader political participation of low-income women and their communities. Some analysts credit the War on Poverty with an increase in the number of African American and Puerto Rican male elected officials in cities like New York and

Philadelphia.[17] However, the CAPs also provided the training ground for resident women community leaders as well. The legacy of their leadership continues in the political commitment of some younger members in their communities—although not as many as the community workers would hope. While the contemporary political and economic context does not encourage progressive political action, the commitment to social justice remains strong in the hearts and voices of the young women I interviewed—a small sample indeed, but an encouraging finding nonetheless.

Certain programs established through the War on Poverty have demonstrated their ongoing effectiveness and continue to receive state support. They include Head Start,[18] Upward Bound, and neighborhood-based legal services. Although these and most other social-welfare programs are also facing cutbacks in funding and political support, CAPs continue to serve low-income residents across the country and have not been specifically targeted for extinction.[19] According to David Bradley (1997), Legislative Director of the National Community Action Foundation, in 1997 almost 99 percent of all U.S. counties were served by community action agencies funded through the Community Services Block Grant, the program through which community action programs have been supported since 1981. This represents an increase of almost nine percent from 1981. Many of these agencies play a central role in providing emergency food, heating assistance, and clothing for those living on the economic edge of our society—although decreases in funding and increases in need are placing great strain on these programs and their staff.

The legacy of the War on Poverty's policy innovations in the areas of New Careers, community action, and maximum feasible participation is particularly manifest in women's community work in low-income communities of color. Many of the community workers employed during the War on Poverty continue to provide essential service and advocacy for members of their communities. They developed special strategies for confronting the problems of poverty, illiteracy, homelessness, and hunger in their neighborhoods which, if utilized, could greatly enhance social welfare policy design and implementation.

## Lessons for a Renewed War on Poverty

Thirty years after this nation declared its War on Poverty, the poor are still with us and those who live and work in poor communities are once again invisible (Harrington 1984)—except when they appear to pose a threat to more privileged individuals or neighborhoods. Poor single mothers with children are currently the targets of coercive welfare-to-work programs. The passage of the Personal Responsibility and Work Opportunity Reconciliation Act in 1996 dims any glimmer of hope for a comprehensive attack on poverty in this country—at least in the foreseeable future. This legislation officially ends Aid to Families with Dependent Children (AFDC), the program established by the Social Security Act in 1935 to provide financial assistance to poor mothers and their children. While the level of assistance varied from state to state and rules for proving eligibility often made claiming state assistance difficult, those who qualified for financial need were entitled to state support. The 1996 legislation requires recipients to work within two years of receiving benefits and limits lifetime receipt of public assistance to five years—no matter what financial need remains. It provides block grants to individual states with little federal oversight, disqualifies legal immigrants from receiving food stamps and Supplemental Security Income, and gives states the option of denying other forms of assistance to noncitizens. The dismantling of AFDC—an important, albeit imperfect, system of financial support to the poor—forms one aspect of a broad-based assault on the welfare state in this country. However, the salience of a discourse emphasizing paid work as one way to end women's dependence on public assistance opens the door for a renewed discussion of the state's role in providing jobs, especially in low-income communities.

Many progressive policy analysts have outlined the economic measures that would help to redistribute resources in this country including: increasing the minimum wage, adopting comparable worth measures,[20] expanding government support for child care, providing paid parental leave, establishing a national health care system, increasing availability of low- and moderate-income housing, improving access to public transportation, cutting corporate welfare, and eliminating tax exemptions that permit high income individuals and corporations to keep large percentages of their wealth. Other measures include enforcing antidiscrimination laws in the workplace and policies against violence against women, extending kindergarten from one-half to a full day, expanding after-school programs, adopting sick-child and elder-care leave policies, and increasing support for drug and alcohol abuse programs. However, the context in which, or processes through which, such policies are developed and implemented rarely receives attention. In fact, without considering what counts as socially meaningful work, how to build and sustain communities, and how to promote democratic processes, antipoverty efforts will ultimately fail to move us toward a more economically equitable and socially just society.

## Supporting Socially Meaningful Labor

Contemporary strategies to fight poverty emphasize behavioral measures such as workfare and render invisible the economic factors that contribute to poverty in America (see Naples 1997). The Personal Responsibility and Work Opportunity Reconciliation Act of 1996 exempts the government from responsibility for ensuring that jobs are available for welfare recipients forced to find paid employment. Given this policy context, policy analysts and antipoverty activists need to explore the state's role in job creation—

particularly jobs that can benefit women on public assistance as well as low-income communities more generally.[21] Community work funded through the War on Poverty accomplished these complimentary goals; although, as discussed above, they were constrained by the processes of social control and institutionalization.

This state-funded form of community work stands out for initially permitting community workers the flexibility to respond to community needs as they defined them. However, several noteworthy antipoverty measures that predated the passage of the EOA also stressed the development of dignified work for unemployed and underemployed residents. As Nancy Rose (1995) details in her historical analysis of U.S. government-funded work programs, the federal government sponsored other approaches that respected individual dignity and choice; understood, to some extent, the need to provide child care for workers with children; and offered above-poverty wages for some workers. These programs can also serve as models for supporting socially meaningful work as well as for countering assumptions that government-sponsored work programs only create "make-work" jobs. Of course, labor organizers remain concerned that the creation of such jobs, especially public-service employment, will be used to replace union-protected labor with low-waged disenfranchised workers.[22] Critics of government-work programs are not mistaken when they worry about this process of worker displacement.[23] However, it is possible to envision government support for socially meaningful work that carries with it the right to unionization, union scale (or at least above poverty) wages and other benefits, and would not create a second tier workforce.

Most community workers emphasized the need for job creation to counter some of the problems of low-income residents. However, many, like African American resident community worker Vera Lane of Philadelphia, were critical of the government's efforts to address this issue. Vera was also skeptical of the job training programs, "unless there's a job at the end of the training." She believed that job training that offered "no place to go" at the end of the training "was worse than no training at all." Vera was more satisfied with the Comprehensive Employment Training Act (CETA) that created jobs for those trained in the programs.[24] Rose (1995, 179) explains that CETA-funded employment included "a variety of socially useful jobs" (also see Hallman 1980). CETA workers found employment in battered women's shelters, neighborhood organizations, and childcare programs and were trained in nontraditional jobs in construction trades, among other fields.[25] But, as Vera observed, most training programs typically did not enhance the employability of those originally trained. And, not surprisingly, many of these training programs included gender-stereotyped assumptions about women's employment.[26]

The racialized and gendered division of labor in contemporary society operates to maintain women, especially women of color, in paid and nonpaid caretaking roles that are devalued both ideologically and economically. The feminist literature on women and work emphasizes the relationship between the work women do in the home and the work they do in the paid labor market.[27] As professionals, women find work as teachers, nurses, and social workers. When they enter male-dominated fields such as law and medicine, they are found in "female-stereotyped" aspects of these fields such as pediatrics or family law.[28] In sex-segregated jobs, women comprise the majority of childcare workers, waitresses, clerical staff, and nurses' aides. Furthermore, women of color, who are disproportionately working as domestic workers and other low-paid service workers, occupy even more disadvantaged economic positions within the segmented and segregated division of labor (see Amott and Matthaei 1991).

Feminists argue for a revaluing of caretaking activity as one strategy to correct the economic inequities between men and women.[29] Women's work lives are intricately bound to their household and family responsibilities. And men's labor force participation benefits from the gender stratification in the paid labor market and depends on women's unpaid service in the home.[30] Social welfare policy historically separates nurturing activity from the category of "productive labor." The work women perform in maintaining the social fabric of neighborhoods, communities, and social institutions is rendered invisible in this separation of productive or wage labor and unpaid social reproductive work. As an extension of their mothering role, women are expected to facilitate their children's homework, support community recreational programs through their volunteer labor, and maintain links with social welfare agencies to obtain necessary resources or support for the family.[31] Women, as the primary caretakers for elderly parents and other sick relatives, are also expected to negotiate with physicians, nursing homes, and health insurance companies. Women are also the main source of unpaid labor for churches and other social institutions. Women living in low-income neighborhoods must work to contest poor housing conditions and inadequate education and health care services while attempting to sustain their own households. All of this unpaid labor sustains the social fabric that constitutes viable communities.

As a consequence of this racialized and gendered division of labor, many women find themselves performing a triple day—as family caretakers, paid workers, and unpaid community workers. For many of the women interviewed for this study, their work on behalf of their communities predated the state's recognition of its importance for low-income communities. Their paid community work strengthened their effectiveness as unpaid community workers and their unpaid community work continued to shape their paid work. However, the triple burden circumscribed the time they had to spend with their families—a loss they often regretted but felt was a necessary price to pay for improving the quality of life in their communities.

The state depends upon women's unpaid work as consumers of social welfare services and as mediators between the state and other targets of social welfare such as children, the elderly, or disabled (Sassoon 1990). In addition, because of women's central role as unpaid and paid community workers, decisions by the state to decrease spending for child care and health care and other services have profound effects on their lives. The community workers I interviewed described how they tried to take up the slack left by the withdrawal of state-supported services in their neighborhoods. Policy designers, whether consciously or unconsciously, expect and rely on women to perform these functions, yet rarely provide childcare or other supports that would assist women in their triple day as family caretakers, paid workers, and unpaid community workers.

To a certain extent, through their hiring practices CAPs recognized the importance of the work women performed for their low-income communities.[32] By distinguishing between the contributions of resident community workers and outside professional experts, New Careers served to legitimate indigenous experience as a form of knowledge, which, in practice, surfaced women's social position as community caretakers. As the New Careers philosophy asserted, due to their close connections to low-income residents, the resident community workers expressed a special sensitivity to the needs of their neighborhoods and recognized how class conflicts and racism further impede the process of social reform. As a result of their unique perspective as women living and working in low-income neighborhoods, they viewed their responsibility to educate community residents as well as social service professionals with the same significance as providing needed material resources and services. They brought their activist mothering into their paid community work and explained how they attempted to counter ineffective approaches used by professionals and bureaucrats employed by the state. They used their paid positions as a resource for their activism although most also described ways in which their employment in state-funded programs interfered with their ability to express more radical political opinions or engage in radical political actions. Over time the nonresident community workers said they deepened their understanding of the economic, social, and political needs of those living in low-income neighborhoods.

Resident community workers in particular felt that the CAPs provided important organizational locations for them to develop political analyses that reflected the different parts of their identities. As the support for the antipoverty programs waned and economic problems increased, the community workers drew on a shifting set of personalized political beliefs in order to make sense of their continued commitment to community work. While some patterns are observable across their narratives, a wide array of ideological perspectives and political practices are also evident. Woven throughout the community workers' discussions of political perceptions and community activism were constructions of community, variously defined in geographic, class, and racial-ethnic terms. The emotionally engaged, albeit shifting, definitions of community offered by the community workers formed the grounds for their political commitments and sustained their activism over periods of disillusionment and economic decline.

## Constituting the Community Context to Fight Poverty

Much of the important community work performed by low-income women remains invisible to the wider society due at least in part to the popular belief that low-income people and poor communities lack social organization and strong community networks. Furthermore, the class bias that characterized most studies of volunteerism and community work overlooked the more informal and loosely defined voluntary community-based work of low-income women.[33] However, as this study demonstrates, low-income urban neighborhoods are often rich in churches, informal neighborhood groups, housing associations, as well as extended family relationships that provide a context for residents to share their personal and political histories as well as analyses of social problems and solutions attempted or envisioned (also see Feldman, Stall, and Wright 1998). Many of the community workers first developed their commitment to fight for social justice on behalf of the poor through these social institutions. Yet as poverty increased in their low-income neighborhoods, informal volunteer efforts became less and less effective.

The state's intervention in low-income urban neighborhoods during the War on Poverty led to the development and elaboration of a network of community-based programs some of which continue to provide vital services, including educational and employment opportunities. More important, these programs play a key role in transmitting knowledge about local history and political struggles that help create and sustain an identifiable sense of community within inner-city areas. Despite evidence that voluntary and community-based organizations offer low-income people an important site for empowerment and continuity of collective action, several factors compromise their effectiveness. To begin with, there has been a decline in the number of community-based organizations since the early 1980s. As John McKnight and John Kretzmann (1984, 17) point out, the organizations that remain "are precisely those publicly funded service agencies that are least capable of producing results no matter how hard a community organization confronts them."

Living conditions have deteriorated in many of the low-income neighborhoods that were the targets of the War on Poverty despite the extensive work accomplished by the community workers. As a friend and previous colleague asked Marcy Barnett of Philadelphia, "Marcy, what do you think we really did while we were out there working?" She recounted her response:

> I said, "You know, when you're on the inside looking out, you feel like you didn't do anything. You really, really feel like you didn't do anything." It almost brings tears to your eyes, thinking of all the negotiating you did with the community…the blood and tears that you've used.

As problems increased in the low-income neighborhoods, women experienced greater difficulties as they attempted to perform or promote community work.

Increased unemployment among the poor intensified the burden on the community workers and contributed to their added frustrations as they attempted to help their neighbors and other community members. African American community worker Dottie Storm recalled that in the 1960s in Philadelphia "it wasn't that difficult to try and find someone employment; but now it is really hard. We don't even have anywhere to refer them." The lack of employment coupled with the increase in housing costs has drastically increased the number of people faced with homelessness. The community workers all agreed that the lack of affordable housing was one of the most consistent problems faced by residents in their low-income communities. The process of gentrification forced many low-income residents from their homes. As Dottie emphasized:

> And people are out there with no income, nothing to pay their rent, no place to live. They're sleeping on the street. There have been lots of changes....It's kind of frustrating because you're not able to refer these people or give these people a helping hand....They can go to the shelter, but only stay in there two or three days.

Because of the loss of low-income housing on the Lower East Side, the only housing that the poor can still afford is in the projects located along East River Drive. However, Francine Evans believes that the low-income residents of the Lower East Side will not give up their community without a fight. She stressed:

> Although we still have the problems we originally screamed about ...we are not about to jump into the river like the lemmings. And what we're saying is that we need to build buildings, about one hundred of them, for those people who live here and are now doubled up and tripled up....We are about the business of redoing our own community and sticking with it.

And like many of the other community workers, Francine believed that too many wealthy people uninterested in the plight of the poor are elected and that "the only way we're going to affect change is for many, many, many people to get involved."

All of the community workers were greatly frustrated by the growth of problems in their neighborhoods especially compared with the great wealth of so many other Americans. African American community worker Naomi Barker believed that although her Philadelphia community "has been going downhill," she reported, the community-based organizations and the churches "all banded together" to provide "food cupboards, clothing, help with fuel." She believed that the antipoverty programs helped enhance this manifestation of community. And, like many of the other community workers interviewed, Naomi emphasized the importance of the community-based organizations controlled by residents for countering the problems of poverty in their neighborhoods.

From the standpoint of the community workers in New York City and Philadelphia it also becomes clear how fragmentation of social life into discrete policy arenas fails to capture the mutually constitutive relationships between family income, childcare, health care, housing, education, employment, and so forth. One significant feature of the state's approach to social welfare is the treatment of social life through disparate and, oftentimes, contradictory policies. Childcare is shaped by provisions for the enforcement of child abuse, foster care guidelines, state funding of childcare, enforcement of standards for childcare programs, tax credits, among other legislation. Health care is influenced by Medicaid and Medicare policies and insurance and tax legislation. Employment policies are also fragmented into separate areas: minimum wage legislation, antidiscrimination policies, health and safety guidelines, unemployment compensation, and tax abatements—to name just a few. Related programs are often administered by different government agencies through conflicting bureaucratic guidelines. And all have an impact on the lives of low-income families. Clearly, a strategy designed to fight poverty in America must recognize the interrelationship between all areas of social life.

The Economic Opportunity Act incorporated a mechanism for assessing the multiplicity of community needs from the point of view of local residents. Initially community workers were granted greater authority to define and respond to these complex needs. The local CAPs were envisioned as sites through which residents could gain help with myriad of problems, from employment training to parent education to counseling to health care. These comprehensive multiservice and neighborhood-based programs attempted to address the full range of needs, including political empowerment, that would help people living in poverty improve their lives. However, the community workers quickly encountered a series of social, structural, and economic problems that could not be resolved at the grassroots level. As the community workers labored to implement strategies to address the political, social, and economic problems of their neighborhoods, they confronted resistance from public officials as well as the social service establishment. However, they continued to envision new ways of solving the problems faced by their neighbors, friends, and family members, although bureaucratic pressures and funding cuts often interfered with their ability to implement many of their innovative strategies.

Visions for the future emphasized by the community workers included predominantly people-centered economic development and humanitarian insights. The community workers offered specific recommendations that they believed would help sustain and improve their communities. Vera Lane, for example, discussed the need to create jobs and improve the housing in her neighborhood in order to "build up communities." She also stressed the importance of giving community residents a say in how their neighborhoods should be developed. Vera emphasized the need to connect the new residents of her neighborhood to the established social network in her geographic community. The social changes that accompany deterioration of housing stock, redevelopment, and gentrification, she argued, interfere with the important informal ties among residents. These ties provide a crucial source of emotional support and economic sustenance as well as political strength for a community.

One of the most fascinating and contradictory findings of this study involves the extent to which most of the resident community workers maintained an optimism about the future of America despite the lack of concern for the poor currently exhibited by the wider society. Ann Robinson described America as "a blessed country." Her religious conviction is evident in the following quote:

> There's so much that we can do if we really treated our neighbors as if
> we were the ones who would be treated that way in that situation. And
> we're not doing it. And I think one of these days we're going to be pun-
> ished for it. We cannot go into other places and impose our wishes of
> how we expect them to function when we are not doing right right
> here in our own places. There's no need for broken-down buildings,
> garbage in the street. We have just lost the respect for each other.
> ...And I think we're going to have to begin, those of us who...believe
> in God or we don't, if we just say we believe in people, then we have
> to stand up and be counted. And we have to begin to help people
> shore up their foundation, to let them know that they are worthwhile.
> They are valuable.

All the community workers believed, as Ann explained, that "to help people shore up their foundation" involves more than individual self-esteem building. It involves a collective process in which people come to feel that they have a stake in their community and in the wider political environment—in Angela Garcia's words, "there's a consciousness that has to be done."

This consciousness-raising process involves creating a "community of memory" (Bellah et al. 1985, 153) that connects members with a recognizable past and provides a collective base from which to envision and strive for a more hopeful future. However, constructions of community used as a basis for political mobilization were often constrained by local patterns of segregation as well as rigid definitions of political identities, especially as they related to race, gender, and class.

Due to the structural conditions that contribute to poverty in American cities, the resident workers knew that they alone could not rectify the multitude of problems confronting their low-income communities. Therefore, many of the women could not see any significant improvements for their communities without major structural changes in the economic and political context of American society. They could not envision such changes without the development of a strong vocal coalition among the poor and progressive allies, although they disagreed on which tactics would be more effective given the conservative political era of the 1990s.

## Putting Democracy Into Practice

The antipoverty programs provided a legitimate site for ongoing organizing activities of the community workers although the commitment to maximum feasible participation for the poor was of limited duration. These programs also created a context for women with no training in community work to develop their political skills and for those with previous experiences to share their political analyses and expand their political networks. Many community workers, resident and nonresident alike, developed their political perspectives to the point where they organized on a much broader basis than when they first began as community workers. Recent federal proposals to prohibit organizations who apply or receive government funds from engaging in political activities (broadly defined) reveals a complete abandonment of the principal of maximum feasible participation provided for in the Economic Opportunity Act.[34] However, organizations set up to respond to local community needs cannot avoid their role as advocates for residents in poor neighborhoods. Since solutions to neighborhood problems generally lie outside the local community,[35] the extent to which the government is responsive to different demands from advocates in community-based organizations varies across time and space, thus providing different grounds for political action.

Furthermore, differences in organizational structure and political history of the CAAs in Philadelphia and New York City contributed to varying contexts for the community workers' political activism. The decentralized structure of New York City's organizational approach enhanced the development of sites for the politicization and grassroots mobilization of low-income residents. However, such political spaces were further and further circumscribed as the state withdrew support for maximum feasible participation and community action. The community workers continued to include advocacy and other political activities as a necessary part of their work on behalf of low-income residents. Many supervisors, politicians, and funders did not share their view as evident in the swift move to limit CAP staff's political activism. Echoing the sentiments of other community workers in this study, Josephine Card of East Harlem recalled how great limitations were placed on the implementation of the maximum feasible participation component of the legislation: "It all sounded great on paper, but...when they said maximum feasible participation and the poor decided that they meant on every level, including the policy-making level, no way!"

The community workers understood the administrative practices as efforts to control their activism and undermine collective protests in the low-income communities. Most said they strove to find a balance between their activism and their positions as employees of the state. Angela Garcia emphasized that "the hardest thing is a community activist coming into a bureaucracy, it has problems, and they're painful ones, very painful ones." Angela recounted her difficulty working with community groups once she accepted a position in a government agency. She found that sometimes her role as community activist overshadowed her position as a state worker "because you sometimes forget that you're working for the government, and you're bitching about it, and you're...[challenging] another state agency." Angela remembered a story she loved to tell:

> I went with a group of [community] people to a meeting, and they said, "We're not going to stand here and take this." And they got up and walked out, and I said, "Yeah," and I got up and walked out, and then I realized, "Oh, my God, what did I do?" So we discussed it, and I know I won't walk out anymore, but they know that I still will react: "Look, I think there's something wrong. I think we need to discuss this." But then I have to be careful. That's the one part that hurts.

She added that paid community workers must "walk on cracked eggs; and it's very sensitive, getting involved in the political arena, getting involved in the educational arena. You have to be careful!"

Despite the depoliticization strategies employed by the state to circumscribe workers' political activism, all the women emphasized that such activities were essential to their community work. In fact, they believed that advocacy and other forms of political activism should be expanded rather than curtailed. According to Nina Reyes, the community agencies must take more initiative in the 1990s to help organize the residents of the surrounding neighborhood, improve housing and other services, and enhance the participation of local residents in the political arena. She complained that most social service agencies have a narrow definition of their role in organizing the local community. However, since agencies situated in low-income neighborhoods are vulnerable to funding cuts, those working in these organizations often find themselves fighting intense political battles to ensure their continued existence. Nina described how she attempted to involve residents in her neighborhood in an effort to prevent funding cuts to her program in 1995. When she received word that her community program for the elderly was to be phased out, she informed community members who in turn helped to thwart the attempt.

> We started writing to our clients and getting people to know what was going on because that's one of the problems of the community....If someone in an agency doesn't, or community person doesn't get involved in telling them, they're not aware of what's really going on. They hear "cuts," but they don't know where they're going to be cut and how they're going to be affected. So my director and I said we have to let our community know....We started writing letters to the clients, getting the [staff] to write letters to all the legislators....So we just found out that we're going to have funds for another year.

Recognizing the need for ongoing organizing to prevent further cuts in subsequent years, Nina and her co-organizers established a coalition of different groups who would be affected by funding cuts in the future. As she explained, "People are getting older, people are getting sicker so we have to keep our faith. We have to because we can't let the government run us."

Despite the major limitations involved in implementation of the participatory component of the Economic Opportunity Act, participation in the state-funded CAPs increased the community workers' sense of personal and political power. Numerous critics of the War on Poverty representing a range of political perspectives emphasized the limits of maximum feasible participation as a strategy to enhance democratic practice. Saul Alinsky (1968), who described the War on Poverty as "political pornography," was particularly critical when he attacked the number of consulting firms and high paid administrators drawing inflated salaries from the antipoverty programs. Daniel Patrick Moynihan (1969), used the term "maximum feasible misunderstanding" in his assessment of the program.[36] However, from the community workers' vantage point, we can see how the War on Poverty, with its emphasis on maximum feasible participation, transformed their previously unpaid community work into paid work and, at the same time, empowered them as residents of low-income communities—resulting in a merging of social and political citizenship.

Experience with oppressive bureaucracies gained through their everyday activities provided the community workers with knowledge of the "actual workings" of the state (Rowbotham 1989, 156). The skills they gained in struggling against insensitive and ineffective public agencies contributed to their political efficacy and many demonstrated their resistance on a daily basis (also see Ames 1996). In the process of resisting these oppressive forces, the women experienced personal empowerment and contributed to the empowerment of others. Since many viewed maximum feasible participation through the lens of the Civil Rights Movement, they saw it as an opportunity to increase the political efficacy of low-income and racial-ethnic minorities. However, as they considered retiring from their jobs or were forced to leave their paid positions as a consequence of cutbacks or reorganization, they grew increasingly concerned that the legacy of their efforts would be lost. While working to pass on the torch, they confronted the limits of the contemporary political and economic context for promoting grassroots leadership among younger generations of low-income community residents. The loss of community-based organizational sites promoting progressive commuinity activism also hampered the transmission of political analyses and strategies from the community workers' generation to the next.

## Negotiating the Contradictions of the State

State intervention in the lives of low-income women, especially single mothers, in the 1990s involves a complicated set of contradictory messages and irreconcilable tensions.[37] On the one hand, to care for their families they must find some means of financial support, yet the low-wage jobs available to them fail to provide the income or the flexibility needed to accomplish the demands of unpaid social reproductive labor. On the other hand, to raise a child with the help of state support is defined as a sign of unhealthy dependence and of their failure as "good" mothers. The community workers from low-income backgrounds challenge the state's construction of what constitutes "good" mothering. In their view, good mothering includes all activities that address the needs of their children and community. Social activism as well as creative use of state resources form central components of their activist mothering. Over the years, they shared their analysis with other mothers living in poverty and affirmed their right to receive support from the state for mothering work. Many participated in the National Welfare Rights Organization[38] and helped promote the sense that mother work, broadly defined, is basic to the development of a vital citizenry and viable communities.

The community workers' resistance to the bureaucratic organization of the state in many instances illustrates the contradictions of state-sponsored, community-based employment. The contradictions result, in part, from the community workers' opposition to the state's false assumptions about the social disorganization of poor communities, low-income women's lack of work ethic, and the racist constructions of a so-called culture of poverty. Since many of the community workers positioned themselves and their labor within historically specific struggles for community self-determination variously defined by intricate relationships of class, gender, race, ethnicity, and locality, their resistance to the oppressive features of state intervention in their lives was only one manifestation of broader-based struggles for social justice and economic security. While the nature of the struggles changed over time, the community workers expressed continued affinity for the goals of community self-determination and equality. As a result of their unique perspective as workers paid by the state, beneficiaries of social-welfare programs, and unpaid caretakers and activists, the resident community workers, in particular, offered an alternative vision of "the just society" that was creatively expressed and passionately lived in their fight against the forces that impoverish their communities.

According to the community workers, much of their initial community work was dedicated to community empowerment from the grassroots—a significant measure of the way they defined maximum feasible participation to mean participatory democracy in its fullest sense. Overall, analysis of the community work of women in low-income urban communities in

Philadelphia and New York City reveals how knowledge generated from the standpoint of women living and working outside the dominant framework can provide a more nuanced and tempered understanding of what creates and sustains poverty in America. The analysis also illustrates how dominant ideology infuses political analysis and political practice of marginalized actors as well as limits how claims can be made within the political arena—as highlighted in the resident community workers' discussion of their work as "civic work" rather than "politics."

The next round of research on the significance of women's community work in low-income communities should address whether or not grassroots warriors can link local activism to larger struggles for social change. How have they successfully worked across the racial, ethnic, and class differences that circumscribe segregated urban neighborhoods? Where, and in what ways, have they been able to incorporate other community members, such as gay and lesbian residents, into their political community? How successful have they been in ensuring the continuity of their work over time?

The extent to which the community workers' activism transformed the state is another subject for future investigation. What strategies have the community workers developed to resist social control practices that are manifest in contemporary welfare policy? To what extent do these women serve as policy innovators at the local level? The extent to which the state can still be viewed as the primary target for such political struggles remains uncertain given the anti-statist political climate of the 1990s. Yet, for low-income communities, few alternatives to state support exist. If antipoverty activists and policymakers wish to wage a successful renewed War on Poverty in the U.S., they must incorporate processes by which low-income women and other working-class people and their communities can participate in policy construction as well as advocate on their own behalf. Socially meaningful employment, community action, and maximum feasible participation—in its fullest democratic interpretation—offer conceptual tools by which to help implement such democratic strategies.

# Appendices

# A. METHODOLOGICAL CONSIDERATIONS

The following guidelines were used to determine which resident community workers would be included in the study: (1) the community worker was born into a low-income family; (2) the community worker was a resident of a low-income community before 1964; and (3) she was employed as a community worker by an antipoverty program between 1964 and 1974, so that she would have a minimun of ten years community work experience at the time of the first interview.

The sampling techniques used to identify the women were designed in response to the different organizational structures of the antipoverty programs in each city (see Bailey 1973; Ershkowitz and Zikmund 1973). Philadelphia created a centralized commission to oversee the work of twelve area offices. A sample of twenty-one resident community workers were chosen from a central list of staff, representatives, and recently retired or laid-off workers. Only one nonresident worker was identified. This worker was serving in an administrative position in the citywide office.

The decentralized structure of New York City's antipoverty programs required a different sampling procedure. The Lower East Side and neighborhoods in Harlem and the South Bronx were identified for their active antipoverty programs. Researchers and professional community workers who had been active in these communities during the early years of the CAPs were asked to identify women they had known in their own community work. I then contacted those who had been named and asked them for additional recommendations. These workers were asked to name women they had known during the years 1964–74. These women were contacted and asked for additional recommendations. Through the process of snowball sampling, twenty-one resident and ten nonresident community workers who were employed through the New York City CAPs and continued to perform community work in the 1980s were interviewed. In addition, I identified and interviewed eleven nonresident community workers who were employed in other community-based organizations but had not worked for CAPs during the years 1964–74, as a way to expand the representation of nonresident workers in the study. See Table 1 for a description of the employment status of the resident community workers at the time of the first interview. See Appendix B for a complete listing of the community workers first interviewed in the mid-1980s.

TABLE 1. EMPLOYMENT STATUS OF RESIDENT COMMUNITY WORKERS AT TIME OF FIRST INTERVIEW, 1983–1985

|  | No. | Percent |
|---|---|---|
| Director, community agency | 7 | 16.7 |
| Area coordinator, PAAC* | 7 | 16.7 |
| Program director, community agency | 4 | 09.5 |
| Outreach, intake or I&R worker** | 6 | 14.2 |
| Administrator, citywide agency | 7 | 16.7 |
| Other community work | 3 | 07.1 |
| Assistant teacher | 1 | 02.4 |
| Retired | 4 | 09.5 |
| Unemployed/laid off | 3 | 07.1 |
| TOTAL | 42 | 99.9 |

*PAAC = Philadelphia Area Action Commission, the Antipoverty Agency estab-lished in Philadelphia
**I&R worker = Information and Referral worker, PAAC

The nonresident women were working in CAPs or similar programs and had either worked as unpaid or paid community workers during 1964–1974. Six of the twenty-two nonresident community workers oper-ated in a social work or social reform tradition and during the mid-1980s were working with a community-based or citywide agency to help support the social service or political advocacy work of these organizations or city agencies. Five were involved in education or the arts. Two worked for city government and two were legal services attorneys. Three were directing advocacy programs in housing, day care, or welfare rights, respectively. Three were directing women's rights organizations. See Table 2.

The resident community workers ranged in age from thirty-six to seventy-two. Given the range of ages, the community workers had been employed in CAPs at different times in their life cycles. Consequently, the younger women had fewer years of unpaid community work experience prior to paid communi-ty work. The resident women were, on average, older than the nonresident community workers. The nonresident community workers were between the ages of thirty-five and sixty at the time of the first interviews scheduled dur-ing the mid-1980s. The Latina resident workers, on average, were younger and had a higher level of formal education than their African American counter-parts. See Table 3 for a summary of the ages of the resident community work-ers by race-ethnicity.

TABLE 2. THE AREA OF EMPLOYMENT OF THE NONRESIDENT COMMUNITY WORKERS AT TIME OF FIRST INTERVIEW, 1983–1985

| Area of Employment | N | Percent |
|---|---|---|
| Social work | 6 | 27.2 |
| Education | 4 | 18.1 |
| Arts | 1 | 4.5 |
| City government | 2 | 9.0 |
| Legal services | 2 | 9.0 |
| Women's rights | 3 | 13.6 |
| Other advocacy | 3 | 13.6 |
| Small business | 1 | 4.5 |
| TOTAL | 22 | 99.5* |

TABLE 3. THE AGE OF THE RESIDENT COMMUNITY WORKERS BY RACE-ETHNICITY AT TIME OF FIRST INTERVIEW, 1983–1985

| | African American | | Latina | | White/Other** | |
|---|---|---|---|---|---|---|
| Age | N | % | N | % | N | % |
| 35–44 | 3 | 11.5 | 5 | 45.4 | 1 | 20.0 |
| 45–54 | 7 | 26.9 | 6 | 54.5 | 1 | 20.0 |
| 55 and up | 16 | 61.5 | 0 | 0.0 | 3 | 60.0 |
| TOTAL | 26 | 99.9 | 11 | 99.9 | 5 | 100.0 |

*This category includes ten Puerto Rican women and one who immigrated from the Dominican Republic.
**This category includes four white European–American women and one Japanese–American woman.

Only two of the women interviewed said they were receiving public assistance at the time; however, seven said they might have gone on welfare had the paid community work position not become available to them. Sixteen were not working for pay when they accepted paid community work; ten were clerical workers and seven had factory jobs at the time. Six had related paid community or social service work. Another two were nurses aides. Of the women who were still employed as paid community workers at the time of the interview in the mid-1980s, about one-quarter earned less than $15,000 per year; thirty-one percent earned between $15,000 and $20,000; and about one-quarter earned between $20,000 and $29,000. One woman, who had completed a master's degree in social work while working for a CAP, earned $40,000 as a director of a social service program in her community. See Table 4.

TABLE 4. INCOME OF THE RESIDENT COMMUNITY WORKERS AT THE
TIME OF FIRST INTERVIEW, 1983–1985

| Income | N | Percent |
|---|---|---|
| Under $15,000 | 10 | 24 |
| $15,000–19,999 | 13 | 31 |
| $20,000–29,999 | 11 | 26 |
| $30,000–40,000 | 1 | 2 |
| Retired/Unemployed | 7 | 17 |
| TOTAL | 42 | 100 |

Nine (or twenty-one percent) of the resident community workers interviewed
for this study were without a high school diploma when they were hired by a CAP.
Of the nine who did not have a high school diploma, eight finished their General
Equivalency Diplomas (GEDs) while employed in a CAP. An additional twenty-
six (or sixty-two percent) had only a high school diploma when they first accepted
CAP employment. Three women had some college education. Only four had
graduated from college before they were employed by a CAP. Of the seven women
who had prior college experience, three continued to further their education while
working for a CAP. One resident community worker recently completed a master's degree in social work, another finished a Ph.D. in education. See Table 5.

TABLE 5. THE EDUCATIONAL ATTAINMENT OF THE RESIDENT COMMUNITY
WORKERS BY RACE-ETHNICITY AT TIME OF FIRST INTERVIEW, 1983-1985

| | African American | | Latina* | | White/ Other** | |
|---|---|---|---|---|---|---|
| Level of Education | N | % | N | % | N | % |
| Less than high school | 1 | 3.8 | 0 | 0.0 | 0 | 0.0 |
| Some high school | 5 | 19.2 | 1 | 9.1 | 2 | 40.0 |
| High school graduate | 17 | 65.4 | 6 | 54.5 | 2 | 40.0 |
| Some college | 2 | 7.7 | 2 | 18.2 | 0 | 0.0 |
| College graduate | 1 | 3.8 | 2 | 18.2 | 1 | 20.0 |
| TOTAL | 26 | 99.9 | 11 | 100.0 | 5 | 100.0 |

*This category includes ten Puerto Rican women and one who immigrated from
the Dominican Republic.*

**This category includes four white European American women and one
Japanese American woman.*

The nonresident community workers had a higher level of educational
attainment when they first accepted paid employment as community workers. All completed college; three of the eleven had master's degrees in social
work. All were directing community-based programs and earning above
$20,000 a year when first contacted in the mid-1980s.

# B. A DEMOGRAPHIC PROFILE OF THE COMMUNITY WORKERS INTERVIEWED, 1983–1985

## Resident Community Workers

| Pseudonym | City/Area | Race/Ethnicity | Approx. Age in 1984 |
|---|---|---|---|
| Mary Adams | Philadelphia | African American | 56 |
| Gloria Alvarez | Lower East Side | Puerto Rican | 39 |
| Naomi Barker | Philadelphia | African American | 51 |
| Marcy Barnett | Philadelphia | African American | 58 |
| Josephine Card | Harlem | African American | 51 |
| Othelia Carson | Philadelphia | African American | 62 |
| Carmela Calas | Lower East Side | Puerto Rican | 50 |
| Maria Calero* | New York City | Dominican | 41 |
| Mrs. Ruth Dever* | Philadelphia | African American | 65 |
| Estelle Downs* | Harlem | African American | 54 |
| Pat Easterly* | Philadelphia | African American | 39 |
| Francine Evans* | Lower East Side | African American | 60 |
| Grace Reynolds* | New York City | White/Jewish | 50 |
| Martha Framer* | Philadelphia | African American | 35 |
| Angela Garcia* | Harlem | Puerto Rican | 54 |
| Samantha Grant | Philadelphia | African American | 61 |
| Carmen Hernandez | Lower East Side | Puerto Rican | 50 |
| Theresa Higgins | Philadelphia | African American | 72 |
| Harriet Jonas | Harlem | African American | 48 |
| Vera Lane | Philadelphia | African American | 55 |
| Mrs. Louise Long | Lower East Side | African American | 45 |
| Rita Martinez* | Harlem | Puerto Rican | 48 |
| Carlotta Mendez* | New York City | Puerto Rican | 52 |
| Theresa Miguel | New York City | Puerto Rican | 40 |
| Wilma North | Philadelphia | African American | 55 |
| Eve Parker | Lower East Side | African American | 53 |
| Mrs. Delia Parsons | Harlem | African American | 36 |
| Ethel Pearls | Philadelphia | African American | 57 |

| Pseudonym | City/Area | Race/Ethnicity | Approx. Age in 1984 |
|---|---|---|---|
| Alice Porter | Philadelphia | African American | 60 |
| Nina Reyes* | Lower East Side | Puerto Rican | 45 |
| Grace Reynolds | Philadelphia | White | 70 |
| Frances Rider | Philadelphia | African American | 60 |
| Barbara Rivers | Philadelphia | White | 55 |
| Ann Robinson* | Harlem | African American | 61 |
| Elsie Rodriguez | Philadelphia | Puerto Rican | 51 |
| Rebecca Russo | Harlem | Puerto Rican | 40 |
| Paula Sands | New York City | Japanese American | 44 |
| Catherine Smith | Philadelphia | African American | 70 |
| Elena Soto | Harlem | Puerto Rican | 39 |
| Dottie Storm | Philadelphia | African American | 61 |
| Clara Thompson | Philadelphia | African American | 55 |
| Harriet Towers | Philadelphia | White | 70 |

## Nonresident Community Workers

| Pseudonym | City/Area | Race/Ethnicity | Approx. Age in 1984 |
|---|---|---|---|
| Joyce Amato | New York City | White/Jewish | 48 |
| Jill Anders | New York City | White/Jewish | 35 |
| Susan Barns* | New York City | White/Jewish | 35 |
| Sabrina Brock* | New York City | White | 48 |
| Shelly Burns | New York City | White/Jewish | 50 |
| Diane Cresser | New York City | White | 41 |
| Sandra Cole | Brooklyn | White | 42 |
| Michelle Dodge* | Philadelphia | African American | 37 |
| Noreen Everest | New York City | White | 38 |
| Dorothy Evers | New York City | White | 35 |
| Sr. Margaret Fogarty* | South Bronx | White | 52 |
| Betty Glass | Harlem | White | 42 |
| Liz Grasser | New York City | White | 37 |
| Edith Harper | New York City | African American | 40 |
| Georgia Havens | New York City | White | 40 |
| Cindy Heller | New York City | White | 45 |
| Beverly Towner | New York City | White | 40 |
| Kathryn Mayor | New York City | White | 38 |
| Lydia Montalvo* | New York City | Puerto Rican | 38 |
| Sr. Helen North | East Harlem | White | 45 |
| Karen Roth | New York City | White/Jewish | 60 |
| Nina Voyage | New York City | White | 45 |

*Also interviewed in 1995

# C. DON'T BOTHER VOTING IN POVERTY ELECTIONS, 1966

# DON'T BOTHER VOTING IN POVERTY ELECTIONS

Mayor Tate runs the Poverty program. Whoever wins the election, Mayor Tate will still be running the Poverty program.

## The "War On Poverty" Is a Fraud

They have spent 13 million to end poverty in Philadelphia.

This amounts to $65 for every poor person which is chicken feed.

What do you have to show for it?

Are you really any better off now than before?

Every week they spend $1 billion $481 million for war. Why don't they use this money to really end poverty?

## END POVERTY!

We can never end poverty under the present system which is making the poor become poorer. What we really need to end poverty is decent high-paying jobs for everyone who wants work.

We want to rebuild the ghetto with poor people making the decisions.

Greatly increased public welfare given to all who need it without red-tape and personal investigations.

We want our men returned from Viet Nam and war money used to end poverty.

# DEMONSTRATION and RALLY
## Thursday July 21 5 to 7 pm City Hall

Sponsors: Freedom George, Young Militants; Bill Mathias, CORE; Fred Mealy, SNCC; Robert Brazzwell, NAACP Youth Council.

# D. AMENDING THE WAR ON POVERTY

The U.S. War on Poverty quickly subsided as costs for the Vietnam War escalated (see Moynihan 1969). Commitment to maximum feasible participation of the poor waned as federal and state officials denounced community action. Challenges to the status quo at the local level finally eroded most support for the participatory ethos that informed the original model for the Community Action Program (see Piven and Cloward 1977).

The history of CAPs under the auspices of OEO spans less then a decade. During these years the autonomy of the CAAs was progressively eroded. Before 1970, approximately eighty percent of the CAAs were private nonprofit community organizations. In 1967, Congress passed the Green Amendments, which required that all CAAs be set up as political subdivisions of the city government with one third of the board consisting of public officials (Marshall 1971, 45). Rep. Edith Green (D Ore.) introduced this "local control feature" into the 1967 authorization for the antipoverty programs to gain support from Southerners as well as to mollify some representatives from Northern cities "where militant antipoverty groups had come in conflict with the city administration" (Congressional Quarterly Service 1969, 766). The final version of the authorization bill (S 2388) included a "bypass" provision that allowed "direct OEO administration of programs if public officials did not develop a satisfactory plan" (p. 766).

As it became clear that the CAPs and local participation posed a threat to the established political order in each city, the federal government gradually brought CAPs under federal control. Funding was initially provided in a lump sum with specific programmatic decisions to be made at the local level. But by 1965, specific programs, primarily Head Start and legal services, were federally designated. The 1966 Amendments further cut the CAPs' discretionary funds in order to limit community organizing activities (D. R. Marshall 1971). In 1967, Congress amended the EOA to prohibit legal services from defending anyone who was indicted for criminal activities. The 1968 amendments required eight specific programs: Head Start, Follow Through, legal services, comprehensive health services, Upward Bound, emergency food and medical services, and senior citizen programs (U. S., OEO 1968a). In 1969, family planning was also included (U.S. OEO 1970a).

The amendments also included provisions for further bureaucratic procedures. These changes are reflected in the annual reports published between 1965 and 1971. For example, the 1967 report described that year as "a period of consolidation and internal strengthening of the CAAs in response to tightened and refined OEO procedures" (U.S. OEO 1967, 9). The 1968 report also included a description of a "comprehensive new grant application process" designed so that "all grants will be based on a standard set of program objectives'" (U.S. OEO 1968a, 12). OEO's budget reached a high point during the fiscal years 1969 and 1970, with annual funding of $1.9 billion, and then steadily declined.

The 1969–1970 fiscal report included a statement by President Richard Nixon that emphasized the "new organizational structures, new operating procedures, and a new sense of precision and direction" which would enable OEO to "be one of the most creative and productive offices in the government (U.S. OEO 1970a, VI-I). This report noted that "mature operating programs run by the OEO have been turned over to other Federal departments and agencies, leaving the OEO free to develop and demonstrate different ideas" (U.S. OEO 1970a, 1). In other words, most of the ongoing programs of OEO were eliminated from the agency's jurisdiction. The FY 1971 report continued to emphasize efficiency, "greater accountability, increased program effectiveness, [and] strengthened management" (U.S. OEO 1971a, 1).

By 1970, community action and VISTA were the only programs operated by OEO. The other programs were delegated to the Departments of Labor, HEW, Agriculture, etc. OEO was disbanded in 1975 and the remaining CAPs, coordinated by the newly established Community Services Administration (CSA), were administratively situated under the Department of Health and Human Services (U.S. Congress, House 1981a).

Nixon tried to dismantle OEO in 1973 but was thwarted by a court decision. A 1975 report commissioned by the Nixon administration was used to restructure the agency and included provisions for further tightening controls over grantee agencies. CSA received little support from President Carter and was finally dismantled on September 30, 1981 by the Reagan administration. During its last year of existence, fiscal year 1981, CSA's operating budget had reached a low of $526.4 million. CSA was abolished as part of the Omnibus Budget Reconciliation Act of 1981 (P.L. 97–35), which also established the Community Services Block Grant (CSBG) to the States (U.S. House 1981b). The CSBG has been funded through 1998. The remaining funds for community action are now administered by the Office of Community Affairs at the Department of Health and Human Services.

# E. PERMISSIBLE AND PROHIBITED ACTIVITIES, PAAC 1966

(Excerpt from PAAC, *Conduct and Administration Report*, Philadelphia, June 25, 1966a)

*Permissible Activities*. An employee may voluntarily:
-Cast his vote at any election.
-Express privately his opinions on any political candidate.
-Be a member of a political party, club or organization.
-Be a member or officer or participate in the activities of non-partisan civic organizations.
-Sign any petition.
-Initiate or circulate petitions provided that such petitions are not identified with a political party, or body, or partisan political club and do not call for the nomination or election of particular candidate to public or party office.
-Participate in the public debate of questions which may be submitted to referendum vote or of other issues of public interest, provided such activity is not in support of any political party or body or partisan political club, and is not identified with any particular political party, body, or candidate.
-Attend as a spectator any political meeting or convention.
-Attend dinners or social functions of a political character.
-Address any meeting, dinner, or social function on local, state, or national issues that are not particularly identified with any particular political party, body, or candidate and do not call for the nomination or election of any candidate to public or party office.
-Distribute printed matter, badges, or buttons in support of any political issue provided that such issue is not identified with any particular political party, body, or candidate and does not call for the nomination or election of any particular candidate to public or party office.
-Participate in any non-partisan campaign for the registration for voters.
*Prohibited Political Activities*. An employee shall not:
-Be an officer or member of a committee of a political party or body.
-Be an officer or member of a committee of a partisan political club or organization.

-Address, make motions, prepare or assist in preparing resolutions, maintain records, or take any other active part in a meeting or convention of a political party or partisan political club.

-Initiate or circulate public petitions, or canvass for the signatures of others, if such petitions are identified with or call for the nomination or election of any particular candidate to public or party office.

-Distribute printed matter, badges, or buttons in support of any candidate for public or party office or political party or body.

-Wear on his person display badges, emblems, signs, posters and the like which are in favor of or against a political party, body or candidate.

-Participate in or help organize a political party.

-Solicit money from any person for the support of any issue, for the support of any political purpose that is identified with or calls for the nomination or election of any particular candidate to public or party office.

-Arrange, or help to arrange a public meeting, rally, dinner, or social function of a political character.

-Sell or distribute tickets for sale for political meetings or dinners.

-Serve at party headquarters or otherwise engage in campaign activities on behalf of a party or candidate in any political campaign or election.

-Write for public or publish any letter or article, signed or unsigned in favor of or against any political party, body or candidate for public office.

-Engage in transportation of voters to the polls on election day on behalf of any candidate or party.

-Act as the accredited watcher of any political party, body, or candidate, or engage in any political activities at the polls except the casting of his own vote.

-Be eligible to continue his Agency employment if he shall become a candidate for nomination or for election to any public office. Any employee who shall become a candidate for a nomination or election to any public office shall be considered to have resigned his employment.

-Give any consideration to the political affiliation of any person in making appointments under the provisions of these regulations.

-Directly or indirectly use or promise or threaten to use the authority or influence of his position in order to coerce or influence the vote of any person.

-Directly or indirectly use or promise to use the authority or influence of his position in order to dismiss, promote, or demote, or in any matter change the official rank or compensation of any employee or promise or threaten to do so for withholding or refusing to make any contribution of money or service or other valuable thing in support of or in opposition to any political party, body, or candidate for public office or issue.

-Directly or indirectly use or promise to use the authority or influence of his position in order to coerce or influence an employee to pay or promise to pay any assessment, subscription or contribution in support of or in opposition to any political party, body, or candidate for public office or issue.

-Address any rally, dinner or social function of a political character on any subject that is identified with or calls for the nomination or election of any candidate to public or party office.

-Participate in a campaign of a political party for registration of voters in that party.

-Perform any of those activities referred to in this regulation during his scheduled hours of employment for the Agency. Those political activities prohibited in this regulation are not permitted before, during and after hours of work for the Agency.

-By collusion or indirectly through another person attempt to accomplish what is prohibited by these regulations.

# F. MAP OF PHILADELPHIA'S TWELVE POVERTY AREAS, 1965

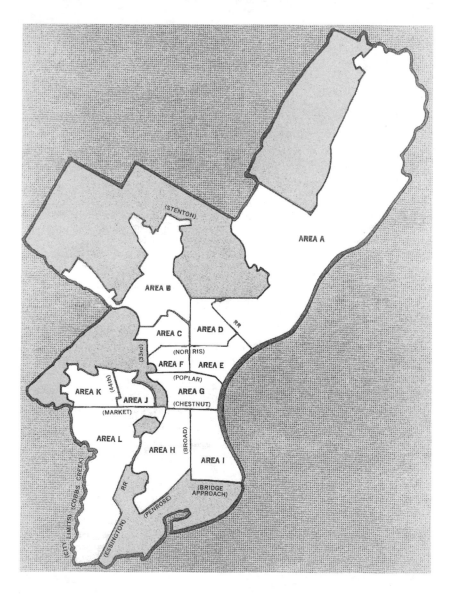

# G. MAXIMUM PARTICIPATION MOVEMENT, PHILADELPHIA 1966

## Position Paper

The poor should have a greater say in the anti-poverty program of Philadelphia. The poor were promised "maximum feasible participation" by the Federal Government. Instead, the poor have gotten a maximum-run around and all the feasible foolishness imaginable. Until representatives of the poor force a series of reforms in the Philadelphia Anti-Poverty Action Council, the poor will continue to be the big losers inside a losing war on poverty.

The MPM is a new citizens group dedicated to the idea that the poor should have real power in the shaping of their own destinies. The MPM is made up of Philadelphians, poor and non-poor alike, who have paid careful attention to the promises and the performance this year of PAAC. After discussions with anti poverty fights in other cities and in Sargent Shriver's Office of Economic Opportunity, the MPM membership has decided to urge consideration by Philadelphians of the following reforms:

1. To strengthen the Community Action Councils-

   (a) each Council should be allocated at least $250,000, as in Boston, to help it launch a series of direct attacks on local problems;

   (b) each Council should have power to hire and fire its own staff, rather than having to go to the PAAC Staff Director, as at present;

   (c) each Council should have at least two weeks to consider a proposal scheduled for a PAAC vote; and

   (d) each Council should have the power to evaluate programs in its neighborhood paid for by PAAC.

2. To strengthen the voice of the poor in PAAC-

   (a) a PAAC sub-committee should hold public hearings on the usefulness of changing PAAC into a private, non-profit corporation, as in New Haven;

   (b) the Community Action Council representatives to PAAC should behave as if strongly guided by the advice of fellow CAC members—and not as if independent of CAC influence, as at present;

c) the chairman of the CAC's should be allowed to participate (on a non-voting basis) at PAAC meetings, thereby adding 12 more voices for the poor; and

(d) the chairman of the two all-powerful PAAC Sub-Committees on CAC's and on Program Review should be restricted to one-year, non-repeating terms.

3. To strengthen the role of the interested public-

(a) public hearings should be held prior to a PAAC vote on program proposals;

(b) the age limit of 21 on CAC membership should be lowered to 18;

(c) the Mayor should reduce his representation on PAAC from five back to two, adding the Citizens Concerned with Public Assistance, the Friends Service Committee, and the Philadelphia Re-Development Authority; and

(d) all PAAC votes should be recorded by individual voter and included as part of the public minutes available to all in each CAC office.

The Maximum Participation Movement intends to fight for these reforms until they are secured. The MPM intends to recommend other reforms as its on-going evaluation of PAAC and its study of the successes and failures of other city programs points up new reforms. The MPM intends to gadfly PAAC's every effort, recognizing successes as well as exposing shortcomings. The MPM welcomes all Philadelphians in membership—and asks only a willingness to share in our work.

# NOTES

## Chapter 1

1. Some aspects of this work appear elsewhere (see Naples 1991a, 1991b, 1992).
2. Analysts credit a complex of economic, social, and political explanations for the War on Poverty. Social scientists who explore the origins of the antipoverty programs often privilege one of three different features: class (see, e.g., Katz 1989; Piven and Cloward 1971, 1993, 1977); race politics (see, e.g., Morone 1990; Quadagno 1994); or modified liberal reform spearheaded by social scientists like Lloyd Ohlin and Richard Cloward, Ford Foundation social planners (notably Paul Ylvisaker), and progressive federal officials like David Hackett and other White House staff of President John F. Kennedy (see Aaron 1978; Davies 1992; Donovan 1980; Levitan and Taggart; Wighorn 1984). Daniel Patrick Moynihan (1969) emphasized the relevance of the economic theories prevalent during the latter part of the 1950s and early 1960s for the War on Poverty. However, Michael Harrington (1962) took issue with the dominant economic analysis that optimistically saw a gradual decrease in the numbers of those living in poverty as the American economy expanded unabated. His book, *The Other America*, offered an analysis of poverty that captured the interest of President John F. Kennedy who began to craft an antipoverty program that was to be a central part of his 1964 legislative agenda (see Sundquist 1969). After his assassination, President Lyndon Johnson enthusiastically carried forward the antipoverty initiative and launched the War on Poverty as the first major act of his administration.
3. The Economic Opportunity Act (EOA) established the Office of Economic Opportunity (OEO). Sar Levitan (1969, 53) outlines the direct and delegated authorities of EOA programs for 1968. In addition to CAPs, OEO administered: Job Corps: Men's and women's Training Centers; Civilian Conservation Centers (operated under interagency agreements with Departments of Agriculture and Interior and agreements with states); Foster Grandparents (Department of HEW Administration on Aging—operated under interagency agreement); Special Impact Programs (Interagency operating agreement with other federal agencies); Emergency Food and Medical Service (Departments of HEW and Agriculture operated under interagency agreement); Migrant Assistant program; Day Care (interagency operating agreement with Departments of HEW and Labor); Information Center; and Domestic Volunteer Service Programs (VISTA). The following programs were delegated to the Department of Labor, Bureau of Work Training Programs: Work Training for Youth and Adults (includes: Neighborhood Youth Corps, Operation Mainstream (delegation does not include Foster Grandparents

Program) and New Careers Programs, Concentrated Employment program, Jobs and Community Service Programs). The Department of Health Education and Welfare was responsible for administering the Follow Through Program. The Department of Agriculture (Farmers Home Administration) was responsible for the Rural Loan Program. The Department of Health, Education, and Welfare (Social and Rehabilitation Service) administered the Work Experience Trainting Program.

4. The Great Society is a term used to describe antipoverty and civil rights legislation passed during President Lyndon Johnson's administration. Johnson's Great Society extended President John F. Kennedy's New Frontier initiatives, which operated under the assumption that by expanding access to health care, education, employment, and training opportunities, the poor could benefit from the then-projected growth of the United States economy. Johnson announced the "War on Poverty" in his 1964 State of the Union Address. One of the most significant pieces of legislation to pass during this period was Title VII of the 1964 Civil Rights Act, which prohibited discrimination in employment on the basis of race and sex. Great Society programs that targeted poor communities included the Area Redevelopment Act of 1961 and the Economic Development Act of 1965, designed to encourage new industries to move into economically depressed areas. Housing and community development programs included the 1965 rent-supplement program and the 1966 Demonstration (Model) Cities and Metropolitan Development Act. The 1962 Manpower Development and Training Act offered retraining for displaced workers and the Food Stamp Act of 1964 provided eligible individuals and families with cash vouchers to purchase basic food and related items. Education measures included the Elementary and Secondary Education Act of 1965 and the Higher Education Act of 1965. Among other key programs associated with the Great Society were the 1965 Title XVIII (Medicare) and Title XIX (Medicaid) amendments to the Social Security Act.

5. The community action title of the OEA of 1964 was intended primarily to provide services to the poor with one major distinction—the poor themselves would identify the specific needs of the community and design the programs they believed would best meet those needs. A CAP was defined as one which develops a comprehensive and multiservice approach to the problem of poverty, drawing on existing public and private community resources (U.S. Congress 1964a). Four different forms of citizen participation were included in the implementation of the EOA: policy making; social service utilization; social action; and job experience (Kramer 1969). The initial legislation did not specify what would constitute adequate participation of the poor. In 1966, the Scheurer Amendments specified that the poor should comprise at least one-third of the Community Action Agency (CAA) board. It also specified that representatives should live in the area and be designated by those living "in areas of concentration of poverty, with special emphasis on participation by the residents of the area who are poor" (Marshall 1971, 11).

6. Boyte 1985. See, e.g., Alinsky 1968; Greenstone and Peterson 1972; D.R. Marshall 1971; Morone 1990; Moynihan 1969; Quadagno 1994. While many of the extensive reports on the CAPs mentioned that women were in the majority at the lower-level positions (see Grosser 1973), only Kenneth Clark and Jeanette Hopkins (1969) and Curt Lamb (1975) detailed the important leadership roles that women played in these programs. Clark and Hopkins (1969) noted that a

greater number of women ran for and, subsequently, won seats on the Community Action Councils (CACs) that were set up to oversee the operation of the twelve area offices of the Philadelphia Anti-Poverty Action Committee (PAAC). (Each CAC consisted of twelve members elected by the community residents.) Furthermore, twice as many women were elected as CAC representatives to PAAC.

7. See Fraser and Gordon 1994a, 1994b.

8. Robert Pruger (1966, 13–14) explained the rationale used to establish a "New Careers" program in a public school in 1964. Policy makers determined that there existed "a reciprocally problematic stalemate...between the low-income commuinity and the established service bureaucracies of that community." In order to break this stalement, "new careerists" were hired as community workers to serve as a bridge between the poor and the different agencies serving the community. Also see Melvin Mogulf 1970a and 1970b.

9. R. Cohen 1976, 8. In 1966, Title II of HR 15111, that extended the antipoverty program through 1970, provided $36.5 million for New Careers and was entitled Public Service Employment. Funds for New Careers was consolidated with other work and training programs such as the Neighborhood Youth Corps and Operation Mainstream by the 1967 amendments to the EOA Congressional Quarterly Service 1969). Other legislation provided additional funding in the areas of health, education, and crime prevention. This legislation includes, for example, the Allied Health Professions Personnel Training Act of 1966, Elementary and Secondary Education Act of 1967, Higher Education Act Amendments of 1967, Social Security Amendments of 1967, Health Manpower Act of 1968, Vocational Education Act Amendments of 1968, Vocational Rehabilitation Act Amendments of 1968, Juvenile Delinquency Prevention and Control Act of 1968, Omnibus Crime Control and Safe Streets Act of 1968, and the Drug Abuse Education Act of 1969.

In 1969, Congress extended funds for New Careers opportunities for unemployed and low-income persons. New Careers included jobs "designed to improve the physical, social, economic, or cultural condition of the community or area served in fields of public service, including without limitation to health, education, welfare, recreation, day care, neighborhood redevelopment, and public safety, which provide maximum prospects for on-the-job training, promotion, and advancement and continued employment without Federal assistance, which give promise of contributing to the broader adoption of new methods of structuring jobs and new methods of providing job ladder opportunities, and which provide opportunities for further occupational training to facilitate career advancement" (p. 834).

10. See Katz 1989.

11. My use of the term "empowerment" here differs from the conceptualization political scientist Barbara Cruikshank (1995) offered in her critique of the War on Poverty. She criticized "the uncritical use of 'empowerment'" (p. 30) as describing a process through which individuals are said to move "from powerlessness to full citizenship, from subjection to subjectivity" (p. 31) with the aid of "experts" or community organizers who are not part of the community (p. 35). My use of the term, however, intentionally includes the personal as well as collective recognition of the power to fight for equality and an improved quality of life. Many of the community workers themselves articulated this particular definition of empowerment, not as an outcome of "expert" intervention but as an

ongoing interactive process occurring in dynamic relationships with those who struggled on their own behalf and for others in their communities. Rather than a top-down view characterized by unequal relations, this conceptualization is rooted in the perspectives and analyses of the women who themselves witnessed processes of personal and collective changes that they termed empowerment. Some community workers, particularly those with professional credentials, did use the term to describe the individual competence building strategies that Cruikshank criticizes. However, in all the community workers' narratives, I found evidence of both individual and collective constructions of empowerment. In fact, most argued that since collective empowerment required individual competence building, the two processes were intrinsically linked.

12. Drawing on postsuffrage social reformers who "connected the achievement of women's full citizenship to the needs of the most vulnerable women," Wendy Sarvasy (1992, 361) offers a similar analysis. She explains: "It is not accidental that the postsuffrage feminists focused on poor women, working-class women, and immigrant women; the needs of these women justified the welfare state and the expansion of women's public role." Also see Kathleen Jones 1990.

13. In a special issue of Social Politics: International Studies in Gender, State, and Society on "Gender and Welfare Regimes," Jane Lewis (1997, 169) criticizes the limits of her earlier work (Lewis 1992) for neglecting to include attention to "caring regimes" (defined as "policies that have constituted women's unpaid work"). However, in her more recent attempt to address this issue she limits the arena of care to the household division of labor and economics. My analysis argues for the expansion of welfare-state analysis to include community-based care as well as family and household-based caring work, paid work, and welfare. I further suggest that these dimensions also should be explored with reference to practices of participatory democracy and therefore take into account both social and political citizenship. Building on Ann Orloff's (1993) analytic framework, my work highlights the significance of (1) community-based organization of welfare services, (2) paid and unpaid work performed for the benefit of communities, and (3) the "racialized gender" organization of work in communities (namely, women are drawn into community work by processes of race as well as gender and class and these differences influence the type of work performed) (see Mink 1995). My analysis also shifts focus from individual households to communities asking parallel questions about the access to economic resources and autonomy.

14. T. H. Marshall (1950) differentiated between civil, political, and social citizenship rights. Civil citizenship refers to the enjoyment of freedom that accompany membership in a political community but does not necessarily include the franchise. Political citizenship is defined as the right to participate in the political process through voting and other political acts such as serving on juries. Social citizenship refers to access to resources like welfare and health care which enable one to sustain a household and "to live the life of a civilized being according to the standards prevailing in the society" (Marshall 1950, 11, quoted in Orloff 1993, 306). During the War on Poverty, state-sponsored programs like the CAPs provided resources to low-income communities as well as offered sites designed to expand poor residents' political participation. Wendy Sarvasy and Birte Siim (1994, 253) suggest the term "pluralistic citizenship" to provide a conceptual framework for analyses of "the interconnections between social and political citizenship."

15. See Boris 1995; Siim 1994.
16. See, e.g., Katz 1986; Trattner 1974. Recent literature on women social reformers, however, demonstrates several parallels with the community workers. For example, Robyn Muncy (1991) emphasizes how female social reformers' values differed from their male colleagues in making expert knowledge accessible to women as consumers and mothers. According to Sarvasy (1997), the feminist social reformers she studied were keenly aware of the ways that bureaucratic forms of administration failed to respond effectively to the needs of the poor. These "citizen social servants" valued indigenous caretaking and argued for expansion of democratic participation in service delivery.
17. See Dill 1988; Gilkes 1988; Johnson 1987; Martin and Martin 1985; Morris 1992; Sanchez-Ayendez 1995; Stack 1974. Historical research by feminist scholars stresses the role of African American women in the struggle to provide social services, education, and health care to low-income residents. (See, e.g., Barnett 1995; Giddings 1984; Gordon 1991; Hine 1990; Jones 1985; Scott 1991.) Latinas, Native American women and Asian American women also have a long tradition of community-based work designed to protect and improve the lives of their racial-ethnic communities. (See, e.g., Acosta-Belen 1986; Aguilar-San Juan 1994; Castello 1986; Glenn 1986; Green 1990; Hewitt 1990.)
18. Also see Fisher 1994; Garland 1988; Kaplan 1982, 1997; Susser 1988; Woliver 1993. In her analysis of women's grassroots campaigns for social justice, Temma Kaplan (1997, 1–2) defines "grassroots" as "being outside the control of any state, church, union, or political party. To the women claiming its provenance, being from the grassroots generally means being free from any constraining political affiliations and being responsible to no authority except their own group." I use the term to highlight the contradictions that arise when community workers who are indigenous to low-income communities are incorporated into the state through the antipoverty programs in their neighborhoods. While their political engagement was circumscribed by processes of bureaucratization and professionalization, the grassroots warriors continued to defy the authority of the state when it interfered with their ability to respond effectively to their defined communities.
19. See, e.g., Aaron 1978; Alinsky 1968; Cloward 1968; Harrington 1971; Piven and Cloward 1971,1993; Rose 1972; Wilensky 1983.
20. See, e.g., Brager and Purcell 1967.
21. Many authors also stress the importance of the urban and racial unrest of the 1960s (see, e.g., Matusow 1984; Piven and Cloward 1971; 1977; S. Rose). The first in a sequence of riots that erupted in low-income African American communities occurred in New York City in 1963, but the social tension was building earlier. Piven and Cloward (1971, 1993, 259) provide further support for their analysis with reference to the initial funding patterns of OEO. Rather than distribute funds across rural and urban regions, OEO targeted the urban areas of New York, Chicago, Los Angeles, Philadelphia, Detroit, St. Louis, Washington, D.C., Boston, Atlanta, and Pittsburgh. Furthermore, the fact that the funds were channeled directly to poor urban neighborhoods further supports their argument that the antipoverty program was designed to "deal with political problems in the cities" resulting from discontent among blacks and other racial-ethnic minorities in inner-cities (p. 256). In contrast, Gareth Davies (1992, 206) argues that "[the] War on Poverty was primarilty the product neither of political expediency nor of racial imperative." Davies asserts that

"it was the autonomous expression of a genuine faith in the traditional American ideal of equal opportunity. That such a faith also served the political interests of President Johnson and his allies need not detract from its authenticity." In his analysis, Davies affirms the perspectives of James T. Patterson (1981), Henry J. Aaron (1978, 1983), Sar A. Levitan (1969) and James L. Sundquist (1974) in arguing for a "naive faith in individual rehabilitation" (p. 207) as the major contributing factor for President Johnson's War on Poverty.

22. In some cities, civil rights organizations actively challenged the administration of the antipoverty programs as evident by the flyer announcing a boycott against the poverty elections in Philadelphia sponsored by Freedom George of the Young Militants, Bill Mathias of CORE, Fred Mealy of SNCC, and Robert Brazzwell of the NAACP Youth Council. See Appendix C.

23. See Abramovitz 1988; Boris 1995; Fraser 1989; Mink 1995; Naples 1991a; Smith 1984.

24. For example, Barbara Nelson (1990, 124, 133) described what she termed the "two-channel welfare state" where white-male industrial workers received benefits through the "judicial, public, and routinized" Workman's Compensation program while "impoverished, white, working-class widows with young children" received state support through the "administrative, private, and nonroutinized" Mothers' Aid program. The racialized gender subtext of the state was further elaborated in the Social Security Act where white widows could claim state support through the less stigmatized Social Security Insurance program while unmarried or divorced mothers received less financial support through the Aid to Dependent Children (see Boris 1995; Mink 1995).

25. See Abramovitz 1988; Boris 1995; Chang 1994; Mink 1995; Mohanty 1991; Nelson 1990.

26. See, e.g., Baulstein and Woock 1968; Donovan 1967; and D.R. Marshall 1971.

27. Since only one community worker interviewed was of Asian American descent, her experiences will not be included in the comparative racial-ethnic analyses of community work.

28. In fact, the terms "resident/nonresident" are more consistently accurate and were less value laden than other distinctions considered (e.g., insider/outsider; indigenous/nonindigenous; or noncredentialed/credentialed).

29. Also see M.L. Anderson 1983; Buss 1985; Geiger 1986; Ginsberg 1989; Kelly 1979; Mohanty 1991; the Personal Narratives Group 1989; Roberts 1981a; D. Smith 1979.

30. Broadly defined, feminist standpoint epistemology includes Nancy Hartsock's (1983) "feminist historical materialist" perspective, Donna Haraway's (1988) analysis of "situated knowledges," Patricia Hill Collins's (1990) "black feminist thought," Chela Sandoval's (1991) explication of third-world feminists "oppositional consciousness," and Dorothy Smith's (1987, 1990) "everyday world" sociology for women, among others. Also see Jaggar 1983; James and Busia 1993; Harding 1986, 1991; Mohanty 1991. Those writing within this broad tradition of feminist standpoint epistemologies draw on three different definitions of standpoint: standpoint viewed (1) as embodied in particular knowers who possess certain racial, ethnic, class, and gender identities as in certain aspects of Collins's approach; (2) through communal or relational processes through which a standpoint is achieved as in Haraway's approach; and (3) as an axis point of investigation as in Smith's "everyday world" perspective. In my use of the term "standpoint," I incorporate all three approaches for a multidimensional standpoint analysis (see Naples 1998b).

31. Linda Alcoff (1988, 433) uses the concept "positionality" to describe "the subject as nonessentialized and emergent from a historical experience...[to] say at one and the same time that gender is not natural, biological, universal, ahistorical, or essential and yet still claim that gender is relevant because we are taking gender as a position from which to act politically." In this study I simultaneously take as the starting point the intersection of gender, race, class, and political context in community workers' political praxis.

32. As a result of her research on activists in the abortion controversy, Faye Ginsberg (1989, 60) recommends the use of "narratives about individual transformations, cast as conversions in life stories" since they "serve as models for envisioned changes in the social and cultural order that accommodate female activists' self understandings." Also see Chase 1995; Geiger 1986; Gluck and Patai 1991; Rollins 1995; Sacks 1988a, 1988b.

33. See Eckstein 1988; Snow and Benford 1992; Tarrow 1992; Wildavsky 1987.

34. Howard Hallman (1969, 1) notes that the call for "community control emerged as a demand of black nationalists as a means of achieving 'black power,' a slogan that gained popularity during the Meredith Mississippi Freedom March of June 1966. As a reaction to the ineffectiveness of programs controlled by stagnant, big-city bureaucracies, neighborhood control became a major interest of Mayor John Lindsay's administration in New York City during the same period."

35. Also see Abu-Lughod 1993; Behar 1993; M. Wolf 1992.

36. Yet, as Kathleen Canning (1994) points out, "Scott's argument foregrounds the discursive in the construction of women's work while leaving obscure its relationship to the social context in which it emerged."

37. In his concluding chapter to his fascinating account of identity formation and contructions of nationhood, Benedict Anderson (1991, 204) writes: "All profound changes in consciousness, by their very nature, bring with them characteristic amnesias. Out of such oblivions, in specific historical circumstances, spring narratives." Much has happened over the course of the community workers' social lives and, therefore, one would expect that their narratives are constructed in ways that render some events and experiences outside the frame. However, what remains within the narrative frames are significant markers of how they integrated their past into a contemporary vision that makes sense of the changes in their social and political environment. Therefore, their oral narratives reveal much about their personal political priorities as they are formulated to connect their past with their present. While details of the stories and events might have differed in their accounts, what is striking in this research is the consistency of certain themes across many of the narratives of the women I interviewed in the mid-1980s and the mid-1990s—a consistency that can partially explain their persistence in this form of work from the 1960s.

38. Borland 1991. Also see D. Wolf 1996.

39. Mario Fantini, Marilyn Gittell, and Richard Magat (1970, x) describe the goals of the community control of schools as...

> a demand for school accountability by parents to whom the schools have never accounted, particularly those parents of low-status groups in Northern cities. It is a demand that their children be respected as human beings with the potential all normal children have and that they be taught by those hired for the purpose of teaching. It is a demand that the schools cease finding scapegoats and stop making excuses for their failure by

claiming that these children are uneducable or too "disruptive" or too "culturally deprived" to respond. It is a desperate response to the subtle and flagrant racism that afflicts so many of the institutions of American education.

For further information on the community control of school movement in New York City also see Maurice Berube and Marilyn Gittell (1969); Mario Fantini and Marilyn Gittell (1973); and Diane Ravitch (1974).

40. See, e.g., Frazier 1963; Lincoln 1984.
41. See, e.g., Katz 1989; Mead 1986; Murray 1984; Naples 1997a.
42. Also see Collins 1990; S. Evans 1979; Fraser 1989; Haraway 1988; Hawkesworth 1989; Peattie and Rein 1983; Smith 1987.
43. See Berube and Gittell 1969; and Ravitch 1974.
44. Temma Kaplan (1997) emphasizes the power of spectacle and shaming rituals for enhancing women's political effectiveness. What might appear as signs of unruliness in one sphere could be utilized to make a stronger statement when taken into the public arena to demonstrate a political point. In diverse settings, women have adopted gendered practices in the domestic or social sphere for broader political purposes to dramatize their concerns and to protest injustice (also see Pardo 1998).
45. See, e.g., Brown 1988; Butler and Kondratas 1987;Carballo and Bane 1984; Katz 1989; Phillips 1990.
46. Community workers associated with Students' for a Democratic Society (SDS) which initiated community organizing programs known as Economic Research and Action Projects (ERAP) in 1963 and the Student Nonviolent Coordinating Committee (SNCC) organized in 1960, along with organizers trained by Saul Alinsky were achieving some success in mobilizing low-income communities (see, e.g., Miller 1994).
47. Spanish Harlem comprises the Manhattan neighborhoods located between East 110th Street and East 125th Street from Fifth Avenue to the East River.
48. New York City's Lower East Side broadly defined encompasses the area from Third Avenue to Avenue D and 14th Street to Chinatown.
49. The racial-ethnic and class segregation of housing, health care, education, and employment in New York City and Philadelphia provided a material ground upon which the community workers constructed differing conceptions of community. Experiences in the social movements of the 1960s and 1970s further reinforced their constructions of community as an intersection of racial, ethnic, class, gender, and spatial relations. Despite these varied conceptualizations, the community workers all defined community through their involvement with others in activities that heightened their experience of communion. According to Schmalenbach, the experience of communion "is formed by an actual experience of common feeling" (quoted in McCourt 1977, 232; also see Erikson 1976; and Mayo 1977). This experience of social bonding sustained them in their work. Their experience of communion is key to understanding why many of these women remained active in their community for years despite the low pay, the precarious nature of the funding for community work, and the deteriorating conditions of their communities.
50. The text of the pledge that Nation of Islam leader Louis Farrakhan asked black men to take at the Million Man March is as follows:

I pledge that from this day forward I will strive to love my brother as I love myself, morally, spiritually, mentally, socially, politically and economically for the benefit of myself, my family and my people. I pledge that I will strive to build businesses, build houses, build hospitals, build factories and enter into international trade for the good of myself, my family and my people

I pledge that from this day forward I will never raise my hand with a knife or a gun to beat, cut, or shoot any member of my family or any human being except in self-defense. I pledge from this day forward I will never abuse my wife by striking her, disrespecting her, for she is the mother of my children and the producer of my future. I pledge that from this day forward I will never engage in the abuse of children, little boys or girls for sexual gratification. For I will let them grow in peace to be strong men and women for the future of our people.

I will never again use the "B word" to describe any female. But particularly my own black sister. I pledge from this day forward that I will not poison my body with drugs or that which is destructive to my health and my well-being. I pledge from this day forward I will support black newspapers, black radio, black television. I will support black artists who clean up their acts to show respect for themselves and respect for their people and respect for the ears of the human family. I will do all of this so help me God.

51. Also see Gilkes 1980, 1988.
52. See Barbara Omolade (1994) and Kisho Scott (1991) for discussions of some of the psychological and social costs paid by professional African American women community workers who struggle on behalf of others in their communities.
53. See, e.g., Lipsky 1980; Piven and Cloward 1971,1993; Schram 1995.
54. Feminist and social movement scholars have carefully explored how bureaucratization and professionalization circumscribe progressive movements for social change (see Ferguson 1984; Piven and Cloward 1977; Pope 1992) as well as constitute inevitable outcomes of movement efforts (see Feree and Martin 1995; Reinelt 1995; Spalter-Roth and Schreiber 1995; Whittier 1995).

# Chapter 2

1. Gilkes 1988; Jones 1985; Kaminer 1984.
2. See, e.g., Marris and Rein 1967; Matusow 1984; Moynihan 1969; Piven and Cloward 1971; Roby 1974; Rose 1972.
3. Saul Alinsky, who played a crucial role in developing community-based organizing strategies and training a generation of community organizers began work with Clifford Shaw after graduating from the University of Chicago in 1931. His book, *Reveille for Radicals* (1946), chronicles the lessons he learned from his work with the Industrial Areas Foundation, a community organization he began in 1940 in "Back of the Yards" in Chicago. See Harry Boyte's discussion of Alinsky's work in *Common Wealth* (1989). Also see Robert Fisher 1994.
4. James Sundquist (1969, 11) reports: "By 1963, the work of the President's

Committee on Juvenile Delinquency and Youth Crime had become in the words of one observer, 'a $30 million test of Ohlin's "opportunity theory.""' Also see Daniel Patrick Moynihan's (1969, 58) discussion of the MFY "social experiment."

5. In addition to their theoretical contribution, Cloward and Ohlin played active roles in the design and implementation of the Grey Areas Projects funded by the Ford Foundation and the early CAAs models (Marris and Rein 1972). The five Grey Areas Projects were initially designed to expand the public school system's role in the community. The Ford Foundation's innovative move into community organization accompanied a new emphasis on local participation (S. Rose 1972).

6. Also influential in the development of community action were Leonard Cottrell and Richard Boone, founder and student, respectively, of the Chicago School of Sociology. Cottrell was executive director of the Russell Sage Foundation, "sometime mentor" to Ohlin, and chaired the Demonstration Review Panel for the delinquency program (Matusow 1984, 112). Boone was hired by Hackett to head the committee that developed Robert Kennedy's "pet project," a National Service Corps (p. 117). Both Cottrell and Boone were "persuasive voice[s] urging participation of the poor."

7. Matusow 1984, 122. Sundquist (1969, 20), quoting Theodore Sorensen (1965, 753) notes that Kennedy had his staff "working on a 'comprehensive, coordinated attack on poverty' more than a month before he went to Dallas—or sometime in October." He credits Assistant Budget Director Charles L. Schultze with suggesting that the antipoverty programs be renamed "action programs" preferring this to the term under consideration by the William B. Cannon of the Budget Bureau, "development corporation." Sundquist reports that some unidentified staff added the word "community" to the phrase.

8. Quoted in Sundquist 1969, 23. See Tocqueville 1969.

9. President Johnson moved quickly to incorporate community action as a main component of the War on Poverty (Sundquist 1969). Matusow (1984, 123) reports:

> In one stroke Johnson escalated community action from an experimental program to precede the War on Poverty into the very war itself. No one at the Texas White House told the president that Hackett's delinquency projects—community action's model—had so far yielded no promising results, that a major purpose of the projects was institutional reform, and that at least one project was dreaming up ways to enlist the poor in a struggle against entrenched local power. No one told Johnson because no one who knew was there.

10. See, e.g., Davies 1992; Sviridoff 1989; Yarmolinsky 1969.

11. For background, critical analysis, and oral historical data on the Peace Corps, see Coates Redmon 1986; T. Zane Reeves 1988; Karen Schwartz 1991; P. David Searles 1997.

12. The National Service Corps was conceived by Robert Kennedy as the domestic version of the Peace Corps. The final proposal included training for a corps of workers who would lend their skills to areas where there was insufficient human services available. The House defeated the National Service Corps bill in 1963 before President Kennedy's assassination (Matusow 1984, 117–188).

13. Piven and Cloward (1971/1993, 281-282) argue that

> ...to reach, placate, and integrate a turbulent black constituency, the national Democratic administration of the 1960s acted to help blacks get more from local government. To accomplish this goal, it reached past state and local governments—including Democratic ones—to stimulate black demands for services, and in that process it directed rising black volatility into service protests against local government.

Also see Davies 1992; Haveman 1977; Kramer 1969a; Marris and Rein 1967,1973; Matusow 1984; Piven and Cloward 1971,1993; Quadagno 1994; Weir 1988.

14. It must also be emphasized that these efforts to constitute the poor as a political constituency were embedded in the historical period when low-income blacks and other racial-ethnic groups were demanding political and economic justice from the dominant white society (see Morone 1990; Quadagno 1994).

15. As a result of pressure placed on President Johnson, the Executive Office worked to limit to the poor's policy-making role. As Daniel Patrick Moynihan (1969, 145) reports:

> On Nov. 5, 1954, a front-page story appeared in The New York Times, stating:
> > The Budget Bureau, fiscal arm of the White House, has told the Office of Economic Opportunity that it would prefer less emphasis on policy making by the poor in planning community projects.
> > "Maximum feasible participation" by the poor in the antipoverty program is called for by the law. In the bureau's view, this means primarily using the poor to carry out the program, not to design it.

Also see Cruikshank 1995; Kramer 1969a; Marris and Rein 1967,1973; Matusow 1984; Morone 1990; Piven and Cloward 1971,1993.

16. See M.J. Austin 1978; Bryan 1981; Levitan 1969.

17. Ironically, the turnover at the administrative level frequently gave the community workers the autonomy to operate with little ongoing interference from the central offices. This, in turn, contributed to greater satisfaction with their paid community work.

18. Lipsky 1980; Pearl and Reissman 1965. The criteria for professionalism in social work include adherence to the following: "...a knowledge base derived from a systematic body of theory; (2) the degree of commitment to professional authority; (3) attainment of community sanction for what social workers do; (4) a [distinct] code of ethics; (5) [distinct] values, norms, and symbols of a professional social work community" (Greenwood 1957 quoted in Burghardt 1982b, 221). Burghardt criticizes social work's claim to professional status given the lack of control most social workers have over their work due to the "harsh organizational realities" they confront in the workplace (p. 222). Further, he argues, "Through the adroit use of 'professional sanction' and appeals to particular values and norms (usually of the kind that demand self-sacrifice)... administrators are able to maintain their dominance of the work situation without the use of more direct but less professionally tolerable requirements of

more work for less pay" (p. 223). The example he offers is when hospitals "'reward' a professional after three years of consistent performance with a student for supervision. This position of supervisor, lacking any increase in pay or organizational authority, does not carry with it the lessening of one's work load in other areas" (p. 223). Burghardt insists that unionization is the more appropriate strategy for social workers to gain greater control over their work.

19. Two of the seven resident community workers who finished their GEDs while working for a CAA also completed some college. Of the twenty-six women who only had a high school degree, twelve completed some college. Eight finished their college degrees while working full time for a CAA. Of these eight, five went on to graduate school. Three completed advanced degrees in social work, public administration, and education, respectively.

20. By 1984, three other community workers had lost their positions or advancements they achieved as a result of funding cutbacks.

21. Also see Fainstein and Fainstein 1974; Piven and Cloward 1971, 1993, 1977.

22. A controversy arose within PAAC over whether paid workers serving on the policy board had a conflict of interest. As a result, many paid workers resigned their elected positions. I further discuss this issue in chapter 3.

23. Matusow 1984; Perlman and Ferman 1981; Wofford 1974.

24. Stephen Rose (1972, 166) concludes from his analysis of the implementation of CAPs in twenty cities:

> The organizational model designed by the CAP planners, stipulating the involvement of existing service systems, created an organizational framework which reduced uncertainty by channeling the decisions required to create the new agencies through the filtering device of coordinated planning. By including the interorganizational field within the organizational structure of the new community action agency, the Community Action Program planners provided the opportunity to re-create the local domain consensus or reinforce it with Federal funds.

25. Sundquist (1969, 13) reports that in 1963 Paul Ylvisaker, then head of Ford Foundation's Public Affairs Program, which first funded community action agencies as new organizational entities within poor communities said: "There is some feeling that this decision to establish new instrumentalities is an attack on the present system of community health and welfare councils. If so, it came not by intent nor with malice, but as a commentary on the gap that exists between the job to be done and the capacity of our urban communities as presently structured to accomplish it."

# Chapter 3

1. See Appendix D. Also see Clark and Hopkins 1969; Matusow 1984; Roby 1974.

2. In fact, some observers argue that the CAPs were designed to co-opt the social protests generated by the Civil Rights Movement and prevent further urban unrest (see Alinsky 1968; Piven and Cloward 1971).

3. Acknowledging the drawbacks of Almond and Verba's construct (i.e., lack of agreed-upon unit of analysis and content and the extent to which it was a result

of individual choice or structural conditions), Tarrow then proceeds to compare the notion of "political culture" with "collective action frames" discussed by David Snow and Robert Benford (1992, 136). "Collective action frames" refer to how social- movement organizations produce and maintain meaning "for constituents, antagonists, and bystanders or observers."

4. See Myra Marx Ferree's (1992) excellent analysis of the limits of rational choice assumptions within resource mobilization approaches. In contrast, she argues, that social-movement theorists should resist reducing "individuals to unthinking resources to be manipulated by a movement organization as it sees fit" (p. 31).

5. In their efforts to recruit others to join a political movement or to gain sympathy for a specific campaign, political actors often construct "collective action frames" (Snow and Benford 1992, 136). However, this process of framing often renders invisible the inconsistencies and contradictions within social-movement organizations or among political allies.

6. Also see William Gamson (1992) for a useful discussion of social-psychological perspectives on collective action. In particular, Gamson highlights processes of micromobilization outlined in his coauthored text *Encounters With Unjust Authority* (Gamson, Fireman, and Rytina 1982). Also see Breines 1982; Giddings 1984; Melucci 1989. While this literature provides fruitful discussion of the factors that contribute to micromobilization, the unit of analysis centers on specific social-movement organizations rather than individual political biographies as characterizes my approach.

7. Greenstone and Peterson 1973; Kramer 1969a; Lowi 1969; Mogulof 1970b.

8. See, e.g., Clark and Hopkins 1969; Kramer 1969a; Matusow 1984; Mogulof 1970b; Peterson 1970; Piven 1966; Rodgers 1982.

9. The twelve area offices of PAAC were identified as Areas A through L. See Appendix F for a map of the twelve area offices in Philadelphia.

10. See Piven 1990; Piven and Cloward 1971,1993; S. Rose 1972.

11. Like MFY, HARYOU's initial focus was on the problem of juvenile delinquency. Funding was secured from President Kennedy's Commission on Juvenile Delinquency and Youth Crime (PCJD), set up in 1961, and the City of New York. Congressman Adam Clayton Powell, who headed the House Education and Labor Committee that funded the PCJD, supported another central Harlem group, Associated Community Teams (ACT). Both organizations were funded. ACT was designated to test the value of Volunteers in Service to America (VISTA) and HARYOU was funded to implement its proposal to serve delinquent youth in Harlem. After eighteen months the groups were to merge. Since the merging organizations could not agree on an executive director, the process was delayed considerably. Tensions heated up between Clark and Powell leading to Clark's departure from HARYOU and Powell's insertion of Livingston Wingate as director of the newly merged HARYOU-ACT (Matusow 1984).

12. Marris and Rein 1972; Matusow 1984.

13. In less than a year, HARYOU-ACT became a focus of investigations by the district attorney of Manhattan, OEO, and the Justice Department. The accusations and subsequent investigations did not reveal any intentional wrongdoing on the part of HARYOU-ACT, but did reduce HARYOU-ACT's status as a progressive and effective CAA. Most of the innovative leaders left the organization. The City of New York as well as the federal government took a more

active role in determining HARYOU-ACT's organizational structure and program services.

14. Lowi 1969; Sennott 1974; also see Ershkowitz and Zikmund 1973.

15. Matusow (1984, 256). Matusow reports: "OEO bravely hailed the election as an example of grassroots democracy and subsequently repeated the experiment in eight other cities—until Shriver, embarrassed by a 0.7 percent turnout in Los Angeles, called a halt" (p. 256).

16. In 1966, one fifth of all Philadelphian families and unrelated individuals were living in poverty; of those living in poverty, eighty-three percent were African American. One in ten potential workers were unemployed (PAAC 1966a). See Appendix C for flyer calling for boycott against the antipoverty elections in Philadelphia in 1966.

17. The Maximum Participation Movement (MPM) was organized as a watch-dog group by university professor Dr. Arthur Shostak and others frustrated by the heavy-handed tactics of Samuel Evans. Shostak was enlisted by Evans to design a War on Poverty Institute to provide training and research for PAAC. Evans and Shostak parted ways over Shostak's vision of the Institute which included guest lectures by Saul Alinsky and other radical community organizers. According to Nancy Sennott (1974, 16–17), Shostak informed OEO that Evans "was converting the Institute into a forum for political propaganda and that they, the framers of the proposal, were withdrawing in protest." OEO refused to fund the Institute. MPM met approximately one year and "issued a series of 'white papers' criticizing the activities of PAAC and advocating more power and authority for the Community Action Councils (Sennott 1974, 17)." See Appendix G.

18. See Hand 1966; Stroh 1966.

19. The Commission would continue to follow the guidelines of the Home Rule Charter which prohibits partisan political activities (see Appendix E). In 1996, Pennsylvania's stipulation against participation in political activities followed the regulations spelled out in the Omnibus Budget Reconciliation Act of 1981:

> No community action agency or limited purpose agency receiving funds pursuant to this act may engage in organized political activity, including, but not limited to, endorsement of candidates for public office, political fundraising or provide similar assistance in connection with an election, nor shall funds received pursuant to this act be expended for providing transportation of voters or prospective voters to the polls on a nonpartisan basis, or providing any nonpartisan voter registration activity or lobbying efforts at the local, State, or Federal level. [Commonwealth of Pennsylvania, General Assembly, 1995, 1996b]

20. CSBG was funded through the Omnibus Budget Reconciliation Act of 1981. The CSBG allocation to the states was based on the states' relative number of unemployed, welfare recipients, and children living in families below the poverty level. The states were charged with the responsibility for distributing the funds to local Community Action Agencies. States determined the allocations to local agencies through an application process based on "such individual state formulas and criteria as the number of people living below the poverty level or the geographic location (urban versus rural) of the local agency" (Givel 1991, 3–4).

21. See U.S. Department of Housing and Urban Development, Office of

Community Planning, and U.S. Department of Agriculture, Office of Small Community and Rural Development 1993.

22. Marilyn Marks Rubin (1994) presents a history of enterprise zones and argues that President Clinton's EZEC program draws on themes that were evident in policy approaches that date back to the Model Cities community-planning projects of the 1960s. The Model Cities Program, a key program of President Johnson's Great Society, was created by the Demonstration Cities and Metropolitan Act of 1966. It provided resources to encourage urban redevelopment. According to Rubin (1994, 166), the program never received adequate funding to accomplish its legislative mandate. The program was funded until 1972 when President Nixon's administration failed to include a budget request for continued Model Cities funding. Also see Sarah Liebschutz 1995.

23. Gerry Riposa (1996, 536) analyzes the extent to which the Empowerment Zones and Enterprise Communities Program fosters "the community context necessary for greater local participation in economic development." However, with no mechanisms to ensure local community participation, it is unlikely that the EZEC programs will involve local residents to the extent that the CAPs initially did. As Riposa (1996, 549–550) reports:

> Because community involvement is solicited, it does not necessarily follow that national and local governments will divide authority and decision-making powers with those whose input is sought....Presently, signs are emerging in empowerment zones that mayors are trying to avoid potential challenges to the existing distribution of power.

24. The 1962 Manpower Development and Training Act included job-training programs in both classroom settings and on-the-job. As Nancy Rose (1995) argues, these programs targeted unemployed and low-skilled fathers.

25. See, e.g., Jonnes 1986; Larner and Howe 1971.

26. MFY received $2.1 million from the Office of Juvenile Delinquency (Matusow 1984, 111). In addition to PCJD, Kennedy was influential in securing the passage of the Manpower Development and Training Act of 1962 and the National Service Corps which are also viewed as precursors of the EOA. The National Service Corps, for example, was proposed by Kennedy in 1963 and formed the basis for Volunteers in Service to America (VISTA) which was funded under the EOA of 1964.

27. The Grey Areas Projects were initially concerned with expanding the public school system's role in the community. The original five Grey Areas Projects were funded in 1962. The Ford Foundation's innovative move into community organization accompanied a new emphasis on local participation in social service and education (S. Rose 1972).

28. Alfred Fried (1969, 137) reports that in 1964 twenty-five percent of MFY funds went to the Work Program and twenty-six percent were allocated to the Education Program.

29. According to Alfred Fried (1969, 141), it was later learned that two MFY staff were paid as informers by the FBI.

30. Marris and Rein 1972; Moynihan 1969. Also see B. Beck 1969; Fried 1969; Weissman 1969a, 1969b, 1969c, 1969d, 1970.

31. For a discussion of welfare-rights organizing sponsored by Mobilization for

Youth see Rabagliati and Birnbaum (1969).

32. As Cruikshank (1995) points out, this "will to empower" within the tradition of social reform often masks the power imbalance between those who position themselves to empower and the targets of such efforts.

## Chapter 4

1. While this section highlights the role of Christian religious institutions, Jewish communities have contributed greatly to the progressive politics in the U.S. For literature on Jewish radicalism in the U.S. that highlights the writings of young radical Jews between the years of 1968 and 1972, see Jack Porter and Peter Dreier (1973).

2. Contributors to the literature on liberation theology include James Cone (1970); Mary Daly (1973); Gustavo Gutiérrez (1973, 1983); Justo L. González (1990); Rosemary Radford Ruether (1973); Mary Sawyer (1994). These authors represent a wide diversity of perspective within liberation theology, emphasizing respectively, black liberation theology, Latin American liberation theology, a radical lesbian perspective, feminist liberation theology, a womanist perspective, an Hispanic perspective, and black ecumenism. Also see Alfred Hennelly, S.J. (1989); Frederick Herzog (1972); and Sharon D. Welch (1985).

3. Dorothy Day was first arrested for her radical activism at age twenty when she marched for women's suffrage and was jailed several years later for her work with the International Workers of the World (Coles 1987, 3). Following her conversion to the Catholic Church, she continued to protest injustice and speak out against war. She criticized Francisco Franco's Spanish civil war losing many Catholic readers of the *Catholic Worker* as a consequence (see Forest 1986). In 1936, she emphasized:"Catholics who look at Spain and think Fascism is a good thing because Spanish Fascists are fighting for the Church against Communist persecution should take another look at recent events in Germany to see how much love the Catholic Church can expect." (Quoted in Coles 1987, 78).

4. According to Nancy Roberts (1984, 10), Day "was jailed four times between 1955 and 1960 for refusing to comply with air raid drills." In 1965, *Catholic Worker* David Miller became the first American to burn his draft card as a protest against the Vietnam War and was jailed for his action. Miller was responding to a call put out by *Catholic Worker* associate editor Thomas Cornell in reaction to a new bill signed by President Johnson that made it illegal to burn or mutilate draft cards (p. 159).

5. Walter Heller, chairman of the Council of Economic Advisors under President John F. Kennedy reported that the President asked for a copy of Michael Harrington's book. According to Arthur Schlesinger, Jr., *The Other America* "helped crystallize his [Kennedy's] determination in 1963 to accompany the tax cut by a poverty program" (Schlesinger 1965, 1009, quoted in Sundquist 1969, 7).

6. Conscientization as defined by Paulo Freire (1970) and first applied in the Latin American context is the process by which people come to understand how their particular situations are shaped by their culture, how they reflect on these new understandings, and act against the circumstances that oppress them to create a more just social world.

7. See, e.g., Breton 1994; Burghardt 1982b; Graber, Haywood, and Vosler 1996;

Rappaport 1986; Solomon 1976; Wagner 1990.

8. Margot Breton (1994, 41) argues that "competence and empowerment-oriented practice starts with the willingness of workers (especially professionals) to share power." Sharing power presumes a separation between the "professional" and the "client." The changing relationship of the resident and nonresident community workers to the communities in which they work further challenges the dichotomy between client/professional that is often drawn in the literature on empowerment approaches to social work practice (also see Burghardt 1982b).

9. One of the major disadvantages of the male-led and fierce infighting evident in the South Bronx (see Jonnes 1986) was that women leaders were circumscribed to more marginal roles within the CAAs.

10. See, e.g., Barnett-Cash 1987; Frazier 1963; Giddings 1984; Lincoln 1984.

11. See, e.g., Carson 1981; Morris 1984; Zinn 1965.

12. Ann Robinson's discussion here evokes Dorothy Day's critique of those who "use the Bible to bring more fear and hate in the world" (quoted in Coles 1987, 29).

13. See, e.g., Boyte, Booth, and Max 1986; Burghardt 1982a, 1982b; Kahn 1982; Naples 1998a; Ohri, Manning, and Curno 1982; Taylor and Randolph 1975. Also see publications from the Center for Community Change, Washington, D.C.; and *Citizen Participation* and *Journal of Community Action* among other journals published through the 1970s and 1980s.

14. See, Curno 1978; Delgado 1982; J. Jacobs 1982; Max 1978, 1977; Rosenbloom 1981. Robert Fisher and Joseph Kling (1990, 81) describe Saul Alinksy, who organized in Chicago from the late 1930s to the late 1940s, as "the father of modern community organizing." His approach included: "(1) a shift from the workplace to the community as the locus of organization, and (2) a move from consciously ideological organization to an approach assumed to be 'nonideological.'" Critics of his approach argue that the emphasis on tactics rather than ideology contributes just as likely to reactionary community actions as progressive ones. Fisher and Kling state that "nonideological organizing" gained popularity among organizers during the 1960s and 1970s (p. 85).

15. See, e.g., Gilkes 1988; Johnson 1987; Martin and Martin 1985.

16. Quoted in Giddings 1984, 97; also see Terrell 1980.

17. The Charity Organization Society (COS) was developed in England to systematize poor relief. The predominant leadership of the COS came from the ranks of upper-income men who were intent upon creating a "business-like" approach to social philanthropy. Many founders of COS were concerned with "pauperism," which assumed that the poor were responsible for their own plight (Hallman 1984). Charity workers were, for the most part, middle- and upper-income women or children of clergy. They were expected to investigate each family and determine who were the "deserving poor" (Bremner 1972). Initially the majority of those who performed the daily work of the COS were volunteers. Paid staff were utilized for program development, fundraising, and supervision. As social needs increased with immigration and migration to the cities by the end of the 1900s, it became evident that volunteers could not adequately maintain the daily functioning of charity work. By 1907, more than fifty percent of the larger COS had abandoned the use of the unpaid "friendly visitors" (Reisch and Wenocur 1981). By the 1920s, professionals were performing most of the tasks originally designed as volunteer.

18. Anne Firor Scott (1991, 91) emphasizes the importance of African American women's missionary societies for helping to improve the educational advance-

ment of poor blacks. She also describes the work of several white women who, through their own missionary work, began to recognize the "discrimination and suffering...in black neighborhoods." Scott reports, "In the face of apathy or outright hostility among the white people," Mary DeBardeleben, a worker employed by the Methodist Home Missionary Society founded a settlement house in a black community in Augusta, Georgia.

19. Collins 1990; Troester 1984.
20. Barnett-Cash 1987; Garcia 1987; Johnson 1987; Smith 1997; Yee 1987.
21. See, e.g., Martin and Martin 1985; A. F. Scott 1991.
22. Robert Fisher and Joseph Kling (1990, 80) discuss the diverse approaches to community organizing in the U.S. They point out that the Communist Party established block committees and other vehicles to organize at the grassroots level. However, these "local campaigns and techniques could be manipulative rather than sincere, and were subject at a moment's notice to reversal by higher party organs and, ultimately, by Comintern determination of overall policy."
23. See James Miller (1994) for a discussion of the political rhetoric and community organizing of the Students for a Democratic Society (SDS). See Stewart Burns (1990) and Sara Evans (1979) for a discussion of sexism within the New Left.
24. See King 1987; Omolade 1994.
25. See Evans 1979; King 1987.
26. Resurrection City was constructed by participants of the "Poor People's Campaign" in an attempt to dramatize the needs of the poor. This shantytown campsite was constructed of plywood and canvas on the grounds of the Washington Monument. Approximately three thousand set up camp in Resurrection City from April 29 to June 23, 1968. Rev. Martin Luther King, Jr., conceived of the Poor People's Campaign before his assassination and Rev. Ralph David Abernathy, who succeeded King as head of the Southern Christian Leadership Conference, led the campaign. On June 24, when the police terminated Resurrection City, Abernathy was arrested. The Congressional Quarterly Service (1969, 776) reports that:

> The Campaign has three major legislative priorities. Among these was repeal of the welfare restrictions added to the 1967 Social Security Act—particularly the freeze on the number of aid to families with dependent children (AFDC) recipients and a new compulsory work program. The freeze was postponed one year, but the work programs were unchanged (S 3063). The other two legislative priorities were passage of the Administration housing bill (S 3497). Only the latter was enacted, and funds were reduced.

27. See Aptheker 1982; Carson 1981; Giddings 1984; Jones 1985; Morris 1984; Piven and Cloward 1977; Robinson 1987; West 1981.
28. Also see Evans 1979; Frankenberg 1993.

# Chapter 5

1. In December of 1963, nineteen hundred members of Local 813 of the International Brotherhood of Teamsters went on strike. The strike affected removal of refuse from commercial establishments like restaurants and other

large businesses. The first day was marked by some violence between the strikers and owner-operators who continued to pick up garbage (Apple 1963). An accord was reached after four days (Stetson 1963).

2. As R.W. Connell (1987, 259) points out: "In ordinary speech 'politics' is a narrow and faintly disreputable term, meaning elections, parliaments, presidents and party antagonisms. 'Politician' can be a term of abuse, 'political' a label for distrust." In fact, women activists have long criticized traditional "politics." In 1927, Winifred Starr Dobyns, who was first chair of the Republican Women's Committee in Illinois, remarked:

> Let us be frank, with some possible exceptions, the aim of the political organization is not good government, patriotic service, public welfare. These are but phrases used for campaign purposes. Political organizations are, for the most part, designed to fill the pockets of politicians at public expense, to give jobs to thousands who find politics an easy way to make a living, to maintain men in office who can do favors for business (Andersen 1990, 182; also quoted in Flammang 1997, 98–99).

3. During the 1970s and early 1980s, feminists debated the significance of capitalism and patriarchy as dual systems of oppressions contributing to women's inequality in contemporary society (see Hartmann 1981; Young 1981). Gloria Joseph (1981), among other feminists of color, argued that this dual formulation did not provide adequate theoretical space for analyzing the role of racism in shaping women of color's oppression.

4. See Griffith and Smith 1990; Sokoloff 1984.

5. Maternalist politics were used by many middle-class women of the later part of the 1800s and early 1900s to justify their movement into the political or public sphere. Seth Koven and Sonya Michel (1993,4) define maternalism as "ideologies and discourses that exalted women's capacity to mother and applied to society as a whole the values they attached to the role: care, nurturance, and morality." Maternalist claims were frequently made on the behalf of others—children, working women, immigrants, the poor. In contrast, activist mothers defined themselves as members of the communities they sought to help, thus breaking with the class and racial-ethnic divisions that often limited maternalist politics of earlier eras. See Molly Ladd-Taylor 1995; Gwendolyn Mink 1995. Furthermore, as this study demonstrates, these women were often already active in the so-called public realm of their neighborhoods as a consequence of their engagement with welfare or health care bureaucracies, housing projects, or neighborhood watch groups, and therefore, they did not need an explicit ideology to justify further involvement. Yet appels to their identities as mothers and community caretakers did circumscribe their self-presentation as political actors thus limiting their efficacy in the formal political arena.

6. See Bookman and Morgen 1988; Gilkes 1988; Kaplan 1982; Krauss 1993; McCourt 1977; Orleck 1995; Pardo 1995; Sacks 1988a.

7. Also see Lind 1992. This point is especially clear when we turn our attention to the feminist activism of the Puerto Rican resident community workers. See chapter six.

8. See, e.g., Moynihan 1967. See Glenn, Chang, and Forcey (1994) and James and Busia (1993) for analyses that contest the traditional constructions of mothering based on white, middle-class, nuclear family models.

9. Latinas, Native American women, and Asian American women have well-estab-
lished traditions of community-based work designed to defend and enhance the
quality of life within their communities. See, e.g., Acosta-Belen 1986; Allen
1986, 1995; Glenn 1986; Glenn, Chang, and Forcey 1994; Gluck et al. 1998;
Green 1990; Hewitt 1990; Sanchez-Ayendez 1995; Torres 1986.
10. hooks 1990, 41. Also see, e.g., Gilkes 1988; Moraga 1981; Rollins 1995; K.
Scott 1991.
11. Essed 1990, 144; also see Carothers 1990.
12. Also see James 1993; Stack 1974; Stack and Burton 1994; Troester 1984.
13. It is possible to view women's activism on behalf of others in their communities
as a form of altruism (Monroe 1996); however, since the resident workers
defined themselves as an integral part of these communities, they felt that they
directly benefitted from these efforts as well. Rather than view women's community work through the bipolar lens of self-interest versus selflessness or
altruism, I explore the workers perception of their relationships with others in
their communal network. In this way, it is possible to explore how these ties
both motivate and sustain the workers commitment. Also see Teske 1997.
14. See Giddings 1984; J. Jones 1985; Stack 1974.
15. See Hochschild, 1995.
16. The shift away from the collective action focus of community work is also evident in some of the community work literature. For example, James Taylor and
Jerry Randolph (1975, 7) emphasized the individual level goal of "coping" as
the primary target for community work. In what they define as a "how-to" book
for new community workers, they offer the following definition:

> Community work is an attempt to help with human needs, and to increase
> people's success in coping with their problems. The person in trouble is
> imbedded within a network of family processes and community systems.
> Your help will be most effective when you can use those systems to sup-
> port your efforts—or at least, not stand in the way of what is needed.
> Although this way of looking at problems can be applied to all class levels
> and groups, in practical fact most of your work will be carried on with the
> poor, the stigmatized, and the deprived.

17. Schram 1995, 63. Also see Piven and Cloward 1971,1993.
18. See, e.g., Daniels 1988; Kaminer 1984.

# Chapter 6

1. Also see hooks 1984; Ferree and Martin 1995; King 1988.
2. Women have also applied their social networking skills to organization on
behalf of racist campaigns. See Blee 1996; Jeansonne 1996; Klatch 1992. For
example, Kathleen Blee (1996) found that a combination of socialization, community context, and specific "transformative" experiences defined through
"racial" lenses motivated women to participate in Ku Klux Klan and other
white-supremacist groups. However, Blee explains: "such racial 'awareness' is
more often a *consequence* of association with members of racist groups than a
*cause* motivating participation" [emphasis in original]. Blee's analysis includes

some significant parallels with analyses of women's political activism more generally. Like the community workers I interview, racist activists describe their active political engagement in racist groups as a logical extension of their becoming "aware" of racial dynamics. However, while the antiracist community workers I interviewed often defined their participation as both personally empowering and politically beneficial to their communities, racist activists expressed a sense of "resignation" and lack of agency. Blee explains that "the declarations of resignation convey both hopelessness in the face of outside social or political forces and powerlessness to reconcile the contradiction between what they see as lofty movement goals of white, Aryan supremacy, and the actual experiences of white, Aryan women within the racist movement" (p. 697).

3. The Ellen Lurie School is located at 3703 Tenth Avenue in Manhattan.

4. Herbert Marcuse (1898–1979) fled Nazi Germany and settled in the United States in 1933. His work emphasized the self-indulgence and excesses of industrial capitalist society. His critical philosophy argued for an analysis of revolutionary change to include factions of society beyond the proletariat—the Marxist revolutionary subject. He was most encouraged by the student movements of the 1960s. See, e.g., Marcuse 1968, 1969.

5. In fact, African American women have been central to the articulation of feminism and offered incisive critiques of the white middle-class Women's Movement (see, e.g., Collins 1990; Combahee River Collective 1982; hooks 1981, 1984).

6. Racism continues to plague white-dominated women's organizations. For example, in 1990, members of the Women of Color caucus walked out of the National Women's Studies Association meetings to protest racism within the organization. Robin Leidner (1991, 266) reports that:

> An African American woman who was fired from her job in NWSA's national office in late 1989 charged that her dismissal was illegal race discrimination and that NWSA's history was one of institutional racism. At the annual convention held in Akron, Ohio, in June 1990, the women of color caucus, angered by the firing, by the association's handling of the subsequent controversy, and by the gap it perceived between NWSA's stated antiracist positions and its organizational practices, withdrew from NWSA with the intention of forming a new organization.

Also see Leidner 1993; Sirianni 1993.

7. The concept "community" brings with it a host of associations. Ira Katznelson (1981, 198) notes that "in 1955, George Hillery counted ninety-four definitions of community in the sociological literature alone." The complexity of the term "community" also relates to the historically changing definitions of community and to the various historically specific forms of social organization of community (see R. Williams 1976; also see Suttles 1972). A distinction must also be made between the ideal-typical construct of community as Gemeinschaft or "localitybound, close-knit network" and Schmalenbach's (1885–1950) notion of "communion" which "is formed by an actual experience of common feeling" (quoted in McCourt 1977, 232; also see Erikson 1976; Mayo 1977). Kathleen McCourt (1977), who studied working class women's activism, attributes the development of a sense of communion to the participation of working-class women in "assertive community organizations" (also see Haywoode 1991).

8. Also see Stern 1998.

9. R.W. Connell (1987, 268–69) also analyzes "working-class feminism" and includes three categories around which working-class feminists might organize: (1) claiming equality in the division of labor in the household and in the paid workplace; (2) gaining independence, freedom from violence, and control over decisions within the family as well as achieving equal representation in unions and freedom from arbitrary authority in the workplace; and (3) attaining control over reproduction, access to contraception, and freedom from sexual harassment.

10. Feminist standpoint theorists influenced by Karl Marx's historical materialist analysis argue that "epistemology grows in a complex and contradictory way from material life" (Hartsock 1983, 117). As a consequence of this analysis, some feminist theorists argue that specific actors who are located in less privileged positions within the social order and who, because of their social locations, are engaged in activities that diverges from others who are not so located will develop analyses of social life that differ from the dominant political perspective (see, e.g., Belenky et al. 1986; Gilligan 1982; Ruddick 1989). These theorists are often criticized for drawing on an essentialized view of women and for equating women's "ways of knowing" with their social identities as women (see Clough, 1994; Flax, 1990).

# Chapter 7

1. Steve Burghardt (1982b, 2) writes about the need for activists "to take joy from politics." He explained:

> After all, if we are trying to change the world to make it a better place in which to work and live, our vision had better encompass a personal capacity that brings part of that vision to life before it miraculously appears somewhere in the distant future.
>
> In the 1980s community practitioners will need to approach their work with appreciation of the personal and political dynamics it involves; to fail in this is to court demoralization and defeat. [Emphasis in original.]

2. Hartsock 1983, 117.

3. Michael Omi and Howard Winant (1986) use the term "racialization" to capture "the processes by which racial meanings are attributed, and racial identities assigned" and infused in material practices and institutional arrangements in a particular society (Winant, 1994, 23). According to racial formation theory, race is "a constituent of the individual psyche and of relationships among individuals...an irreducible component of collective identities and social structures" and "contested throughout social life" (p. 23).

4. In February 1997, the *Utne Reader* reported that a new generation of Black Panthers had emerged in cities like New York. However, reporter Craig Cox points out:

> The new Panthers have not...been warmly welcomed—even in the black communities they seek to serve. And some members of the original Panthers are particularly peeved. [Bobby] Seal, a lecturer at Temple University, has decried the new party's emphasis on guns and vigilante-style

community patrols over the community organizing he and his followers advocated. Kaleef Hasan, one of the original founders of the Dallas chapter of the Panthers, has gone so far as to sue the revivalists in his hometown to prevent them from besmirching the party's good name (p. 25).

5. See, e.g., Jencks 1992; Wilson 1987, 1997.

## Chapter 8

1. See, e.g., Ackelsberg 1988; Ferree and Hess 1985; Flammang 1997; Jonasdottir 1988; K. Jones 1990; MacKinnon 1989; Morgan and Bookman 1988; Sarvasy 1992; Shapiro 1981; Susser 1988.
2. See Aulette and Mills 1988; Baver 1989; Bookman and Morgen 1988; Elshtain 1981; J. Evans 1986; Flammang 1997; Garland 1988; Gordon 1986; Pateman and Gross 1987; Phillips 1987; Shapiro 1983; West 1981.
3. Antonio Gramsci, writing between 1929 and 1935 from an Italian prison, critisized political projects produced by intellectuals "out of thin air" (Sassoon 1987, 252). In contrast, he argued, "organic intellectuals" derive their political analyses from a more direct link "to the dominant mode of production" (p. 137). Gramsci believed that an organic intellectual "performs ideological and organizational functions based on a practical intervention to change the real world. It is this concrete activity which is the foundation of the elaboration of a philosophy which is a new and integral conception of the world."
4. The concept of "racialization (Omi and Howard Winant 1986) helps us go beyond simple reified categories typically used to describe race so that we can focus on shifts in identities as well as the processes through which racial categories are created and maintained over time and space. Racialization processes position people of diverse race and ethnic backgrounds differently. Relations of class, gender, and sexuality also infuse the processes of racial formation.
    However, personal political analyses of the structural conditions that contour social life—often referred to as the process of politicization—is not a simple outcome of particular experiences or an unmediated result of specific social identities. It derives from conscious reflection on how such experiences and social positions are organized by, what Dorothy Smith has termed, the "relations of ruling." According to Dorothy Smith (1987, 2), "relations of ruling" include "the intersection of the institutions organizing and regulating society" and the power relations formed in and through these institutions. In her usage, the term "ruling" refers to the "complex of organized practices, including government, law, business and financial management, professional organization, and educational institutions as well as the discourse in texts that" organize power within these institutions. Everyday activities are organized through administrative procedures codified in texts and bureaucratic forms and procedures. These regulatory practices are devived far from the actual experiences of those whose lives these texts are designed to control. Also see Marie Campbell and Ann Manicom 1995. Since the relations of ruling permeate daily life in ways that are often hidden from immediate view, the development of particular political perspectives derives, in large measure, from lessons the community workers learned through their attempts to challenge inequality or gain social justice—and as "sit-

uated knowledges" (Haraway 1988) were only partial accounts of these ruling processes (also see Collins 1990).

5. Attention to the relationship of gender, race, and class in this analysis of women's community work further accents how these dimensions are mutually constitutive rather than autonomous social phenomena. This research further illustrates Patricia Hill Collins's (1990) discussion of Afrocentric feminist consciousness and affirms the need to incorporate experiences and perspectives of working-class women into feminist analysis. Collins argues that black feminist thought embraces "a paradigm of race, class, and gender as interlocking systems of oppression" (p. 222).

6. Virginia Shapiro (1990, 37) notes that women's social reform activities included:

> ...the efforts in the 1840s of Dorothea Dix to get Congress to provide money and land for the construction of mental institutions (the bill passed but President Franklin's Pierce's veto was sustained); the establishment of the United States Sanitary Commission; Josephine Shaw Lowell's New York Charity Organization Society and its counterparts...Florence Kelley's National Consumers' League...the instigators of the Children's Bureau; and the authors and primary promoters of the 1921 Infancy and Maternity (Sheppard-Towner) Bill.

Also see Berg 1978; Giddings 1984; Gordon 1991; Kaminer 1984; Sklar 1985; Skocpol 1992.

7. For example, in recognition of her unpaid activism, Frances Perkins was appointed Labor Secretary by Franklin Delano Roosevelt with Eleanor Roosevelt's encouragement (Katz 1986). According to Audrey McClusky (1994,76), Mary McLeod Bethune "was already well known by the time she accepted the directorship of the Negro section of the National Youth Administration (NYA) in the Roosevelt administration in 1936."

8. Writing about feminists employed by the Australian welfare state, Hester Eisenstein (1991, 1996) demonstrates that feminists can make a progressive difference in policy design and implementation when located in strategic positions within the welfare state bureaucracy. She argues that feminist bureaucrats or "femocrats" helped place feminist issues on the political agenda and established "a range of feminist institutions funded by governments" in Australia during the early 1970s and later 1980s—the period she reports on (1995, 70). Such feminist interventions are not a natural outgrowth of women's social location as employees of the state, nor are they limited to high-level managers as this analysis of urban women's community work in the United States demonstrates. However, regardless of political perspective, the community workers' scope of influence remains more constrained than the Australian femocrats. As the process of welfare state disinvestment proceeds in the United States, community workers are further marginalized.

9. For example, Johnnie Tillmon helped found the the Aid to Needy Children (ANC) Mothers in Watts in 1963 (see Gluck et al. 1998; West 1981).

10. See, e.g., Evans 1979; King 1987.

11. Hester Eisenstein (1995, 67) explains that the term femocrats was coined "when members of the Australian women's movement first developed the strategy of entering federal and state bureaucracies as a way of bringing femenist concerns

onto the public policy arena."

12. When a community-based group becomes reliant on outside funding for economic survival, the goals of the funding source frequently determine program design. In addition, the process of researching and applying for funds often consumes a great deal of organizational time and resources. Funding requirements inhibit program flexibility and undermine an organization's ability to meet new community problems as they arise. See, e.g., Grosser 1973; Hallman 1984; Perlman and Ferman 1981; Piven and Cloward 1977.

13. The growing impression that these programs primarily supported non-white minorities created further disaffection among white voters. See Michael K. Brown (1988) and Frances Fox Piven and Richard Cloward (1971, 1993).

14. James L. Sunquist (1969, 24) reports that in response to President Johnson's community action plan, Labor Secretary W. Willard Wirtz argue:

> ...that improvement of health and education services, while desirable, would produce no immediate visible results. Poverty was, by definition, lack of income. Income came from jobs. To have impact among the poor, the War on Poverty must begin with immediate, priority emphasis on employment. Fresh from another battlefront—the war on structural employment—Wirtz could find in the community action program few new jobs apart from summer and part-time employment for students working their way through school.

Sargent Shriver quickly came to side with Wirtz and added several new titles to the bill including among others Job Corps, Neighborhood Youth Corps, a work and training program for welfare recipients, and a work program for college students. Shriver did attempt to introduce a job-creation proposal reminiscent of the Works Progress Administration of the 1930s but President Johnson rejected the idea "because it would have added to the budget (a tobacco tax was proposed to finance it) at a time when taxes were being cut" (Sundquist 1969, 26–27). Margaret Weir (1988, 151–52) argues that the lack of a broad-based coalition to support wide-ranging employment strategies, coupled with the fragmented "national administrative structure" undermined the possibility of creating a national unemployment policy. She reports that Secretary of Labor Willard Wirtz argued unsuccessfully "to make adult employment the centerpiece of" the War on Poverty (p. 178). Weir criticizes the 1967 decision to make CAPs responsible for operating the Concentrated Employment Program because they lacked the "experience or capacity to create jobs and had little sway over employers, whose cooperation would have been essential to the program's success"(p. 185). Nancy Rose (1995, 87) explains that the Concentrated Employment Program was "designed to reach the 'severely disadvantaged'" and "provided a multiple set of remedial manpower services, including counseling, employment-skills training, job development, and outreach." Between 1967 and 1972 "almost half a million people, two-thirds of them African American and two-fifths of them women, were served."

15. Furthermore, other analysts argue, certain strategies of decentralization utilized in urban communities "could shatter the global challenge that race presented to the urban system and restore the territorial boundaries of regular urban conflict" (Katznelson 1981, 179, paraphrasing Altshuler 1970, 203). Ira

Katznelson (1981, 179–180) found evidence for this process in his own analysis of the Neighborhood Action Program and the District School Board in northern Manhattan during the 1970s.

Frances Fox Piven and Richard Cloward (1980, 140) point to additional limitations of decentralization in their discussion of the "decentralized apparatus of school administration"; namely, how this structure serves

> to obscure the centralized and hierarchical imposition of school policy, while lending democratic legitimation to centralized and hierarchical imposition. But it does more. The features of school structure which lend the appearance of local accessibility and local control not only generate ideas about politics, they generate politics as well....This politics is incapable of influencing crucial educational policies, which are decided elsewhere through other processes; nevertheless, the existence of a local school board, its relative visibility and accessibility, helps to promote local interest and activity in the politics of the schools. Most of the time, this politics follows conventionalized patterns, dictated by the rules and traditions of school structures.

Yet, they point out, this process can also provide the grounds for resistance. Piven and Cloward continue: "Some of the time, however, people are driven by hardship and indignation to act outside these rules and traditions. Even then, however, the very existence of a structure and tradition of local participation acts to channel indignation into [limited] educational protest."

Norma Fainstein and Susan Fainstein (1974, 53) also emphasize how "assertive community organizations" (McCourt 1977) "sometimes perform functions of political socialization and provide a ready-made communications network" in low-income neighborhoods that can be mobilized for urban social movements.

16. Just to highlight how far we have come from the emphasis on maximum feasible participation of the poor in the political arena, only one of the two hundred and forty-six witnesses who appeared during the legislative hearings preceding the passage of the Family Support Act in 1988 had been a recipient of welfare (Naples 1997). Ironically, this witness, Shirley Lawson, explained to Representative Henry Waxman, chair of the Subcommittee on Health and the Environment of the House Energy and Commerce Committee, that she was forced to apply for public assistance after she lost her job with the Department of Social Services (U.S. Congress, House 1987). The subsequent "welfare reform" bill, the 1996 Personal Responsibility and Work Opportunity Reconciliation Act, includes no federal oversight to protect the poor against arbitrary bureaucratic decisions and other problems with implementation, therefore, further narrowing the citizenship rights of our most vulnerable citizens. Since legislation now prohibits Legal Aid attorneys from filing class action suits on behalf of groups like welfare recipients, the ability of poor residents to protect their rights is further constrained. The 1996 welfare legislation also prohibits legal immigrants from receiving food stamps and other state resources, an unprecedented shift in legislative practice in this country's history that constricts the rights of legal residents to make claims on the state for essential support.

17. Of course, the growth in the number of black and Puerto Rican elected officials is also intrinsically tied to the Civil Rights Movement, which helped generate the social context and political pressure for the War on Poverty as well as for the expansion of community-based organizations (e.g., Quadagno 1990).

18. For example, the popularity of Project Head Start persists into the 1990s, although analysts argue that the long term benefits of the program has yet to be demonstrated (see Besharov 1992; Zigler, Styfco, and Gilman 1993). Among the documented successes of the program are short-term educational gains and improved health of Head Start children. Parent involvement in the programs is also cited as a valuable contribution to Head Start parents' self-esteem, career training, and political empowerment (Ames with Ellsworth 1997; Kennedy 1993; Valentine 1979).

19. With the support of the Republican-dominated Congress and over President Bill Clinton's opposition, $489.6 million was appropriated for 1997, a twenty-six percent increase ($100 million) over fiscal year 1996 and $95 million more than the appropriation for 1981 when the CSBG was first established (Bradley 1997).

20. Campaigns for comparable worth concern "correcting for the underpayment of wages to those performing such historically female jobs as registered nurse, legal secretary, clerk, food-service worker, and housekeeper because that work has been and continues to be performed primarily by women" (Steinberg 1996, 225).

21. Ironically, the work performed by the community workers mirrors some of the community services jobs supported through the National and Community Service Trust Act of 1993 [H.R. 2010; P.L. 103-82] which established the Commission on National and Community Service to administer $73 million for community services jobs over a period of two years. However, unlike New Careers, this legislation, initiated by President Bill Clinton, targets college-bound youth. Consequently, community service is viewed both as a temporary employment opportunity and provided to others, rather than on behalf of one's own community—an approach that mirrors the Peace Corps rather than the New Careers model. In fact, the Peace Corps served as the stated model for this new program rather than the War on Poverty. This new national service corps for America is called Americorps.

22. Union representatives and other advocacy groups who testified in the Congressional Hearings on welfare reform that preceded the passage of the Family Support Act of 1988 which included the first federal mandated work requirement for recipients of public assistance were particularly concerned about the way workfare could be used to replace other workers (see Naples 1997). For example, Morton H. Sklar, former director of Jobs Watch, described how workfare threatens existing civil-service jobs (U.S. Congress, House 1987).

23. Gerald W. McEntee, international president of the American Federation of State, County, and Municipal Employees, noted that in addition to displacement of regular workers, "workfare creates a working underclass in the public sector" with "no rights, benefits or access to grievance procedures" (U.S. Congress, Senate 1987, 320). He emphasized that five to ten thousand people in New York City were working off their welfare grant alongside workers with higher pay and benefits.

24. CETA was passed in 1973 to promote the establishment of employment and training programs designed and implemented in local community organiza-

tions. CETA merged training funds from the Manpower Development and Training Act of 1962 and the Economic Development Act thus removing substantial control over the content and direction of employment and training activities from CAAs. By the end of the 1970s, Howard Hallman (1980, 47–8) reports, "800 of the 830 community action agencies" operated some form of employment and training program funded by CETA.

25. As mentioned, the contemporary Americorps program also provides funds for service jobs in community-based programs. However, unlike CETA, the Americorps program forms part of a general shift from state responsibility for maintaining commnity services to volunteers and private- sector initiatives. In the remarks President Clinton made when he signed the bill establishing the program, he stated:

> This morning our Cabinet and the heads of our Federal Agencies were directed to redouble their efforts to use service, community grassroots service, to accomplish their fundamental missions. We want them to help reinvent our Government, to do more and cost less, by creating new ways for citizens to fulfill the mission of the public. We believe we can do that. Already departments have enlisted young people and not so young people to do everything from flood cleanup to housing rehabilitation, from being tour guides in our national parks to being teachers' aides in our schools. (p. 1824)

Echoing a central theme of the new welfare bill, Clinton added, "And I hope it [Americorps] will remind every American that there can be no opportunity without responsibility" (p. 1824).

26. See Quadagno and Fobes (1995) who describe the gender stereotyping of Job Corps training programs.

27. See, e.g., Bose 1985; Kanter 1977; Sokoloff 1980.

28. See Epstein 1981; Lorber 1984.

29. See, e.g., Pascall 1986; Sarvasy 1988.

30. Hillsman and Levison 1982; Kanter 1977; Pleck 1982.

31. See, e.g., Devault 1991; Griffith and Smith 1990; Smith and Griffith 1990.

32. Certain occupational categories supported by the War on Poverty, such as health and education aide, are now established parts of the state (as well as private institutions) although they are gender segregated, low paid, and the first to be eliminated during times of financial crisis. The quick redefinition of community work positions as paraprofessional contributed to the elaboration of jobs within health and social welfare organizations and hastened the deskilling of certain forms of work in the health, legal, and social work professions. Because many of these positions were filled by women, this de-skilling process also increased the gender segregation in these occupations. Since women of color are disproportionately represented in these positions, they were (and continue to be) disproportionately affected by the downsizing of the welfare state.

33. See Gittell and Shtob 1980; Kaminer 1984.

34. In April 1995, Jeff Shear reported in the *National Journal* that conservative House Republicans were "aiming to 'Defund the Left' by stopping the flow of federal money to not-for-profit organizations that have been associated with liberal causes" (p. 924). Those organizations that were identified as the target for this campaign included the Association of Head Start Grantees, the Child

Welfare League, the Children's Defense Fund, the NAACP Legal Defense and Education Fund Inc., the National Council of La Raza, and the National Council of Senior Citizens.

35. Another primary dilemma for community-based organizations is the extent to which resources can be devoted to political advocacy versus service provision (see Burghardt 1982b; Withorn 1984). While movement organizations can, to a certain extent, freely debate the degree of allocation of resources to devote to service provision, CAPs established with federal funds have much less freedom. Low-income groups more generally cannot survive without some external funds and, therefore, are more constrained by these external pressures to conform to a social service model (Piven and Cloward 1992).

36. Moynihan (1969, 168) wrote: "The essential problem with community action was that the one term concealed at least four quite distinct meanings: organizing the power structure, as in the Ford Foundation programs of Paul Ylvisaker; expanding the power structure, as in the delinquency program of Cloward and Ohlin; confronting the power structure, as in the Industrial Areas Foundation Program of Saul Alinsky; and finally, assisting the power structure, as in the Peace Corps of Sargent Shriver."

37. See Edin 1991; Oliker 1995. See Abramovitz 1988 and Gordon 1993 for a discussion of similar tensions experienced by women in the early part of the twentieth century.

38. Frances Fox Piven and Richard Cloward (1977, 276) outlined "A Strategy to End Poverty" in a 1966 article that appeared in The Nation. Piven and Cloward's proposal was taken up by George A. Wiley who had worked with them in the Congress on Racial Equality (CORE) and together with welfare-rights workers in New York City founded the National Welfare Rights Organization (NWRO). For further information on NWRO see Piven and Cloward 1974; Pope 1990; Best 1981, 1990.

# REFERENCES

Aaron, Henry J. 1978. *Politics and the Professors: The Great Society in Perspective*. Washington, D.C.: The Brookings Institute.

Abramovitz, Mimi. 1988. *Regulating the Lives of Women: Social Welfare Policy From Colonial Times to the Present*. Boston: South End Press.

Abu-Lughod, Lila. 1993. *Writing Women's Worlds: Bedouin Stories*. Berkeley and Los Angeles: University of California Press.

Ackelsberg, Martha A. 1988. "Communities, Resistance, and Women's Activism: Some Implications for a Democratic Polity." Pp. 297–313 in *Women and the Politics of Empowerment*, eds. Ann Bookman and Sandra Morgen. Philadelphia: Temple University Press.

Acosta-Belen, Edna, ed. 1986. *The Puerto Rican Woman's Perspectives on Culture, History and Society*. 2d. Ed. New York: Praeger Press.

Aguilar-San Juan, Karin, ed. 1994. *The State of Asian American Activism and Resistance in the 1990s*. Boston: South End Press.

Alcoff, Linda. 1988. "Cultural Feminism Versus Post-Structuralism: The Identity Crisis in Feminist Theory." *Signs* 13(3): 405–36.

Alinsky, Saul. 1946. *Reveille for Radicals*. Chicago: University of Chicago Press.

————. 1968. "The War on Poverty: Political Pornography." Pp. 171–79 in *Poverty: Power and Politics*, ed. Chaim I. Waxman. New York: Grosset and Dunlap.

Allen, Paula Gunn. 1986. *The Sacred Hoop: Recovering the Feminism in American Indian Traditions*. Boston: Beacon Press.

————. 1995. "Angry Women Are Building: Issues and Struggles Facing American Indian Women Today." Pp. 32–36 in *Race, Class, and Gender: An Anthology*, ed. Margaret Andersen and Patricia Hill Collins. Belmont, Calif.: Wadsworth Publishing Company.

Almond, Gabriel, and Sidney Verba, eds. 1964. *The Civic Culture Revisited*. Boston: Little Brown.

Altshuler, Alan. 1970. *Community Control: The Black Demand for Participation in Large American Cities*. New York: Pegasus.

Ames, Lynda J. 1996. "Contrarieties at Work: Women's Resistance to Bureaucracy." *NWSA Journal* 8(2):37–59.

Ames, Linda J., with Jeanne Ellsworth. 1997. *Woman Reformed, Women Empowered: Poor Mothers and the Endangered Promise of Head Start*. Philadelphia: Temple University Press.

Amott, Teresa. 1993. *Caught in the Crisis: Women and the U.S. Economy Today*. New York: Monthly Review Press.

Amott, Teresa, and Julie Matthaei. 1991. *Race, Gender, and Work: A Multicultural Economic History of Women in the United States*. Boston: South End Press.

Andersen, Kristi. 1990. "Women and Citizenship in the 1920s." Pp. 177–98 in *Women, Politics, and Change*, eds. Louise A. Tilly and Patricia Gurin. New York: Russell Sage.

Andersen, Margaret L. 1983. *Thinking About Women: Sociological and Feminist Perspectives*. New York: Macmillan Publishing Company.

Anderson, Benedict. 1991. *Imagined Communities*. London and New York: Verso.

Apple, R. W., Jr. 1963. "Violence Erupts in Refuse Strike as Owner-Drivers Still Operate." *New York Times* December 3, pp. 1, 46.

Aptheker, Bettina. 1982. *Women's Legacy: Essays on Race, Sex, and Class in American History*.

Amherst, Mass.: University of Massachusetts Press.

Arches, Joan. 1985. "Don't Burn, Organize: A Structural Analysis of Burnout in the Human Services." *Catalyst* 5(17/18): 15–20.

Aulette, Judy, and Trudy Mills. 1988. "Something Old, Something New: Auxiliary Work in the 1983–1986 Copper Strike." *Feminist Studies* 14(2): 251–68.

Austin, Michael J. 1978. *Professional and Paraprofessionals*. New York: Human Sciences Press.

Bailey, Harry A., Jr. 1973. "Poverty, Politics, and Administration: The Philadelphia Experience." Pp. 168-87 in *Black Politics in Philadelphia*, eds. Miriam Ershkowitz and Joseph Zikmund II. New York: Basic Books.

Bar On, Bat-Ami. 1993. "Marginality and Epistemic Privilege." Pp. 83–100 in *Feminist Epistemologies*, eds. Linda Alcoff and Elizabeth Potter. New York: Routledge.

Barber, Benjamin. 1984. *Strong Democracy: Participatory Politics for a New Age*. Berkeley and Los Angeles: University of California Press.

Barnett, Bernice McNair. 1995. "Black Women's Collectivist Movement Organizations: Their Struggles During the 'Doldrums.'" Pp. 199–219 in *Feminist Organizations*, ed. Myra Marx Ferree and Patricia Yancey Martin. Philadelphia: Temple University Press.

Barnett-Cash, Floris. 1987. "Sisterhood Across Generations: Black Women and Community Activism, 19th Century to the Present." Paper presented at the National Women's Studies Association Annual Conference, Spelman College, Atlanta, GA, June 24–28.

Baulstein, Arthur I., and Roger R. Woock, eds. 1968. *Man Against Poverty: WWIII: A Reader on the World's Most Crucial Issue*. New York: Random House.

Baver, Sherry L. 1989. "Political Participation of Puerto Rican Women: Mapping a Research Agenda." *Affilia: Journal of Women and Social Work* 4(1): 59–69.

Beck, Bertrum. 1969. "Mobilization For Youth: Reflections About Its Administration," Pp. 145–66 in *Justice and the Law*, ed. Harold Weissman. New York: Association Press.

Behar, Ruth. 1993. *Translated Woman: Crossing the Border With Esperanza's Story*. Boston: Beacon Press.

Belenky, Mary Field, Blythe McVicker Clincy, Nancy Rule Goldberger, and Jill Matuck Tarule. 1986. *Women's Ways of Knowing*. New York: Basic Books.

Bellah, Robert N., Richard Madsen, William M. Sullivan, Ann Swidler, and Steven M. Tipton. 1985. *Habits of the Heart: Individualism and Commitment in American Life*. Berkeley and Los Angeles: University of California Press.

Berg, Barbara J. 1978. *The Remembered Gate: Origins of American Feminism: The Women and the City 1800–1860*. Oxford: Oxford University Press.

Berube, Maurice R., and Marilyn Gittell, eds. 1969. *Confrontation at Ocean Hill-Brownsville; The New York School Strikes of 1968*. New York: Praeger.

Besharov, Douglas J. 1992. "A New Start for Head Start?" *The American Enterprise* 3(2): 52–57.

Blee, Kathleen M. 1996. "Becoming a Racist: Women in Contemporary Ku Klux Klan and Neo-Nazi Groups." *Gender & Society* 10(6): 680–702.

Block, Fred, Richard A. Coward, Barbara Ehrenreich, and Frances Fox Piven. 1987. *The Mean Season: The Attack on the Welfare State*. New York: Pantheon Books.

Bookman, Ann, and Sandra Morgen, eds. 1988. *Women and the Politics of Empowerment*. Philadelphia: Temple University Press.

Boone, Richard. 1972. "Reflections on Citizen Participation and the Economic Opportunity Act." *Public Administration Review* 32(September/October): 444–56.

Booth, Heather, Harry Boyte, and Steve Max. 1986. *Citizen Action and the New Populism*. Philadelphia: Temple University Press.

Boris, Eileen. 1995. "The Racialized Gendered State: Constructions of Citizenship in the United States." *Social Politics* 2(2): 160–80.

Borland, Katherine. 1991. "'That's Not What I Said': Interpretive Conflict in Oral Narrative Research." Pp. 63–75 in *Women's Words: The Feminist Practice of Oral History*, Sherna Berger Gluck and Daphne Patai, eds. New York: Routledge.

Bose, Christine E. 1985. *Jobs and Gender: A Study of Occupational Prestige*. New York: Praeger.

Boyte, Harry. 1980. *Backyard Revolution: Understanding the Citizen Movement*. Philadelphia: Temple University Press.

———. 1984. *Community Is Possible: Repairing America's Roots*. New York: Harper and Row.

———. 1985. "Review of No Ceasefires: The War on Poverty in Roanoke Valley" by

Edwin L. Cobb. *Contemporary Sociology* 14(5): 638–39.

———. 1989. *Common Wealth: A Return to Citizen Politics*. New York: Free Press.

Boyte, Harry, Heather Booth, and Steve Max. 1986. *Citizen Action and the New American Populism*. Philadelphia: Temple University Press.

Boyte, Harry, and Frank Riessman, eds. 1986. *The New Populism: The Politics of Empowerment*. Philadelphia: Temple University Press.

Brager, George A., and Frances P. Purcell, eds. 1967. *Community Action Against Poverty: Readings From the Mobilization Experience*. New Haven, Conn: College and University Press.

Bradley, David. 1995. Interviewed by author. August 17.

———. 1997. Interviewed by author. October 10.

Braverman, Harry. 1972. *Labor and Monopoly Capital*. New York: Monthly Review Press.

Breines, Wini. 1982. *Community and Organization of the New Left, 1962–1968: The Great Refusal*. New York: Preager.

Bremner, Robert H. 1972. "The Origins of Charity Organization." Pp. 39–44 in *Poverty and Social Welfare in the United States*, ed. Roy Lubove. New York: Holt, Rinehart, and Winston Company.

Breton, Margot. 1994. "Relating Competence-Promotion and Empowerment." *Journal of Progressive Human Services* 5(1): 27–44.

Brewer, Rose M. 1994. "Race, Class, Gender and US State Welfare Policy: The Nexus of Inequality of African American Families." Pp. 115–27 in *Color, Class and Country: Experiences of Gender*, eds. Gay Young and Bette J. Dickerson. London: Zed Books.

Bridges, Amy. 1984. *A City in the Republic: Antebellum New York and the Origins of Machine Politics*. New York: Cambridge University Press.

Brown, Michael K. 1988. "The Segmented Welfare State: Distributive Conflict and Retrenchment in the United States, 1968–1984." Pp. 182–210 in *The Making the Welfare State: Retrenchment and Social Policy in America and Europe*, ed. Michael K. Brown. Philadelphia: Temple University Press.

Brown, Robert McAfee. 1993. *Liberation Theology: An Introductory Guide*. Louisville, Ky.: Westminster/John Knox Press.

Bryan, William L. 1981. "Preventing Burnout in the Public Interest." *The Grantsmanship Center News*. 9(March/April): 15–27; 66–75.

Burghardt, Steve. 1982a. *Organizing for Community Change*. Beverly Hills, Calif.: Russell Sage.

———. 1982b. *The Other Side of Organizing: Resolving the Personal Dilemmas and Political Demands of Daily Practice*. Cambridge, Mass.: Schenkman Publishing Company.

Burns, Stewart. 1990. *Social Movements of the 1960s: Searching for Democracy*. Boston: Twayne.

Buss, Fran Leeper. 1985. *Dignity: Lower Income Women Tell of Their Lives and Struggles*. Ann Arbor, Mich.: University of Michigan Press.

Butler, Stuart, and Anna Kondratas. 1987. *Out of the Poverty Trap: A Conservative Strategy For Welfare Reform*. New York: The Free Press.

Campbell, Marie, and Ann Manicom, eds. 1995. *Knowledge, Experience, and Ruling Relations: Studies in the Social Organization of Knowledge*. Toronto: University of Toronto Press.

Canning, Kathleen. 1994. "Feminist History after the Linguistic Turn: Historicizing Discourse and Experience." *Signs* 19(Winter): 368–404.

Carballo, Manuel, and Mary Jo Bane, eds. 1984. *The State of the Poor in the 1980s*. Boston: Auburn House.

Carothers, Suzanne. 1990. "Catching Sense: Learning from Our Mothers to Be Black and Female." Pp. 232–47 in *Uncertain Terms: Negotiating Gender in American Culture*, eds. Faye Ginsburg and Anna Lowenhaupt Tsing. Boston: Beacon Press.

Carson, Claybourne. 1981. In *Struggle: SNCC and the Black Awakening of the 1960's*. Cambridge, Mass.: Harvard University Press.

Castello, Ana. 1986. "The Watsonville Women's Strike: A Case of Mexicana Activism." Pp. 43–62 in *Massacre of the Dreamers: Essays on Xicanisma*, by Ana Castello. Albuquerque: University of New Mexico Press.

Center for the Study of Social Policy. *1983. A Dream Deferred: The Economic Status of Black Americans*. Washington, D.C.: Center for the Study of Social Policy.

Center on Social Welfare Policy and Law. 1995. *Left to the Tender Mercies of the States: The Fate of the Poor Families Under a Cash Assistance Block Grant*. Washington, D.C.: Center on Social Welfare Policy and Law.

Chambers, Clarke A. 1963. *Seedtime of Reform: American Social Service and Social Action, 1918–1933*. Minneapolis, Minn.: University of Minnesota Press.

Chang, Grace. 1994. "Undocumented Latinas: Welfare Burdens or Beasts of Burden?" *Socialist Review* 93(3): 151–85.

Chase, Susan E. 1995. *Ambiguous Empowerment: The Work Narratives of Women School Superintendents*. Amherst, Mass.: University of Massachusetts Press.

Chodorow, Nancy. 1978. *The Reproduction of Mothering: Psychoanalysis and the Sociology of Gender*. Berkeley and Los Angeles: University of California Press.

*Citizen Participation* 1–5 (1980–1984).

*City Limits* 1–9 (1976–1984).

Clark, Kenneth. 1965. *Dark Ghetto: Dilemmas of Social Power*. New York: Harper and Row.

Clark, Kenneth, and Jeannette Hopkins. 1969. *A Relevant War Against Poverty: A Study of Community Action Programs and Observable Social Change*. New York: Harper and Row.

Clough, Patricia Ticineto. 1994. *Feminist Thought*. Oxford and Cambridge: Blackwell.

Cloward, Richard A. 1964. "Community Organization Program of Mobilization for Youth." New York: Mobilization for Youth.

———. 1968. "The War on Poverty: Are the Poor Left Out?" Pp. 159–79 in *Poverty: Power and Politics*, ed. Chaim Isaac Waxman. New York: Grosset and Dunlap.

Cloward, Richard, and Lloyd Ohlin. 1960. *Delinquency and Opportunity*. Glencoe, Ill.: Free Press.

Cobb, Edwin L. 1984. *No Ceasefires: The War on Poverty in Roanoke Valley*. Cabin John, Md.: Seven Locks Press.

Cohen, Audrey C. 1981. "Human Service." Pp. 1–17 in *The Modern American College: Responding to the New Realities of Diverse Students and a Changing Society*, ed. Arthur W. Chickering and Associates. San Francisco: Josey Boss.

Cohen, Robert. 1976. *"New Careers" Grows Older: A Perspective on the Paraprofessional Experience, 1965–1975*. Baltimore: Johns Hopkins University Press.

Coles, Robert. 1987. *Dorothy Day: A Radical Devotion*. Reading, Mass.: Addison-Wesley Publishing Company.

Collins, Patricia Hill. 1990. *Black Feminist Thought: Knowledge, Consciousness, and the Politics of Empowerment*. Boston: Unwin Hyman.

———. 1991a. "Learning From the Outsider Within: The Sociological Significance of Black Feminist Thought." Pp. 35–59 in *Beyond Methodology*, eds. Mary Margaret Fonow and J. A. Cook. Bloomington: Indiana University Press.

———. 1991b. "The Meaning of Motherhood in Black Culture." In *The Black Family: Essays and Studies*, ed. R. Staples. Belmont, Calif.: Wadsworth.

———. 1994. "Shifting the Center: Race, Class, and Feminist Theorizing about Motherhood." Pp. 45–65 in *Mothering: Ideology, Experience, and Agency*, eds. Evelyn Nakano Glenn, Grace Chang, and Linda Rennie Forcey. New York: Routledge.

Combahee River Collective. 1982. "A Black Feminist Statement." Pp. 13–22 in *All the Women are White, All the Blacks Are Men, But Some of Us Are Brave: Black Women's Studies*, eds. Gloria T. Hull, Patricia Bell Scott, and Barbara Smith. Old Westbury, NY: The Feminist Press.

Commonwealth of Pennsylvania, General Assembly. 1995/1996 a. Community Services Act, Section 4. 1996 Pa. Laws 166; Pa. SB 1397.

Commonwealth of Pennsylvania, General Assembly. 1995/1996 b. Community Services Act, Section 5c. 1996 Pa. Laws 166; 1995 Pa. SB 1397.

Cone, James. 1970. *A Black Theology of Liberation*. Philadelphia, Penn.: J. B. Lippincott Company.

Congressional Quarterly Service. 1969. *Congress and the Nation: Volume II 1965–1968*. Washington, D.C.: Congressional Quarterly Service.

Connell, R. W. 1987. *Gender and Power: Society, the Person and Sexual Politics*. Cambridge: Polity Press.

Cox, Craig. 1997. "Copycats: The New Black Panthers Struggle for Street Credibility." *Utne Reader* February, pp. 25–27.

Cruikshank, Barbara. 1995. "The Will to Power: Technologies of Citizenship and the War on Poverty." *Socialist Review*. 23(4): 29–55.

Curno, Paul, ed. 1978. *Political Issues and Community Work*. London: Routledge and Kegan Paul.

Daly, Mary. 1973. *Liberation Theology*. Mahwah, NJ: Paulist Press.

Daniels, Arlene Kaplan. 1988. *Invisible Careers: Women Civic Leaders from the Volunteer World*. Chicago: University of Chicago Press.

Davies, Gareth. 1992. "War on Dependency: Liberal Individualism and the EOA of 1964." *Journal of American Studies* 26(2): 205–31.

Davis, Angela. 1981. *Women, Race, and Class*. New York: Random House.

Day, Dorothy. 1952. *The Long Loneliness*. New York: Harper and Row.

Delgado, Gary. 1982. "Talking It to the Streets: Community Organizing and National Politics." *Socialist Review* 12(3–4): 49–84.

Devault, Marjorie L. 1991. *Feeding the Family: The Social Organization of Caring as Gendered Work*. Chicago: University of Chicago Press.

Dill, Bonnie Thornton. 1988. "Our Mothers' Grief: Racial Ethnic Women and the Maintenance of Families." *Journal of Family History*. 13(4): 415–31.

———. 1995a. "Our Mothers' Grief: Racial Ethnic Women and the Maintenance of Families." Pp. 237–60 in *Race, Class, and Gender: An Anthology*, eds. Margaret Andersen and Patricia Hill Collins. Belmont, Calif.: Wadsworth Publishing Company.

———. 1995b. "Race, Class, and Gender: Prospects for an All-inclusive Sisterhood." Pp. 277–95 in *U.S. Women in Struggle: A Feminist Studies Anthology*, eds. Heidi Hartmann and Claire Goldberg Moses. Urbana and Chicago: University of Illinois Press.

Donovan, John C. 1967. *The Politics of Poverty*. New York: Pegasus.

———. 1980. *The 1960s: Politics and Public Policy*. Lanham, MD: University Press of America.

Dressel, Paula, and Michael Lipsky. 1989. "Political Socialization in Social Welfare Work." Pp. 143–71 in *Political Learning in Adulthood: A Source Book of Theory and Research*, ed. Ruth Sigel. Chicago: University of Chicago Press.

Dressel, Paula, Michelle Waters, Mike Sweat, Obie Cayton, Jr., and Amy Chandler-Clayton. 1988. "Deprofessionalization, Proletarianization, and Social Welfare Work." *Journal of Sociology and Social Welfare* 15(2): 113–31.

Eckstein, Harry. 1988. "A Culturalist Theory of Political Change." *American Political Science Review* 82: 789–804.

Economics Education Project of the Union for Radical Political Economics. 1981. *Crisis in the Public Sector*. New York: Monthly Review Press.

Edin, Kathryn. 1991. "Surviving the Welfare System: How AFDC Recipients Make Ends Meet in Chicago." *Social Problems* 38(4): 462–74.

Eisenstein, Hester. 1991. *Gender Shock: Practicing Feminism on Two Continents*. Boston: Beacon Press.

———. 1995. "The Australian Femocratic Experiment: A Feminist Case for Bureaucracy." Pp. 69–83 in *Feminist Organizations*, eds. Myra Marx Ferree and Patricia Yancey Martin. Philadelphia: Temple University Press.

———. 1996. *Inside Agitators: Australian Femocrats and the State*. Philadelphia: Temple University Press.

Elshtain, Jean Bethke. 1981. *Public Man, Private Women*. Princeton, NJ: Princeton University Press.

Epstein, Barbara. 1982. "Family Politics and the New Left: Learning from Our Own Experience." *Socialist Review* 12(3–4): 141–61.

Epstein, Cynthia. 1981. *Women in Law*. Garden City, NY: Doubleday and Anchor.

Erikson, Kai T. 1976. *Everything In Its Path*. New York: Simon and Schuster.

Erlich, John L. 1977. "Organization Building in Working-Class Communities." Pp. 181–86 in *Tactics and Techniques of Community Practice*, eds. Fred M. Cox, John L. Erlich, Jack Rothman, and John E. Tropman. Itasca, Ill.: F. E. Peacock Publishers.

Ershkowitz, Miriam, and Joseph Zikmund II, eds. 1973. *Black Politics in Philadelphia*. New York: Basic Books.

Essed, Philomena. 1990. *Everyday Racism: Reports from Women of Two Cultures*. Claremont, Calif.: Hunter House, Inc.

Evans, Judith. 1986. "Feminism and Political Theory." Pp. 1–16 in *Feminism and Political Theory*, eds. J. Evans et al. Beverly Hills, Calif.: Sage.

Evans, Sara. 1979. *Personal Politics: The Roots of Women's Liberation in the Civil Rights Movement and the New Left*. New York: Vintage Books.

Evans, Sara M., and Harry C. Boyte. 1986. *Free Spaces: The Sources of Democratic Change in America*. New York: Harper and Row Publishers.

Fainstein, Norma I., and Susan S. Fainstein. 1974. *Urban Political Movements: The Search for Power By Minority Groups in American Cities*. Englewood Cliffs, N.J.: Prentice-Hall.

Fantini, Mario, and Marilyn Gittell. 1973. *Decentralization: Achieving Reform*. New York: Praeger.

Fantini, Mario, Marilyn Gittell, and Richard Magat. 1970. *Community Control and the Urban School*. New York: Praeger Publishers.

Feldman, Roberta M., Susan Stall, and Patricia A. Wright. 1998. "'The Community Needs to Be Built by Us': Women Organizing in Chicago Public Housing." Pp. 257–74 in *Community Activism and Feminist Politics: Organizing Across Race, Class, and Gender*. New York: Routledge.

Ferguson, Kathy E. 1984. *The Feminist Case Against Bureaucracy*. Philadelphia: Temple University Press.

Ferree, Myra Marx. 1992. "The Political Context of Rationality: Rational Choice Theory and Resource Mobilization." Pp. 29–52 in *Frontiers in Social Movement Theory*, eds. Aldon D. Morris and Carol McClurg Mueller. New Haven, Conn.: Yale University Press.

Ferree, Myra Marx, and Beth Hess. 1985. *Controversy and Coalition: The New Feminist Movement*. Boston: Twayne Publishers.

Ferree, Myra Marx, and Patricia Yancey Martin. 1995. "Doing the work of the movement: Feminist organizations." Pp. 3–23 in *Feminist Organizations: Harvest of the New Women's Movement*, eds. Myra Marx Ferree and Patricia Yancey Martin. Philadelphia: Temple University Press.

Fisher, Robert. 1994. *Let the People Decide: Neighborhood Organizations in America*. Boston: Twayne Publishers.

Fisher, Robert, and Joseph M. Kling. 1990. "Leading the People: Two Approaches to the Role of Ideology in Community Organizing." Pp. 71–90 in *Dilemmas of Activism: Class, Community, and the Politics of Local Mobilization*, eds. Joseph M. Kling and Prudence S. Posner. Philadelphia: Temple University Press.

Flammang, Janet A. 1997. *Women's Political Voice: How Women are Transforming the Practice and Study of Politics*. Philadelphia: Temple University Press.

Flax, Jane. 1990. *Thinking Fragments: Psychoanalysis, Feminism, & Postmodernism in the Contemporary West*. Berkeley and Los Angeles: University of California Press.

Forcey, Linda Rennie. 1994. "Feminist Perspectives on Mothering and Peace." Pp. 355–75 in *Mothering: Ideology, Experience, and Agency*, eds. Evelyn Nakano Glenn, Grace Chang, and Linda Rennie Forcey. New York: Routledge.

Forest, Jim. 1986. *Love Is the Measure: A Biography of Dorothy Day*. New York: Paulist Press.

Frankenberg, Ruth. 1993. *White Women, Race Matters*. Minneapolis, Minn.: University of Minnesota Press.

———. 1994. "Whiteness and Americanness: Examining Constructions of Race, Culture, and Nation in White Women's Life Narratives." Pp. 62–77 in *Race*, eds. Steven Gregory and Roger Sanjek. New Brunswick, N.J.: Rutgers University Press.

Fraser, Nancy. 1989. *Unruly Practices: Power, Discourse and Gender in Contemporary Social Theory*. Minneapolis, Minn.: University of Minnesota Press.

Fraser, Nancy, and Linda Gordon. 1994a. "'Dependency' Demystified: Inscriptions of Power in a Keyword of the Welfare State." *Social Politics* 1(1): 4–31.

———. 1994b. "A Genealogy of Dependency: Tracing a Keyword of the U.S. Welfare State." *Signs: Journal of Women in Culture and Society* 19(2): 309–36.

Fraser, Nancy, and Linda J. Nicholson. 1990. "Social Criticism Without Philosophy: An Encounter Between Feminism and Postmodernism." Pp. 19–38 in *Feminism/Postmodernism*, ed. Linda J. Nicholson. New York: Routledge.

Frazier, E. Franklin. 1963. *The Negro Church in America*. New York: Schocken Books.

Freeman, Jo, ed. 1983. *Social Movements of the Sixties and Seventies*. New York: Longman.

Freire, Paulo. 1970. *Pedagogy of the Oppressed*. New York: Continuum.

Fried, Alfred. 1969. "The Attack on Mobilization." Pp. 137–62 in *Community Development in the Mobilization for Youth Experience*, ed. Harold Weissman. New York: Association Press.

Gamson, William A. 1992. "The Social Psychology of Collective Action." Pp. 53–76 in *Frontiers in Social Movement Theory*, eds. Aldon D. Morris and Carol McClurg Mueller. New Haven, Conn.: Yale University Press.

Gamson, William A., Bruce Fireman, and Steven Rytina. 1982. *Encounters with Unjust*

*Authority*. Homewood, Ill.: Dorsey.

Garcia, Mikel Mary. 1987. "Black Female Social Networks and Community Development: Los Angeles Black Community, 1914." Paper presented at the National Women's Studies Association Annual Conference, Spelman College, Atlanta, Georgia (June 24–28).

Garland, Anne Witte. 1988. *Women Activists: Challenging the Abuse of Power*. New York: The Feminist Press.

Gartner, Alan, Russel A. Nixon, and Frank Riessman, eds. 1973. *Public Service Employment: An Analysis of its History, Problems, and Prospects*. New York: Praeger Publishers.

Geiger, Susan N.G. 1986. "Women's Life Histories: Method and Content." *Signs: Journal of Women in Culture and Society*, 11(2): 334–51.

Giddings, Paula. 1984. *When and Where I Enter: The Impact of Black Women on Race and Sex in America*. New York: William Morrow and Company.

Gilkes, Cheryl Townsend. 1980. "Holding Back the Ocean With a Broom: Black Women and Community Work." Pp. 217–31 in *The Black Woman*, ed. L. Rodgers-Rose. Beverly Hills, Calif.: Sage.

———. 1988. "Building in Many Places: Multiple Consciousness and Ideologies in Black Women's Community Work." Pp. 53–76 in *Women and the Politics of Empowerment*, eds. Ann Bookman and Sandra Morgen. Philadelphia: Temple University Press.

Gilligan, Carol. 1982. *In a Different Voice: Psychological Theory and Women's Development*. Cambridge: Harvard University Press.

Ginsburg, Faye D. 1989. *Contested Lives: The Abortion Debate in an American Community*. Berkeley and Los Angeles: University of California Press.

Gittell, Marilyn. 1967. *Participants and Participation*. New York: Frederick A. Praeger Publishers.

———. 1971. *Demonstration for Social Changes: An Experience in Local Control*. New York: Institute for Community Studies, Queens College of the City University of New York.

———. 1980. *Limits to Citizen Participation: The Decline of Community Organizations*. With Bruce Hoffacker, Eleanor Rollins, Samuel Foster, and Mark Hoffacker. Beverly Hills, Calif.: Russell Sage.

Gittel, Marilyn, and Nancy Naples. 1982. "Activist Women: Conflicting Ideologies." *Social Policy* 13(4): 25–27.

———. 1983. "Coalition Building among Activist Women: Strategies for the 1980s." Report to the Carnegie Foundation, New York.

Gittel, Marilyn, and Teresa Shtob. 1980. "Changing Women's Roles in Political Volunteerism and Reform of the City." *Signs: Journal of Women in Culture and Society*. 5 (Spring) Supplement: S67–78.

Givel, Michael. 1991. *The War on Poverty Revisited: The Community Services Block Grant Program in the Reagan Years*. New York: Lanham.

Glenn, Evelyn Nakano. 1986. Issei, Nisei, *War Bride: Three Generations of Japanese Women in Domestic Service*. Philadelphia: Temple University Press.

———. 1991. "White Women/Women of Color: Historical Continuities in the Racial Division of Women's Work." Paper presented at the Meetings of the American Sociological Association, Cincinnati, Ohio (August 24).

———. 1992. "From Servitude to Service Work: Historical Continuities in the Racial Division of Paid Reproductive Labor." *Signs: Journal of Women in Culture and Society*. 18(1): 1–43.

———. 1994. "Social Constructions of Mothering: A Thematic Overview." Pp. 1–29 in *Mothering: Ideology, Experience, and Agency*, eds. Evelyn Nakano Glenn, Grace Chang, and Linda Rennie Forcey. New York: Routledge.

Glenn, Evelyn Nakano, Grace Chang, and Linda Rennie Forcey, eds. 1994. *Mothering: Ideology, Experience, and Agency*. New York: Routledge.

Gluck, Sherna Berger, with Maylei Blackwell, Sharon Cotrell, and Karen Harper. 1997. "Whose Feminism, Whose History? Reflections on Excavating the History of (the) US Women's Movement(s)." Pp. 31–56 in *Community Activism and Feminist Politics: Organizing Across Race, Class, and Gender*. New York: Routledge.

Gluck, Sherna B., and Daphne Patai, eds. 1991. *Women's Words: The Feminist Practice of Oral History*. New York: Routledge.

González, Justo L. 1990. *Mañana: Christian Theology from a Hispanic Perspective*. Nashville: Abingdon Press.

Gordon, Linda. 1986. "What's New in Women's History." Pp. 20–30 in *Feminist Studies/Critical Studies*, ed. Teresa de Lauretis. Bloomington: Indiana University Press.
———. 1990. "The New Feminist Scholarship on the Welfare State." Pp. 9–35 in *Women, the State, and Welfare*, ed. Linda Gordon. Madison, Wis.: University of Wisconsin Press.
———. 1991. "Black and White Visions of Welfare: Women's Welfare Activism, 1890–1945." *Journal of American History* 78(September): 559–90.
———. 1993. *Pitied But Not Entitled: Single Mothers and the History of Welfare*. New York: The Free Press.
Graber, Helen V., Sally Haywood, and Nancy R. Vosler. 1996. "An Empowerment Model for Building Neighborhood Community: Grace Hill Neighborhood Services." *Journal of Progressive Human Services* 7(2): 63–76.
Gramsci, Antonio. 1971. *Selections from the Prison Notebooks*. New York: International Publishers.
Green, Rayna. 1990. "American Indian Women: Diverse Leadership for Social Change." Pp. 61–73 in *Bridges of Power: Women's Multicultural Alliances*, eds. Lisa Albrecht and Rose M. Brewer. Philadelphia: New Society Publishers.
Greenstone, J. David, and Paul E. Peterson. 1972. "Reformers, Machines, and the War on Poverty." Pp. 21–46 in *Community Organizing: Studies in Constraint*. ed. Irving A. Spergel. Beverly Hills, Calif.: Russell Sage.
———. 1973. *Race and Authority in Urban Politics: Community Participation and the War on Poverty*. New York: Russell Sage.
Greenwood, Ernest. 1957. "Attributes of a Profession." *Social Work* 2(3).
Gregory, Steven. 1994. "Race, Rubbish, and Resistance: Empowering Difference in Community Politics." Pp. 366–91 in *Race*, eds. S. Gregory and R. Sanjek. New York: Routledge.
Griffith, Alison I., and Dorothy E. Smith. 1990. "What Did You Do in School Today?: Mothering, Schooling, and Social Class." Pp. 3–24 in *Perspectives on Social Problems* Vol. 2, eds. Gale Miller and James A. Holstein. Greenwich, Conn.: JAI Press.
Grosser, Charles. 1967. "Community Organization and the Grass Roots." *Social Work* 12(4): 61–67.
———. 1973. *New Directions in Community Organizations*. New York: Praeger Publishers.
Gutiérrez, Gustavo. 1973. *A Theology of Liberation: History, Politics and Salvation*. Trans. and eds. Sister Caridad Inda and John Eagleson. Maryknoll, N.Y.: Orbis Books.
———. 1983. *The Power of the Poor in History: Selected Writings*. Translated by Robert R. Barr. Maryknoll, N.Y.: Orbis Books.
Hallman, Howard W. 1969. *Community Control: A Study of Community Corporation and Neighborhood Boards*. Washington, D.C.: Washington Center for Metropolitan Studies.
———. 1970. *Neighborhood Control of Public Programs*. New York: Praeger Publishers.
———. 1980. *Community-Based Employment Programs*. Baltimore: Johns Hopkins University Press.
———. 1984. *Neighborhoods: Their Place in Urban Life*. Beverly Hills, Calif.: Russell Sage.
Hamilton, Richard F. 1972. *Class and Politics in the United States*. New York: Wiley.
Hand, Judson. 1966. "Most Elected Aides on PAAC Panel Turn Up On Payroll." *Philadelphia Inquirer* (20 July).
Haraway, Donna. 1988. "Situated Knowledges: The Science Question in Feminism and the Privilege of Partial Perspective." *Feminist Studies* 14(3): 575–99.
Harding, Sandra. 1986. *The Science Question in Feminism*. Ithaca, N.Y.: Cornell University Press.
———. 1991. *Whose Science? Whose Knowledge?* Ithaca, NY: Cornell University Press.
Harlem Youth Opportunities Unlimited, Inc. 1964. *Youth in the Ghetto: A Study of the Consequences of Powerlessness and a Blueprint for Change*. New York: Harlem Youth Opportunities Unlimited.
Harrington, Michael. 1962. *The Other America: Poverty in the United States*. New York: Macmillan.
———. 1971. "The Politics of Poverty." Pp. 13–38 in *Poverty: Views from the Left*, eds. Jeremy Larner and Irving Howe. New York: William Morrow and Company.
———. 1984. *The New American Poverty*. New York: Holt, Rinehart and Winston.
Hartmann, Heidi I. 1981. "The Unhappy Marriage of Marxism and Feminism: Towards a More Progressive Union." Pp 1–41 in *Women and Revolution*, ed. Lydia Sargent.

Boston: South End Press.

Hartsock, Nancy C. M. 1983. *Money, Sex and Power: Toward a Feminist Historical Materialism*. Boston: Northeastern University Press.

Hatton, Barbara R. 1977. "Schools and Black Community Development: A Reassessment of Community Control." *Education and Urban Society* 9(2): 215–33.

Haveman, Robert H., ed. 1977. *A Decade of Federal Antipoverty Programs: Achievements, Failures and Lessons*. New York: Academic Press.

Hawkesworth, Mary E. 1989. "Knowers, Knowing, Known: Feminist Theory and Claims of Truth." *Signs: Journal of Women in Culture and Society*. 14(3) (1989): 533–57.

Haywoode, Terry. 1991. "Working Class Feminism: Creating a Politics of Community, Connection, and Concern." Ph.D. dissertation, the City University of New York.

Health and Welfare Council, Inc. 1964. "Fact Book on Poverty: A Study of Selected Population Characteristics Related to Poverty: Bucks, Chester, Delaware, Montgomery, and Philadelphia Counties, 1960." Special Report Series. No. 23. Research, Department, Health and Welfare Council, Inc., Philadelphia (November).

Hennelly, Alfred S. J. 1989. *Theology for a Liberating Church: The New Praxis of Freedom*. Washington, D.C.: Georgetown University Press.

Herzog, Frederick. 1972. *Liberation Theology: Liberation in Light of the Fourth Gospel*. New York: The Seabury Press, Inc.

Hewitt, Nancy A. 1990. "Charity or Mutual Aid?: Two Perspectives on Latin Women's Philanthropy in Tampa, Florida." Pp. 55–69 in *Lady Bountiful Revisited: Women, Philanthropy, and Power*, ed. Kathleen D. McCarthy. New Brunswick, N.J.: Rutgers University Press.

Higginbotham, Evelyn Brooks. 1992. "African-American Women's History and the Metalanguage of Race." *Signs: Journal of Women in Culture and Society*. 17(2): 251–74.

Hillery, George A. 1955. "Definitions of Community: Areas of Agreement." *Rural Sociology* 20(2): 117.

Hillsman, Sally T., and Bernard Levinson. 1982. "Job Opportunities of Black and White Working-Class Women." Pp. 218–33 in *Women and Work: Problems and Perspectives*, eds. Rachel Kahn-Hut, Arlene Kaplan Daniels, and Richard Colvard. New York: Oxford University Press.

Hine, Darlene Clark. 1990. "We Specialize in the Wholly Impossible: The Philanthropic Work of Black Women." Pp. 70–93 in *Lady Bountiful Revisited: Women, Philanthropy, and Power*, ed. K. D. McCarthy. New Brunswick, N.Y.: Rutgers University Press.

Hochschild, Arlie Russell, with Anne Machung. 1989. *The Second Shift: Working Parents and the Revolution at Home*. New York: Viking.

Hochschild, Arlie Russell. 1995. "The Culture of Politics: Traditional, Postmodern, Cold-modern, and Warm-modern Ideals of Care." *Social Politics* 2(3): 331–46.

hooks, bell. 1981. *Ain't I a Woman: Black Women and Feminism*. Boston: South End Press.

———. 1984. *Feminist Theory: From Margin to Center*. Boston: South End Press.

———. 1989. "Overcoming White Supremacy: A Comment." Pp. 112–19 in *Talking Back*. Boston: South End Press.

———. 1990. *Yearning: Race, Gender, and Cultural Politics*. Boston: South End Press.

Horowitz, Claudia. 1993. "What Is Wrong with National Service." *Social Policy* 24(1): 37–43.

Howe, Louise Kapp. 1977. *Pink Collar Workers Inside the World of Women's Work*. New York: G. P. Putnam and Sons.

Jackson, Larry, and William Johnson. 1974. *Protest By the Poor: The Welfare Rights Movement in New York City*. Lexington, Ky.: Lexington Books, D.C. Health and Company.

Jacobs, Jim. 1982. "DARE to Struggle: Organizing in Urban America." *Socialist Review* 12(3–4): 85–104.

Jaggar, Alison. 1983. *Feminist Politics and Human Nature*. Totowa, N.J.: Rowman & Allanheld.

Jencks, Christopher. 1992. *Rethinking Social Policy: Race, Poverty, and the Underclass*. Cambridge, Mass.: Harvard University Press.

James, Stanlie M. 1993. "Mothering: A Possible Black Feminist Link to Social Transformation?" Pp. 44–54 in *Theorizing Black Feminisms: The Visionary Pragmatism of Black Women*, eds. Stanlie M. James and Abena P. A. Busia. New York: Routledge.

James, Stanlie M., and Abena P. A. Busia, eds. 1993. *Theorizing Black Feminism: The*

*Visionary Pragmatism of Black Women.* New York: Routledge.

Jeansonne, Glen. 1996. *Women of the Far Right: The Mothers' Movement and World War II.* Chicago: University of Chicago Press.

Jenson, Jane. 1997. Presentation for Conference on "Comparative Research on Gender and States," held at the University of Wisconsin, Madison (January 31–February 2).

Joe, Tom and Cheryl Rogers. 1985. *By the Few for the Few: The Reagan Welfare Legacy.* Lexington, Ky.: Lexington Books.

Johnson, Audreye E. 1987. "The Movers and the Shakers: African-American Women and Social Welfare Development." Paper presented at the National Women's Studies Association Annual Conference, Spelman College, Atlanta, Georgia (June 24–28).

Johnson, Cathryn. 1992. "Gender, Formal Authority, and Leadership." Pp. 29–49 in *Gender, Interaction, and Inequality,* ed. Cecilia L. Ridgeway. New York: Spring-Verlag.

Jonasdottir, Anna G. 1988. "On the Concept of Interest, Women's Interests, and the Limitations of Interest Theory." Pp. 33–65 in *The Political Interests of Gender,* eds. Kathleen B. Jones and Anna G. Jonasdottir. London: Sage.

Jones, Hettie. 1969. "The Use of Indigenous Personnel as Service Givers." Pp. 62–73 in *Individual and Group Services in the Mobilization for Youth Experience,* ed. Harold Weissman. New York: Association Press.

Jones, Jacqueline. 1985. *Labor of Love, Labor of Sorrow: Black Women, Work and the Family, From Slavery to the Present.* New York: Vintage Books.

Jones, Kathleen B. 1990. "Citizenship in a Woman-Friendly Polity." *Signs: Journal of Women in Culture and Society.* 15(4): 781–812.

Jones, McKinley Alfred. 1976. *Black Consciousness and Political Socialization.* Urbana and Chicago:University of Illinois Press.

Jonnes, Jill. 1986. *We're Still Here: The Rise, Fall, and Resurrection of the South Bronx.* New York: The Atlantic Monthly Press, 1986.

Joseph, Gloria. 1981. "The Incompatible Menage á Trois: Marxism, Feminism, and Racism." Pp. 91–108 in *Women and Revolution,* ed. Lydia Sargent. Boston: South End Press.

*Journal of Community Action.* 1983.

Kahn, Si. 1982. *Organizing: A Guide for Grassroots Leaders.* New York: McGraw-Hill.

Kaminer, Wendy. 1984. *Women Volunteering: The Pleasure, Pain and Politics of Unpaid Work From 1830 to the Present.* Garden City, N.Y.: Doubleday.

Kaplan, Marshall, and Peggy Cuciti, eds. 1986. *The Great Society and Its Legacy: Twenty Years of U.S. Social Policy.* Durham, NC: Duke University Press.

Kaplan, Temma. 1982. "Female Consciousness and Collective Action: The Case of Barcelona, 1910–1918." *Signs: Journal of Women in Culture and Society.* 7(3): 545–66.

———. 1997. *Crazy for Democracy: Women in Grassroots Movements.* New York: Routledge.

Katz, Michael. 1986. *In the Shadow of the Poorhouse: A Social History of Welfare in America.* New York: Basic Books.

———. 1989. *The Undeserving Poor: From the War on Poverty to the War on Welfare.* New York: Pantheon.

Katznelson, Ira. 1981. *City Trenches: Urban Politics and the Patterning of Class in the United States.* New York: Pantheon Books.

Kaufman, Leslie. 1993. "P. C. Corps: Clinton's national service prototype was largely a poverty program disguised as a sensitivity seminar." *The Washington Monthly* October, pp. 9–11.

Kelly, Joan. 1979. "The Doubled Vision of Feminist Theory: A Postscript to the 'Women and Power' Conference." *Feminist Studies* 5(1): 216–27.

Kennedy, Edward M. 1993. "The Head Start Transision Project: Head Start Goes to Elementary School." Pp. 97–109 in *Head Start and Beyond: A Ntional Plan for Extended Childhood Intervention,* eds. Edward Zigler and Sally J. Styfco. New Haven: Yale University Press.

Kennedy, Susan Estabrook. 1979. *If All We Did Was to Weep at Home: A History of White Working-Class Women in America.* Bloomington, Ind.: Indiana University Press.

King, Deborah K. 1988. "Multiple Jeopardy, Multiple Consciousness: The Context of a Black Feminist Ideology." *Signs: Journal of Women in Culture and Society.* 14(1): 42–72.

King, Many. 1987. *Freedom Song: A Personal Story of the 1960s Civil Rights Movement.* New York: William Morrow and Company.

Klatch, Rebecca. 1992. "The Two Worlds of Women of the New Right." Pp. 529–52 in

*Women, Politics, and Change*, eds. Louise A. Tilly and Patricia Gurin. New York: Russell Sage.

Korbrin, S. 1959. "The Chicago Area Project: A 25 Year Assessment." *Annals of the American Academy of Political and Social Science* 322(March):19–27.

Koven, Seth, and Sonya Michel. 1993. "Introduction: 'Mother Worlds'." Pp. 1–42 in *Mothers of a New World: Maternalist Politics and the Origins of Welfare States*. New York: Routledge.

Kramer, Ralph M. 1969a. *Participation of the Poor: Comparative Community Case Studies in the War on Poverty*. Englewood Cliffs, N.J.: Prentice-Hall Inc.

———. 1969b. "Why Organize the Poor? The Dilemma of Services Versus Organization." Pp. 215–38 in *Participation of the Poor*. Englewood Cliffs, NJ: Prentice-Hall Inc.

Krause, Elliott A. 1968. "Functions of a Bureaucratic Ideology: Citizen Participation." *Social Problems* 16(2): 129–43.

Krauss, Celene. 1993. "Women and Toxic Waste Protests: Race, Class and Gender as Resources of Resistance." *Qualitative Sociology* 16(3): 247–62.

Ladd-Taylor, Molly. 1994. *Mother-Work: Women, Child Welfare, and the State, 1890–1930*. Urbana: University of Illinois Press.

Lamb, Curt. 1975. *Political Power in Poor Neighborhoods*. New York: Schenkman Publishing Company.

Lambert, John. 1978. "Political Values and Community Work Practice." Pp. 3–16 in *Political Issues and Community Work*, ed. Paul Curno. London: Routledge and Kegan Paul.

Lane, Robert E. 1972. *Political Man*. New York: Free Press.

Larner, Jeremy. 1971. "Initiation for Whitey: Notes on Poverty and Riot." Pp. 95–106 in *Poverty: Views from the Left*, eds. Jeremy Larner and Irving Howe. New York: William Morrow and Company.

Larner, Jeremy, and Irving Howe, eds. 1971. *Poverty: Views from the Left*. New York: William Morrow and Company.

Lees, Ray, and Marjorie Mayo. 1984. *Community Action for Change*. London: Routledge and Kegan Paul.

Leidner, Robin. 1991. "Stretching the Boundaries of Liberalism: Democratic Innovations in a Feminist Organization." *Signs: Journal of Women in Culture and Society*. 16(2): 263–89.

———. 1993. "Constituency, Accountability, and Deliberations: Reshaping Democracy in the National Women's Studies Association." *NWSA Journal* 5(1): 4–27.

Levitan, Sar A., ed. 1969. *The Great Society's Poor Law: A New Approach to Poverty*. Baltimore: Johns Hopkins Press.

Lewis, Jane. 1992. "Gender and the Development of Welfare Regimes." *Journal of European Social Policy* 2(3): 159–71.

Lewis, Jane. 1997. "Gender and Welfare Regimes: Further Thoughts." *Special Section: A Discussion of Gender and Welfare Regimes Social Politics* 4(2): 160–81.

Liebschutz, Sarah F. 1995. "Empowerment Zones and Enterprise Communities: Reinventing Federalism for Distressed Communities." *The Journal of Federalism* 25(3): 117–32.

Lincoln, C. Eric. 1984. *Race, Religion, and the Continuing American Dilemma*. New York: Hill and Wang.

Lind, Amy Conger. 1992. "Power, Gender, and Development: Popular Women's Organizations and the Politics of Needs in Ecuador." Pp. 134–49 in *The Making of Social Movements in Latin America: Identity, Strategy, and Democracy*, eds. Arturo Escobar and Sonia E. Alvarez. Boulder, Colo.: Westview Press.

Lipsky, Michael. 1980. *Street-Level Bureaucracy: Dilemmas of the Individual in Public Services*. New York: Russell Sage.

Lorber, Judith. 1984. *Women Physicians: Careers, Status, and Power*. New York: Tavistock Publications.

Loseke, Donileen R. 1992. *The Battered Woman and Shelters: The Social Construction of Wife Abuse*. Albany: State University of New York Press.

Lowi, Theodore J. 1969. *The End of Liberalism: Ideology, Policy, and the Crisis of Public Authority*. New York: W. W. Norton.

Lurie, Ellen. 1970. *How to Change the Schools: A Parents' Action Handbook on How to Fight the System*. New York: Random House.

MacKinnon, Catherine. A. 1989. *Toward a Feminist Theory of the State.* Cambridge, Mass.: Harvard University Press.

Marcuse, Herbert. 1968. *Negations: Essays in Critical Theory.* Boston: Beacon Press.

———. 1969. *An Essay on Liberation.* Boston: Beacon Press.

McClusky, Audrey Thomas. 1994. "Multiple Consciousness in the Leadership of Mary LcLeod Bethune." *NWSA Journal* 6(1): 69–81.

McCourt, Kathleen. 1977. *Working Class Women and Grass Roots Politics.* Bloomington, Ind.: Indiana University Press.

McKnight, John, and John Kretzmann. 1984. "Community Organizing in the '80s: Toward a Post-Alinsky Agenda." *Social Policy* 14(2): 15–17.

Marris, Peter, and Martin Rein, eds. 1972. *Dilemmas of Social Reform: Poverty and Community Action in the United States.* London: Routledge and Kegan Paul.

———. 1967/1973. *Dilemmas of Social Reform: Poverty and Community Action in the United States.* Chicago: Aldine Publishing Company.

Marshall, Dale Rogers. 1971. *The Politics of Participation in Poverty.* Berkeley and Los Angeles: University of California Press.

Marshall, T. H. 1950. *Citizenship and Social Class and Other Essays.* Cambridge, England: Cambridge University Press.

Martin, Biddy, and Chandra Talpade Mohanty. 1986. "Feminist Politics: What's Home Got To Do With It?" Pp. 191–212 in *Feminist Studies/Critical Studies,* ed. Teresa de Lauretis. Bloomington: Indiana University Press.

Martin, Joanne M., and Elmer P. Martin. 1985. *The Helping Tradition in the Black Family and Community.* Silver Springs, MD: National Association of Social Workers.

Martin, Patricia Yancey. 1990. "Rethinking Feminist Organizations." *Gender & Society* 4(4): 182–206.

———. 1992. "Gender, Interaction, and Inequality in Organizations." Pp. 208–31 in *Gender, Interaction, and Inequality,* ed. Cecilia L. Ridgeway. New York: Spring-Verlag.

Massey, Doreen. 1994. *Space, Place, and Gender.* Minneapolis, Minn.: University of Minnesota Press.

Matthews, Nancy. 1994. *Confronting Rape: The Feminist Anti-Rape Movement and the State.* New York: Routledge.

———. 1995. "Feminist Clashes With The State: Tactical Choices by State-Funded Rape Crisis Centers." Pp. 291–305 in *Feminist Organizations,* eds. Myra Marx Ferree and Patricia Yancey Martin. Philadelphia: Temple University Press.

Matusow, Allen J. 1984. *Unraveling of America: American Liberalism During the 1960s.* New York: Harper and Row.

Max, Steve. 1977. "Why Organize?" Chicago: Midwest Academy.

———. 1978. "The Objective Limits of Community Organizing." Chicago: Midwest Academy.

Mayo, Marjorie, ed. 1977. *Women in the Community.* Boston: Routledge and Kegan Paul.

Mead, Lawrence M. 1986. *Beyond Entitlement: The Social Obligations of Citizenship.* New York: Free Press.

Melucci, Alberto. 1989. *Nomads of the Present: Social Movements and Individual Needs in Contemporary Society.* Philadelphia: Temple University Press.

Miller, James. 1994. *Democracy Is in the Streets: From Port Huron to the Siege of Chicago.* Cambridge, Mass.: Harvard University Press.

Miller, S. M., and Pamela Roby. 1971. "The War on Poverty Recon-sidered." Pp. 68–82 in *Poverty: Views from the Left,* eds. Jeremy Larner and Irving Howe. New York: William Morrow and Company.

Mink, Gwendolyn. 1995. *The Wages of Motherhood: Inequality in the Welfare State, 1917–1942.* Ithaca, NY: Cornell University Press.

Mogulof, Melvin B. 1970a. *Citizen Participation: A Review and Commentary on Federal Policies and Practices.* Washington, D.C.: Urban Institute.

———. 1970b. *Citizen Participation: The Local Perspective.* Washington, D.C.: Urban Institute.

Mohanty, Chandra Talpade. 1991a. "Under Western Eyes: Feminist Scholarship and Colonial Discourses." Pp. 51–80 in *Third World Women and the Politics of Feminism,* eds. Chandra Talpade Mohanty, Ann Russo, and Lourdes Torres. Bloomington, Ind.: Indiana University Press.

———. 1991b. "Cartographies of Struggle: Third World Women and the Politics of

Feminism." Pp. 1–47 in *Third World Women and the Politics of Feminism*, eds. Chandra Talpade Mohanty, Ann Russo, and Lourdes Torres. Bloomington: Indiana University Press.

Molyneux, Maxine. 1986. "Mobilization Without Emancipation? Women's Interests, State and Revolution in Nicaragua." Pp. 280–302 in *Transition and Development: Problems of Third World Socialism*, eds. Richard R. Fagen, Carmen Diana Deere, and Jose Luis Goraggio. New York, N.Y.: Monthly Review Press and Center for the Study of the Americas.

Monroe, Kristen Renwick. 1996. *The Heart of Altruism: Perceptions of a Common Humanity*. Princeton, N.J.: Princeton University Press.

Moraga, Cherríe. 1981. "La Guerra." Pp. 27–34 in *This Bridge Called My Back: Writiings by Radical Women of Color*. Watertown, MA: Persephone Press.

Moraga, Cherríe. 1986. "From a Long Line of Vendidas: Chicanas and Feminism." Pp. 173–90 in *Feminist Studies: Critical Studies*, ed. Teresa de Lauretis. Bloomington, Ind.: Indiana University Press.

Morgen, Sandra. 1988. "'It's the Whole Power of the City Against Us!': The Development of Political Consciousness in a Women's Health Care Coalition." Pp. 97–115 in *Women and the Policies of Empowerment*, eds. Ann Bookman and Sandra Morgen. Philadelphia: Temple University Press.

———. 1995. "'It Was the Best of Times, It Was the Worst of Times': Emotional Discourse in the Work Cultures of Feminist Health Clinics." Pp. 234–47 in *Feminist Organizations*, eds. Myra Marx Ferree and Patricia Yancey Martin. Philadelphia: Temple University Press.

Morgen, Sandra, and Ann Bookman. 1988. "Rethinking Women and Politics: An Introductory Essay." Pp. 3–29 in *Women and the Politics of Empowerment*, eds. Ann Bookman and Sandra Morgen. Philadelphia: Temple University Press.

Morone, James A. 1990. *The Democratic Wish: Popular Participation and the Limits of American Government*. New York: Basic Book.

Morris, Adam. 1984. *The Origins of the Civil Rights Movement: Black Communities Programming for Change*. New York: Free Press.

Morris, Aldon D. 1992. "Political Collective Action." Pp. 351–74 in *Frontiers in Social Movement Theory*, eds. Aldon D. Morris and Carol McClurg Mueller. New Haven, CT: Yale University Press.

Moynihan, Daniel P. 1967. *The Negro Family: The Case for National Action*. Washington, D.C.: Government Printing Office.

———. 1969. *Maximum Feasible Misunderstanding: Community Action in the War on Poverty*. New York: The Free Press.

Muncy, Robyn. 1991. *Creating Female Domination in American Reform, 1890–1935*. New York: Oxford University Press.

Murray, Charles. 1984. *Losing ground: American Social Policy, 1950–1980*. New York: Basic Books.

Naples, Nancy A. 1988. "Women Against Poverty: Community Workers in *Anti-Poverty Programs*, 1964–1984." Ph.D. Dissertation, CUNY.

———. 1991a. "Contradictions in the Gender Subtext of the War on Poverty: Community Work and Resistance of Women from Low Income Communities." *Social Problems* 38(3): 316–32.

———. 1991b. "Just What Needed to Be Done: The Political Practice of Women Community Workers in Low-Income Neighborhoods." *Gender & Society* 5(4): 478–94.

———. 1992. "Activist Mothering: Cross-Generational Continuity in the Community Work of Women from Low-Income Communities." *Gender & Society* 6(3): 441–63.

———. 1996. "A Feminist Revisiting of the Insider/Outsider Debate: The 'Outsider Phenomenon' in Rural Iowa." *Qualitative Sociology* 19(1): 83–106.

———. 1997. "The 'New Consensus' on the Gendered 'Social Contract': The 1987–1988 Congressional Hearings on Welfare Reform." *Signs: Journal of Women in Culture and Society*. 22(4): 907–45.

———, ed. 1998a *Community Activism and Feminist Politics: Organizing Across Race, Class, and Gender*. New York: Routledge.

———. 1998b. "Women's Community Activism: Exploring the Dynamics of Politicization and Diversity." Pp. 327–49 in *Community Activism and Feminist Politics: Organizing Across Race, Class, and Gender*. New York: Routledge.

———. Forthcoming. "Towards a Comparative Analysis of Women's Political Praxis: Explicating Mutliple Dimensions of Standpoint Epistemology for Feminist Ethnography." *Women & Politics* 20(1).

Nelson, Barbara J. 1990. "The Origins of the Two-Channel Welfare State: Workman's Compensation and Mothers' Aid." Pp. 123–51 in *Women, the State, and Welfare*, ed. Linda Gordon. Madison, Wis.: University of Wisconsin Press.

———. 1984. "Women's Poverty and Women's Citizenship: Some Political Consequences of Economic Marginality." *Signs: Journal of Women in Culture and Society*. 19(2): 209–31.

Nixon, R. A. 1970. *Legislative Dimensions of the New Careers Program: 1970*. New York: Center for the Study of the Unemployed, Graduate School of Social Work, New York University.

O'Connor, June. 1991. *The Moral Vision of Dorothy Day: A Feminist Perspective*. New York: Crossroad.

Ohri, Askhok, Basil Manning, and Paul Curno, eds. 1982. *Community Work and Racism*. Boston: Routledge and Kegan Paul.

Oliker, Stacey J. 1995. "The Proximate Contexts of Workfare and Work: A Framework for Studying Poor Women's Economic Choices." *The Sociological Quarterly* 36(2): 251–72.

Omi, Michael, and Howard Winant. 1986. *Racial Formation in the United States from the 1960s to the 1980s*. New York: Routledge and Kegan Paul.

Omolade, Barbara. 1994. *The Rising Song of African American Women*. New York: Routledge.

Orleck, Annelise. 1989. *Common Sense and a Little Fire: Working-Class Women's Activism in the Twentieth-Century United States*. Ph.D. dissertation, New York University.

———. 1995. "'We Are That Mythical Thing Called the Public': Militant Housewives During the Great Depression." Pp. 189–213 in *U.S. Women in Struggle: A Feminist Studies Anthology*, eds. Heidi Hartmann and Claire Goldberg Moses. Urbana and Chicago: University of Illinois Press.

Orloff, Ann Shola. 1993. "Gender and the Social Rights of Citizenship: The Comparative Analysis of Gender Relations and Welfare States." *American Sociological Review* 58(3): 303–28.

Pardo, Mary. 1998. "Creating Community: Mexican American Women in Eastside Los Angeles." Pp. 275–300 in *Community Activism and Feminist Politics: Organizing Across Race, Class, and Gender*, ed. Nancy A. Naples. New York: Routledge.

———. 1995. "Doing it for the Kids: Mexican American Community Activists, Border Feminists?" Pp. 356–71 in *Feminist Organizations: Harvest of the New Women's Movement*, eds. Myra Marx Ferree and Patricia Yancey Martin. Philadelphia: Temple University Press.

Pascall, Gillian. 1986. *Social Policy: A Feminist Analysis*. London: Tavistock Publications.

Pateman, Carol, and E. Gross, eds. 1987. *Feminist Challenges: Social and Political Theory*. Boston: Northeastern University Press.

Patterson, James. 1981. *America's Struggle Against Poverty, 1900–1980*. Cambridge, Mass.: Harvard University Press.

Pearl, Arthur, and Frank Riessman. 1965. *New Careers for the Poor: The Nonprofessionals in Human Service*. New York: The Free Press.

Peattie, Lisa, and Martin Rein. 1983. *Women's Claims: A Study in Political Economy*. London: Oxford University Press.

Perlman, Janice E. 1976. *The Myth of Marginality: Urban Policy and Politics in Rio de Janeiro*. Berkeley and Los Angeles: University of California Press.

———. 1979. "Grassroots Empowerment and Government Responses." *Social Policy* 10(2): 16–21.

Perlman, Janice, and Joyce Ferman. 1981. *The Impact of Government Funding on Community Organizations*. Washington, D.C.: Center for Responsive Governance.

Personal Narratives Group, ed. 1989. *Interpreting Women's Lives: Feminist Theory and Personal Narratives*. Philadelphia: Temple University Press.

Peterson, Paul E. 1970. "Forms of Representation: Participation of the Poor in the Community Action Programs." *American Political Science Review* 69(2): 491–507.

Philadelphia Anti-Poverty Action Commission (PAAC). 1966a. Conduct and Administration Report. Philadelphia, June 25.

———. 1966b. *Maximum Participation Movement Recommendations. Open Hearing*. Philadelphia (December 12).

————. 1966c. *Open Public Meeting, Community Conference on the Anti-Poverty Programs.* Philadelphia (July 14).

————. 1966d. *PAAC Organization Chart.* Philadelphia (June).

————. 1967. *Progress Report, 1966–1967.* Philadelphia.

————. 1968a. *Conduct and Administration, January to June 1968. Rev.* Philadelphia (January 11).

————. 1968b. *Resident Participation, January to June, 1968.* Philadelphia (January).

————. 1971. *PAAC Five-Year Progress Report, 1967–1971.* Philadelphia.

Phillips, Anne, ed. 1987. *Feminism and Equality.* New York: New York University Press.

Phillips, Kevin. 1990. *The Politics of Rich and Poor: Wealth and the American Electorate in the Reagan Aftermath.* New York: HarperCollins.

Physician Task Force on Hunger in America. 1985. *Hunger in America: The Epidemic.* Middletown: Wesleyan University Press.

Piven, Frances Fox. 1963. "Low-Income People and the Political Process." A report published by MFY. Reprinted in Cloward and Piven, *The Politics of Turmoil.* New York: Pantheon, 1974.

————. 1966. "Participation of Residents in Neighborhood Community Action Programs." *Social Work* 11(1): 73–80.

————. 1969. "Militant Civil Servants." *Transaction* 7(1). Reprinted in Cloward and Piven, *The Politics of Turmoil.* New York: Pantheon, 1974.

————. 1986. "Women and the State: Ideology, Power, and Welfare." Pp. 326–40 in *For Crying Out Loud: Women and Poverty in the United States,* ed. Rochelle Lefkowitz and Ann Withorn. New York: Pilgrim Press.

————. 1990. "Ideology and the State: Women, Power, and the Welfare State." Pp. 250–64 in *Women, the State, and Welfare,* ed. Linda Gordon. Madison: University of Wisconsin Press.

Piven, Frances Fox, and Richard Cloward. 1971/1993. *Regulating the Poor: The Functions of Public Welfare.* New York: Vintage Books.

————. 1977. *Poor People's Movements: Why They Succeed, How They Fail.* New York: Vintage Books.

————. 1980. "Social Policy and the Formation of Political Consciousness." *Political Power and Social Theory* 1: 117–52.

————. 1982. *The New Class War: Reagan's Attack on the Welfare State and its Consequences.* New York: Pantheon Books.

————. 1992. "Normalizing Collective Protest." Pp. 301–25 in *Frontiers in Social Movement Theory,* eds. Aldon D. Morris and Carol McClurg Mueller. New Haven, CT: Yale University Press.

Pleck, Joseph H. 1982. "The Work-Family Role System." Pp. 101–10 in *Women and Work: Problems and Perspectives,* eds. Rachel Kahn-Hut, Arlene Kaplan Daniels; and Richard Colvard. New York: Oxford University Press.

Polakow, Valerie. 1993. *Lives on the Edge: Single Mothers and Their Children in the Other America.* Chicago: University of Chicago Press.

Polatnick, M. Rivka. 1996. "Diversity in Women's Liberation Ideology: How a Black and a White Group of the 1960s Viewed Motherhood." *Signs: Journal of Women in Culture and Society.* 21(3): 679–706.

Pope, Jacqueline. 1990. *Biting the Hand that Feeds Them.* New York: Praeger.

————. 1992. "The Colonizing Impact of Public Service Bureaucracies in Black Communities." Pp. 141–49 in *Race, Politics, and Economic Development,* ed. James Jennings. London and New York: Verso.

Porter, Jack Nusan, and Peter Dreir. 1973. *Jewish Radicalism: A Selected Anthology.* New York: Grove Press.

Pruger, Robert. 1966. *The Establishment of a "New Careers" Program in a Public School.* Walnut Creek, Calif.: Contra Costa Council of Community Services.

Quadagno, Jill. 1990. "Race, Class and Gender in the U.S. Welfare State: Nixon's Failed Family Assistance Plan." *American Sociological Review* 55(1): 11–28.

————. 1992. "Labor Unions and Racial Conflict in the War on Poverty." *American Sociological Review* 57(5): 616–34.

————. 1994. *The Color of Welfare: How Racism Undermined the War on Poverty.* New York: Oxford.

Quadagno, Jill, and Catherine Fobes. 1995. "The Welfare State and the Cultural Reproduction of Gender: Making Good Girls and Boys in the Jobs Corps." *Social*

*Problems.* 42(2): 171–90.

Radford, Jim. 1978. "Don't Agonise—Organise." Pp. 106–22 in *Political Issues and Community Work*, ed. Paul Curno. London: Routledge and Kegan Paul.

Rabagliati, Mary, and Exra Birnbaum. 1969. "Organization of Welfare Clients." In *Community Development in the Mobilization for Youth Experience*, ed. Harold H. Weissman. New York: Association Press.

Rappaport, Julian. 1986. "Collaborating for Empowerment: Creating the Language of Mutual Help." Pp. 64–79 in *The New Populism: The Politics of Empowerment*, eds. Harry Boyte and Frank Riessman. Philadelphia: Temple University Press.

Ravitch, Diane. 1974. *The Great School Wars: New York City, 1805–1973.* New York: Basic Books.

Redmon, Coates. 1986. *Come as You Are: The Peace Corps Story.* New York: Harcourt Brace Jovanovich.

Reed, Adolph, Jr., ed. 1986. *Race, Politics, and Culture Critical Essays on the Radicalism of the 1960s.* Westport, Conn.: Greenwood Press.

Reeves, T. Zane. 1988. *The Politics of the Peace Corps & Vista.* Tuscaloosa: The University of Alabama Press.

Reinelt, Claire. 1995. "Moving Onto the Terrain of the State: the Battered Women's Movement and the Politics of Engagement." Pp. 84–104 in *Feminist Organizations*, eds. Myra Marx Ferree and Patricia Yancey Martin. Philadelphia: Temple University Press.

Reisch, Michael, and Stanley Wenocur. 1981. "Professionalization and Volunteers in Social Welfare." *Working Paper Series.* Washington, D.C.: Center For Responsive Governance.

Riposa, Gerry. 1996. "From Enterprise Zones to Empowerment Zones: The Community Context of Urban Economic Development." *American Behavioral Scientists* March/April 39(5): 536–51.

Roberts, Dorothy E. 1995. "Race, Gender, and the Value of Mother's Work." *Social Politics* 2(2): 195–207.

Roberts, Helen, ed. 1981. *Doing Feminist Research.* London: Routledge and Kegan Paul.

Roberts, Nancy L. 1984. *Dorothy Day and the Catholic Worker.* Albany, N.Y.: SUNY Press.

Robinson, Jo Ann. 1987. *The Montgomery Bus Boycott and the Women Who Started It.* Knoxville, Tenn.: The University of Tennessee Press.

Roby, Pamela, ed. 1974. *The Poverty Establishment.* Englewood Cliffs, NJ: Prentice-Hall.

Rodgers, Mark Eugene. 1982. "The Small Town Emphasis Program: A Federal Effort in Low-Income Citizen Participation." D.S.W. Dissertation, University of Pennsylvania.

Rollins, Judith. 1995. *All Is Never Said: The Narrative of Odette Harper Hines.* Philadelphia: Temple University Press.

Rose, Gillian. 1993. *Feminism and Geography.* Cambridge, Mass.: Polity Press.

Rose, Nancy E. 1995. *Workfare or Fair Work: Women, Welfare, and Government Work Programs.* New Brunswick, N.J.: Rutgers University Press.

Rose, Stephen M. 1972. *The Betrayal of the Poor: The Transformation of Community Action.* Cambridge, Mass.: Schenkman Publishing Company.

Rosenbloom, Robert A. 1981. "The Neighborhood Movement: Where Has It Come From? Where Is It Going?" *Journal of Voluntary Action Research* 10(2): 4–46.

Rowbotham, Sheila. 1989. *The Past Is Before Us: Feminism in Action Since the 1960s.* London: Pandora Press.

Rubin, Marilyn Marks, 1994. "Can Reorchestration of Historical Themes Reinvent Government? A Case Study of the Empowerment Zones and Enterprise Communities Act of 1993." *Public Administration Review* March/April 54(2): 161–69.

Ruddick, Sara. 1989. *Maternal Thinking: Toward a Politics of Peace.* New York: Ballantine Books.

Ruether, Rosemary Radford. 1973. *Liberation Theology.* Mahwah, N.J.: Paulist Press.

Russell, Letty M. 1974. *Human Liberation in a Feminist Perspective—A Theology.* Philadelphia: The Westminster Press.

Sacks, Karen Brodkin. 1988a. *Caring by the Hour: Women, Work, and Organizing at Duke Medical Center.* Urbana and Chicago, Ill.: University of Illinois Press.

———. 1988b. "Gender and Grassroots Leadership." Pp. 77–94 in *Women and the Policies of Empowerment*, eds. Ann Bookman and Sandra Morgen. Philadelphia: Temple University Press.

———. 1989. "Review Article: Toward a Unified Theory of Class, Race and Gender." *American Ethnologist* 16(3): 534–46.

Sacks, Karen Brodkin, and Dorothy Remy, eds. 1984. *My Troubles Are Going to Have Trouble With Me*. New Brunswick, N.J.: Rutgers University Press.

Sanchez-Ayendez, Melba. 1995. "Puerto Rican Elderly Women: Shared Meanings and Informal Supportive Networks." Pp. 172–86 in *All American Women: Lines That Divide, Ties That Bind*, ed. Johnnetta B. Cole. New York: The Free Press.

Sandoval, Chela. 1991. "U.S. Third World Feminism: The Theory and Method of Oppositional Consciousness in the Postmodern World." *Genders* 10:1–24.

———. 1995. "Feminist Forms of Agency and Oppositional Consciousness: US Third World Feminist Criticism." Pp. 208–26 in *Provoking Agents: Gender and Agency in Theory and Practice*, ed. Judith Kegan Gardiner. Urbana and Chicago: University of Illinois Press.

Sarvasy, Wendy. 1988. "Reagan and Low-Income Mothers: A Feminist Recasting of the Debate." Pp. 253–76 in *Remaking the Welfare State: Retrenchment and Social Policy in America and Europe*, ed. Michael K. Brown. Philadelphia: Temple University Press.

———. 1992. "Beyond the Difference versus Equality Debate: Postsuffrage Feminism, Citizenship, and the Quest for a Feminist Welfare State." *Signs: Journal of Women in Culture and Society*. 17(2): 329–62.

———. 1994. "From Man and Philanthropic Service to Feminist Social Citizenship." *Social Politics* 1(3): 306–25.

———.1997. "Social Citizenship From a Feminist Perspective." *Hypatia: Special Issue on Citizenship* 12(4): 54–73.

Sarvasy, Wendy, and Birte Siim. 1994. "Gender, Transitions to Democracy, and Citizenship." *Social Politics* 1(3):249–55.

Sassoon, Anne Showstack. 1987 "Women's New Social Role: Contradictions of the Welfare State." Pp. 158–88 in *Women and the State*, ed. Anne Showstack Sassoon. London: Hutchinson.

Sawyer, Mary R. 1994. *Black Ecumenism: Implementing the Demands of Justice*. Valley Forge, Pa.: Trinity Press International.

Schlesinger, Arthur H., Jr. 1965. *A Thousand Days*. Boston: Houghton Mifflin.

Schram, Sanford F. 1995. *Words of Welfare: The Poverty of Social Science and the Social Science of Poverty*. Minneapolis, Minn.: University of Minnesota Press.

Schwartz, Karen. 1991. *What You Can Do for Your Country: An Oral History of the Peace Corps*. New York: William Morrow and Company.

Scott, Anne Firor. 1991. *Natural Allies: Women's Associations in American History*. Urbana and Champaign: University of Illinois Press.

Scott, Joan W. 1992. "'Experience'." Pp. 22–40 in *Feminists Theorize the Political* eds. Judith Butler and Joan Scott. New York: Routledge.

Scott, Kisho Y. 1991. *The Habit of Surviving*. New York: Ballantine.

Searles, P. David. 1997. *The Peace Corps Experience: Challenge and Change 1969–1976*. Lexington, Kentucky: The University Press of Kentucky.

Sennott, Nancy. 1974. "Philadelphia's War on Poverty." Unpublished thesis. Philadelphia.

Shapiro, Virginia. 1981. "When Are Interests Interesting? The Problem of Political Representation of Women." *American Political Science Review* 75: 701–16.

———. 1983. *The Political Integration of Women: Roles, Socialization, and Potlics*. Urbana and Champaign: University of Illinois Press.

———. 1984. "Women, Citizenship, and Nationality: Immigration and Naturalization Politics in the United States." *Politics and Society* 13(1): 1–26.

———. 1990. "The Gender Basis of American Social Policy." Pp. 36–54 in *Women, the State, and Welfare*, ed. Linda Gordon. Madison, Wis.: University of Wisconsin Press.

Shaw, Clifford Robe. 1930/1960. *The Jack-Roller: A Delinquent Boy's Own Story*. Chicago: The University of Chicago Press.

Shaw, Clifford Robe, and Henry D. McKay. 1969. *Juvenile Delinquency and Urban Areas: A Study of Rates of Delinquency in Relation to Differential Characteristics of Local Communities in American Cities*. Chicago: University of Chicago Press.

Shear, Jeff. 1995. "The Ax Files." *National Journal* April 15, pp. 924–27.

Sidel, Ruth. 1986. *Women and Children Last: The Plight of Poor Women in Affluent America*. New York: Viking Penguin, Inc.

Sigel, Ruth, ed. 1989. *Political Learning in Adulthood: A Source Book of Theory and Research*. Chicago: University of Chicago Press.

Siim, Birte. 1994. "Engendering Democracy: Social Citizenship and Political Participation for Women in Scandinavia." *Social Politics* 1(3): 286–305.

Sirianni, Carmen. 1993. "Feminist Pluralism and Democratic Learning: The Politics of Citizenship in the National Women's Studies Association." *NWSA Journal* 5(3): 367–84.

Sklar, Kathryn Kish. 1995. *Florence Kelley and the Nation's Work*. New Haven, Con.: Yale University Press.

———. 1985. "Hull House in the 1890s: A Community of Women Reformers." *Signs: Journal of Women in Culture and Society*. 10(4): 658–77.

Skocpol, Theda. 1992. *Protecting Soldiers and Mothers: The Political Origins of Social Policy in the United States*. Cambridge, Mass.: Harvard University Press.

Slessarev, Helene. 1997. *The Betrayal of the Urban Poor*. Philadelphia: Temple University Press.

Smith, Dorothy E. 1979. "Toward a Sociology for Women." Pp. 135–87 in *Prism of Sex*, eds. Julia A. Sherman and Evelyn Torton Beck. Madison, Wis.: University of Wisconsin Press.

———. 1984. "The Gender Subtext of Power." Toronto: Ontario Institute for Studies in Education.

———. 1987. *The Everyday World as Problematic: A Feminist Sociology*. Toronto: University of Toronto Press.

———. 1990a. *The Conceptual Practices of Power: A Feminist Sociology of Knowledge*. Boston, Mass.: Northeastern University Press.

———. 1990b. *Texts, Facts, and Femininity: Exploring the Relations of Ruling*. New York: Routledge.

Smith, Dorothy E., and Alison I. Griffith. 1990. "Coordinating the Uncoordinated: Mothering, Schooling, and the Family Wage." Pp. 25–43 in *Perspectives on Social Problems* Vol. 2, eds. Gale Miller and James A. Holstein. Greenwich, Conn.: JAI Press.

Smith, Susan L. 1997. "Welfare for Black Mothers and Children: Health and Home in the American South." *Social Politics* 4(1): 49–64.

Snow, David, and Robert Benford. 1992. "Master Frames and Cycles of Protest." Pp. 133–54 in *Frontiers in Social Movement Theory*, eds. Aldon D. Morris and Carol McClurg Mueller. New Haven, Conn.: Yale University Press.

Sokoloff, Natalie J. 1980. *Between Money and Love: The Dialectics of Women's Home and Market Work*. New York: Praeger.

———. 1984. "On Motherwork and Working Mothers." Pp. 259–66 in *Feminist Frameworks: Alternative Theoretical Accounts of the Relations Between Women and Men*, eds. Alison M. Jaggar and Paula Rothenberg. New York: McGraw-Hill.

———. 1992. *Black Women and White Women in the Professions: Occupational Segregation by Race and Gender, 1960–1980*. New York: Routledge.

Solomon, Barbara Bryant. 1976. *Black Empowerment: Social Work in Oppressed Communities*. New York: Columbia University Press.

Solmon, Lewis, and Tamara W. Schiff. 1993. "National Service: Is It Worth Government Support?" *Change* September/October, pp. 37–41.

Sorensen, Theodore C. 1965. *Kennedy*. New York: Harper and Row.

Spalter-Roth, Roberta, and Ronnee Schreiber. 1995. "Outsider Issues and Insider Tactics: Strategic Tensions in the Women's Policy Network During the 1980s." Pp. 105–27 in *Feminist Organizations*, eds. Myra Marx Ferree and Patricia Yancey Martin. Philadelphia: Temple University Press.

Stack, Carol B. 1974. *All Our Kin: Strategies For Survival in a Black Community*. New York: Harper and Row.

Stack, Carol, and Ling M. Burton. 1994. "Kinscripts: Reflections on Family, Generation, and Culture." Pp. 33–44 in *Mothering: Ideology, Experience, and Agency*, eds. E. Nakano Glenn, G. Chang, and L. Rennie Forcey. New York: Routledge.

Steinberg, Ronnie J. 1996. "Advocacy Research for Feminist Policy Objectives: Experiences with Comparable Worth." Pp. 225–55 in *Feminism and Social Change: Bridging Theory and Practice*, ed. Heidi Gottfried. Urbana and Chicago: University of Illinois Press.

Sterling, Dorothy, ed. 1984. *We Are Your Sisters: Black Women in the Nineteenth Century*. New York: W. W. Norton.

Stern, Susan P. 1998. "Conversation, Research, and Struggles over Schooling in an African American Community." Pp. 107–27 in *Community Activism and Feminist Politics: Organizing Across Race, Class, and Gender*. New York, NY: Routledge.

Stetson, Damon. 1963. "Strike Is Ended, Refuse Picked Up." *New York Times* December 7, p. 22.

Stroh, Nicholas W. 1966. "U.S. Reaffirms Ban on Elected Officials of PACC and Kin Holding Paid Jobs." *The Evening Bulletin* 27 June, 13(G).

Sundquist, James L. 1969. "Origins of the War on Poverty." Pp. 3–33 in *On Fighting Poverty: Perspectives from Experience*, ed. James L. Sundquist. New York: Basic Books.

———, ed. 1974. *On Fighting Poverty: Perspectives on Experience*. New York: Basic Books.

Susser, Ida. 1988. "Working-class Women, Social Protest, and Changing Ideologies." Pp. 257–71 in *Women and the Politics of Empowerment*, eds. Ann Bookman and Sandra Morgen. Philadelphia: Temple University Press.

Suttles, Gerald D. 1968. *The Social Order of the Slum: Ethnicity and Territory in the Inner City*. Chicago: University of Chicago Press.

———. 1972. *The Social Construction of Communities*. Chicago: University of Chicago Press.

Sviridoff, Mitchell. 1989. "The Local Initiatives Support Corporation: A Private Initiative for a Public Problem." Pp. 207–34 in *Privatization and the Welfare State*, eds. Sheila B. Kamerman and Alfred J. Kahn. Princeton, N.J.: Princeton University Press.

Tarrow, Sidney. 1992. "Mentalities, Political Cultures, and Collective Action Frames: Constructing Meanings Through Action." Pp. 174–202 in *Frontiers in Social Movement Theory*, eds. Aldon D. Morris and Carol McClurg Mueller. New Haven, Conn.: Yale University Press.

Taylor, James B., and Randolph, Jerry. 1975. *Community Worker*. New York: Aronson.

Terrell, Mary Church. 1980. *A Colored Woman in a White World*. New York: Arno Press.

Teske, Nathan. 1997. *Political Activists in America: The Identity Construction Model of Political Participation*. New York: Cambridge University Press.

Tocqueville, Alexis de. 1969. *Democracy in America*, eds. J. P. Mayer and A. P. Kerr. Garden City, N.Y.: Doubleday.

Torres, Lourdes. 1986. "The Construction of the Self in U.S. Latina Autobiographies." Pp. 271–87 in *Third World Women and the Politics of Feminism*, eds. Chandra Talpade Mohanty, Ann Russo, and Lourdes Torres. Bloomington and Indianapolis: Indiana University Press.

Trattner, Walter I. 1974. *From Poor Law to Welfare State: A History of Social Welfare in America*. New York: The Free Press.

Troester, Rosalie Riegle. 1984. "Turbulence and Tenderness: Mothers, Daughters and 'Othermothers' in Paule Marshall's Brown Girl, Brownstones." *Sage: A Scholarly Journal on Black Women* 1(2): 13–16.

Turner, John B., ed. 1969. *Neighborhood Organization for Community Action*. New York: National Association of Social Workers.

Turner, Ralph, and Lewis Lillian. 1987. *Collective Behavior*. Englewood Cliffs, N.J.: Prentice-Hall.

U.S. Congress. 1964a. *Congressional Record*. August 7.

U.S. Congress. 1964b. 88th Congress, 2nd Session. *Economic Opportunity Act of 1964*, Public Law 88-452.

U.S. Congress. 1967. *Congressional Record*, 90th Congress, 1st Session.

U.S. Congress. 1969. Public Law 91-177—December 30, 833–834. Title II—Special Work and Career Development Programs. 1st Session, 91st Cong.

U.S. Congress. 1970. *United States Statutes at Large, Volume 83*. Washington, D.C.: Government Printing Office.

U.S. Congress. Joint Economic Committee. 1986. *The Growth in Poverty: 1979–1985 Economic and Demographic Factors*. Washington, D.C.: A Democratic Staff Study Prepared for the Joint Economic Committee United States Congress (December).

U.S. Congress. House. 1964. Committee on Education and Labor. *Economic Opportunity Act of 1964. Hearings before the Subcommittee on the War on Poverty Programs*, 88th Cong., 2nd sess. Washington, D.C.: Government Printing Office.

U.S. Congress. House. 1965. Committee on Education and Labor. *Antipoverty Programs in New York City and Los Angeles. Hearings before the Subcommittee on the War on Poverty Programs*, 89th Cong, 1st sess. Washington, D.C.: Government Printing Office.

U.S. Congress. House. 1967. *EOA: Amendments of 1967. Hearings before Special Ad Hoc Subcommittee*, 90th Cong., 1st sess. Washington, D.C.: Government Printing Office.

U.S. Congress. House. 1981a. Committee on Economic and Educational Opportunities. *Community Services Block Grant Act as Amended Through December 31, 1994*. Serial No.

104-B. Pp. 78-96. 104th Cong., 1st sess. Washington, D.C.: U.S. Government Printing Office.

U.S. Congress. House. 1981b. Committee on Government Operations. *Community Actinon and the CSA Closure Decision.* Report No. 97-116. Washington, D.C.: U.S. Government Printing Office.

U.S. Congress. House. 1987. *Welfare Reform, Hearings Before the Subcommittee on Public Assistance and Unemployment Compensation. House Ways and Means Committee.* 100th Cong., 1st sess. January 28; February 19; March 4, 6, 10, 11, 13. Washington, D.C.: Government Printing Office.

U.S. Congress. Senate. 1965. Committee on Labor and Public Welfare. *Expand the War on Poverty. Hearings Before the Select Subcommittee on Poverty,* 89th Cong., 1st sess. Washington, D.C.: Government Printing Office.

U.S. Congress. Senate. 1967. Subcommittee on Employment, Manpower, and Poverty of the Committee on Labor and Public Welfare. *Examination of the War on Poverty,* 90th Cong, 1st sess. Washington, D.C.: Government Printing Office.

U.S. Congress. Senate. 1987. *Welfare: Reform or Replacement? (Work and Welfare). Hearings before the Subcommittee on Social Security and Family Policy, Senate Finance Committee.* 100th Cong., 1st sess. February 23. Washington, D.C.: Government Printing Office.

U.S. Department of Housing and Urban Development, Office of Community Planning; and U.S. Department of Agriculture, Office of Small Community and Rural Development. 1993. *Building Communities: Together. The President's Community Enterprise Board.* Washington, D.C.: U.S. Department of Housing and Urban Development, Office of Community Planning; and U.S. Department of Agriculture, Office of Small Community and Rural Development.

U.S. Office of Economic Opportunity. 1965a. *Community Action Program Guide.* Washington, D.C.: Government Printing Office.

U.S. Office of Economic Opportunity. 1965b. *Community Action Program Guide,* Vol. 1 *Instructions for Applicants.* Vol. 1, February. Washington, D.C.: Govt. Printing Office.

U.S. Office of Economic Opportunity. 1965c. *A Nation Aroused: First Annual Report.* Washington, D.C.: Government Printing Office.

U.S. Office of Economic Opportunity. 1966. *The Quiet Revolution: Second Annual Report.* Washington, D.C.: Government Printing Office.

U.S. Office of Economic Opportunity. 1966–1969. *Communities in Action* 1–5 (May 1966–April 1969). Washington, D.C.: Government Printing Office.

U.S. Office of Economic Opportunity. 1967. *The Tide of Progress: Annual Report.* Washington, D.C.: Government Printing Office.

U.S. Office of Economic Opportunity. 1968a. *As the Seed is Sown: Annual Report.* Washington, D.C.: Government Printing Office.

U.S. Office of Economic Opportunity. 1968b. *Community Action Memorandum 80. Designation and Recognition of CAA, Under the 1967 Amendments.* Washington, D.C.: Government Printing Office.

U.S. Office of Economic Opportunity. 1968c. *Community Action Memorandum 81. The Organization of Community Action Boards and Committees under the 1967 Amendments.* Washington, D.C.: Government Printing Office.

U.S. Office of Economic Opportunity. 1968d. *Instruction #6907–1. Restrictions on Political Activism, Community Action Programs,* September 6. Washington, D.C.: Government Printing Office.

U.S. Office of Economic Opportunity. 1968e. *OEO Publications: A Bibliography, 1965–1968.* Compiled by John B. Regnell. Miscellaneous Paper #4. Bureau of Governmental Research. University of Nevada, Reno, Nevada.

U.S. Office of Economic Opportunity. 1968f. *Participation of the Poor in the Community Decision—Making Process.* (Ref. OEO Instruction 6005–1 Participation of the Poor in the Planning, Conduct and Evaluation of Community Action Programs, December 1.) Washington, D.C.: Government Printing Office.

U.S. Office of Economic Opportunity. 1968g. *Planning for Community Action. Planning Development Program.* Reference Notebook for CAAs, CAA Board Members, CAA State, Neighborhood Groups. Washington, D.C.: Government Printing Office.

U.S. Office of Economic Opportunity. 1969a. *Communities in Action* 1–5 (May 1966–April 1969).

U.S. Office of Economic Opportunity. 1969b. *CAP Atlas as of 3/1/69,* Washington, D.C.:

Government Printing Office.

U.S. Office of Economic Opportunity. 1969c. *Participation of the Poor in the Community Decision-Making Process.* (August). (Ref. OEO Instruction 6005–1 Participation of the Poor in the Planning, Conduct and Evaluation of Community Action Programs, December 1, 1968.) Washington, D.C.: Government Printing Office.

U.S. Office of Economic Opportunity. 1969d. *Women in the War on Poverty.* Washington, D.C.: Government Printing Office.

U.S. Office of Economic Opportunity. 1970a. *Annual Report: Fiscal Years 1969-1970.* Washington, D.C.: Government Printing Office.

U.S. Office of Economic Opportunity. 1970b. *Instruction #6320-1. The Mission of the Community Action Agency,* November 16. Washington, D.C.: Government Printing Office.

U.S. Office of Economic Opportunity. 1971a. *Annual Report: Fiscal Year 1971.* Washington, D.C.: Government Printing Office.

U.S. Office of Economic Opportunity. 1971b. *CAP Atlas as of May 1971,* Washington, D.C.: Government Printing Office.

Valentine, Jeanette. 1979. "The Social Context of Parent Involvement in Head Start." Pp. 291–314 in *Project Head Start: A Legacy of the War on Poverty,* eds. Jeanette Valentine and Evan Stark. New York: The Free Press.

Wager, Deborah. 1967. "Womanpower." *Communities in Action* 2 (October–November): 24–26.

Wagner, David. 1990. *The Quest for a Radical Profession: Social Service Careers and Political Ideology.* Lanham, MD: University Press of America.

Watson, Frank Dekker. 1922. *The Charity Organization Movement in the United States: A Study in American Philanthropy.* New York: Arno Press, a New York Times Company.

Waxman, Chaim Isaac, ed. 1968. *Poverty: Power and Politics.* New York: Grosset and Dunlap.

———. 1983. *The Stigma of Poverty: A Critique of Poverty Theories and Politics.* New York: Pergamon.

Weir, Margaret. 1988. "The Federal Government and Unemployment: The Frustration of Policy Innovation from the New Deal to the Great Society." Pp. 149–97 in *The Politics of Social Policy in the United States,* ed. by Margaret Weir, Ann Shola Orloff, and Theda Skocpol. Princeton, N.J.: Princeton University Press.

Weissman, Harold, ed. 1969a. *Community Development in the Mobilization for Youth Experience.* New York: Association Press.

———. 1969b. *Employment and Education Services in the Mobilization for Youth Experience.* New York: Association Press.

———. 1969c. *Individual and Group Services in the Mobilization for Youth Experience.* New York: Association Press.

———. 1969d. *Justice and the Law.* New York: Association Press.

———. 1970. *Community Councils and Community Control: The Workings of Democratic Mythology.* Pittsburgh, Pa.: University of Pittsburgh Press.

Welch, Sharon D. 1985. *Communities of Resistance and Solidarity: A Feminist Theology of Liberation.* Maryknoll, N.Y.: Orbis Books.

West, Guida. 1981. *The National Welfare Rights Movement: The Social Protest of Poor Women.* New York: Praeger Publishers.

———. 1990. "Cooperation and Conflict Among Women in the Welfare Rights Movement." Pp. 149–71 in *Bridges of Power: Women's Multicultural Alliances,* eds. Lisa Albrecht and Rose M. Brewer. Philadelphia: New Society Publishers.

West, Guida, and Rhoda Lois Blumberg. 1990. "Reconstructing Social Protest From a Feminist Perspective." Pp. 3–36 in *Women and Social Protest,* eds. Guida West and Rhoda Lois Blumberg. New York: Oxford University Press.

White, E. Frances. 1990. "Africa On My Mind: Gender, Counter Discourses and African-American Nationalism." *Journal of Women's History* 2(1): 73–97.

White, Elliott. 1973. "Articulateness, Political Mobility, and Conservatism: An Analysis of the Philadelphia Antipoverty Election." Pp. 188–205 in *Black Politics in Philadelphia,* eds. Miriam Ershkowitz and Joseph Zikmund II. New York: Basic Books.

Whittier, Nancy. 1995. *Feminist Generations: The Persistence of the Racial Women's Movement.* Philadelphia: Temple University Press.

Wildavsky, Aaron. 1987. "Choosing Preferences by Constructing Institutions: A Cultural

Theory of Preference Formation." *American Political Science Review* 81: 3–22.

Wilensky, Harold L. 1983. "Political Legitimacy and Consensus: Missing Variables in the Assessment of Social Policy." Pp. 51–74 in *Evaluating the Welfare State: Social and Political Perspectives*, eds. Shimon E. Spiro and Ephraim Yuchtman-Yaar. New York: Academic Press.

Williams, Raymond. 1976. *Keywords: A Vocabulary of Culture and Society*. New York: Oxford University Press.

Wilson, Elizabeth. 1976. "Women in the Community." Pp. 1–11 in *Women in the Community*, ed. Marjorie Mayo. London: Routledge and Kegan Paul.

Wilson, William Julius. 1987. *The Truly Disadvantaged: The Inner City, the Underclass, and Public Policy*. Chicago: University of Chicago Press.

———. 1997. *When Work Disappears*. New York: Random House.

Winant, Howard. 1994. *Racial Conditions*. Minneapolis, Minn.: University of Minnesota Press.

Withorn, Ann. 1982. *The Circle Game: Services For the Poor in Massachusetts, 1966–1978*. Amherst, Mass.: The University of Massachusetts Press.

———. 1984. *Serving the People: Social Services and Social Change*. New York: Columbia University Press.

———. 1986. "For Better and For Worse: Women Against Women in the Welfare State." Pp. 220–34 in *For Crying Out Loud: Women and Poverty in the United States*, ed. Rochelle Lefkowitz and Ann Withorn.

Wofford, John G. 1974. "The Politics of Local Responsibility." Pp. 70–102 in *On Fighting Poverty: Perspectives From Experience*, ed. James L. Sundquist. New York: Basic Books.

Wolf, Diane L., ed. 1996. *Feminist Dilemmas in Fieldwork*. Boulder, CO: Westview Press.

Wolf, Margery. 1992. *A Thrice-Told Tale*. Stanford, Calif.: Stanford University Press.

Woliver, Laura R. 1993. *From Outrage to Action: The Politics of Grass-Roots Dissent*. Urbana and Chicago: University of Illinois Press.

Yarmolinsky, Adam. 1969. "The Beginnings of OEO." Pp. 34–51 in *On Fighting Poverty: Perspectives from Experience*. New York: Basic Books.

Yee, Shirley J. 1987. "Self-Help: Black Women Abolitionists and Their Community, 1818-1860." Paper presented at the National Women's Studies Association Annual Conference, Spelman College, Atlanta, Georgia (June 24–28).

Young, Iris. 1981. "Beyond the Unhappy Marriage: A Critique of Dual Systems Theory." Pp. 71–90 in *Women and Revolution*, ed. Lydia Sargent. Boston: South End Press.

Zigler, Edward, Sally J. Styfco, and Elizabeth Gilman. 1993. "The National Head Start Program for Disadvantaged Preschoolers." Pp. 1–42 in *Head Start and Beyond: A National Plan for Extended Chilhood Intervention*, eds. Edward Zigler and Sally J. Styfco. New Haven: Yale Univrsity Press.

Zinn, Howard. 1965. *SNCC: The New Abolitionists*. Boston: Beacon Press.

Zinn, Maxine Baca. 1989. "Family, Race, and Poverty in the Eighties." *Signs: Journal of Women in Culture and Society*. 14(4): 856–74.

———. 1990. "Family, Feminism, and Race in America." *Gender & Society* 4: 68–82.

# INDEX